Audiobooks, Literature, and Sound Studies

Routledge Research in Cultural and Media Studies

1. Video, War and the Diasporic Imagination
Dona Kolar-Panov

2. Reporting the Israeli-Arab Conflict
How Hegemony Works
Tamar Liebes

3. Karaoke Around the World
Global Technology, Local Singing
Edited by Toru Mitsui and
Shuhei Hosokawa

4. News of the World
World Cultures Look at Television News
Edited by Klaus Bruhn Jensen

5. From Satellite to Single Market
New Communication Technology and
European Public Service Television
Richard Collins

6. The Nationwide Television Studies
David Morley and Charlotte Bronsdon

7. The New Communications Landscape
Demystifying Media Globalization
Edited by Georgette Wang, Jan Servaes,
and Anura Goonasekera

8. Media and Migration
Constructions of Mobility and Difference
Edited by Russel King and Nancy Wood

9. Media Reform
Democratizing the Media,
Democratizing the State
Edited by Monroe E. Price, Beata
Rozumilowicz, and Stefaan G. Verhulst

10. Political Communication in a New Era
Edited by Gadi Wolfsfeld and
Philippe Maarek

11. Writers' Houses and the Making of Memory
Edited by Harald Hendrix

12. Autism and Representation
Edited by Mark Osteen

13. American Icons
The Genesis of a National
Visual Language
Benedikt Feldges

14. The Practice of Public Art
Edited by Cameron Cartiere and
Shelly Willis

15. Film and Television After DVD
Edited by James Bennett and
Tom Brown

16. The Places and Spaces of Fashion, 1800–2007
Edited by John Potvin

17. Communicating in the Third Space
Edited by Karin Ikas and
Gerhard Wagner

18. Deconstruction After 9/11
Martin McQuillan

19. The Contemporary Comic Book Superhero
Edited by Angela Ndalianis

20. Mobile Technologies
From Telecommunications to Media
Edited by Gerard Goggin and
Larissa Hjorth

**21. Dynamics and Performativity
of Imagination**
The Image between the Visible
and the Invisible
Edited by Bernd Huppauf and
Christoph Wulf

**22. Cities, Citizens, and
Technologies**
Urban Life and Postmodernity
Paula Geyh

23. Trauma and Media
Theories, Histories, and Images
Allen Meek

24. Letters, Postcards, Email
Technologies of Presence
Esther Milne

**25. International Journalism and
Democracy**
Civic Engagement Models from
Around the World
Edited by Angela Romano

**26. Aesthetic Practices and Politics
in Media, Music, and Art**
Performing Migration
Edited by Rocío G. Davis, Dorothea
Fischer-Hornung, and Johanna C.
Kardux

**27. Violence, Visual Culture, and the
Black Male Body**
Cassandra Jackson

**28. Cognitive Poetics and Cultural
Memory**
Russian Literary Mnemonics
Mikhail Gronas

**29. Landscapes of Holocaust
Postmemory**
Brett Ashley Kaplan

**30. Emotion, Genre, and Justice in
Film and Television**
E. Deidre Pribram

**31. Audiobooks, Literature,
and Sound Studies**
Edited by Matthew Rubery

Audiobooks, Literature, and Sound Studies

Edited by Matthew Rubery

First published 2011
by Routledge
711 Third Avenue, New York, NY 10017

Simultaneously published in the UK
by Routledge
2 Park Square, Milton Park, Abingdon, Oxfordshire OX14 4RN

First issued in paperback 2014

Routledge is an imprint of the Taylor & Francis Group, an informa business

© 2011 Taylor & Francis

The right of Matthew Rubery to be identified as author of this work has been asserted
by him in accordance with sections 77 and 78 of the Copyright, Designs and Patents
Act 1988

Typeset in Sabon by IBT Global.

All rights reserved. No part of this book may be reprinted or reproduced or utilised
in any form or by any electronic, mechanical, or other means, now known or hereafter invented, including photocopying and recording, or in any information storage or
retrieval system, without permission in writing from the publishers.

Trademark Notice: Product or corporate names may be trademarks or registered trademarks, and are used only for identification and explanation without intent to infringe.

Library of Congress Cataloging-in-Publication Data

Audiobooks, literature, and sound studies / edited by Matthew Rubery.
   p. cm. — (Routledge research in cultural and media studies ; 31)
   Includes bibliographical references and index.
   1. Literature and technology—History.   2. Mass media and literature—History.
3. Audiobooks.   4. Sound in literature.   5. Literature—Appreciation.   6. Books and
reading—History—20th century.   I. Rubery, Matthew.
   PN56.T37A83 2011
   302.23—dc22
   2011006330

ISBN 13: 978-0-415-88352-8 (hbk)
ISBN 13: 978-1-138-83337-1 (pbk)

Contents

List of Figures	ix
Acknowledgments	xi
Foreword	xiii
CHARLES BERNSTEIN	
Introduction: Talking Books	1
MATTHEW RUBERY	

PART I
Sound Experiments

1	The Three-Minute Victorian Novel: Remediating Dickens into Sound JASON CAMLOT	25
2	A Library on the Air: Literary Dramatization and Orson Welles's *Mercury Theatre* JAMES JESSON	44
3	The Audiographic Impulse: Doing Literature with the Tape Recorder JESPER OLSSON	61
4	Poetry by Phone and Phonograph: Tracing the Influence of Giorno Poetry Systems MICHAEL S. HENNESSEY	76
5	Soundtracking the Novel: Willy Vlautin's *Northline* as Filmic Audiobook JUSTIN ST. CLAIR	92

viii *Contents*

PART II
Close Listenings

6 Novelist as "Sound-Thief": The Audiobooks of John le Carré   109
GARRETT STEWART

7 Hearing Hardy, Talking Tolstoy: The Audiobook Narrator's
Voice and Reader Experience   127
SARA KNOX

8 Talking Books, Toni Morrison, and the Transformation of
Narrative Authority: Two Frameworks   143
K. C. HARRISON

9 Obama's Voices: Performance and Politics on the *Dreams from
My Father* Audiobook   159
JEFFREY SEVERS

10 Bedtime Storytelling Revisited: Le Père Castor
and Children's Audiobooks   178
BRIGITTE OUVRY-VIAL

11 Learning from LibriVox   199
MICHAEL HANCHER

12 A Preliminary Phenomenology of the Audiobook   216
D. E. WITTKOWER

Contributors   233
Index   237

Figures

I.1 The Phonographic Book: "The phonograph at home reading out a novel." From "The Papa of the Phonograph," *Daily Graphic* (New York), April 2, 1878, 1 (The Western Reserve Historical Society, Cleveland, Ohio).   4

I.2 The Talking Book: "Blinded Airman Listening to Talking Book" (1944). Official First Air Force photograph, Base Photo Lab, Bradley Field, Connecticut (Courtesy of the Library of Congress, LC-USZ62–107565).   7

I.3 The Audiobook. Woman listening to an audiobook on a portable listening device with earbuds (2010) (©iStockphoto.com/CandyBox Photography).   9

1.1 Image of William Sterling Battis from *The Platform: The Lyceum and Chautauqua Magazine* (1913) (Library and Archives Canada, Harold D. Smith fonds, MUS 113, volume 1, folder 11).   31

1.2 Image from Victor Record Co. pamphlet *The Victrola in the Schools* (1918) (Library and Archives Canada, Harold D. Smith fonds, MUS 113, volume 3, folder 17).   36

1.3 Pages from catalogue *Victor Records Suitable for Use in the Teaching of English Literature* (Camden, N.J.: Victor Talking Machine Company, 1916) (Library and Archives Canada, Harold D. Smith fonds, MUS 113, volume 9, file 253).   37

10.1a-e Sample audiobook covers from the series Albums-disques, Les classiques du Père Castor (Paris: Flammarion, 1976–2002) (Courtesy of Editions Père Castor-Flammarion).   180-82

x *Figures*

10.2   Reading Beaver: the current company logo printed on the last page of all titles from the Secondes lectures series, Les Classiques du Père Castor (Paris: Flammarion, 1934–) (Courtesy of Editions Père Castor-Flammarion).   188

10.3   Beaver reading over child's shoulder. From the cover to a promotional document for Paul Faucher, *A L'enseigne du Père Castor* (Paris: Flammarion, 1982) (Courtesy of Editions Père Castor-Flammarion).   195

11.1   LibriVox downloads from Internet Archive by March 22, 2010: copies (complete or partial) plotted against titles.   204

Acknowledgments

There are a number of people to whom I am indebted for sound advice while putting together this book. I would like to start by thanking my contributors for their patience with my occasional tin ear as editor. Robert Jones helped me out with the selection process in the early stages of this project. Stephen Donovan, Peter Howarth, and Jeff Severs gave much needed feedback on the introduction. Thanks also to Hugh McGuire for an ongoing correspondence. The English Department at Queen Mary provided financial and moral support for this project after my arrival in 2010. Numerous colleagues there have offered me informal advice during this time. My thanks also to participants in lively discussions of audiobooks at the MLA, Université du Maine, Royal Holloway English Research Forum, and Queen Mary Postgraduate Research Seminar. At Routledge, I am grateful to Erica Wetter, Liz Levine, and Polly Dodson for giving the collection a hearing and to the production team for the many takes needed to get this book ready for publication.

As always, Victoria Riley supported me throughout this project with her usual grace despite a number of upheavals to our life including the birth of our son, Joseph. The sounds of a newborn baby in the next room were a welcome distraction during the completion of this book.

Foreword

Charles Bernstein

> And the men which iourneyed with him, stood speechlesse, hearing a voice [*phōnē* (φωνή)], but seeing no man.
>
> —Actes 9:7, King James Version (1611)[1]

This summer, 133 years after Thomas Edison made the first sound recording of "Mary Had a Little Lamb," the *New York Times*, which published its first issue just twenty years before the invention of grammaphony,[2] described Woody Allen, who had just released an audiobook, as an "adopter of cutting edge technology."[3] In the introduction to a brief interview with Allen publicizing the release of the audiobooks of his "humorous essays," Allen himself turned the unintended comedy of this remark into farce:

> I don't own a computer, have no idea how to work one, don't own a word processor, and have zero interest in technology.

Allen is not alone in blithely discounting the fact that the alphabet and the book are themselves technologies, even relatively new technologies, depending on your time frame. Certainly the Greek phonetic alphabet, clocking in at about twenty-five hundred years old, is still on the newer end of human history. But Woody is speaking in straight lines, not time lines. He gives the impression that audio recordings are a recent invention of the computer age, more recent than the television technology that gave him his start in the biz or the movies he grew up watching and with which he fell in love. One of Allen's first jobs was writing scripts for the likes of Sid Caesar. His own early, scripted monologues were released on 33 1/3 rpm "LP" (long playing) vinyl records. Here's Allen (*Woody*, not *Gracie*) speaking via alphabetic transcription of his voice, via email:

> I can only hope that reading out loud does not contribute to the demise of literature, which I don't think will ever happen.

Maybe not, now that poetry and theater have survived the demise of orality after the advent of alphabetic writing. The presence of the word seemed to come through despite script's absence of presence. (My worry is not the absence of presence in writing but the presence of absence in presence.)

xiv *Charles Bernstein*

The story inevitably goes back to Homer: did alphabetic transcription spoil the oral epic, which was, as Eric Havelock and Gregory Nagy tell us, the culmination of a very sophisticated oral technology for storage and retrieval of cultural memory via reperformance and variation?[4]

Is Homer's *Iliad* the first novelization?

Woody's not *that* troubled (the italics is a script code to tell you that if you read this out loud you should give an extra emphasis to *that*, pausing slightly before it). Literature, he notes, somehow survived the audio recordings of poetry he heard on Caedmon records, and he rather likes those LPs, as long as we remember they were a "little treat" that did not "encroach" on the mastery of the texts themselves. (*Literature*, after all, comes from the Latin word for *letter*.)

Don't get me wrong: *I love Woody*. So I find it funny—his clinging to such a literal understanding of *literature*, as if verbal art was joined at the hip to the new (depending on your time line) silent reading user interface (SRUI). (Augustine is credited with the first citing of SRUI, about sixteen hundred years ago.[5]) But Woody Allen's point, amidst the strategic technophobia, is that he wrote his books for SRUI, not as a script to be performed and listened to on an LP record or cassette tape or compact disc, or VHS videotape, or digital video disc, or RealAudio, waveform, audio interchange, or Moving Picture Experts Group file format:

> The discovery I made was that any number of stories are really meant to work, and only work, in the mind's ear and hearing them out loud diminishes their effectiveness. Some of course hold up amusingly, but it's no fun hearing a story that's really meant to be read.

And one might say, equally, that it's no fun reading a script meant to be performed, as for example the sheet music for "I Can't Get No Satisfaction" or the printed version of *Iphigenia at Aulis* ('Ιφιγένεια έν Αὐλίδι). One can well imagine Mr. Euripides being a bit put out by the paperback translation of the play that I read in college. I mean, how can you really appreciate Euripides except in Greek? (I wouldn't know.) Or is everything in lit'ra'ture either a transcription (both in the musical sense and in the sense of a textual version of somethin' spoken) or a translation or trancreation (as Haroldo de Campos puts it) or a traduction (Ezra Pound's term) or remediation or . . . well, you get my drift.

Let's switch back over to Woody Live:

> which brings me to your next question, and that is that there is no substitute for reading, and there never will be. Hearing something aloud is its own experience, but it's hard to beat sitting in bed or in a comfortable chair turning the pages of a book, putting it down, and eagerly awaiting the chance to get back to it.

Foreword xv

There is no substitute for substitution either, or another way to say that is that everything is substitution, including the metaphoric senses of *substitution*. There is no translation like the original and the original is the remediated trace of the unknowable.

In other words: if everything is translatable, nothing is.

And verse vica.

I love originality so much I keep copying it.

So why the valorizing ("*You just said the secret word!*") of one technology over another, or why this neoliberal nostalgia that the technology in which you invest your Symbolic Aura Dollars (SAD) is not a technology at all, but the Real Deal? Is printed matter the gold standard of lit'ra'ture? (—If you say so, buddy.)

It's so very Old Testament: the law as immutable scripture and all that. Not muttered and mutable sound. But even the New Testament is old news now.

The term "audiobook" is vexatious and that may be its allure. The etymology of *book* suggests something written or printed, a document (tablet or sheets); in this sense an audiobook is not a book at all. The book is a writing-storage device that usually includes an audio dimension—the implicit sound of phonetic script (*phonotext* is Garrett Stewart's term). Retrievable sound recordings, which used to be called *records*, then *tapes*, then *discs*, are now, in the most generic sense, called *sound files*.

The published, packaged, free-standing audiobook will, as media history goes, have had a relatively short shelf life. As a term of art, *audiobook* suggests, first, books-on-tape; the moniker seems hardwired to the cassette (1963–2003) and averse to poetry. I have often thought, walking into a Barnes & Ignoble superstore and glancing over the audiobooks section: "We blew it!"[6] (We being a somewhat hysterical identification with poetry.) Books-on-tape are now primarily on CD (1982–2015) or downloaded via MP3 (1994–2018). While recorded (nonsinging) voice can be stored and played in many formats, it's a safe bet to say digital files—streamed or downloaded or broadcast—will dominate in what I like to call "the coming digital presence." Amazon's category is "Books on CD," and their bestsellers include a number of distinct genres: mysteries (Stieg Larsson is huge), thrillers, classic fiction, new novels, New Age, self-help, political memoir (Tony Blair vs. Barack Obama), and motivationals (Dale Carnegie is still influencing people). The historical novelty of audiobooks is not the technology but rather the proliferation of multihour recordings in these genres.

Crude but useful demarcations can be made between sound art, poetry, fiction, and nonfiction audiobooks: the terms overlap (I always say poetry is nonfiction), but the boundaries are explicit. The other broad demarcation I'd make is between recordings made by the author and those performed/recited by someone else (actor by definition, "reader" the term of art). After listening to W. B. Yeats reciting "The Lake Isle of Innisfree," a student, used to audiobooks, suggested we give no more authority to Yeats's reading

xvi   *Charles Bernstein*

of his most famous poem (albeit recorded decades after he wrote it) than we would give to another reader/performer/actor or even impersonator (I do a mean Yeats impression). This is a little like saying the Pope's prayers amount to nothing more than those of any other parishioner. Pretty to think so, perhaps, but God surely pays special attention to the Pope, and I advised the student to pay just such special attention to Yeats doing Yeats.

On a computer, the same digital code produces the alphabetic letters on the screen or the voice sound coming through the speakers. It all depends on the output you request. (For the real experience of *this* script play it on your computer's voice reader and set "Ralph" for a rate of 35, pitch of 36, intonation of 82. The piece is about nineteen hundred words and runs about fifteen minutes as audio.)

From the invention of the alphabet to right *now* (only that now was months or years ago), one of its primary uses was *transcriptive*: script to be read out loud (in a play or a newscast) or translation/evocation of speech. ("Transcriptive," like its double "lyric," has two complementary meanings; lyric means both the script of words to be sung and a poem that evokes utterance in its words alone.)

Textuality, sounded, evokes orality.

Textuality is a palimpsest: when you scratch it you find speech underneath. And when you sniff the speech, you find language under that.

The alphabet is frozen sound.[7]

So is the audiobook and all tape-recorded voice.

While the alphabet has to evoke the full range of human voice in just thirty or so characters (including punctuation marks), the audio recording provides a much thicker evocation of tone, pitch, rhythm, intonation, and accent.

Unlike "live" performance, grammophony is a textual experience: you hear it but it doesn't hear you. Like writing, the audio voice is always a voice that conjures the presence of the speaker but marks the speaker's absence. For this reason, all voice recording is at some fundamental, if usually subliminal, level ghostly. The voice of the dead speaking as if alive. Or alive one more time.

Is the long car ride the necessary condition for the business model of the audiobook in our time?

Take my wife.

(Please.)

Susan Bee tells me that on a long solo car trip she was listening to Frank McCourt's reading of *Angela's Ashes* and that she had to pull off the road because she found herself weeping. Marjorie Perloff tells me a story of listening to a download from PennSound, with our low-rent recordings, and, hearing the siren of a fire engine, pulling off the road before realizing that it was an extraneous sound on the recording.

The new frontier for audiobooks and their Web extensions (podcasts, downloads, verbal audio art) isn't filling them with words from the previous medium (think of Marshall McLuhan's wry prediction that movies would

Foreword xvii

fill the TV airways). There will also be new audio works created especially for this medium, sampling the audio archive but also making it new.

There are only two kinds of writing: sound writing and unsound writing. Sound is always the ingénue at the media party.

Sound is grace. We don't earn it, but it is forever there for us, in its plenitude, as the social-material dimension of human language.

Its fleece was white as snow.

New York
September 14, 2010

NOTES

1. *Phōnē* can also be translated *sound*.
2. I prefer keeping *gramma* (letter, written mark) as the root of the word: sound writing.
3. Dave Itzkoff, "Woody Allen's Talk Therapy: Audiobooks by a Technophobe," *New York Times*, July 20, 2010, C6. All subsequent citations are from this piece.
4. See Eric A. Havelock, *The Muse Learns to Write: Reflections on Orality and Literacy from Antiquity to the Present* (New Haven: Yale University Press, 1986); and Gregory Nagy, *Poetry as Performance: Homer and Beyond* (Cambridge: Cambridge University Press, 1996).
5. See the account of silent reading in Augustine's *Confessions*, bk. 6, chap. 3.
6. We didn't. PennSound <http://writing.upenn.edu> gets almost 9 million file downloads per year; that's over 700,000 per month, 24,000 per day. Our files can be a single poem or a full reading.
7. This foreword riffs off of four recent essays of mine: "The Art of Immemorability" (2000); "Making Audio Visible: Poetry's Coming Digital Presence" (2003); "Hearing Voices" (2007); and "The Bound Listener" (2009), all of which are collected in *Attack of the Difficult Poems: Essays & Inventions* (Chicago: University of Chicago Press, 2011). See also my introduction to *Close Listening: Poetry and the Performed Word* (New York: Oxford University Press, 1998).

Introduction
Talking Books

Matthew Rubery

"Welcome, nonreader" are the opening words to the audio edition of Jon Stewart's *America*.[1] Is an audiobook listener really a "nonreader"? Literary critics have been curiously silent on the topic of audiobooks despite the fundamental questions this format raises about the act of reading. This volume aims to bring the silence to an end by starting a conversation about recorded literature. Challenging conventional ways of thinking about the reading experience, the essays in this collection treat the audiobook as a distinct medium that in many instances has had a marked influence on the reception of literary texts. In other words, this collection addresses the question of what it means to read a book by giving audiobooks a chance to speak for themselves.

Audiobooks, Literature, and Sound Studies is the first scholarly book to consider the significance of the audiobook, defined here as any spoken word recording of books, periodicals, or other printed materials.[2] As such, it examines the tradition of recorded literature since Thomas Edison's invention of the phonograph in 1877, the earliest machine to enable the reproduction of the human voice. No sooner than it was invented, the phonograph was put to use for literary ends, capturing the verse of Alfred Tennyson and Robert Browning. With the growing popularity of auditory literature since Edison's time, readers can no longer turn a deaf ear to the ways in which oral delivery has influenced the reception of literature. Recent advances in sound technology—not to mention the conspicuous presence of an audiobook narrator in the White House—make this an opportune moment to reflect on the evolution of our reading practices since those earliest instances of recorded literature. Some of the questions addressed by this collection include: What is the relationship between printed and spoken texts? What methods of "close listening" are appropriate to the reception of auditory literature? What new formal possibilities are opened up by the use of sound-recording technology? How have attitudes toward recorded literature changed over the past century? What are the social consequences of new listening technologies?

There are a number of reasons for the renewed critical interest in—or at least diminishing hostility toward—audiobooks. One is the growing

2 Matthew Rubery

influence of scholarly investigations into sound loosely organized under the rubric of "sound studies." This emerging field brings together scholars from numerous disciplines to consider the role played by sound in the formation of culture. In documenting the ways sound has changed throughout history, pioneering work called attention to the privileging of vision over other senses since the Enlightenment.[3] Despite an eclectic range of approaches, subsequent studies agree that sound has been neglected as an object of historical inquiry despite its crucial role in our apprehension of the world. Such studies reach well beyond an initial focus on music to consider the full scale of sounds.[4] The work of Michael Bull, Steven Connor, Douglas Kahn, James Lastra, Jonathan Sterne, and Emily Thompson in particular investigates from various disciplinary perspectives the transformation of sound from the 1870s onward.[5] In doing so, sound studies have reinvigorated interest across the humanities in sonic matters such as the voice, the ears, and talking machines.

At the same time, cultural studies have extended the scope of academic inquiry to forms of popular literature formerly dismissed as insufficiently serious or meaningful. Such approaches have shown a number of neglected works to be potentially as complex as established forms of literature and to reach a readership hitherto overlooked by scholarship. Overly deterministic accounts of the degraded forms of mass media consumption generated by the culture industry have likewise been challenged by studies documenting how audiences actually make use of media. The passive listener in these accounts is increasingly recognizable as a caricature of consumers who respond to media in highly individualized ways. It is clear that audiences are growing accustomed to numerous media formats beyond the printed book, from electronic books to hypertext, even if audiobooks lag behind other remediated forms—that is, material adapted from one medium into another—in terms of the respect accorded to them by universities.[6]

Critical attention to audiobooks has also arisen from changing attitudes toward disability. Accusations against talking books as "shortcuts" are almost always directed at sighted readers with a choice of textual formats; rarely are blind or otherwise disabled readers accused of "not really reading." As we will see, the history of the medium from the outset has been intimately connected to disability. The growing prominence of reviews of audiobooks alongside those of printed books in major newspapers today is one sign of their changing status.[7] The allegation of "not really reading" is also not usually extended to illiterate or impoverished audiences who have historically lacked access to other forms of textual transmission.

It is easy to forget in a culture saturated by print that reading aloud is a far older mode of transmission than silent reading. Few call into question that listening audiences are involved in the imaginative apprehension of a literary tale, even if the listening experience may differ in key ways from the reading experience. The discipline of Book History has succeeded in drawing attention to the changing nature of books and reading practices over

Introduction 3

recent centuries and in disputing claims for a normative practice of reading. Studies of the material book illustrating how the medium influences the message impart the lesson that books rarely exist in a single, inviolable format in the first place. Such studies have been invaluable in their attention to the actual formats through which readers encounter literature, contesting the familiar conception of the silent reader.[8] It is just such experiences that this volume aims to restore to the historical record.

This volume takes the initial steps toward rethinking what it means to read an audiobook despite the formidable objections that have been made against it. One of the most serious challenges to the format's legitimacy comes from Sven Birkerts, who has accused audiobooks of posing a threat to concentrated attention or what he calls "deep reading," the unhurried, meditative immersion in the language of the printed page.[9] By contrast, listening to a book makes its counterpart "deep listening" improbable, according to Birkerts, because it is difficult to surrender to the spoken word to the same extent without having any say over the pace of narration. The validity of this opposition between sound and print is taken up by each of the following twelve chapters as they explore the potential for deep listening in audiobooks.[10] This introduction will frame the conversation by providing a brief overview to the topic. The first part situates this relatively recent format amid a much longer history of recorded literature extending back to the use of sound technology in the late-nineteenth century. The second part reviews familiar objections to the audiobook format that will be taken up at greater length in the chapters to follow.

A LIBRARY OF TALKING BOOKS

Spoken word recordings first became possible with the invention of the phonograph by Thomas Edison in 1877. "Phonographic Books" were among the original applications envisioned by Edison for his new talking machine, which would "speak to blind people without effort on their part."[11] Books recorded for the blind could now be "read by ear," as one newspaper put it.[12] No longer would the centuries-old tradition of reading aloud depend on the physical presence of an actual speaker. The initial words spoken into the tinfoil phonograph were Edison's recital of "Mary Had a Little Lamb," the first instance of recorded verse—if not the first talking book. A demonstration of the phonograph at the Royal Institution in Britain the following year likewise began with verse including "Hey Diddle Diddle, the Cat and the Fiddle" and a line of Tennyson's poetry. The verse recorded on the phonograph during its initial trials unwittingly established a tradition of recorded literature still flourishing today.[13]

The talking machine has generally been remembered as a singing machine by historians of sound. Yet one of the first questions asked about Edison's invention by the editors of *Scientific American* concerned the impact of

Figure I.1 The Phonographic Book: "The phonograph at home reading out a novel." From "The Papa of the Phonograph," *Daily Graphic* (New York), April 2, 1878, 1 (The Western Reserve Historical Society, Cleveland, Ohio).

sound-recording technology on the spoken word: "Are we to have a new kind of book? There is no reason why the orations of our modern Ciceros should not be recorded and detachably bound so that we can run the indented slip through the machine, and in the quiet of our apartments listen again, and as often as we will, to the eloquent words."[14] Glimpses of just such a new kind of book were offered through early recordings of lyric poetry by Alfred Tennyson, Robert Browning, and Henry Irving captured by Edison's representatives in an effort to establish a "Library of Voices."[15] Yet calls for a spoken literature were premature because the capacity to record a substantial work of literature in its entirety was still several decades away, despite Edison's prediction that Dickens's novel *Nicholas Nickleby* would fit onto several phonograph cylinders.

Edison's original talking machine required technical improvements in order to make recordings of literature a viable option. Limited to storage capacity of four minutes each, phonograph cylinders best suited brief spoken recordings excerpted from longer works. Hence Mark Twain gave up recording his novel *The American Claimant* on a rented phonograph after filling four dozen cylinders in 1891.[16] At the turn of the century, records were too heavy, fragile, and expensive to be suitable for library or postal distribution. The recording of an entire book remained impractical even after the replacement of Edison's revolving cylinders with flat platters because the record play speed permitted only about twelve minutes of recorded sound. One early listener complained that he would need a wheelbarrow to carry around talking books recorded on discs with such limited storage capacity.[17] In the 1930s, the development of the slow-speed, close-grooved record capable of playing for at least twenty minutes made it possible to record longer narratives.

The first recordings of unabridged novels were made in Britain and the United States in the 1930s. The need for recorded literature in both countries arose in response to soldiers returning from the First World War with eye injuries and to others with vision impairments who were unable to read Braille. The recording of books began in America as part of the American Foundation for the Blind (AFB) and Library of Congress Books for the Adult Blind Project. The Talking Books Program pioneered their development in 1932 with test recordings including a chapter from Helen Keller's *Midstream* and Edgar Allen Poe's "The Raven." The organization produced an electric playback machine the following year and received congressional approval for exemption from copyright and for free postal distribution of talking books.[18] In a letter to President Franklin D. Roosevelt, Helen Keller described recorded books as the most valuable tool for the blind since the development of Braille.[19]

The first recordings made for the Talking Books Program in 1934 included sections of the Bible; the Declaration of Independence and other patriotic documents; plays and sonnets by Shakespeare; and fiction by Gladys Hasty Carroll, E. M. Delafield, Cora Jarrett, Rudyard Kipling, John Masefield, and P. G. Wodehouse. Other charitable organizations also contributed to the growing library of talking books; in 1936, the American Printing House for the Blind produced its first with a recording of Jonathan Swift's *Gulliver's Travels*. The Works Progress Administration (WPA) assisted in the manufacture and repair of talking book machines during the 1930s while a campaign was undertaken to raise funds for the Talking Books service. The service benefited from the participation of celebrity authors reading aloud from their own work, including W. Somerset Maugham's *Of Human Bondage*, Stephen Vincent Benét's *John Brown's Body*, and Eleanor Roosevelt's *This Is My Story*. The use of celebrity narrators has continued ever since to play a prominent role in the audiobook publishing industry.[20]

6 Matthew Rubery

In Britain, the Royal National Institute for the Blind (RNIB) began experimenting with different formats for the production of talking books in the 1920s. In 1934, Ian Fraser, chairman of the Sound Recording Committee formed by the RNIB and St. Dunstan's, announced, "I do not want to excite undue hopes, but I think that in the future it may be possible to establish a library of Talking Books."[21] The first novels recorded by the RNIB on long-playing records for the gramophone reached blind and partially sighted people in 1935. The first two titles were Agatha Christie's *The Murder of Roger Ackroyd* and Joseph Conrad's *Typhoon*. Other recordings from 1935 included two of the Gospels, selections from Shakespeare's plays, and works by John Buchan, Elizabeth Gaskell, Thomas Hardy, George Bernard Shaw, and William Thackeray. One blinded veteran described his reading habits in a letter to the Sound Recording Committee in 1936:

> This is how I enjoy the talking book. Every night about 10 o'clock I shoot the wife off to bed, then make the fire up, draw my armchair near after having got a bottle of Worthington and a cigar going, then I switch on the talking book. Don't you think this is real luxury? If the book is particularly interesting it's possible I may have another disk and another Worthington, retiring to bed about midnight. . . . Not being able to sleep much and being very poor at Braille you can imagine how useful the talking book is to me.[22]

The American Foundation for the Blind and the Royal National Institute for the Blind worked together in subsequent years in order to share research, exchange titles, and avoid duplicating recordings. Similar libraries of recorded books were opened in Canada, Australia, New Zealand, and South Africa. Plans for collections in Rhodesia, India, Spain, Argentina, El Salvador, Mexico, Russia, and, eventually, Saudi Arabia, Libya, Jordan, and Ceylon represented the RNIB's ambition to establish an "international talking book library of world literature."[23]

For many people, their first encounter with literature would have been over the airwaves rather than through print. Talking books could be heard on the radio from the beginning of the twentieth century. In Britain, live recitations and dramatizations of classic literature reflected the British Broadcasting Corporation's (BBC) mandate to broadcast for purposes of instruction as well as entertainment. Excerpts from Shakespearean drama were among the first to be broadcast over the wireless in Britain in 1923. Adaptations of novels for radio followed the next year with Charles Kingsley's *Westward Ho!* and Joseph Conrad's *Lord Jim*. Scenes such as "Barkis Is Willin'" from *David Copperfield* indicate the preference for abridged classic literature and Dickens in particular during the initial decades of radio. *A Christmas Carol* was performed nearly every year on the airwaves after its initial broadcast in 1925. The first serial reading of an entire Dickens novel took place in 1930 with V. C. Clinton Baddeley's narration of

Figure I.2 The Talking Book: "Blinded Airman Listening to Talking Book" (1944). Official First Air Force photograph, Base Photo Lab, Bradley Field, Connecticut (Courtesy of the Library of Congress, LC-USZ62–107565).

Great Expectations in sixteen installments, followed by renditions of six other Dickens novels over the next decade. Adaptations of classic novels became a regular feature in the broadcast schedule from March 1939.[24] Novelists, poets, and playwrights frequently read their own work aloud on BBC radio.[25]

Literary adaptation into sound was less common in the United States because radio producers were not free from commercial restraints in the way their government-funded British counterparts were. Still, adaptations, abridgments, and dramatizations of literature flourished on many stations in the 1930s and 1940s prior to competition from television. Serious drama programs became increasingly prominent from the mid-1930s with programs like Orson Welles's *Mercury Theater on the Air*, which brought a variety of classic fiction to radio beginning with Bram Stoker's *Dracula*. One press release for the program boasted that "the list of its broadcasts reads like a library of the world's best books."[26] From the earliest broadcasts, literary adaptations for radio cultivated in audiences skills of "story listening," an orientation demanding close attention to speech, language, wordplay, verbal

8   *Matthew Rubery*

imagery, and sound effects.[27] The earliest literary recitations went unrecorded, but a substantial sound archive of recorded radio broadcasts remains intact. Without radio, a long tradition of archival recordings of writers would have gone unheard by the majority of listeners in exclusive series made by Harvard, Yale, Stanford, and the Library of Congress.[28]

Improved recording technology from inexpensive gramophones to long-playing records renewed commercial interest in spoken-word recordings. Caedmon Records was one of the first commercial enterprises to publish recordings of contemporary writers beginning in 1952. The company's first release was a collection of poems recorded by Dylan Thomas. Because the poems filled only one side of the record, Thomas agreed to record on the reverse side the short story "A Child's Christmas in Wales," recently published in *Harper's Bazaar*. Unheralded in print, the tale went on to become one of the most popular stories recorded in the twentieth century. Caedmon Records recorded other notable writers reading their own works including W. H. Auden, T. S. Eliot, Robert Frost, Ernest Hemingway, and Gertrude Stein. The label subsequently expanded its range to include other types of spoken word recordings from speeches to children's stories. According to Caedmon's founders, recordings were not substitutes for reading but rather, in their words, a means to "deepen experience rather than originating it."[29] Such early recordings by Caedmon, Spoken Arts, and Argo proved that the potential audience for talking books reached well beyond the visually impaired.

The availability of talking books continued to improve along with developments in sound technology during the second half of the twentieth century. Whereas the term "talking book" had emerged with government programs designed for blind readers in the 1930s, the term "audiobook" came into use during the 1970s with the use of audiocassettes as an alternative to records. The ease of using audiocassettes quickly established them as the preferred medium for those listening to recorded literature in automobiles with built-in cassette players and on portable listening devices like the Walkman. Consumer mail-order rental services introduced by companies such as Books on Tape, Recorded Books, and Books in Motion began to reach the growing number of commuters and travelers with spare time, if not hands. Use of audiobooks by the general public increased as they became accessible in libraries, bookstores, and mail-order rental programs. The audiocassette remained the preferred medium for listening to talking books until the development of the compact disc in the 1980s, a decade in which major trade publishers such as HarperCollins, Random House, and Simon & Schuster began publishing recorded literature. In 1994, the Audio Publishers Association established the term "audiobook" as the industry standard.[30]

By 2002, talking books had become available for download from the Internet through digital audio formats such as MP3 files. Whereas an unabridged recording of Tolstoy's *War and Peace* once required 119 records, 45 cassettes, or 50 compact discs, the entire novel could now be

Figure I.3 The Audiobook. Woman listening to an audiobook on a portable listening device with earbuds (2010) (©iStockphoto.com/CandyBox Photography).

stored in digital format on a portable listening device such as an iPod. Improved ease of use is one reason why listening to audiobooks is among the minority of reading practices found to be increasing in popularity as the number of overall readers continues to decline. Whereas audiobooks are still responsible for only a small fraction (4–10 percent) of the total book publishing market, this is a substantial number of readers amounting to estimated sales figures of over $2 billion. A consumer survey conducted by the Audio Publishers Association in 2005 estimated that nearly a quarter (24.6 percent) of the population had listened to at least one audiobook during the previous year.[31]

The audiobook is a format that continues to develop since its evolution from wax cylinder to shellac disc to vinyl record to cassette tape to compact disc to, most recently, digital file. In fact, recent developments suggest that the talking book may no longer be a talking book at all in the sense imagined by Edison. The latest incarnations lack a defining feature: the human voice. Just as the phonograph replaced the human body, so the latest sound technology replaces the human speaker with a synthetic voice—truly a talking machine. The New York Public Library experimented with synthetic voice as early as 1978 through the Kurzweil Reading Machine, an optical scanning device that converted printed text into synthetic speech. Today the mechanized narrator is a standard feature on many electronic reading devices. Since 2009, Amazon's Kindle includes a text-to-speech feature—a synthetic voice capable of reading aloud any electronic book. The largest online collection of free electronic books divides its audiobooks into two categories: "human-read" and "computer-generated."[32] Text-to-speech programs are still in their infancy when it comes to replicating the expressiveness of an actual human voice, however, as anyone who listens to an audiobook read aloud by one will attest.[33] It remains to be seen whether text-to-speech will be met with enthusiasm by audiences in the coming decades as our ears become accustomed to the synthetic voice. Such potentially radical changes make this an opportune moment to reflect on what it means to read an audiobook.

READING WITH OUR EARS

Critical evaluation of the audiobook is long overdue. The audiobook has struggled to gain acceptance among the humanities as a legitimate aesthetic form despite its growing popularity. The absence of critical discussion of a format that has been around for over a century is one indication of its marginal status. When audiobooks are discussed, it is usually to compare them unfavorably to the experience of reading printed books or to rehash the controversy over their legitimacy through reports framed by such skeptical titles as "Can We Really Read with Our Ears?"[34] If it is true that reading with our ears is different from reading with our eyes, then this distinction should serve as the starting point for critical inquiry into alternative modes of textual reception—as it does for the contributions to this volume. In an attempt to move beyond a reductive "for" or "against" stance, this section identifies the most common objections made against audiobooks in preparation for subjecting them to critical appraisal—if not refutation—in the subsequent chapters. To this end, what follows is a review of the major complaints heard by audiobook listeners.

1. Listening to an audiobook is a passive activity.
The alleged passivity of audiobook reception is largely responsible for suspicions that it is "not really reading." Whereas reading a printed text demands active forms of behavior including decipherment, interpretation, and judgment, merely listening seems to designate a passive state of absorption often described in terms of lulling the reader into an uncritical state of relaxation. The vocabulary used to characterize audiobook consumption in terms of seduction, submission, or transfixion reinforces this perception of the audiobook as a sonic opiate. Scholars have even resorted to neuroimaging techniques to confirm that listening and reading use different parts of the brain.[35] The defensiveness of audiobook listeners is evident in their frequent apologies for listening to rather than reading a book. Why should this be the case?

Such defensiveness stems in part from the enduring idea that literature is under threat from new forms of technology. A nostalgic preference for the material book underpins the discomfort many readers feel toward an act of reception involving no tangible manuscript. Listening to a book is not a sensuous experience in the same way as is holding a book in one's hands, with the heft of its binding and the texture of its pages. The proximity of the audiobook to the printed book is unsettling because it threatens the very identity of reading in a way that is not true of other forms of adaptation easily set apart as secondary to the printed text.

The reader's "vocalization" of the printed page has been taken by many to be a fundamental part of the imaginative apprehension of literature.[36] In the eyes of critics, the removal from the reader's control of this internal act of constructing the author's "voice" makes listening to an audiobook little better than watching television, an analogy implying an inert, unreflective act of reception: the audiovisual counterpart to Stewart's nonreader. Birkerts speaks of the "captive listener" who surrenders control over key elements of the reading experience including pace, timbre, and inflection; for him, audiobook narration is a form of "vocal tyranny" in its denial of the reader's inner voice invoked by the printed page.[37] The external narrator's intrusion suggests to skeptics that the story has already been interpreted in advance. Yet such claims have not been examined by literary critics. The case studies in Part II of this volume test the validity of these claims through their firsthand accounts of reading audiobooks.

2. Audiobooks do not require the same level of concentration as printed books.

Related objections point to the inattentive nature of audiobook consumption. The very features promoted by audiobook vendors as selling points—their convenience, portability, and supplementary status to other activities—are the same ones used by critics to denigrate the format as a diluted version of the printed book. Literature heard on the radio is especially susceptible to this charge because radio is seldom the sole focus of attention but rather background accompaniment to other tasks. The opposition is a disingenuous one, however, for just as audiobooks can be consumed in states of distraction, printed texts can be read in inhospitable environments such as cafés and buses, inviting frequent disruption.

Conversely, the serious listener is likely to create an acoustic environment set apart from distraction. Sociologist Michael Bull uses the term "cocoon" to describe the use of headphones to cordon off the listener from the outside world.[38] Indeed, the private acoustic world created by sound technology makes it possible for the listener to discern multiple layers of meaning embedded in the spoken word that might otherwise go undetected by readers of the printed text. The acts of reading and listening may not be equivalent, but it is misleading to promote one as superior to the other in terms of concentration.

12 Matthew Rubery

3. Audiobooks distort the original narratives through abridgment.
Commercial audiobooks are frequently abridged by publishers in order to lower production costs and to appeal to busy readers. In fact, abridgment is not a requisite feature of the audiobook format but rather an option available to any textual format, whether in print or out loud. The content is exactly the same in spoken and printed texts; what is at issue is the mode of reception.

4. The pace of the audiobook is removed from the reader's control.
It is certainly true that the rhythm of listening to an audiobook is very different from that of reading a printed book. Much like the "page turner" in print, the audiobook narrator forces the reader forward at a pace that is blithely indifferent to individual interest in the narrative. The relentless momentum of the external narrator can be an impediment to the reader who wishes to linger over a passage or to pause for a reverie. The audiobook reader whose mind wanders momentarily risks sacrificing comprehension when the narrator moves briskly on to the next sequence of events. The choreographed narration of the audiobook is not for daydreamers.

Yet there are also benefits to the narrator's pace. Words susceptible to skimming on the printed page cannot be hurried past when read aloud. There is no "speed listening" equivalent to "speed reading." Spoken narratives restore the rhythm and cadence of prose in ways reminiscent of early storytelling reliant on verse as a mnemonic device, even if these performances are based on a tradition of written literature that incorporates increasing levels of difficulty in terms of sequence, syntax, and wordplay comprehensible only to the reader of the printed page.

5. Reading aloud is for children.
A familiar defense of the audiobook points out that spoken word recordings have the potential to restore literature to its oral roots. Whether or not audiobooks signal a return to the Homeric tradition of storytelling is matter for debate, however. For some, recorded literature promises to restore the spoken word to printed forms of literature that ceased to circulate by word of mouth long ago and that modern audiences hear read aloud only in childhood. One of the earliest academic studies of the audiobook proposed that "envoicing" the narrator brings back the intimacy of the storyteller: "the communicative paradigm—storyteller to listener—that underlies printed texts has again become flesh."[39] The very terms "talking books" and "audiobooks" encapsulate this paradoxical combination of orality and print.

Others contend that audiobooks invoking a bygone oral culture simultaneously displace that very culture through their dependence on impersonal, unfleshed media. Walter Ong has argued that modern communications technologies deliver only "secondary orality," a mere simulation of the conditions of oral society in a culture pervaded by the written word.[40] In other words, listening to a recorded tale differs in numerous ways from the act of listening to an ancient storyteller as human consciousness has evolved alongside the printed word. Many of the most recent assessments—most volubly, those influenced by the critiques of Jacques Derrida—challenge the very dichotomy between oral and written cultures underlying accounts of a nostalgic decline into silence. For these critics, the divide between oral and written cultures is not nearly as wide as such accounts presume. The voice persists throughout cultures of print despite the best efforts to silence it.[41]

6. *The audiobook speaker interferes with the reader's reception of the text.*

This objection deserves to be dealt with at length. Audiobooks are set apart from other literary formats by the presence of a literal rather than metaphoric voice. Whereas printed texts possess a voice in a figurative sense, as a metaphor for the illusion of authorial presence available through the printed word, the situation is very different in the case of literature made audible by an actual speaking voice. The spoken delivery of the audiobook is a departure from the familiar conception of the narrator as an imagined voice in the reader's mind. In an influential discussion of poetry recitals, Charles Bernstein has proposed a useful distinction between the printed text and the "audiotext," the speaker's acoustic performance of a literary work.[42] Bernstein's work delivers an important challenge to the priority of the original printed text over its subsequent performances, which in many cases constitute new versions of the existing work. Hence Bernstein advocates a critical method of "close listening" appropriate for sound recordings.

Little attention has been given to the ways in which spoken narration is capable of enhancing a text. Sounding out the words may be an element of silent reading, but the sensuousness of language is impossible to overlook in spoken narration. Spoken words can suddenly take on unexpected import, resonance, even opacity when read aloud. Nearly all readers report understanding identical texts differently in spoken and silent formats as various elements stand out depending on the mode of reception. The external narrator can be especially useful in giving voice to unfamiliar accents, dialects, or languages. Narratives singled out in this regard range from Flo Gibson's rendering of Yorkshire dialect in *Wuthering Heights* to Lisette Lecat's Botswanan accents for the No. 1 Ladies' Detective Agency series and Frank Muller's rendition of a detective with Tourette's syndrome in Jonathan Lethem's *Motherless Brooklyn*. The vocalization of such distinctively aural texts would otherwise be impoverished for many readers poorly equipped to sound out the linguistic effects for themselves.

Audiobook narrators may be classed into four main categories. The narrator may be the book's author (Stephen King, Toni Morrison, Barack Obama), a professional voice actor (Scott Brick, Jim Dale, Barbara Rosenblat), a celebrity (Johnny Cash, Jeremy Irons, Oprah Winfrey), or an amateur. On the borderline between performance and adaptation, a fifth possibility often heard on radio is the dramatized recording by a full cast of actors.

14 Matthew Rubery

The prominence of celebrity actors narrating audiobooks has tended to reinforce suspicions toward the format's commercial nature. Rob Reiner's *This Is Spinal Tap* humorously satirized the practice through its hypothetical Namesake series of audiobooks read by celebrities sharing the same last name as the author (for example, professional basketball player Julius "Dr. J" Irving reading the tales of Washington Irving). However, publishers who enlist famous voices are simply participating in a centuries-old tradition of celebrity recitals of literature.[43] The wish for a celebrity narrator reflects the listener's desire to put a face to the disembodied, acousmatic voice emanating from the machine that has been a source of uncanny fascination since Edison's era. The audiobook narrator may enhance or interfere with the reading experience to varying degrees, but there is no question that the speaker's voice has a profound influence over textual reception.

Voicing an otherwise silent narrative introduces a number of potential interpretive issues. The voice narration may affect the narrative in simple stylistic ways otherwise left to the reader's discretion when confronted by the printed page. For instance, the narrator's voice may or may not approximate the imagined sound of the narrative in the reader's mind. The pronunciation or inflection of certain phrases may diverge from the reader's expectations, or the tone of certain passages may strike the ear as discordant. The listener may become too aware of the narrator's voice if it does not achieve a sufficient level of neutrality, instead becoming an unwelcome third party intruding between author and reader. The narrator's differentiation of voices, particularly those of characters of the opposite sex, is another potential obstacle. The silent reader does not risk disliking a narrator's voice at an irrational, visceral level in a way that can make concentration on a story next to impossible.

In addition, the spoken narration of a printed text introduces a potentially ideological dimension through its aural rendering of such controversial categories as class, ethnicity, gender, race, and nationality. Characteristics often thought of in terms of visual representation are inflected in audio formats by the narrator's voice. As Lisa Gitelman has pointed out, early sound-recording devices such as the phonograph and radio were never "colorblind media" in their efforts to reproduce racial qualities in distinctly aural terms.[44] The choice of narrator for an audio recording is a delicate matter as a result. Voice actors are often selected as much for their perceived fidelity to the politics of a text as for their vocal talents. This is particularly evident in recordings of African American literature exhibiting a heightened sensitivity to the sounding of race. Critical dismissals of the audiobook format as too commercial risk overlooking the complex ways such formats engage with and revise notions of authorial identity in today's literary marketplace.

7. Audiobooks lack form.

Spatial arrangement has become an increasingly important dimension to literary composition since the avant-garde and Modernist experimentation of the early-twentieth century, although visual effects have been essential in varying degrees to all forms of printed literature. This raises the question: what do the famous black and blank pages sound like in *Tristram Shandy*? Paratextual elements of all kinds (including book jackets, chapter titles, epigraphs, illustrations, charts, maps, footnotes, bibliographies, and so forth) pose serious challenges to voiced narration. Even a simple shift to italics can be difficult to convey through tone. Experimental narratives involving multiple voices or interior monologues composed of fragmentary speech can be far more disorienting to the ear than to the eye. It is difficult to imagine how voice alone could ever do justice to Stéphane Mallarmé's free verse experiment with the blank spaces of the page, *Un coup de dés jamais n'abolira le hasard*.

Not that this will stop narrators from trying. After all, excellent recordings of James Joyce's *Ulysses* (including Joyce's own) are available despite its formal complexity. In fact, the recorded version of a printed text might be said to replace one kind of complexity with another. The challenge of aurally rendering visual effects has in some cases been responsible for generating its own formal innovations. For instance, David Foster Wallace retains his signature fondness for the footnote in audiobook recordings by manipulating his voice so that the footnoted material appears in a distant intonation easily distinguished from the primary narration. As Wallace explains, "There is no bottom page in an audiobook, of course."[45]

8. Audiobooks appeal only to the ear, not the eye.

The pageless nature of the audiobook brings us to one of the format's most distinctive and least explored dimensions: its phenomenology. It is well known that audiences frequently listen to audiobooks as a secondary activity in accompaniment to other activities such as jogging through the park or driving to the office. Unlike the coordinated experience of reading a printed book, there is a complete disjunction between the aural and visual senses in such scenarios. Or is there? The degree to which the visual field influences the reception of a literary text is a topic about which little has been written. Yet even an avowed audiobook skeptic such as Birkerts acknowledged the potentially exhilarating "doubleness" occasioned by bringing into contact discrepant visual and virtual worlds while listening to a recording of Thoreau's *Walden* during a walk along Concord's Walden Pond.[46] This anecdote suggests the curious impact that synchronized or discordant visual environments might have on the listening experience for which we currently lack an adequate vocabulary. The potential role played by affect in such instances of aural reception is especially strong, if to this point undocumented. The formal possibilities of the audiobook, which can transform a narrative through the narrator's voice, the dramatization of the text, the incorporation of sound effects, or even the introduction of a personalized visual field will be taken up at greater length by the chapters to follow.

16 *Matthew Rubery*

The twelve chapters in this volume speak to different aspects of recorded literature. They span the earliest adaptations into sound of printed texts by Charles Dickens, Thomas Hardy, and other authors from the nineteenth century to recordings made by John le Carré, Toni Morrison, and Barack Obama in the twentieth and twenty-first centuries. The collection is divided into two parts in order to best evaluate the status of spoken word recordings today: Sound Experiments and Close Listenings.

Part I documents literary experiments with sound-recording technology and competing media including radio, television, and film. In doing so, it sketches a genealogy of the audiobook format with which we are familiar today. The collection opens with a chapter by Jason Camlot recovering the earliest adaptations of Dickens into sound. Bridging the gap between phonographic books and audiobooks, Camlot demonstrates how audiences initially perceived recorded literature to be a more immediate reading experience than the printed page—the reverse of the way audiobooks are perceived by many of today's readers. Chapter 2 addresses the relationship between literature and radio from the 1930s, when Orson Welles's *Mercury Theatre on the Air* dramatized novels over the airwaves. James Jesson captures how Welles's radio broadcasts helped to define the audiobook through their retention of formal features of the printed book including the author's name, title page, and narrator.

The next two chapters consider the role played by new sound technologies in distributing verse. Jesper Olsson traces the impact of tape recording on a wide range of aesthetic practices after the 1950s, from avant-garde sound poetry to the tapes of William S. Burroughs. By contrast, Michael Hennessey focuses on the work of a single artist, John Giorno, whose multimedia experiments including the telephone-based poetry project Dial-A-Poem and recorded poetry albums for Giorno Poetry Systems anticipate today's online poetry archives. Both chapters assert the centrality of sound to our understanding of poetry and reconsider the extent to which sound-recording technology has influenced conceptions of authorial voice.

The book's first part concludes with a chapter showing the continuing influence of sound technology on the printed book (and not just other way around). In chapter 5, Justin St. Clair evaluates recent efforts to provide musical accompaniment or soundtracks to printed books including Mark Z. Danielewski's *House of Leaves*, Thomas Pynchon's *Inherent Vice*, and Willy Vlautin's *Northline*. Such experiments might be said to break the sound barrier between printed books and audiobooks.

Part II presents a series of "close listenings" of individual recordings of verse, fiction, and nonfiction. Chapter 6 carries us forward from the experiments with sound-recording technology through its brief history of analogue tape technology deployed by the military. In support of this counterhistory of the audiobook, Garrett Stewart establishes links between the thematics of tape-recorded surveillance and the carefully calibrated vocal inflection heard throughout John le Carré's fiction. As Stewart puts it (in a shrewd reversal of the familiar sequence), le Carré doesn't just record audiobooks but also writes them. The subsequent chapter on twentieth-century recordings of fiction by Hardy and Tolstoy takes up the link between voice and affect. Weaving together formal analysis with personal anecdote, Sara Knox movingly demonstrates the impact different narrators have on the reception of a single text—in this case, *Tess of the d'Urbervilles* read by Anna Bentinck, Flo Gibson, and Stephen Jack. Knox makes a compelling case that each of these listening encounters is distinctive and indelibly bound up in her memory with the narrator's voice.

The next two chapters reflect the stature of audiobooks in African American literature, where the trope of the talking book first appeared in early transatlantic slave narratives. Drawing on reception studies and informal surveys collected from audiobook readers, K. C. Harrison considers the interpretive frameworks best suited to audiobooks read by Toni Morrison, an author whose emphasis on oral storytelling challenges the divide between printed and spoken narratives. Jeffrey Severs likewise asks whether a vocal poetics and politics are at work in the audiobook version of Barack Obama's best-selling memoir, *Dreams from My Father: A Story of Race and Inheritance*. As Severs recounts, Obama's narration of the audiobook version of this memoir played a prominent role in the presidential campaign of 2008. Both chapters vividly portray the risks and rewards for authors who narrate their own audiobooks.

The final three chapters of the volume focus on the reading practices associated with audiobooks. Brigitte Ouvry-Vial brings a comparative perspective to the collection through her attention to the status of audiobooks in France, namely the series of Père Castor's classics for children that were converted into audiobooks in the 1970s. Her work identifies continuities between recorded literature and reading aloud to children, one of the few remaining occasions for oral storytelling today. Chapter 11 considers another occasion for storytelling presented by LibriVox, an online collection containing thousands of free audiobooks recorded by volunteers since its inception in 2005. Reflecting on the new "canon" formed by this website's contributors, Michael Hancher relates the practices of reading aloud modeled by the LibriVox community back to their eighteenth- and nineteenth-century precedents.

The final chapter's phenomenological account of reading an audiobook brings the book to a close. Drawing on philosophical discussions of aural experience originating with the work of Edmund Husserl, D.E. Wittkower compares the experience of listening to a recorded narrative to that of listening to music or an actual speaker. Wittkower's reflections on the distinctive features of the audiobook point toward directions for future research. In fact, this is the goal of the entire volume: to stimulate further critical interest in the neglected medium of the audiobook. On that note, let us turn our attention to the case studies of particular recordings. Nonreaders welcome.

18 Matthew Rubery

NOTES

1. Jon Stewart, *America (The Audiobook): A Citizen's Guide to Democracy Inaction*, abridged ed. (Hachette Audio, 2004).
2. The only previous studies of the audiobook format are Sarah Kozloff, "Audio Books in a Visual Culture," *Journal of American Culture* 18, no. 4 (1995): 83–95; James Shokoff, "What Is an Audiobook?" *Journal of Popular Culture* 34, no. 4 (2001): 171–181; Jason Camlot, "Early Talking Books: Spoken Recordings and Recitation Anthologies, 1880–1920," *Book History* 6 (2003): 147–173; Deborah Philips, "Talking Books: The Encounter of Literature and Technology in the Audio Book," *Convergence: The International Journal of Research into New Media Technologies* 13, no. 3 (2007): 293–306; Marie-Luise Egbert, "'A Good Book Speaks for Itself': Audiobooks and Reception Aesthetics," in *Intermedialities*, ed. Werner Huber, Evelyne Keitel, and Gunter Süss (Trier, Germany: Wissenschaftlicher Verlag Trier, 2007), 59–68; and Matthew Rubery, "Play It Again, Sam Weller: New Digital Audiobooks and Old Ways of Reading," *Journal of Victorian Culture* 13, no. 1 (2008): 58–79.
3. Two of the most influential accounts of the shift from oral cultures aligned with the spoken word to visual cultures aligned with print include Walter Ong, *Orality and Literacy: The Technologizing of the Word* (New York: Methuen, 1982); and Marshall McLuhan, *The Gutenberg Galaxy: The Making of Typographic Man* (Toronto: University of Toronto Press, 1962). For more recent accounts of the hegemony of vision, see Martin Jay, *Downcast Eyes: The Denigration of Vision in Twentieth-Century French Thought* (Berkeley and Los Angeles: University of California Press, 1993); and David Michael Levin, ed., *Modernity and the Hegemony of Vision* (Berkeley and Los Angeles: University of California Press, 1993).
4. One of the earliest formulations of the phrase "sound studies" in relation to music can be found in Trevor Pinch and Karin Bijsterveld, "Sound Studies: New Technologies and Music," *Social Studies of Science* 34, no. 5 (2004): 635–648.
5. Douglas Kahn, *Noise, Water, Meat: A History of Sound in the Arts* (Cambridge: MIT Press, 1999); Michael Bull, *Sounding Out the City: Personal Stereos and the Management of Everyday Life* (Oxford: Berg, 2000); Steven Connor, *Dumbstruck: A Cultural History of Ventriloquism* (Oxford: Oxford University Press, 2000); James Lastra, *Sound Technology and the American Cinema: Perception, Representation, Modernity* (New York: Columbia University Press, 2000); Emily Thompson, *The Soundscape of Modernity: Architectural Acoustics and the Culture of Listening in America, 1900–1933* (Cambridge: MIT Press, 2002); and Jonathan Sterne, *The Audible Past: Cultural Origins of Sound Reproduction* (Durham, N.C.: Duke University Press, 2003). Notable essays on sound have been reprinted in collections including *The Auditory Culture Reader*, ed. Michael Bull and Les Back (Oxford: Berg, 2003); Veit Erlmann, ed., *Hearing Cultures: Essays on Sound, Listening and Modernity* (Oxford: Berg, 2004); and Mark M. Smith, ed., *Hearing History: A Reader* (Athens: University of Georgia Press, 2004).
6. On the concept of remediation, see Jay David Bolter and Richard Grusin, *Remediation: Understanding New Media* (Cambridge: MIT Press, 1999).
7. See, for instance, Sue Arnold's audiobook reviews for the *Guardian* newspaper that list the reader, recording length, and abridgment status in addition to standard publication details.
8. Many of the most influential accounts of reading practices are reprinted in Shafquat Towheed, Rosalind Crone, and Katherine Halsey, eds., *The History of Reading* (New York: Routledge, 2010).

Introduction 19

9. Sven Birkerts, "Close Listening," in *The Gutenberg Elegies: The Fate of Reading in an Electronic Age* (New York: Fawcett Columbine, 1994), 146.

10. For a defense of "deep listening," see Michael Bull and Les Back, "Introduction: Into Sound," in *The Auditory Culture Reader*, 3.

11. Thomas A. Edison, "The Phonograph and Its Future," *North American Review* 126 (1878): 534; and "The Perfected Phonograph," *North American Review* 146 (1888): 646.

12. "The Talking Book," *New York Times*, March 13, 1934, 20.

13. The largest online collections of recorded poetry include PennSound, http://writing.upenn.edu/pennsound/; The Poetry Archive, http://www.poetryarchive.org/; and UbuWeb, http://www.ubu.com/.

14. Quoted in Walter L. Welch and Leah Brodbeck Stenzel Burt, *From Tinfoil to Stereo: The Acoustic Years of the Recording Industry, 1877–1929*, rev. ed. (Gainesville: University Press of Florida, 1994), 14.

15. John M. Picker, *Victorian Soundscapes* (Oxford: Oxford University Press, 2003), 114.

16. Picker, *Victorian Soundscapes*, 126–127.

17. Eleanor Carroll, "A 'Reader' for the Blind," *New York Times*, December 29, 1935, X11.

18. American Foundation for the Blind Talking Book Exhibit, http://www.afb.org/Section.asp?SectionID=69. The Books for the Adult Blind Project still exists today, although the program has expanded from its original mandate to serve blind adults to include children and individuals with other physical impairments that prevent the reading of printed material. The legislative history of the talking book program is described in detail in Frances A. Koestler, *The Unseen Minority: A Social History of Blindness in the United States* (New York: AFB Press, 2004), 144–169.

19. Helen Keller to President Franklin D. Roosevelt, November 2, 1935, Helen Keller Archives, American Foundation for the Blind, http://www.afb.org/talkingbook/tbmediaviewer.asp?FrameID=154#main.

20. The catalogue of audiobook publisher Silksoundbooks consists exclusively of recordings of classic works of literature by celebrity performers. http://www.silksoundbooks.com.

21. Quoted in "History of RNIB Talking Book Service," http://www.rnib.org.uk/xpedio/groups/public/documents/publicwebsite/public_tbhistory.hcsp (accessed August 14, 2009; site now discontinued).

22. "A Boon to the Blind, the Ex-Soldier, and 'Real Luxury,'" *New York Times*, January 27, 1936, 6.

23. "Talking Books," *The Times*, August 2, 1965, 11.

24. Robert Giddings and Keith Selby, *The Classic Serial on Television and Radio* (Basingstoke: Palgrave, 2001), 10. Histories of the closely related genre of radio drama can be found in John Drakakis, ed., *British Radio Drama* (Cambridge: Cambridge University Press, 1981); and Dermot Rattigan, *Theatre of Sound: Radio and the Dramatic Imagination* (Dublin: Carysfort Press, 2002).

25. For more on the relationship between literature and radio in Britain, see Kate Whitehead, *The Third Programme: A Literary History* (Oxford: Clarendon Press, 1989); and David Hendy, *Life on Air: A History of Radio Four* (Oxford: Oxford University Press, 2007). Studies of individual authors are available in the collection *Broadcasting Modernism*, ed. Debra Rae Cohen, Michael Coyle, and Jane A. Lewty (Gainesville: University Press of Florida, 2009).

26. Quoted in Michele Hilmes, *Radio Voices: American Broadcasting, 1922–1952* (Minneapolis: University of Minnesota Press, 1997), 225. See also Michele Hilmes and Jason Loviglio, eds., *Radio Reader: Essays in the*

20   *Matthew Rubery*

Cultural History of Radio (New York: Routledge, 2002). The Mercury Theatre broadcasts are available online at: http://www.mercurytheatre.info/.

27. Susan J. Douglas, *Listening In: Radio and the American Imagination* (Minneapolis: University of Minnesota Press, 2004), 34.

28. See Robert J. O'Brien, "Literary Recordings," in *Encyclopedia of Recorded Sound*, ed. Frank Hoffman, 2 vols. (New York: Routledge, 2005), 1:618–621.

29. Melvin Maddocks, "The Caedmon Story," *Christian Science Monitor*, June 6, 1962, 10.

30. Robin Whitten, "Growth of the Audio Publishing Industry," *Publishing Research Quarterly* 18, no. 3 (September 2002): 5.

31. These statistics are taken from the Audio Publishers Association's *Audiobook Market Survey: Customer Profile, Usage Patterns, and Experiences*, http://www.audiopub.org/files/public/2006ConsumerSurveyCOMPLETEF INAL.pdf; and the National Endowment for the Arts report "Reading at Risk: A Survey of Literary Reading in America," Research Division Report #46 (June 2004) based on Census Bureau findings in 1982, 1992, and 2002, http://www.nea.gov/pub/ReadingAtRisk.pdf.

32. See Gutenberg: The Audio Books Project, http://www.gutenberg.org/wiki/ Gutenberg:The_Audio_Books_Project.

33. Farhad Manjoo, "Read Me a Story, Mr. Roboto: Why Computer Voices Still Don't Sound Human," *Slate*, March 3, 2009, http://www.slate.com/ id/2212800.

34. Rand Richards Cooper, "Can We Really Read with Our Ears? The 'Wuthering' Truth about Novels on Tape," *New York Times*, June 6, 1993, 15.

35. See the PET brain scans based on reading and listening reprinted in Paul M. Matthews and Jeffrey McQuain, *The Bard on the Brain: Understanding the Mind through the Art of Shakespeare and the Science of Brain Imaging* (New York: Dana Press, 2003), 100.

36. See Camlot's discussion of vocalization in "Early Talking Books," 167.

37. Birkerts, "Close Listening," 147.

38. Bull, *Sounding Out the City*, 26.

39. Kozloff, "Audio Book," 92. See also Walter Benjamin's influential discussion of the decline of storytelling in modern culture, in "The Storyteller," in *Illuminations* (New York: Schocken Books, 1969), 83–109.

40. Ong, *Orality and Literacy*, 133.

41. One of the most persuasive critiques of the relationship between orality and print can be found in David Vincent, *Literacy and Popular Culture: England, 1750–1914* (Cambridge: Cambridge University Press, 1989). The relationship between speech and writing is a frequent topic of discussion throughout the examples of sound studies cited in note 5. Jacques Derrida's arguments on the voice's relationship to writing are outlined in *Of Grammatology*, trans. Gayatri Spivak (Baltimore: Johns Hopkins University Press, 1976).

42. Charles Bernstein, "Introduction," in *Close Listening: Poetry and the Performed Word* (New York: Oxford University Press, 1998), 12. Bernstein's term is opposed to the "phonotext," the array of sound effects embedded within the verbal narrative, formulated in Garrett Stewart, *Reading Voices: Literature and the Phonotext* (Berkeley and Los Angeles: University of California Press, 1990), 28. For more on poetry performance, see Peter Middleton, "How to Read a Reading of a Written Poem," *Oral Tradition* 20, no. 1 (2005): 7–34.

43. For an account of famous actors and actresses who read aloud from works of literature in previous centuries, see Malcolm Andrews, *Charles Dickens and His Performing Selves: Dickens and the Public Readings* (Oxford: Oxford University Press, 2006), 59–67.

44. Lisa Gitelman, *Scripts, Grooves, and Writing Machines: Representing Technology in the Edison Era* (Palo Alto, Calif.: Stanford University Press, 1999), 137.
45. David Foster Wallace, *Consider the Lobster and Other Essays (Selected Essays)*, abridged ed. (Hachette Audio, 2005). Other illustrations can be found in Andrew Adam Newman, "How Should a Book Sound? And What about Footnotes?" *New York Times*, January 20, 2006, 33.
46. Birkerts, "Close Listening," 150.

Part I
Sound Experiments

1 The Three-Minute Victorian Novel
Remediating Dickens into Sound

Jason Camlot

Among Thomas Edison's speculations about the significance of the phonograph in his 1878 essay "The Phonograph and Its Future" was the prediction of audiobooks, or as he called them, "Phonographic books." As he forecast: "A book of 40,000 words upon a single metal plate ten inches square ... becomes a strong probability. The advantages of such books over those printed are too readily seen to need mention. Such books would be listened to where now none are read. They would preserve more than the mental emanations of the brain of the author; and, as a bequest to future generations, they would be unequaled."[1] Edison may have dreamed about having a novel in its entirety (he is said to have referred to Dickens's *Nicholas Nickleby* as his example) on a compact audio record, but it was not until the 1930s, under the initiative of the Library of Congress Books for the Adult Blind project, that books the length of Victorian novels were actually transferred into the medium of sound.[2] And even then, when Victor Hugo's *Les misérables* was produced in talking book format on records that played at 33 1/3 rpm—much slower than the then commercial standard of 78 rpm—it still ran to an unwieldy 104 double-faced disks.[3] The audiobook as we now think of it was not a material possibility in the early days of sound recording. The basic navigation and storage constraints of the Edison cylinder and Victor flat disc record circa 1900 set the parameters for what this medium could mean for literature during the acoustic era of sound recording.

This chapter examines some of the earliest adaptations of Victorian literature into sound and focuses in particular on one case study that is useful for understanding how early spoken recordings were shaped by precedent media and forms of literary expression, and how audio technologies of the early-twentieth century were imagined for use in teaching "new" kinds of literary experience. The story of early adaptations of Victorian literature into sound introduces a variety of diverging plotlines about remediation, although all of them can be understood to display the twin logics of immediacy and hypermediacy—transparency and opacity—outlined by Jay Bolter and Richard Grusin, wherein "immediacy dictates that the medium should disappear and leave us in the presence of the thing represented" and yet simultaneously demands that the user take pleasure in the act of mediation by calling attention to the specificity of the new media form in itself and in relation to other media.[4] The oscillation between immediacy and hypermediacy provides clues about how a new medium refashions older and other contemporary media. Again, as Bolter and Grusin argue, "Although each medium promises to reform its predecessors by offering a more immediate or authentic experience, the promise of reform inevitably leads us to become aware of the new medium as a medium. Thus immediacy leads to hypermediacy."[5]

Sound recording technology was marketed for its immediacy from the day it was introduced.[6] Edison was not alone in identifying his invention of the phonograph as an apparent transcendence of the "technology" of reading (as decipherment), leading to an experience that was even more intimate than that of the reader with his printed book (as he says of talking books, "such books . . . would preserve more than the mental emanations of the brain of the author"). Late-Victorian fantasies concerning a book that talks (some of them promotional in their conception) often focused on the author's individualized presence for the "reader" as a result of the preservation of his or her voice. The phonographic book represented the fantasy of "a spoken literature, not a written one" that would allow writers to communicate "with all the living reality of the present moment."[7] Whereas such effusive testimonials asserted the utter novelty of a technology that could capture the voice and character of an author without the mediation of the printed page, the true novelty of the invention of sound recording lay at least as much in its storage capacity, in its ability to preserve something "practically forever," as in its ability to deliver a new, aural experience of authorial presence or literary immersion.

Much recent scholarship has demonstrated that the voice of the author and storyteller was made available to the Victorian reading public "with all the living reality of the present moment," repeatedly, in the form of "At Home" theatricals and public readings for decades prior to the existence of a talking machine.[8] Any account of the new media claim for an invention like the phonograph—that it supersedes the print-based book in its delivery of vocal presence—must consider the Victorian book not as a silent repository of text awaiting an automated sounding technology but rather as the locus of what Ivan Kreilkamp refers to as Victorian "performative, mass reading," by which he means,

> a mode of literary consumption that is intersubjective, often occurring communally; vocal rather than silent; productive and active rather than passive and receptive; often occurring in public spaces rather than interior, domestic ones; and—perhaps most significantly—somatically responsive, involving a performance or display of physical reaction.[9]

The Three-Minute Victorian Novel 27

With this conception of reading in mind, Edison's bequest might seem somewhat unidirectional and somatically delimited, might sound inflexible, even a little tinny. It is precisely in such qualitative distinctions between mediated modes of literary expression that we can begin to articulate a historicized conception of a medium's relationship with an art form. To tell the story of early phonographic books, both as they were imagined and as they existed, one must consider the kinds of literary practice that informed them as well as the literary works that furnished them with content to replay. In doing so, we come to understand the import and function of a medium. John Guillory has made this point recently in a statement that may also serve to elucidate Bolter and Grusin's argument about hypermediacy: "It is much easier to see what a medium does—the possibilities inherent in the material form of an art—when the same expressive or communicative contents are transposed from one medium to another. Remediation makes the medium as such *visible*."[10]

Early spoken recordings were produced for varied purposes and according to diverse models of generic adaptation, aesthetic and social value, display, dissemination, use, and experience. For example, the story of the numerous recordings made around the turn of the century by professional actors and elocutionists of Alfred Tennyson's poem "The Charge of the Light Brigade" would involve discussion of the origins of the Mechanical versus Natural schools of elocution (John Walker versus Thomas Sheridan) in the eighteenth century; the widespread appearance of Tennyson's poem in Victorian recitation anthologies and elocution manuals and what that meant as a context for social interaction and personal acculturation; the rivalry between gestural versus dramatic/instinctual elocutionary methods at the turn of the nineteenth century (Genevieve Stebbins versus Samuel Silas Curry) and the aesthetic weight attributed to these different schools of oral performance; the commercial and cultural significance of the individuals who made these recordings (elocutionists and actors such as Lewis Waller, Canon Fleming, Henry Ainley, and Rose Coghlan); and the generic identification and placement of these recordings in early record catalogues and speculation about how exactly they were used.

Even among the few examples of Victorian novels that were adapted into early sound recordings, significant distinctions concerning the media, meaning, and marketing trajectories must be acknowledged. If you compare, for example, recordings of the transformation scene from Robert Louis Stevenson's *The Strange Case of Dr. Jekyll and Mr. Hyde* as recorded by Len Spencer for Columbia Records in 1905, Svengali's mesmerism scene as recorded by Herbert Beerbohm Tree for The Gramophone Company (later HMV) in 1906, and the numerous Dickens recordings made by the likes of Bransby Williams (between 1905 and 1912 for Edison, HMV, and Columbia Records) and William Sterling Battis (for Victor in 1916), you encounter three quite different contexts of adaptation and models of remediation.[11]

28   *Jason Camlot*

Tree's *Trilby* recording can be traced as an adaptation from George Du Maurier's 1894 novel to Paul Potter's popular dramatization in which Tree performed the role of Svengali to great acclaim. In this sense, it represents an audio memento to supplement the stage-production photograph albums that were developed for this purpose. The recording was presented in the manner used to market early commercial music recordings by the likes of Enrico Caruso and Adelina Patti. It was sold as one among several of the roles to which Tree applied his distinctive genius, along with Hamlet's soliloquy on death, Falstaff's speech on honor, and Mark Antony's lament over the body of Julius Caesar, all of which were also recorded and released in that same year.

Spencer's *Jekyll and Hyde* recording, another dramatization of a popular work of fiction, stands in contrast as the recording of a seasoned phonograph performer playing a role on record that he had never played on the stage. Spencer and other recording artists like him, including Russell Hunting, John Terrell, and George Graham, had long, successful recording careers making records ranging from early phonograph promotional poems and "high" literary recitations to dialect sketches, recordings of famous historical speeches, and multivoice dramas (both comic and serious). Representative of a domestic, "family circle" genre of recitation, the varieties of materials performed by individual recording artists like Spencer suggest that they were not simply identified as specialists in the elocutionary or ethnic personae that they performed but rather were versatile impersonators and monopolyloguists.[12] The virtuosic demonstration of vocal and characterological plasticity was a key selling point of early spoken recordings. Consequently, it might be more important to understand Spencer's recording of this transformation scene (which entails the performance of two character voices, that of Jekyll and that of Hyde, and brief vocal appearances by Utterson the lawyer and Poole the butler, before the door goes down) in terms of his fame as a master mimic and performer of multiple voices than as a recording from a stage adaptation of Stevenson's novella.

In the present chapter I will focus on the contexts and models that inform our understanding of the last set of recordings mentioned above—the Dickens records made by Bransby Williams and, especially, by Williams's less famous epigone, William Sterling Battis. Whereas Williams (after Dickens himself) may have been the original Dickens imitator—the better Dickens man, so to speak—Battis's story is compelling from the perspective of media history as it relates to literary history and newly mediated ways of teaching literature to students. Despite the distinctive remediation narratives informing the examples of early adaptations from fiction into sound, such recordings were usually categorized together in record catalogues as entertaining novelty items up until the second decade of the twentieth century, when record companies began to develop their own education departments, drawing upon the recordings in their backlist, commissioning new ones, and organizing them all into separate "Educational Records" sections at the back of their regular monthly catalogues. Such educational sections began to appear around 1910 as single-page lists featuring a few dozen records, rerationalized according to the lower educational levels (kindergarten, primary grades, intermediate grades, grammar grades, high school) and with minimal instructions for use. Then, as record companies began to identify schools as a potential market for records and record players, they developed more explicit pedagogical arguments for the use of sound recordings in the classroom, produced new records for this purpose, and published discrete education catalogues designed to serve as manuals with suggested listening programs for use by teachers.[13]

The Dickens records of William Sterling Battis stand as the earliest fiction-based audio adaptations produced specifically for pedagogical application and thus represent an interesting bridge between earlier conceptions of the "talking record"[14] as a novel form of popular entertainment and the later, pedagogically motivated category of the "literary recording."[15] A key element of this historical transition from "Talking Record" to "Literary Recording" is the identification of the sound recording material with the printed book. The production of Battis's Dickens records, and their inclusion in the Victor educational records catalogue, bring us one step closer in the history of spoken recordings to that entity we now call the audiobook.

These recordings also serve as a useful focus for speculation about the particular kind of literary adaptation, excerption, condensation, and remediation that resulted from the earliest recordings that were produced specifically for such pedagogical application. This story about the early uses of educational technologies is interesting in itself, but my own interest in the pedagogical context lies primarily in how it occasioned a conceptual rationalization and material realization of a new kind of sound recording, one that is offered as both supplement to and surrogate for the printed book. Whereas the story of Battis's recordings must, significantly, begin with Dickens himself, as a novelist and as an adaptor, public reader, and performer of his own work, the overarching trajectory of my plot will move from the Lyceum Stage upon which Battis made his reputation as a Dickens impersonator to a discussion of the context in which a certain kind of public, popular entertainment (with pedagogical motives) was redirected and condensed into a new argument for literary encounter in the classroom, into an early form of mechanically audible literature to be used as what we now call educational technology.

The particulars of the scenes I will be setting are drawn from histories of Chautauqua in America, record catalogues, actors' memoirs, education theory, technical information about early sound recording, and especially from a rich archive held at the National Library of Canada, The Harold D. Smith Collection. A "jobber" or manager at the Victor company offices in Camden, New Jersey, from 1913 to 1935, Harold D. Smith worked in Victor's educational department until the mid-1920s (before moving into the foreign languages division) and developed Victor's first comprehensive

30   *Jason Camlot*

educational catalogue. This archive, consisting of more than thirty boxes filled with everything from recording ledgers, in-house publications, sales reports, Victor internal and dealer correspondence, advertising materials, pamphlets, newspaper clippings, and Smith's unpublished autobiography to reams of unused stationary and half-used Victor-stamped pencils, allows us virtually to reconstruct Smith's Camden office where the spirit of commercial strategy and literary enthusiasm led him to develop a vision of an education program with sound recordings, aimed at selling record players and, according to his media arguments, heightening a student's experience of literature.

In the course of my essay I will unpack the significance of these source materials in terms of the assumptions about reading and media that inform them. With these two historical contexts analyzed, I will conclude with some speculation about what Dickens became through this particular process of remediation and condensation that began with a novel and became an audio recording. By tracking "Dickens" from Lyceum stage to Ed. Tech., I want to unpack certain assumptions about reading and media that sometimes seem to place print literature as a degree-zero format, an unmediated raw material for subsequent mediated adaptations. As Guillory has shown, the media concept has developed over time and has held meaning in relation to a great variety of concepts, including mimesis, rhetoric and communication, instrumentality (means), mediation, representation, and so forth. If the idea of media as technological format or platform emerged in earnest in the late-nineteenth century—when, as Guillory states, "[t]he system of the fine arts yielded to a new system, the media"—the story of these sound recordings is especially rich as a site where older rhetorical concepts converge with this newer, more familiar media concept, and where print can be understood to have mediated sound as much as sound remediated print.[16]

FROM LYCEUM STAGE . . .

An individual attending a Chautauqua gathering in the summer of 1907 would have enjoyed "the world's greatest orator" William Jennings Bryan delivering his lecture "The Old World and Its Ways," heard the Chautauqua Orchestra in concert, seen The Vitagraph Company's screening of its nine-minute film *A Modern Oliver Twist* (1906, directed by J. Stuart Blackton),[17] and witnessed "A Most Humorous Entertainment of the Highest Literary Value" by "A Master of Interpretive Impersonation" and literary "Life Portrayals"[18]—an act identified in the program as "Entertainment. 'Masterpieces from Dickens' by William Sterling Battis, impersonator and dramatic orator."[19] Gazing at the stage, one would have seen a regular-looking fellow sit down at a dressing table, apply makeup, a wig, and gradually, before the audience's very eyes, transform himself in person and voice into Daniel Peggotty, Wilkins Micawber, and Uriah Heep.[20]

Following the performance, one might have agreed with the *Peoria Daily Star* that "Mr. Battis appears to his audience not as an impersonator, but as the real living character"; with the *Henderson Journal* that "the people in the audience felt as if they were in the presence of characters in a Dickens story"; and with the *Lyceumite* review, which said, "In his 'Life Portrayals' Mr. Battis . . . does not suggest the characters—[rather] they are flesh and blood creations."[21] One might have concurred with the *Platform Magazine*'s assessment that Mr. Battis was "one of the best posted, most thoroughly acquainted and most practical Dickens scholars in the lyceum."[22]

Figure 1.1 Image of William Sterling Battis from *The Platform: The Lyceum and Chautauqua Magazine* (1913) (Library and Archives Canada, Harold D. Smith fonds, MUS 113, volume 1, folder 11).

32   *Jason Camlot*

The precedent for a Dickens character impersonator like Battis goes back to Dickens himself. As the work of Philip Collins, Edwin Eigner, Malcolm Andrews, Ivan Kreilkamp, and numerous others has shown, Dickens's fiction is fruitfully understood as an art of remediation from the moment it first appears in print, and even from a period that precedes print publication. For example, Eigner makes strong claims for the influence of the popular traveling pantomime theatricals Dickens experienced in his youth on the development of "Dickens' ultimate clown, Wilkins Micawber," a character that "eclipsed even Grimaldi's comic creation."[23] And Andrews traces the influence on Dickens of the great professional impersonator Charles Mathews's "extraordinary technique of impersonation" and his "capacity almost to efface himself in the act of embodying one of his characters."[24] According to Andrews, what Dickens learned from having witnessed the one-man "At Home" theatrical performances of an impersonator like Mathews must have included his narratorial relationship to his readers, the constitution of fictional characters and signal character exaggeration through idiosyncratic dialects and speech styles, the identification of characters by reiterated tag lines, the use of comic dramatic formulae associated with such theater practitioners of the 1830s as John Poole and Richard Brinsley Peake, and, especially, the unique literary allure and performative power of the virtuoso monopolylogue.[25] Such performative and formulae-generating techniques characteristic of popular Victorian theatricals would be adapted by Dickens into print and would, in turn, influence subsequent adaptations of his novels for public reading.

To the list of models Dickens inherited for his public readings, Philip Collins adds "that of the actor or elocutionist giving Shakespearean or other literary selections, and that of the author giving lectures or readings from his own work."[26] Collins identifies "The Victorian Soloist Tradition" as one context through which to approach Dickens as reader and then follows that discussion with another under the heading "The Performer and the Novelist," which rightly acknowledges the fact that Dickens was more than just a soloist; he was an author reading to his public. As the *Illustrated London News* wrote in a report on Dickens's earliest performances, "Mr. Dickens has invented a new medium for amusing an English audience."[27] The novelty of this "new medium"—Charles Dickens reading aloud— seems to have been identified with the way these readings combined virtuosic performance, cultural codes of celebrity, and authorial intimacy. Having delivered close to five hundred readings from his work before large audiences in Britain, France, and the United States during his lifetime, Dickens cultivated in performance his own sense (and the tangible fact) of what he described as "that particular relation (personally affectionate and like no other man's) which subsists between me and the public."[28] These readings represented a performative reinforcement of what Dickens worked to establish in other ways through apostrophe and additional narrative techniques in his fiction and through his use of the periodicals *Household Words*

The Three-Minute Victorian Novel   33

and *All the Year Round* as platforms for exchange between author and reader. They enacted in theater the "strength of a faultless sympathy" that George Gissing understood to be the key ingredient to Dickens's "supreme popularity."[29] In short, by functioning as the performative medium for his own fictional characters, Dickens theatricalized the function of reader as a figure for sentiment in circulation.[30] Or, to take another Garrett Stewart phrase out of context, he functioned as a public figure for private absorption by enacting "an extroversion of the fictional inner life."[31]

In moving from reading text to oralized character-immersion, the Dickens public reading might also be understood as the reverse or playback mode of Ivan Kreilkamp's description of Charles Dickens, the novelist, as voice recorder.[32] Kreilkamp makes a suggestive claim for the inscriptive medium of phonography, or shorthand, as a key to understanding the means by which Dickens delivered such qualities and techniques of oral utterance to the page. "[W]hat is characteristically and newly 'Victorian' about Dickens," says Kreilkamp, "cannot be separated from what is phonographic in his writing: its urge to vocalize writing and to write voice."[33] Dickens's expertise in shorthand, and its connection to the facility with which he could render (or capture) vivid and immediately distinctive voices for his fictional characters, is a familiar element of his authorial biography. As a transcriptive model for writing characteristic voice into fiction, this version of the novelist as voice recorder informs subsequent reality claims made for Dickens's characters and may help explain the emergence of late-Victorian Dickens impersonators even more than the precedent of Dickens's own public readings.

Bransby Williams (whom I have already mentioned as an early recording artist), born the year in which Dickens died (1870), was the most significant one-man Dickens show immediately after Dickens. He became a star of the English music hall in the 1890s with an act that featured imitations of great stage actors of the day including Henry Irving and Beerbohm Tree, and then pioneered the development of a repertoire of Dickens characters, which he played on the music hall stage and took on the road.[34] One would think that the extensive documentation of Dickens as public reader in periodicals like the *Illustrated London News* might have inspired his own Dickens shows, but Williams never mentions Dickens's own performances in the chapter from his memoir entitled "How I Became a Dickens Actor." Instead, Williams credits his career to a belief in versatility as the hallmark of great acting, an early admiration for "wonderful single-handed performer[s]" like Fred Macabe and Fleming Norton, a professional interest in comedic mimicry, and an early love of reading Dickens's novels.[35] It was during his early success as a comedic mimic that the idea of bringing Dickens to the stage arose in his mind:

> During this time I was always reading Dickens's works, and slowly but surely I began to realize what great living characters were all these

34   *Jason Camlot*

people of his brain! No mere figures of straw, but real living personalities, who gradually became to the reader his very friends, so to speak. All their little idiosyncrasies, all their sayings and doings, their very temperaments, developed by their own words and actions, lifted them from lay figures in a book into human beings whom we felt were real friends. That is one of the reasons of Dickens's greatness: he has created men and women for us who are as real and living as any men and women who have walked the earth. And the idea seemed to come to me all at once, that if these characters were all this to me, they must also be as well known to the rest of the world, and that being so, why not present them with their peculiarities, their pathos and humour and tragedy, in the flesh upon stage?[36]

I cite this passage at length because it is so typical of the language that informed the rationale for all subsequent Dickens character impersonators as well as the early Dickens character recordings. The focus now was not on a performance of the narrator or author in relation to his audience, or of Dickens himself, but rather on the corporeal realization of those immediate transcripts of "real living personalities" found in his fiction, with "[a]ll their little idiosyncrasies," "sayings and doings," and "temperaments." A new representation of Dickens's power as a novelist was being formalized in Williams's performances. They were nothing less than enactments of the reader's experience of immersion in a feeling of intimate encounter with the "people" of Dickens's brain.

Whereas Williams claims to have invented the field in 1896, many other Dickens character impersonators followed, and, by 1909, Williams estimated that there were sixteen men and one woman who impersonated Dickens characters. What may sound odd to us now is Williams's insistence on the originality of his art and his dismissal of later Dickens impersonators as mere copyists of his original mode of imitation: "In 1896 I was the only actor presenting Dickens on the stage, now there are many imitators; and what is more strange, they are so indifferent to the fact that they are copyists, that in course of time they think they have been the originators themselves."[37] Williams identified the originality of his own impersonations with the way he adapted the texts of Dickens for performance and with the realization in performance of "what Dickens meant or what he intended to convey."[38] Among the supposed interlopers were William Sterling Battis (about whom, more soon), Frank Speaight (whose 1909 Dickens season was advertised in the *Dickensian Magazine*),[39] and Mortimer Kaphan, who prepared his "realistic portrayals of Dickens' characters" for performance "in the theatre, drawing-room, society entertainments, colleges, clubs, seminaries, lodges and schools," and whose recording of Wilkins Micawber would be released by Pathé Records in 1917.[40]

Materials concerning the abovementioned Dickens men—Williams and the later ones included—were clipped and studied by Harold D. Smith as he worked on the development of his education catalogue for Victor. Bransby Williams was also the model according to which William Sterling Battis's own work as a Dickens man was judged. As W. B. Matz remarks in the *Dickensian Magazine*, "Mr. William Sterling Battis is doing for Dickens in America what Bransby Williams has done for the novelist in England."[41] Precisely what Battis was doing, and could do, for Dickens in America was of great interest to Smith as he formulated the rationale for teaching English literature with the aid of gramophone records.

... TO EARLY ED. TECH.

The listening programs developed by record companies during the 1910s and 1920s were concerned with pedagogical considerations about how recordings of literary recitations and selected musical accompaniment might create a more materially felt and powerful experience of literary works. Such programs embody in rhetoric (if not in actual artifact) some of the key principles articulated by John Dewey in works such as "My Pedagogic Creed" (1897) and *Schools of Tomorrow* (1915) concerning the importance of primary experience and social encounter in education. Dewey's idea of "Learning by Doing" is translated by opportunistic gramophone companies, and by their educational department directors in particular, into a rationale for using new technologies like sound recording and film in the classroom as a means of teaching literature in such a way that it comes alive for students as lived experience. Smith's *A New Correlation* (1915), which has a substantial pedagogical introduction as well as notes and suggestions running throughout the record listings, argues that recitation and music recordings can be used to lift, as he puts it, "a seemingly dry subject from the black and white of the printed page into the realm of human interest."[42] Smith's argument takes the Deweyan tenet that "knowledge that is worthy of being called knowledge ... is obtained only by participating intimately and actively in activities of social life"[43] and identifies the gramophone with such active, social participation, for it allows (as Smith writes) "the bond of sympathy" to be "established between [English students] and the character in [a] story."[44] The speciousness of Smith's argument is my concern only insofar as it reveals the distinctiveness of the medium he was promoting. My main interest is in the nascent conception of literary interpretation that arises with Smith's remediation project, and with the formal implications of these adaptations of Dickens onto audio disc.

A selection of recorded "character impersonations from the leading novels of Charles Dickens" (as these recordings are described in a pamphlet about Victrolas in the schools) represents a prototypical manifestation of Smith's idea of marketing the gramophone as social experience in the classroom through the synecdochal concentration of lengthy narratives into refracted personations of minor characters.[45] It is an approach that stands in interesting contrast to the Hepworth Company's film *David Copperfield* (1913, directed by Thomas Bentley), which was advertised as "an immortalized visualization of Dickens's masterpiece"[46] and, as Joss Marsh notes, "set British film on a long and fruitful course of preoccupation with production design"—that is, with reproducing the world and setting of Dickens in all its elaborate material detail, as opposed to the people of Dickens in all their essential traits.[47]

From one perspective there are parallels to be drawn between the elocutionary models informing some of the Tennyson recordings I mentioned earlier in the chapter that were produced at about the same time as these Dickens recordings. I am referring in particular to what the late-Victorian natural elocutionist Samuel Silas Curry referred to as the "dramatic instinct" in the oral performance of literature, which he defined in his 1896 book *Imagination and Dramatic Instinct* as "the spontaneous realization of ideas in living relations, and of the motive and manifestations of character."[48] According to this theory, the poetry reader approaches the poem as a repository of character in action, and through the practice of his method "the personality of the speaker . . . [enters] into an instinctive assimilation of the character" that is alive there.[49] Or, as Curry puts it in a later book he wrote—not surprisingly—on Browning and the dramatic monologue, "The dramatic instinct is primarily concerned with insight into character. . . . By it we realize another's point of view or attitude of mind towards a truth or situation, and identify ourselves sympathetically with character."[50] It is precisely this kind of interpretive work that Williams identified as the source

Figure 1.2 Image from Victor Record Co. pamphlet *The Victrola in the Schools* (1918) (Library and Archives Canada, Harold D. Smith fonds, MUS 113, volume 3, folder 17).

of his originality and that informs the *Platform* magazine's identification of Battis as a "Dickens scholar" that I cited above.[51] The primary difference between this active mode of literary interpretation and the experience of listening to one of Battis's Dickens recordings, however, is that the model of engagement in the latter is not so much one of sympathetic immersion with the speaker (an "assimilation of the character" of Heep or Micawber) as one of inhabiting the invisible space of David Copperfield (the narrator) as the minor character addresses him, but without the responsive capacity that a narrator possesses simply as a result of his ability to narrate.

The Dickens recordings Battis made for Smith—the only recordings in the Victor catalogue based on a novel (all of the other recordings were either of poems or scenes from plays)—represent at once a more blatant and more estranged version of Curry's conception of literary interpretation. More blatant because the characters that Battis (and other contemporary Dickens impersonators) "interpret"—all minor characters—come already foreshortened, preprocessed, and dolloped into their distinctive molds in which the extremity of their attitudes and the liquidity of their motives have hardened into a "substantive physical phenomenon."[52] They come with the physiognomic traits and linguistic tics that have rendered them "over-significant" in relation to the protagonists of the novels from which they have come to us, seemingly alive.[53] More estranged because the listener

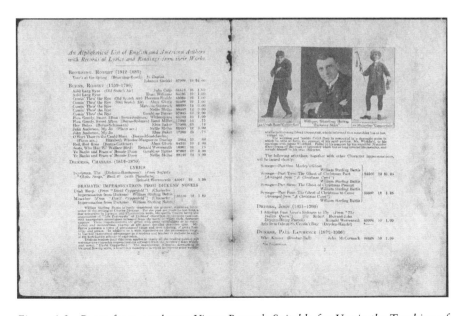

Figure 1.3 Pages from catalogue *Victor Records Suitable for Use in the Teaching of English Literature* (Camden, N.J.: Victor Talking Machine Company, 1916) (Library and Archives Canada, Harold D. Smith fonds, MUS 113, volume 9, file 253).

38 *Jason Camlot*

is disingenuously positioned in the space of interlocutor, but, like Ebenezer Scrooge in audience with his younger self (only without the visuals), the listener cannot respond or evoke a response from the speaker. So, whereas the recordings may have been marketed as providing a more immediate, transparent, and "real" experience of a fictional character—you can experience what it is like to be in conversation with Micawber from the perspective of David Copperfield—the fixed action pattern of the Victor record, the fact that it must turn in one direction at the correct speed and that its grooves are uniformly spaced to play only one set of audible vibrations again and again—betrays its inflexible materiality as a medium.[54]

The same might be said of the fact that these records based on Dickens novels were short, only about three minutes long. As Smith worked with Battis to develop these recordings, the primary issue that arose in their correspondence was concerned with condensation—how to bring out the essence of the character in a monologue of no more than three minutes in duration. Battis worried about "how it will be . . . difficult to reduce" his monologues and what may be lost if they "attempt to cut too much."[55] But Smith was adamant, and the result was a character collage consisting of key sentences and tag lines—the most markedly identifiable idiosyncrasies of speech—that best represented the "person" of a minor character from across a Dickens novel. Although J. Hillis Miller once noted that "it is impossible to give appropriate space to Micawber," expansive space was precisely what Smith and Battis did not have available to them in their project of adapting this character to the incommodious medium of the Victor flat disc record in 1916.[56] More than simple excerption, the Battis recording represents an engagement with the constraints of the Victor twelve-inch disc in the form of an intensive selection of the most typically particular (a paradoxical formulation, I know) speech acts of a Dickens character.

The label of Battis's Micawber recording—the B-side to Battis's performance of Uriah Heep—describes the record contents as "Character impersonation from Dickens: Micawber (from 'David Copperfield')."[57] This monologue consists of sentence fragments (and the rare complete sentence) procured from at least five separate chapters (36, 35, 12, 41, and 11) of *David Copperfield*. These passages have been reassembled without regard to the narrative chronology of their appearance in the novel and have been grafted onto other passages that are sometimes paraphrases of quotations from the novel and sometimes the product of Battis's own sense of what Micawber should say. These various kinds of discursive fragments (each in its own way characteristic of Micawber's distinctive vocabulary, syntax, and speech patterns as they appear in the novel) have then been strung together as if Micawber is engaging in a unified monologue in real time. It is the bullion-cube method of character impersonation, packing all of the already very salty, potent flavors of a minor character's speech into a neat, performable package.

The most explicitly stated occasion for this collaged discourse of Micawber as compiled by Battis is Micawber's imminent embarkment upon the study of the law (through the influence of Heep). However, the more general sense of occasion that arises from such discursive grafting is simply that of departure for any one of the various instances of leave-taking that give Micawber occasion to speak in Dickens's novel: departure for the debtor's prison, departure for Plymouth (where Mrs. Micawber's family live), departure for Canterbury (to work for Heep), departure for Australia to begin a new life. The occasion of the speech in this contrived monologue is both particular and general, just as Micawber's character as manifest in his eccentric manner of speaking is simultaneously compressed and verbose. To work from an observation made by Alex Woloch, insofar as the monologue functions simultaneously as an abstraction of Micawber and a condensation of those verbal eccentricities that make him a distinctive literary representation of an imagined human being, it can be understood to function as the materialization of a typical Dickensian minor character that, existing already in caricature because of its constriction to an extremely reduced space, emerges out of this delimiting flatness as distinctively singular.[58] More important for the purpose of my own argument is the observation that such condensation is enacted upon a Dickensian minor character whose status was already, from the beginning (in Dickens's novel), or even before the beginning (in the character monologues of Charles Mathews), a remediated figure, an impersonator's performance fixed as a speech act into print.

If perspective (the placing of the listener into the position of interlocutor) and erasure (the nonspecificity of the occasion for speech erasing the fact of the recording as a peculiar act of discursive condensation and ultimately the storage limitations of the medium) represent two strategies by which a medium attempts to achieve transparency, automation represents another such strategy. From the beginning, sound recording was presented as the automation of writing, thus supposedly bypassing (actually concealing) the fact and process of production. Kreilkamp's account of the phonographic identity of Dickens the novelist as voice recorder explains the cultural logic of such automation as it relates to the medium of shorthand. In the case of these early Dickens-character recordings (and as manifest in the rhetoric surrounding the marketing of early sound recordings in general) we are presented with the automation of voice capture *as if* the voice that has been captured is itself the voice first heard in Dickens's head, written by Dickens on the page, read by Dickens live to an audience, and so forth. In short, the rhetoric of automation attributed to the technology of sound recording works to instantiate the fictional act that has been recorded as a kind of immediate reality.[59] Smith's interest in Battis's Dickens character impersonations for his catalogue was based on this sense that the major achievement of Dickens as a novelist could be grasped in the sharp dints and expressive singularities of his most paradigmatic minor characters and delivered within the limited format offered by sound recording in 1916.

40   *Jason Camlot*

Like the modern day MP3 file format, which models human hearing so that it can remove as much audio information as possible and still trick the ear into believing it hears a sound with high fidelity to its original source, William Sterling Battis's Dickens recordings may be understood as strategically patchy constructions made of piecemeal discursive bits webbed together in a syntactical structure that hides the gaping holes and suggests the delivery of a complete character. Jonathan Sterne suggests that the MP3 as cultural object might represent "a celebration of the limits of auditory perception."[60] By analogy, then, these earliest examples of fiction-based literary recordings may represent a test case for the limits of the formal category of the audiobook, which, after all, suggests the possibility of a rich and immersive textual encounter through the medium of sound.

NOTES

1. Thomas Edison, "The Phonograph and Its Future," *North American Review* 126 (1878): 534.
2. In 1889, Philip G. Hubert, Jr., reported in the *Atlantic Monthly*, "Edison estimates that Nicholas Nickleby can be transcribed upon six cylinders, six inches in diameter by twelve inches in length." "The New Talking Machines," *Atlantic Monthly* 63 (1889): 259.
3. John Cookson et al., *Digital Talking Books: Planning for the Future* (Washington, D.C.: Library of Congress, 1998), 3–4; Leroy Hughbanks, *Talking Wax* (N.p.: Hobson, 1945), 106.
4. Jay David Bolter and Richard Grusin, *Remediation: Understanding New Media* (Cambridge: MIT Press, 2000), 6, 14.
5. Bolter and Grusin, *Remediation*, 19.
6. For a discussion of early immediacy arguments surrounding the phonograph, see Jason Camlot, "Early Talking Books: Spoken Recordings and Recitation Anthologies, 1880–1920," *Book History* 6 (2003): 147–173.
7. "Julian Hawthorne in 'America,'" *The Phonograph and Phonograph-Graphophone* (New York: Russell Bros., 1888; reprint, London: London Phonograph and Gramophone Society, 1973), 24; J. Mount Bleyer, "Living Autograms," *Phonogram* 1 (1893): 16.
8. See, for example, Deborah Vlock, *Dickens, Novel Reading, and the Victorian Popular Theatre* (Cambridge: Cambridge University Press, 1998); and Ivan Kreilkamp, *Voice and the Victorian Storyteller* (Cambridge: Cambridge University Press, 2005).
9. Kreilkamp, *Voice*, 91.
10. John Guillory, "Genesis of the Media Concept," *Critical Inquiry* 36 (2010): 321.
11. Len Spencer, *Transformation Scene from Dr. Jekyll and Mr. Hyde*, Columbia Phonograph Company, 1905, cylinder 32604; Herbert Beerbohm Tree, *Svengali Mesmerizes Trilby*, The Gramophone Company, 1906, 10-inch disc 1313; Bransby Williams, *The Awakening of Scrooge*, Edison Company, 1905, cylinder 13353.
12. For more on the virtuosic and versatile mimicry of early spoken recording artists, see Camlot, "Early Talking Books," 163–166.
13. The Victor Talking Machine Company at Camden, New Jersey, was the first to found an education department in 1911. "The Thing Talked: Some Memories of the Days Spent inside and outside the Phonograph Business," unpublished

The Three-Minute Victorian Novel 41

manuscript, 123, information from Library Archives Canada, Harold D. Smith fonds, MUS 113, Harold D. Smith Collection, vol. 7, folder 15.

14. Common generic categories for spoken recordings used in early record catalogues included "Descriptive Specialties," "Recitations," "Novelties," or the general "Talking Records." See *Victor Record Catalogue* (Camden, N.J.: Educational Department of the Victor Talking Machine Co., May 1906), 104–111; and *Columbia Records* (New York: Columbia Phonograph Company, June 1897), 12.

15. "Literary Recordings" is the title of a 1966 Library of Congress checklist of audio poetry and literature: *Literary Recordings: A Checklist of the Archive of Recorded Poetry and Literature in the Library of Congress* (Washington, D.C.: Library of Congress, 1966).

16. Guillory, "Genesis," 346–348.

17. "A Modern Oliver Twist," Internet Movie Database, http://www.imdb.com/title/tt0000564/.

18. "Life Portrayals: A Masterpiece of Interpretative Impersonation," pamphlet, n.d., Library and Archives Canada, Harold D. Smith fonds, MUS 113, vol. 1, folder 4.

19. For general information about the Chautauqua movement, see Joseph Edward Gould, *The Chautauqua Movement; An Episode in the Continuing American Revolution* (New York: State University of New York, 1961); Theodore Morrison, *Chautauqua: A Center for Education, Religion, and the Arts in America* (Chicago: University of Chicago Press, 1974). For program information from the July 1907 Chautauqua assembly in Tulsa, Oklahoma, see Jeffrey Scott Maxwell, "Timeline: The Tulsa Chautauqua Assembly, 1905 to 1908," in *The Complete Chautauquan: The Tulsa Chautauqua Assembly*, article posted October 8, 2000, http://www.crackerjackcollectors.com/Jeffrey_Maxwell/alphachautauquan/tulshist.html.

20. "Daniel Peggotty," *The Platform* (The Dickensian Number), n.d., n.p.; "Two Immortal Characters," *The Platform* (The Dickensian Number), n.d., n.p., Library and Archives Canada, Harold D. Smith fonds, MUS 113, vol. 1, folder 4.

21. All quoted in pamphlet "William Sterling Battis: Interpreter of Dickens" (Philadelphia: Scorer Lyceum Bureau), n.d., n.p., Library and Archives Canada, Harold D. Smith fonds, MUS 113, vol. 1, folder 12.

22. "William Sterling Battis," *The Platform* (The Dickensian Number), n.d., n.p., Library and Archives Canada, Harold D. Smith fonds, MUS 113, vol. 1, folder 4.

23. Edwin M. Eigner, *The Dickens Pantomime* (Berkeley and Los Angeles: University of California Press, 1989), 4, 157.

24. Malcolm Andrews, *Charles Dickens and His Performing Selves: Dickens and the Public Readings* (Oxford: Oxford University Press, 2006), 114.

25. Andrews, *Charles Dickens*, 109–125.

26. Philip Collins, "Introduction," in *Charles Dickens: The Public Readings*, ed. Philip Collins (Oxford: Clarendon Press, 1975), li.

27. Quoted in Collins, "Introduction," xlvi.

28. Quoted in Collins, "Introduction," xxii.

29. George Gissing, *Charles Dickens* (London: Blackie and Son, 1898), 83.

30. In describing the reader as he or she is addressed by the narrator in Victorian fiction, Garrett Stewart writes, "As everywhere else in the fiction of the period, and never more openly, the 'you to whom I write,' the reader, is only a code name, only a figure, for sentiment itself in circulation." Garrett Stewart, *Dear Reader: The Conscripted Audience in Nineteenth-Century British Fiction* (Baltimore: Johns Hopkins University Press, 1996), 49.

42 *Jason Camlot*

31. The larger phrase from which this formulation is borrowed states, "[N]arrative reading is made possible by an extroversion of the fictional inner life: a mimesis of emotion as well as milieu whose only point of occlusion is the scene of reading itself when set off within plot." Stewart, *Dear Reader*, 75.
32. Kreilkamp, *Voice*, 76.
33. Kreilkamp, *Voice*, 78.
34. Robert Giddings, "The Mystery of Ackroyd and Callow," Dickens on the Web, http://charlesdickenspage.com/ackroyd_callow_dickens-giddings.html.
35. Bransby Williams, *An Actor's Story* (London: Chapman and Hall, 1909), 61–63. Williams's account suggests that the novels themselves, and not Dickens's reading copies (published editions of which were limited), served as his primary source material. On the publication history of Dickens's reading copies, see Collins, "Introduction," xlii–xlv.
36. Williams, *An Actor's Story*, 62–63.
37. Williams, *An Actor's Story*, 75–66.
38. Williams, *An Actor's Story*, 83.
39. Advertisement, *The Dickensian: A Magazine for Dickens Lovers and Monthly Record of the Dickens Fellowship* 4, no. 8 (August 1908): 198, Library and Archives Canada, Harold D. Smith fonds, MUS 113, vol. 1, folder 4.
40. "Walter J. Lowenhaupt Presents Mr. Mortimer Kaphan: Realistic Portrayals of Charles Dickens Characters," pamphlet, 1–2, Library and Archives Canada, Harold D. Smith fonds, MUS 113, vol. 1, folder 11.
41. W. B. Matz, *The Dickensian Magazine*, Library and Archives Canada, Harold D. Smith fonds, MUS 113, vol. 1, folder 12.
42. Harold D. Smith, "Foreword," *A New Correlation* (Camden, N.J.: Educational Department of the Victor Talking Machine Co., 1915), 3, Library and Archives Canada, Harold D. Smith fonds, MUS 113, vol. 10.
43. John Dewey and Evelyn Dewey, *Schools of Tomorrow* (1915; New York: E. P. Dutton & Co., 1962), 47.
44. Harold D. Smith, "Foreword," *A New Correlation*, 4, Library and Archives Canada, Harold D. Smith fonds, MUS 113, vol. 10.
45. *The Victrola in the Schools* (1918), n.p., Library and Archives Canada, Harold D. Smith fonds, MUS 113, vol. 3, folder 17.
46. Brochure, Hepworth Co., back page, Library and Archives Canada, Harold D. Smith fonds, MUS 113, vol. 1, folder 12. .
47. Joss Marsh, "Dickens and Film," in *The Cambridge Companion to Charles Dickens*, ed. John O. Jordan (Cambridge: Cambridge University Press, 2001), 207.
48. S. S. Curry, *Imagination and Dramatic Instinct: Some Practical Steps for Their Development* (Boston: Expression Company, 1896), 235.
49. Curry, *Imagination and Dramatic Instinct*, 236.
50. S. S. Curry, *Browning and the Dramatic Monologue* (New York: Haskell House, 1965), 30.
51. "William Sterling Battis," *The Platform* (The Dickensian Number), n.d., n.p., Library and Archives Canada, Harold D. Smith fonds, MUS 113, vol. 1, folder 4.
52. Alex Woloch, *The One vs. The Many: Minor Characters and the Space of the Protagonist in the Novel* (Princeton: Princeton University Press, 2004), 149.
53. The idea of the "over-significance" of Dickens's minor characters is discussed in Woloch, *The One*, 125–176.
54. Victor introduced the twelve-inch flat disc record in 1904 (the previous flat disc standard was ten inches). The standardized size of the twelve-inch records and the speed at which they had to be played limited the playing time

of a recording to three minutes and thirty seconds per side. For discussion of cylinder and flat disc formats in the acoustic era of recording, see Walter L. Welch and Leah Brodbeck Stenzel Burt, *From Tinfoil to Stereo: The Acoustic Years of the Recording Industry, 1877–1929* (Gainesville: University Press of Florida, 1995), 111–117.

55. W. S. Battis to Harold D. Smith, February 15, 1915, Library and Archives Canada, Harold D. Smith fonds, MUS 113, vol. 1, folder 4.
56. J. Hillis Miller, *Charles Dickens: The World of His Novels* (Cambridge: Harvard University Press, 1958), 151.
57. William Sterling Battis, *Micawber (from "David Copperfield")*, 12-inch disc, Victor 35556-B (Camden, N.J.: Victor Talking Machine Co., 1916).
58. Woloch, *The One*, 14, 129.
59. Bolter and Grusin discuss perspective, erasure and automation as strategies by which media seek immediacy. *Remediation*, 24–28.
60. Jonathan Sterne, "The MP3 as Cultural Artifact," *New Media & Society* 18 (2006): 828.

2 A Library on the Air
Literary Dramatization and Orson Welles's *Mercury Theatre*

James Jesson

> I can even envisage the day when we shall put a book onto a mechanism as now we put on a gramophone record, and the whole thing will be enacted for us. Sitting in our armchairs at home, we shall see and hear and smell the author's characters. But whether this performance could be called "literature," or our share in it "reading," are questions quite beyond my reeling imagination.
>
> —Cecil Day Lewis

Speaking on British Broadcasting Corporation (BBC) radio about writing's future, Cecil Day Lewis offered one vision of literature unbound from the book by electronic media. Two years after Day Lewis published these thoughts in *Revolution in Writing* (1935), English actor Eustace Wyatt's radio play *Public Domain* dramatized a similar scenario of the literary work freed from its material form.[1] In the play, broadcast on the American CBS network, characters from *The Pickwick Papers*, Lewis Carroll's *Alice* books, and other literary classics have "escaped through copyright lane into the limitless expanse of the public domain," according to a narrator's introduction.[2] Having been confined for years to the "well-worn covers of books," these characters, the narrator says, "yearn for release from monotony."[3] The play's action involves Dickens's Sam Weller, Carroll's Alice, Shakespeare's Hamlet, and other characters meeting in the formless space of the public domain and declaring their rights to live "free and unhampered by the sickly sentiments and sloppy phrases assigned to us by the selfish interests of the unsolicited authors of our lives."[4] In both Day Lewis's talk and Wyatt's play, new media technologies free the book's characters from the material objects containing them, but the results are variously humorous or unsettling. The characters' unmoored state entertains in Wyatt's play, but Day Lewis struggles to conceptualize the artifact that emerges from the book's encounter with audiovisual media. Read together, Day Lewis's and Wyatt's broadcasts suggest that writers and performers in the 1930s were attempting to reenvision the literary work in the absence of the printed book. If today we can speak easily of "audiobooks" as literary entities roughly comparable to textual ones (so that "reading a book" is interchangeable with "listening to a[n] [audio]book"), these connections between print and sound reproduction still needed to be formed during this early age of electronic mass media.

In this chapter I will use one particular meeting of literary texts and new media, Orson Welles's *Mercury Theatre on the Air* radio series (1938–1940), to suggest how radio drama helped define the audiobook in relation to printed texts. As a series that dramatized literary classics—with a notable focus on novels—*Mercury* represents one of the most direct examples of radio drama's "pivotal position between written text and oral performance."[5] That is, by dramatizing novels—works typically identified in twentieth-century culture with the material book—the series explored the relationship between the written or printed word and its necessarily performative expression on radio. In doing so, the series took advantage of the formal and phenomenological similarities between radio drama and the novel genre that several critics have observed. Narrators, a staple of the novel, are common in radio drama (although rare on the stage), and radio critic Ian Rodger speculates that radio-play narrators "have their origin in the novel in the days when novels were written to be read aloud."[6] And whereas stage plays allow viewers to choose where to direct their gazes, the stageless radio play, like the novel, allows writers to control strictly their audience's point of view.[7] Radio listening also has been compared frequently to the experience of reading, with radio plays said to "[invade] the listener's own solitude" and stimulate an "illusion inside his own head" as novels do for readers.[8] Radio drama, therefore, can often resemble the novel formally as well as in the experience it provides listeners.

And this affinity between a print-based literary genre and radio also points to historical connections between sound reproduction and writing. Timothy C. Campbell, Lisa Gitelman, and other critics have recently explored sound-recording and sound-transmission technologies' early development as *writing* machines that promised to improve on existing modes of *graphic* representation.[9] As Campbell notes, the association of "wireless" with radio *sound* technologies that developed during the twentieth century obscures the history of *writing* via older wireless devices such as the radio telegraph. With our current understanding of *wireless* again encompassing textual transmission (for example, e-mail, text messaging), we can consider how radio drama used wireless transmission to extend literary genres traditionally identified with print. As I will argue, Welles's series played a significant part not only in extending the printed word into the wireless realm but also, and perhaps more importantly, in making the audible book comprehensible to the listening public during the late age of print.

THE MERCURY THEATRE: REMEDIATING THE NOVEL

The Mercury Theatre on the Air—also called *First Person Singular* when the series began in July 1938 and *Campbell Playhouse* when the soup

46   *James Jesson*

company began sponsoring the show that December—adapted a different work each week for one-hour broadcasts. Before Campbell's sponsorship, the properties adapted tended to be nineteenth- or early-twentieth-century literary "classics." These included novels and novellas by Charlotte Brontë (*Jane Eyre*), Booth Tarkington (*Clarence* and *Seventeen*), and Joseph Conrad (*Heart of Darkness*) as well as occasional stage plays (Shakespeare's *Julius Caesar* and John Drinkwater's *Abraham Lincoln*). Campbell sought higher ratings through more adaptations of recent novels, Broadway plays, and films, but some older novels like *The Count of Monte Cristo* and *The Adventures of Huckleberry Finn* remained on the schedule.

Significantly, the series' adaptations of novels were not simply dramatizations, in the sense of enacting episodes from the novels with an ensemble cast; they also remediated the genre of the novel and the medium of the book. Media theorists Jay David Bolter and Richard Grusin define remediation as "the representation of one medium in another."[10] One can think, for example, of ekphrasis—representing visual art in literature, as in the description of Breughel's painting *The Fall of Icarus* in W. H. Auden's poem "Musée des Beaux Arts." Adaptations of works between media are not necessarily remediations. As Bolter and Grusin note, many films adapt novels without "any overt reference to the novel on which they are based." In such cases, "[t]he content has been borrowed"—the plot, characters, and settings—"but the medium has not been appropriated or quoted."[11] In contrast, Welles's adaptations frequently quote the medium and genre from which they derive, much as *Public Domain* does by explicitly citing its bookish origins. Quotations of one medium in another provide audiences with experiences of "hypermediacy"—intense awareness of mediation. According to Bolter and Grusin, hypermediacy paradoxically promotes a new medium's immediacy (an impression of direct access to reality) to consumers, who "take pleasure in the act of mediation."[12] For example, the multiple windows of a computer operating system, while foregrounding their heterogeneity and mediation of content, seem to "reproduce the rich sensorium of human experience" with the range of media they present: still and moving images, text, and sound.[13] As a result of this sensory diversity—the visual element of still photographs, the tactility of moving images, the audibility of music or voice recordings—the cumulative effect of the desktop interface can resemble the variety of lived experience. Hypermediacy also frequently calls attention to the competitive relationship between old and new media; by quoting the old medium, a new one can argue for its superior immediacy. Similarly, by remediating the book, Welles encouraged listeners to make sense of the *Mercury*'s broadcast performances in comparison to textual expression.

An early example of Welles's remediation of writing is the adaptation of *Treasure Island* that Welles wrote along with coproducer John Houseman for the *Mercury*'s second broadcast.[14] The script employs the *Mercury*'s characteristic mix of narration (performed here, as in many episodes, by

A *Library on the Air*   47

Welles) and scenes enacted by a full company of actors. The play's opening follows the beginning of Robert Louis Stevenson's novel almost exactly, with Welles narrating in the character of the elder Jim Hawkins:

> Squire Trelawney, Dr. Livesey, and the rest of the gentlemen having asked me to write down the whole particulars about Treasure Island, from the beginning to the end, keeping nothing back but the bearings of the island, and that only because there is still treasure not yet lifted, I take up my pen in the year of grace 1783 and go back to that time nineteen years ago when my father kept the Admiral Benbow Inn and the brown old seaman with the saber cut first took up his lodging under our roof. I was fourteen, but I remember him as if it were yesterday.[15]

The final sentence cues the first of many dramatic scenes interspersed with Welles's narration, as the younger Jim Hawkins hears Billy Bones approaching the inn singing "Fifteen men on the dead man's chest—Yo-ho-ho, and a bottle of rum!" *Treasure Island* illustrates the combined immediacy and hypermediacy that Bolter and Grusin identify as a characteristic of remediation. The immediacy of dramatic scenes involving Billy Bones, Long John Silver, and others contrast with the narrator's reference to writing, which emphasizes mediation while recalling the novel's original, textual incarnation.

Many of the *Mercury* broadcasts similarly remediate writing. Examples include the series' first broadcast, *Dracula*, which retains the novel's use of diary entries and letters to tell the story; an adaptation of Edward Ellsberg's *Hell on Ice*, which reconstructs a doomed nautical voyage through the ship captain's diary entries; and even *The War of the Worlds*, better known for its first act's fake radio newscast than for its second act, which begins with a narrator "set[ting] down . . . notes on paper" about the Martian invasion and ends with the narrator in his "peaceful study at Princeton writing down this last chapter" on the war's resolution.[16] Each of the original novels includes these quotations of other forms of writing (the diary and the memoir) and thus exhibits the hypermediacy commonly found in the novel genre, which Mikhail Bakhtin argues is characterized by its heterogeneous combinations of literary forms and modes of discourse.[17] Welles and his collaborators easily could have removed these citations of textual forms in adapting the novels' stories. That they did not suggests an interest in exploring the effect on print forms of being transferred to radio. Moreover, by recapitulating the original works' remediations of textual forms, the broadcasts mimic the novel genre, providing listeners with the impression not only of hearing a radio play but also of listening to a book.

Welles's remediations not only replicated the formal heterogeneity of novels but also attended to their material construction as books. Gerard Genette's concept of the book's "paratext" can focus our attention on how Welles's broadcasts constructed the radio adaptation as an alternate book of sorts. Genette's term refers to all the features of the book surrounding

48 *James Jesson*

the text itself: for example, the book's title, table of contents, chapter titles, jacket cover, and so on. These features, which gradually have been ratified into a set of publishing conventions, help frame the reader's encounter with any book. Genette writes that paratext not only informs readers of the book's contents but also enables a work "to become a book and to be offered as such to its readers and, more generally, to the public."[18] Paratext makes a novel recognizable as a book, and it is appropriate, therefore, that, in attempting to make audible novels similarly recognizable, Welles's remediations of the book often focused on paratext in two senses. First, Welles remediated the book by figuring elements of paratext in his broadcasts. His most consistent focus was on the author's name and identity—the authorial attribution found in most contemporary printed works of literature—but certain plays also cite other parts of a book's title page and other paratextual elements in the broadcast. In a production of *Huckleberry Finn* (1940), for example, Welles precedes the play by introducing the actors, who "await their cues to play as many of the Mark Twain characters as we could cram into a single broadcast. . . . But right now they would like me to read to you in a loud clear voice *the words printed on the title page* of tonight's story."[19] Welles then reads Twain's notice discouraging his readers from finding a motive, moral, or plot in the story. This reference to the title page evokes the material book and enforces the comparison between book and broadcast implicit in Welles's earlier statement about "cram[ming] into a single broadcast" as many of Twain's characters as possible.

Welles figures both the book and the dramatization as physical containers for the story's elements and emphasizes their similarity by reproducing the author's title-page address to readers. He also, however, indicates the obvious differences between these containers' capacity: the hour-long broadcast can cram in only so much of the book. These quotations of the book's conventions not only remediate paratextual elements of the adapted novels but also do so during moments that might be called the broadcasts' paratext—the frame around the play that includes Welles's introductory comments and closing remarks. These paratextual moments highlight the bookness of the original novel and function also as the paratext for a new, audible version of the book. The rest of this essay will focus on these paratextual moments around the figurative margins of the *Mercury* broadcasts, which reflect on Welles's conception of his own broadcasts' relationship to literary and print traditions.

THE RADIO PLAY AS AUDIOBOOK

One important component of the *Mercury* plays' remediations of the novel genre is their format. As other critics have observed, although *Mercury* was a dramatic series, Welles downplayed the broadcasts' connections to the stage and instead stressed their kinship with the novel.[20] Introducing the *Campbell*

Playhouse production of Daphne du Maurier's novel *Rebecca,* for example, Welles claimed the adaptation was "not a play; it's a story," and he reminded listeners, "The Campbell Playhouse is situated in a regular studio, not a theater. . . . There's only one illusion I'd like to create: the illusion of a story."[21] Two years later, Welles wrote, "The less a radio drama resembles a play the better it is likely to be. . . . [R]adio drama is more akin to the form of the novel, to storytelling, than to anything else of which it is convenient to think."[22] To compensate for the radio audience's inability to see settings and characters, Welles proposed a narrator to "introduc[e] other characters" and "weld the various episodes together," as a press release described his plans for the series.[23] Paul Heyer has pointed out that Welles's radio plays did not invent radio-play narration (*The Lone Ranger, Lux Radio Theatre,* and other programs used the device for transitions between scenes), but Welles's trademark was making the narrator a character in the story, whenever possible.[24] Blending the roles of narrator and character often created near-seamless transitions between narration and enacted scenes, with the result that dramatized novels arguably came "out in something very close to their original form."[25] Therefore, whereas his plays altered the adapted novels in obvious ways (dramatizing and condensing them), the broadcasts projected impressions of novels rendered audibly.

Another component of Welles's remediation of novels is his much-discussed focus on literary authorship. Part of Welles's "practice of self-creation" as a mass-media celebrity involved associating himself with the "master authors" whose works he adapted,[26] and the CBS network helped Welles's audiences perceive him as an authorlike figure by promoting *Mercury* as "his show in every sense of the word: 'Written, directed, produced and performed by Orson Welles.'"[27] Michele Hilmes writes that the "prestige status" that *Mercury* conferred on CBS depended on Welles's "genius persona," which could only be sustained if audiences perceived Welles as an autonomous creator—a confirmation of cultural assumptions that "a work of art possesses a sole creative author from whose individual genius the work stems."[28] The figure of the novelist fit this model of the individual creator perfectly, and the *Mercury*'s format allowed Welles to embody the author as he narrated the plays. Moments like the *Treasure Island* broadcast's opening implicitly associated Welles with the story's author by casting his narration as an act of *writing,* and other broadcasts made this connection even more explicitly. Before a dual presentation of Joseph Conrad's *Heart of Darkness* and Clarence Day's *Life with Father,* for example, announcer Dan Seymour declared, "Tonight Mr. Welles will not only appear in several parts but will also *speak for the two authors* as narrator."[29]

Welles's self-identification with the literary author reinforced his reputation as an artistic genius, which eventually helped Welles land his famously generous film contract with RKO during the *Mercury*'s second year. Often, however, rather than merely self-aggrandizing, Welles's reflections on authorship interrogated that concept's construction through the old media technologies

50 *James Jesson*

of publishing and his new media adaptations. One broadcast from the series' presponsorship period (*Treasure Island*) and one *Campbell* production (*I Lost My Girlish Laughter*) illustrate how Welles used his broadcasts' paratext to examine the bibliographic construction of authorship.

Before the *Treasure Island* play begins with Welles figuratively "tak[ing] up [his] pen" to write/narrate the story, Welles compares the *Mercury*'s dramatization to the source book, telling listeners, "it's [*Treasure Island*] in your library because it's a great English classic, and this evening, because it's a great story, it's on your radio."[30] Welles's chiastic sentence suggests parallels between a book and its adaptation on the airwaves. As the antecedent of *it* subtly shifts between the printed and the audible story (the one "in your library," the other "on your radio"), Welles's sentence seems to elide the differences between book and broadcast. The gesture toward equating his radio broadcast with the book suggests a reverence for the older literary tradition, but a closer look at Welles's opening remarks reveals him to be destabilizing the printed word's ostensible authority. Like many of Welles's "lead-ins," this one offers a brief biographical sketch of the author. Also characteristically, Welles's biography of Stevenson focuses on the latter's creation of the novel and places special attention on the work's publication and the paratextual attribution of authorship. Welles begins the sketch by describing "a small boy who asked his stepfather . . . please to write something interesting."[31] Welles then describes how the resulting story was originally serialized as *The Sea Cook* and credited to the pseudonymous Captain George North, and he discusses the story's collaborative creation: "The small boy himself helped a lot, even though Captain North got the credit, and so did a third and equally incurable small boy, the author's father."[32] Welles's introductory comments narrate not only the story's collaborative invention but also its development into a textual object bearing the false attribution to Captain North.

As the introduction progresses, Welles further complicates the authorial attribution and suggests that the story's materialization as a book obscures certain complexities of literary creation. Welles does not name Stevenson until just before the play's beginning, when Welles assumes the role of author-narrator. This confluence of events—the revelation of the author's identity and Welles's assumption of the authorial role—helps Welles associate himself with the author. Welles also suggests, however, that Stevenson's authorial identity in the novel is nearly as constructed as Welles's authorial identity is in the broadcast. Welles sets a mysterious tone earlier in the introduction by mentioning the author's death among the Samoans, who "laid [him] to rest in the hills of their own faraway treasure island," and he speculates that the author somehow may be "tuned in on this broadcast."[33] The author's mysterious end and Welles's hints at his haunting presence make the revelation of his name all the more dramatic.

Welles ends the introduction and leads into the play's opening by commenting on the luck of Stevenson's stepson, remarking, "There are

A Library on the Air 51

millions of small boys. But only one of us had Robert Louis Stevenson for a stepfather."[34] Appearing for the first time, Stevenson's name punctuates the introduction and occupies the center of attention just as squarely as an author's name on a title page. Welles's narrative has gradually approached this definitive identification, which develops from the nonliterary identities of stepfather and son through the pseudonym of Captain George North and finally to the ostensibly authoritative attribution to Robert Louis Stevenson. Although Welles's narrative thus treats this final identity as definitive truth, other elements of Welles's biography subvert this image of individual authorship. Given the novel's collaborative creation, the single-name attribution can appear to obscure the truth rather than reveal it. Welles also challenges Stevenson's primacy by appearing to be a duplicate author. Welles implies a parallel between his *Mercury* cohorts ("we who are *retelling* this story") and Stevenson (known to the Samoans as "the great *teller* of tales"). This association suggests that the tale as it is materialized in the book and attributed to Stevenson is just one of its many possible iterations. By reanimating the process of the novel's writing and its enshrinement as a book, Welles reveals how the single-author attribution can gloss over less straightforward cases of literary invention.

As Campbell shifted the series' focus to newer works, Welles increasingly interviewed live authors either before or after the plays. The adaptation of *I Lost My Girlish Laughter*, a satirical novel about Hollywood by Jane Schor and Silvia Schulman (but published under the pseudonym Jane Allen), again allowed Welles to explore the mystery and complexity of authorial identity.[35] Even more than his introduction to *Treasure Island* had, Welles's interview with the reputed Jane Allen focused on the novel's paratext and the publishing industry's role in defining the literary work and its author. And, with his own program increasingly serving to promote authors and guest actors, Welles also suggested parallels between the influence of the novel's and his broadcasts' paratext.

After the *Girlish Laughter* dramatization, Welles and his cast spoke by telephone with the novel's purported author. Before the conversation, Welles plays up the author's mysterious identity, as he had in the *Treasure Island* broadcast: "We only know that *I Lost My Girlish Laughter* was credited on its title page to somebody who calls herself or himself or themselves Jane Allen."[36] This reference to the book's title page follows Welles's declaration that the author's actual identity is "a well-kept secret with its publishers"—"a good trick if Random House Incorporated can do it."[37] As with *Treasure Island*, publication has obscured multiple authors' identities with a singular attribution. Welles promises to reveal the truth and enlists each listener as "a full member of our special secret service sworn to unmask all authors and authoresses to the last poison penname."[38] Naturally, however, this mystery's preservation makes for better radio, and Welles pursues the author's identity lightly and with tongue in cheek. The play's cast assumes the roles of "inspectors" but hardly delivers the "unrelenting

52   James Jesson

efforts" that Welles promises to listeners:[39] one, playwright George Kaufman, first asks facetiously if the author is "animal, vegetable, or mineral," and then whether she has seen any good plays lately, a question clearly designed to elicit praise for his latest play, *The American Way*, rather than to uncover her identity.[40] Instead of undermining Random House's publicity efforts, therefore, Welles's mock investigation actually amplifies them. Welles further mystifies the novelists' identities while publicizing both their book and Kaufman's work. The broadcast, therefore, not only traces the fictional author's developing public persona but also contributes to it through Welles's dramatization and audible paratext.

Like the *Treasure Island* lead-in, *Girlish Laughter*'s conclusion suggests that behind the image of a single author lie multiple people's combined agency: the writer or writers, performers like Welles, and publishers like Random House. The work's existence owes not only to the person whose name appears in the title page but also to the book's extended paratext, which now encompasses Welles's broadcasts. The final example I will consider further complicates not only the concept of authorship but also the conception of the literary work when another agent is involved: Welles's sponsor. As I will discuss, Welles's and Campbell's competing definitions of both the authorial role and the audible literary artifact emerged during the production of Charles Dickens's *A Christmas Carol* and revealed the high stakes over defining the broadcasts' paratext.

As Marguerite H. Rippy has observed, Dickens was a "perfect source" for Welles, whose association with the "fellow populist showman . . . established his entertainment brand as both geared to the masses and culturally respectable."[41] Of the *Mercury* series' seventy-eight broadcasts, five adapted Dickens works, more than those of any other author: *A Tale of Two Cities* (July 25, 1938), *Oliver Twist* (October 2, 1938), *The Pickwick Papers* (November 20, 1938), and *A Christmas Carol* (December 23, 1938, and December 24, 1939). Dickens's dual identity as author and performer suggested similarities between Welles and the Victorian writer. As I will discuss, however, Campbell also benefited from association with Dickens and, particularly, with the family traditions his Christmas story portrayed. The soup company had begun sponsoring Christmastime radio dramatizations of *Carol* three years before joining Welles's series. Having established a tradition with its *Carol* programs, the company had reason to restrict Welles's assertions of creative control in his introductory and closing remarks, which might detract from Campbell's image as the creator of this annual holiday event. Two draft introductions written for Welles's first *Carol* broadcast—one apparently by Welles and one by Campbell's advertising agency—illustrate both parties' attempts to claim the play as the product of their respective creative efforts.

Welles's draft lead-in, preserved in an untitled typescript, characteristically focuses on authorial biography.[42] In the event, Welles's on-air introduction included no biography of Dickens but began with an excerpt from

A Library on the Air 53

Luke's account of Christ's birth, which Welles followed with a discussion of Christmastime storytelling. Welles's one brief reference to Dickens ended the broadcast version of the introduction, as he read from the author's comments on the title page of *A Christmas Carol* and then noted that this title page is signed, "Your faithful friend and servant Charles Dickens." The broadcast introduction, therefore, characteristically delayed naming the author— Welles even paused dramatically before saying "Charles Dickens"—while remediating the book's paratext. The alternate draft includes many more biographical details and focuses on the Victorian writer's public readings while implicitly comparing Welles's and Dickens's popular performances. Dickens, whom Welles once described as "not a writer who acted" but "an actor who wrote,"[43] combined writing and performance, as did Welles, who continued into the mid-1930s to think of himself as a writer more than an actor and director, according to Heyer.[44] Welles's draft biography also connects Dickens's public readings to the *Mercury* broadcasts' characteristic mode of storytelling. The draft begins by noting that "Many of our grandfathers' [sic] may have heard Charles Dickens read his 'Christmas Carol.' He did it often enough."[45] The large audiences at these readings (so big that "[m]any of our grandfathers" may have been included) suggest comparisons to Welles's mass-media listenership, but the intimacy of *grandfathers* also personalizes Dickens's audience in Welles's description. This combination of intimacy and multiplicity encapsulates Welles's notion that radio storytelling forms personal connections with individual members of a mass listenership. As he once stated, the "invisible [radio] audience should never be considered collectively, but individually."[46]

Having implied comparisons between Dickens's performances and the *Mercury*'s radio storytelling, Welles's biographical notes then associate the broadcasts with Dickens's books—the other manifestations of the author's creations. Concluding his discussion of Dickens's public appearances, Welles quotes from the end of the "touching speech" that closed Dickens's final reading of *A Christmas Carol*: "Ladies and gentlemen, in but two short weeks from this time I hope that you may enter, in your own homes, on a new series of readings, at which my assistance will be indispensable; but from these garish lights I now vanish forevermore, with a heartfel [sic], grateful respectful and affectionate farewell."[47] The biography's focus shifts here from performance to the material objects—the books—facilitating this "new series of readings" in the home. Welles's draft introduction, therefore, associates his broadcasts—also enjoyed domestically—with the novel in two of its possible manifestations: as public performances and as the privately read book. As an implied equivalent of each of these manifestations, Welles's audible book appears to be not a single object so much as a diverse range of experiences enabled by the novel.

In contrast to Welles's expansive view of authorship and the book, Campbell's alternative introduction illustrates the company's interest in limiting definitions of the literary product and its creator. Like Welles, Campbell

54   James Jesson

sought to associate itself with Dickens and the literary tradition and social customs represented by his Christmas story. In his draft introduction, Welles conveyed his series' combination of tradition and innovation—its updating of literary classics for a new medium. Campbell's alternate opening—outlined in a typescript titled "Suggested Carol Opening"—displays the company's similar efforts to present itself as an innovator with links to tradition.[48] But in contrast to Welles's depiction of audible books imbued with characteristics of oral performance, Campbell's conception of the broadcasts suggested commodities resembling the company's products.

Campbell's suggested opening—like Welles's draft, ultimately not used in the broadcast—sketches a preplay dialogue for Welles and Lionel Barrymore, who had starred as Scrooge in Campbell's three previous productions of *Carol* but eventually backed out of the 1938 broadcast because of illness. The suggested opening scripts Barrymore's speeches but offers only general suggestions for many of Welles's introductory remarks, including "planting [the] fact that this is Campbell's Christmas present to the listener—that it's the fourth year of its presentation, etc."[49] As Hilmes writes, during Campbell's sponsorship Welles "increasingly distanced himself from even [a] limited role in promoting the sponsor's product," and although *A Christmas Carol* was only his third *Campbell Playhouse* broadcast, Welles appeared already wary of his promotional duties.[50] Welles did not mention Campbell's earlier productions of *A Christmas Carol* in the broadcast's opening, although his concluding remarks referred briefly to his part in "this happy tradition of the *Campbell Playhouse*."[51] The suggested opening charges Barrymore with subtly linking this relatively short tradition to longer ones. In the draft, the actor, born eight years after Dickens's death, provides part of this link by recalling "the first time my mother read [the story] to us—to John and Ethel and myself, as children" and using Victorian imagery in reminiscing about "tripp[ing] all over . . . my father's frock coats."[52] Here the *Carol* links the Victorian, domestic experience of communal reading to the radio audience's contemporary listening. In the broadcast, CBS announcer Ernest Chappell states that "throughout the country today in thousands of homes it has become an important and beloved Christmas custom to *listen* to this story."[53] Having alluded to the familial setting of these performances and the Barrymore family tree, Campbell's suggested opening draws another genealogy from Barrymore to Welles. The document suggests that Welles make "use of the phrase we have used for three years, in describing [Barrymore as] 'America's grandest character actor,'" and Barrymore would then describe Welles as "Radio's grandest actor."[54] Thus an image of tradition emerges through the artistic lineage of Dickens, Barrymore, and Welles.

Associating its product with family traditions was crucial for Campbell, which used its advertisements during *Campbell Playhouse* broadcasts to reassure housewives that it was acceptable to serve soup from a can. The first promotional spot in the 1938 *Carol* broadcast associated holiday gatherings with the canned soup's modern convenience:

> Women like to have plenty of good soups on hand all through the holidays so that they can serve piping-hot, nourishing platefuls at any family mealtime. The youngsters are on the go all day long, making the most of the Christmas vacation, and soup can be ready for them in a jiffy. There's health and happiness in good, hot soup. Your grocer has Campbell's soups—twenty-one delicious kinds awaiting your selection.[55]

The advertisement connects the family holiday traditions evoked by Dickens's story to the choice and convenience delivered by modern commerce. Significantly, this comparison extended to the company's portrayal of the broadcast as an embodiment of literary tradition merged with consumer goods. In the 1938 introduction, Chappell tells listeners, "Four years ago, the makers of Campbell's Soups went shopping for a Christmas present to give to all their friends. They found it in this story—Charles Dickens's embodiment of the very spirit of Christmas."[56] Welles's draft introduction presents the story not as an object or product but as a range of possible experiences, from public performance to private reading. In contrast, as an "embodiment" of the Christmas spirit, Campbell's version of the story depicts it as a material good that can be shopped for like a can of soup. In the following year's *Carol* broadcast, Chappell's introduction retains this sense of the broadcast as a physical artifact. Now the gift has not been purchased on a shopping trip but appears like a gift under a Victorian Christmas tree: "Off come the wrappings, off come the tags that say, 'Please do not open till Christmas,' out comes the card, 'To you, from Campbell's.' And here's the gift itself"—that is, the play, which begins immediately after this announcement.[57] Notably, Campbell structures its lead-in much as Welles frequently did his opening commentaries. In moments like the end of his *Treasure Island* lead-in, Welles conflated the author's identity (an intense focus due to Welles's delayed naming of Stevenson until just before Welles assumed the narrator's role) with his own performance. Campbell's proposed lead-in similarly culminates by cuing a transition that equates its gift to listeners (the play) with its gift to consumers ("twenty-one delicious" kinds of soup "awaiting your selection").

These contrasting introductions to the *Carol* broadcast suggest each party's interest in controlling the definition of the broadcasts. Campbell exerted control by limiting Welles's role, in contrast to the actor-director-writer's tendency to shift freely between multiple creative functions. Campbell's proposed conclusion to the broadcast, also included in the "Suggested Carol Opening" typescript, illustrates the company's efforts to regulate Welles's creative role. The script states that "[a]t the end of the play Barrymore does not again step out of character" and delivers his last lines as Scrooge before Welles "comes in again . . . to sign off." As the document notes, "This preserves Welles as Campbell's spokesman—personalizes Barrymore before the play starts, and does not break the mood at the end."

56 *James Jesson*

The sponsor's attempt to delineate rigidly the role of presenter (Welles) and actor (Barrymore) seems the opposite of Welles's strategy of downplaying distinctions between his roles as he transitioned from presenter to narrator to multiple characters in the plays.

As the above discussion also suggests, however, Welles and Campbell used similar strategies to frame the dramatizations: balancing images of continuous tradition with claims of innovation and associating their innovative products (radio storytelling and canned soup) with the older and more culturally established object of the book. That a radio performer and a canned soup company would similarly seek to associate themselves with audible novels may not be surprising given the connections that Jonathan Sterne has posited between sound recording and food preservation—between canned sound and canned food. As radio transmissions, the *Mercury* productions represented live rather than recorded sound, but they nonetheless bear comparison to the cultural history of sound recording that Sterne traces. Sterne argues that new technologies for preserving food and embalming corpses influenced how sound recording was perceived and used. Like embalming, recording was conceived as a means of preserving the dead so that the recorded voice, like the embalmed body preserved for public viewings, "could continue to perform a social function after life."[58] By recording the voices of the living and replaying them after their death, however, the phonograph and gramophone altered those voices, which became exterior to the body and thus lacked the deceased speaker's interior consciousness. Just as embalming removed inner organs to preserve the body's external appearance, with sound recording the "inside of sound was transformed so that it might continue to perform a cultural function."[59] Welles's construction of the audible book resembles sound reproduction as Sterne describes it. Evoking the book through the authorial attribution on its title page, Welles suggested that his plays updated the book to preserve its social function. Dickens's stories, as Welles's draft introduction represented them, fulfilled multiple social functions through their adaptability to public performance or private reading, and Welles's broadcasts extended them into yet another social context created by radio. As in Sterne's depictions of sound recording, something of the original entity remains in altered form as the story travels from one medium or context to another. Stevenson's *Treasure Island* begins in family storytelling and then becomes a serialized publication and later a book. But the book is not the story's essential, perfected identity, as the logic of a literary culture centered on print reproduction might have it; rather, it is one manifestation of many possible ones, including the story's appearance on "your radio," as opposed to in "your library."

Welles's description of the author exhibits a similar mutability that is related to the story's adaptability. Stevenson, the "great *teller* of tales," gives way to Welles and company who are "*retelling* this story." The story, again, appears as the nexus of a creator-audience relationship rather than a fixed object, and Welles can therefore adopt Stevenson's authorial role, just as Stevenson perhaps stole some of the credit from his collaborators. Like the stories Welles adapts, the authors are reproduced in the broadcasts, preserved in altered form to extend their social function. As Welles summons Stevenson as a ghostly eavesdropper on the broadcast and quotes Dickens's farewell address, he reanimates them. These ghostly authors exemplify the uncanny reproduction of bodies that Edward D. Miller describes as a characteristic effect of radio disembodiment, in which the broadcast voice "suggests a body, but . . . not necessarily the *original* or the remainder of what was once . . . the actual body."[60] The body is reproduced in the listener's mind but altered by the great spatial or temporal distance it travels.

The book in Welles's broadcasts is similarly uncanny, conspicuously reproduced and altered. As remediations, many of Welles's broadcasts quote the written word and even the components of the book that present literature in recognizable form to readers. As a result, the broadcasts at times seem to re-create the book audibly. But like more recent media that provide experiences of hypermediacy, Welles's dramatizations "privilege fragmentation, indeterminacy, and heterogeneity and . . . emphasize process or performance rather than the finished art object," as William J. Mitchell has described digital imaging.[61] The contrast between focusing on "process or performance," on the one hand, and "the finished art object," on the other, encapsulates the difference between Welles's and Campbell's view of the broadcasts. Campbell presents them as objects akin to the cans of soup the company produced. In contrast, Welles—who once claimed he could not watch any of his completed films because each is "not only dead, it's not even very *fresh*. It comes in a can"—presents his broadcasts as part of the literary works' evolving identity.[62] His remediations of the book, focusing on the paratext and particularly on the authorial attribution, reveal how those components of the printed text construct the book's identity. The "paratext" of the broadcasts themselves, therefore, participates in the ongoing re-creation of the literary work and reveals the work's instability but also its ability to endure.

As William B. Worthen has recently argued, drama has always "been an anomaly in print culture" because the identity of the dramatic work exists both in print and "elsewhere, in the incommensurable practices of the stage."[63] This anomaly makes dramatic works ideal vehicles for reexamining the literary work and the printed text. Radio, with its verbal focus and development from writing technologies like the gramophone and wireless telegraphy, occupies a position like that of drama between print and nonprint cultures. These characteristics of the medium and genre perhaps explain why some of the best-known and most innovative radio plays remediate written and printed texts—including American radio plays such as Norman Corwin's dramatization of the Bill of Rights, *We Hold These Truths* (1941), and British works such as Dylan Thomas's *Under Milk Wood* (1954), with its talking Guide-Book and dialogic letters delivered and enacted by the village postman, and Tom Stoppard's *In the Native*

58   *James Jesson*

State (1991), which remediates scholarly publishing through its footnote-reciting Professor Eldon Pike. Whereas we have yet to see Day Lewis's imagined mechanism for translating books into full performances, complete with sounds and smells, the book has been inserted into radio many times over. Welles's broadcasts comprise perhaps the most deliberate and sustained effort to remediate the book on radio. Many others remain to be studied as part of the audible book's twentieth-century history.

NOTES

1. Cecil Day Lewis, *Revolution in Writing* (London: Hogarth Press, 1935), 15.
2. Eustace Wyatt, *Public Domain*, *Columbia Workshop*, CBS, January 2, 1937, *Internet Archive*, http://www.archive.org/details/ColumbiaWorkshop.
3. Wyatt, *Public Domain*, 0:26.
4. Wyatt, *Public Domain*, 24:29.
5. Everett C. Frost, "Mediating On: Beckett, *Embers*, and Radio Theory," in *Samuel Beckett and the Arts: Music, Visual Arts, and Non-print Media*, ed. Lois Oppenheim (New York: Garland, 1999), 316.
6. Ian Rodger, *Radio Drama* (London: Macmillan, 1982), 28.
7. Howard Fink, "The Sponsor's v. the Nation's Choice: North American Radio Drama," in *Radio Drama*, ed. Peter Lewis (London: Longman, 1981), 192. Fink writes that the "secret in both radio and the novel is the generation of 'point of view'" (192).
8. Donald McWhinnie, *The Art of Radio* (London: Faber and Faber, 1959), 36.
9. Timothy C. Campbell, *Wireless Writing in the Age of Marconi* (Minneapolis: University of Minnesota Press, 2006), x–xii; Lisa Gitelman, *Scripts, Grooves, and Writing Machines: Representing Technology in the Edison Era* (Stanford, Calif.: Stanford University Press, 1999), 12–13. Also see Douglas Kahn and Gregory Whitehead, eds., *Wireless Imagination: Sound, Radio, and the Avant-Garde* (Cambridge: MIT Press, 1992). Kahn and Whitehead call the phonograph "a machined fusion of orality and literacy" (5).
10. J. David Bolter and Richard A. Grusin, *Remediation: Understanding New Media* (Cambridge: MIT Press, 1999), 45.
11. Bolter and Grusin, *Remediation*, 44.
12. Bolter and Grusin, *Remediation*, 14.
13. Bolter and Grusin, *Remediation*, 34.
14. John Houseman and Orson Welles, *Treasure Island*, *Mercury Theatre on the Air*, CBS, July 18, 1938. Recordings of most of the *Mercury* broadcasts are widely available online and on phonograph record and compact disc. A thorough collection of these and many other recordings of broadcasts featuring Welles can be found at the Web site "The Museum of Orson Welles," http://museumoforsonwelles.blogspot.com/. In this chapter, all citations to Welles's broadcasts refer to the recordings available on this Web site.
15. Houseman and Welles, *Treasure Island*, 4:29.
16. John Houseman and Orson Welles, *Dracula*, *Mercury Theatre on the Air*, CBS, July 11, 1938; Howard Koch, *Hell on Ice*, *Mercury Theatre on the Air*, CBS, October 9, 1938; Howard Koch, *The War of the Worlds*, *Mercury Theatre on the Air*, CBS, October 30, 1938, 41:12, 56:25.
17. M. M. Bakhtin, *The Dialogic Imagination*, ed. Michael Holquist, trans. Caryl Emerson and Michael Holquist (Austin: University of Texas Press, 1981), 49–51.

A *Library on the Air*   59

18. Gerard Genette, *Paratexts: Thresholds of Interpretation*, trans. Jane E. Lewin (Cambridge: Cambridge University Press, 1997), 1.
19. Herman Mankiewicz, *Huckleberry Finn, Campbell Playhouse*, CBS, March 17, 1940, 1:07 (emphasis added).
20. Paul Heyer, *The Medium and the Magician: Orson Welles, the Radio Years, 1934–1952* (Lanham, Md.: Rowman & Littlefield, 2005), 47; Simon Callow, *Orson Welles: The Road to Xanadu* (London: Jonathan Cape, 1995), 373–374.
21. Howard Koch, *Rebecca, Campbell Playhouse*, CBS, December 9, 1938, 5:08, 5:16.
22. Orson Welles, "Progress of Radio Drama in Broadcasting," *Radio Annual* 3 (1940): 55.
23. Columbia Broadcasting System, "Welles to Dramatize Great First Person Stories in CBS Series," press release, June 15, 1938. Orson Welles Manuscripts. Courtesy Lilly Library, Indiana University, Bloomington, Indiana (hereafter cited as Welles MSS).
24. Heyer, *The Medium and the Magician*, 35.
25. James Naremore, *The Magic World of Orson Welles* (Dallas: Southern Methodist University Press, 1989), 14.
26. Marguerite H. Rippy, *Orson Welles and the Unfinished RKO Projects: A Postmodern Perspective* (Carbondale: Southern Illinois University Press, 2009), 6–7.
27. John Houseman, *Run-Through: A Memoir* (New York: Simon and Schuster, 1972), 360.
28. Michele Hilmes, *Radio Voices: American Broadcasting, 1922–1952* (Minneapolis: University of Minnesota Press, 1997), 213, 212.
29. Howard Koch, *Heart of Darkness/Life with Father, Mercury Theatre on the Air*, CBS, November 6, 1938, 0:55 (emphasis added).
30. Houseman and Welles, *Treasure Island*, 1:57.
31. Houseman and Welles, *Treasure Island*, 2:06.
32. Houseman and Welles, *Treasure Island*, 2:42.
33. Houseman and Welles, *Treasure Island*, 3:28, 3:19.
34. Houseman and Welles, *Treasure Island*, 3:49.
35. Howard Koch, *I Lost My Girlish Laughter, Mercury Theatre on the Air*, CBS, January 27, 1939.
36. Koch, *Girlish Laughter*, 50:08.
37. Koch, *Girlish Laughter*, 48:23, 43:34.
38. Koch, *Girlish Laughter*, 48:50.
39. Koch, *Girlish Laughter*, 51:51.
40. Koch, *Girlish Laughter*, 51:28.
41. Rippy, *Orson Welles*, 7, 46.
42. The untitled, unattributed, two-page draft is located in Welles MSS. Although its author is unknown, the draft is likely Welles's creation, given its resemblance to the author biographies that Welles wrote as lead-ins to other broadcasts. Hereafter cited as "draft introduction to Dickens broadcast."
43. Orson Welles and Peter Bogdanovich, *This Is Orson Welles*, ed. Jonathan Rosenbaum (New York: HarperCollins, 1992), 262.
44. Heyer, *The Medium and the Magician*, 12. Heyer argues that Welles's authorship of original plays and contributions to the *Everybody's Shakespeare* book in the early 1930s led him "to think of himself more as a writer than an actor" and to introduce himself as such when he met Thornton Wilder in 1933.
45. Welles, draft introduction to Dickens broadcast.
46. Quoted in Naremore, *The Magic World of Orson Welles*, 13.

47. Welles, draft introduction to Dickens broadcast.
48. "Suggested Carol Opening," Welles MSS.
49. "Suggested Carol Opening."
50. Hilmes, *Radio Voices*, 224.
51. Howard Koch, *A Christmas Carol*, *Campbell Playhouse*, CBS, December 23, 1938, 57:30.
52. "Suggested Carol Opening."
53. Koch, *A Christmas Carol*, 1:09 (emphasis added).
54. "Suggested Carol Opening."
55. Koch, *A Christmas Carol*, 1:50.
56. Koch, *A Christmas Carol*, 0:55.
57. Koch, *A Christmas Carol*, *Campbell Playhouse*, CBS, December 24, 1939, 2:54.
58. Jonathan Sterne, *The Audible Past: Cultural Origins of Sound Reproduction* (Durham, N.C.: Duke University Press, 2003), 292.
59. Sterne, *The Audible Past*, 307.
60. Edward D. Miller, *Emergency Broadcasting and 1930s American Radio* (Philadelphia: Temple University Press, 2003), 6.
61. William J. Mitchell, *The Reconfigured Eye: Visual Truth in the Post-photographic Era* (Cambridge: MIT Press, 1994), 8.
62. Welles and Bogdanovich, *This Is Orson Welles*, 8.
63. William B. Worthen, *Print and the Poetics of Modern Drama* (Cambridge: Cambridge University Press, 2005), 5–6.

3 The Audiographic Impulse
Doing Literature with the Tape Recorder

Jesper Olsson

In the spring of 1951, the Swedish electronics company Luxor—founded in the 1920s, as the excavation of Tutankhamun's tomb made headlines across the world—began to put out a publication called *Trådnytt* (Wire news). More of a pamphlet than a magazine, the publication employed, during its four years of existence, a variety of textual genres and modes. Reportage, interviews, short stories, reader queries, and contests covered the pages, juxtaposed with information about Luxor's latest product, which was the actual incentive behind the publishing venture. Interestingly, the initial task of introducing this technological gadget to a public of consumers was given to the art of fiction. The first text in the first issue (apart from editorial preludes) is a crime story, whose very first and generically overdetermined lines present to us a new machine:

> The lips of Sam Lobster curled into a sardonic smile, and a half-choked laughter burst up from his throat as he heard the familiar voice in the loudspeaker of the Magnephone.—What a jerk, he thought. Without flinching he had walked straight into the exquisite trap. And now the closing line, clear and loud on the wire: "There's only one way out of my misery. I've been a bad person and, what's worse, I've been a bad actor." And then—the gun shot.[1]

The actual topic of *Trådnytt*, as well as of the short story "Magnefonmordet" (The Magnephone murder), was thus a new wire recorder called the Magnephone, introduced by Luxor after the Second World War. It was presented as an amazing device capable of transforming everyday life. Retrospectively we know that this would not happen. The magnetic wire recorder, which dates as far back as 1897, when Valdemar Poulsen invented his telegraphone, was a thing of the past.[2] The future belonged to the Magnephone's flexible and more manageable ancestor, the tape recorder.

Still, the story of Sam Lobster and his enemy, the murdered actor Barnard, while far from being aesthetically challenging—rather, it is unintentionally comical—is in many ways an instructive piece of literature. First of all, it offers an early example of how magnetic recording would become

62   Jesper Olsson

a recurrent theme in postwar fiction—from Paul Bowles and Heinrich Böll to Marcel Beyer and Paul Auster—and, in this regard, it brings up a range of issues such as time, memory, identity, voice, and narrative that would be reconceptualized in the vicinity of sound technology. Secondly, "Magnefonmordet" gives a clue to how magnetic recording would be marketed, how the technology at the time, in spite of seventy years of phonography, had to be discursively framed in manuals, advertisements, and pamphlets as a viable and desirable object for consumers who should be taught how and why to use it.

Finally, the fate of Sam Lobster, in the end convicted for murder, offers a fascinating allegory of literature in the age of media. By no coincidence, the story's main character, Lobster, is a writer who has put pen and paper aside to start dabbling with the media of the modern age. That is—to use the well known terms of Jacques Lacan invoked by media theorists such as Friedrich Kittler—Lobster has left the world of the *symbolic* (literature, fiction, alphabetic signs) to enter the world of the *real* (actual voices on magnetized wire).[3] The result of this decision is, indeed, very real: a dead body, whose disembodied voice can still be heard among the living. But Lobster was far from alone in making this media-technological move. A multitude of artists and writers would do the same in the years to come, if usually with a less lethal outcome. Sound recording technology was to enter the sphere of literary practice in the 1950s and 1960s, and it would have an impact on writerly methods and forms as well as on issues of representation, distribution, and the reception of literature.

This history of "recorded literature"—as Nicholas Zurbrugg has suggested we designate the field of aural literature, from modern radio plays to sound poetry—offers an archaeological site for reflection on sound and literature, and in particular on its most well known and succesful progeny, the audiobook.[4] This chapter takes a first step toward such an archaeological project. More specifically, it will enter a discussion on voice, narrative, and the dissemination of literary works evoked by the artistic exploration of tape recording during the 1950s, 1960s, and 1970s. The intention is mainly to point out the historical layers of recorded literature just beyond the horizon of the contemporary circulation of audiobooks, and to give an idea of a more heterogeneous "tape recorder poetics" than the established notion of an audiobook might evoke today.

CAPTURING THE SOUND OBJECT

The genealogy of recorded literature and audiobooks can be traced farther back in history than the postwar tape recorder suggests—after all, Thomas Edison saw the "phonographic book" as a privileged area of application for his invention in the late-nineteenth century.[5] However, the emergence of the tape recorder, whose enhanced capabilities were a

The Audiographic Impulse 63

consequence of German military research during the Second World War, radically altered the conditions for recording in everyday life. The machine was, and was marketed as, a layman's technology, a device accessible to amateurs. To record, erase, rewind, play, and even to edit a recording on tape was an "operation extremely easy to perform," and "since a tape can be cut at any point and any two sections joined together by plastic tape," as a manual of 1964 states, "an immense field of possibilities [was] yours for the taking."[6]

To be sure, both manuals and actual users of the tape recorder mapped out an immense field of activity, and it is important to recall that the tape recorder at this early stage was not exclusively an apparatus for the recording and playback of music. Instead, it was used in a number of contexts, from so-called sound hunting (the hobby of collecting and exchanging weird and hard-to-capture sounds) to wiretapping, hypnopedia, language instruction, voice therapy, and even audio portraits of you, your friends, and your family—"more than twelve hundred applications," as one manual claimed.[7] A recurring suggestion in the discourse of tape-recording technology was to record celebrations and holidays—a tip that might have reached Samuel Beckett, who made the protagonist in *Krapp's Last Tape* (1958) base his archive of voices on birthday recordings.[8]

The accessibility and versatility of tape soon insinuated itself into professional activities of various kinds (teaching, police work, therapy, journalism, academic research), and it would find its way into the field of aesthetic practice, making composers, writers, and artists prone to engage *directly* with the registering of voice and sound. Among the arts, it was in music that the technology first made an imprint. If composers such as Edgard Varèse and John Cage had experimented with technical recording earlier in the century, it was through the invention of *musique concrète* by French composer and radio engineer Pierre Schaeffer that recorded sound became established as compositional material for music.[9] Schaeffer started out his work with a set of serially connected turntables, which made it possible for him to transform material that he had recorded.[10] But soon after the war, the tape recorder became his instrument of choice.

Schaeffer would also develop a theory of music based on his compositional practice.[11] The implications of this theory cannot be analyzed here, but its foundation—the creation of an *objet sonore*—is relevant to an understanding of how literature approached recording in the decades to come. With audiotape, the technical objectification of sound, already in the making through phonography, became a concrete experience.[12] Sound and music were *spatialized*, so to speak, as was recognized early on by Cage, who in a comment on his first tape composition, *Williams Mix* (1952), remarked, "What was so fascinating about tape possibility was that a second, which we had always thought was a relatively short space of time, became fifteen inches. It became something quite long that could be

64 *Jesper Olsson*

cut up."[13] Sound turned into a visible and tangible object, a plastic entity, accessible to technical operations and transformations.

However, in this context of early tape recording, an ambiguity in the understanding of and in the rhetoric surrounding the technology took shape that was to affect the poetics engendered by the machine as well. On the one hand, tape seemed to capture and make possible the retrieval of *actual* sounds and voices. The magnetic pattern on tape, evoked by the transduction of a soundwave into an electric signal, came forth as a *trace of the real*, as an *indexical* sign, in C. S. Peirce's sense. This capacity to store real sonic events is what gives credence to Sam Lobster's crime, and it is the crucial observation behind the recurring comparisons between tape and photography.[14] On the other hand, the tape abduction of sound and voice, as practiced in *musique concrète*, for example, inevitably turned these phenomena into technical objects to edit and *manipulate*. Consequently, the apparently real was threatened by artifice, virtuality, and deception—the document was also, so to speak, a construct.

VOCAL MATTERS

Composers began to work with audiotape in the early 1950s, and a multitude, from Karlheinz Stockhausen to Pauline Oliveros, Alvin Lucier, and The Beatles followed suit, as did poets and artists who likewise began to investigate the technology. Whereas Andy Warhol used audiotape as an instrument for mapping everyday life—manifested, for example, in his *a: a novel* (1968)—other artists such as Vito Acconci, Allan Kaprow, Robert Morris, and Bruce Nauman introduced it as a prop or tool in performances, sculptures, and installations. Similarly, a host of writers approached the medium as both a tool and collaborator in their work. Most notably, it became a storage device for poetry readings. But it was often applied to the compositional process too—as is shown, to mention just one example, in the work of American poet Paul Blackburn. Blackburn was the master recorder of recitals in bars and cafés in Manhattan during the 1960s, but he also used the machine as an invaluable instrument for gathering material to be inscribed or transcribed in his own books of poetry.[15] Furthermore, the tape recorder was a new object to be represented in and reflected on in novels and poems, and sometimes it even contributed to the formal imagination of literature, as the examples of poetic loops and the idea of poetry on strips and tape from the period suggest.[16]

For poets it was primarily the possibility of recording the voice that caught their attention, and the genre or mode that most insistently engaged with the recorded voice was without doubt *sound poetry*. Such poetry had been a significant stratagem in the activities of Futurism and Dada, but it experienced a new boom with the advent of tape recording. As one of the

The Audiographic Impulse 65

genre's most prolific practitioners during the second half of the twentieth century, French poet Henri Chopin claimed, "It is made by the sound of the voice and recovers orality which, with the use of the tape recorder, is quite different from what we might imagine with the simple use of words alone, which means that, without this machine, **sound poetry**, as I publish it in OU [Chopin's magazine] would not exist."[17]

Sound poetry is, as the name suggests, an attempt to push the weight of language closer toward the second of the two poles that Paul Valéry once circumscribed in his definition of the poetic genre as a "prolonged hesitation between sense and sound."[18] Even though extrahuman sonic material is sometimes used, the primary source has usually been the voice, and its register was definitely enriched with recorders, microphones, and loudspeakers. When sound poets during midcentury—from the French post-Lettrists to the Vienna Group poets Ernst Jandl and Gerhard Rühm to the Brazilian concrete poets, among others—began to employ the machine, it made possible the storage and dissemination of such notoriously difficult-to-score sounds as cries, whispers, and sobs, those borderline cases that must be taken into account, as Mladen Dolar has observed, in defining the voice.[19]

Although poets sometimes framed tape-recorded lyrics as a return to the ancient foundation of poetry as an oral art, there were, of course, distinct differences between older forms of poetry and the tape-based research into vocality that sound poets set out to do. Even though one sometimes encounters a problematic rhetoric about how the spoken language is more authentic than writing, most poets were aware of the naivité entailed by a simple *return* to orality and would instead approach—in thought and deed—what Marshall McLuhan, Walter Ong, and other media theorists characterized as a *secondary* orality shaped by the context of modern media technologies.[20]

Such was the stance of Henri Chopin, for example, who in the late 1960s declared that "the verbal upheaval that we [the *poètes sonores*] are causing . . . goes far beyond orality as it was understood in the ancient civilisation" due to the "electrical means" now available.[21] And even if Chopin charged this orality with qualities not attainable in writing, the contrast to a primary orality would come forth with force in his work. As is the case with much sound poetry, Chopin's poems move toward the margins of language, and they are almost always dependent on the properties of the tape recorder.[22] Chopin used the microphone to record breath, cries, and murmurs, but he also stuck the microphone into his mouth (or used a contact microphone) to capture subvocal sounds which were later manipulated through changes in tape speed, superimposition, and loops. Typical here is the modus operandi Chopin describes in his performance of the poem "Vibrespace" (1964), in which droning sounds, whispers, whistling, breath, clicks, smacks, and slight verbal echoes traverse and construct a vast suggestive sound space. "I unhook myself,"

66 *Jesper Olsson*

Chopin writes, "vibrate in space with the one voice, accompanied by some concrete sounds of the microphone struck violently on a small denture that I don't much like. You've got to use your body factory! Forget this storytelling body with its words to turn into music of the voice."[23]

In an illuminating way, a piece such as this, as well as the comment, show how Chopin distanced himself from the anecdotal or narrative dimensions of poetry, away from semantics, toward what Steve McCaffery has designated as the "protosemantic."[24] But apart from exploring a sensual dimension of language and speech, there is also a conceptual aspect of Chopin's work that cannot be submerged. In recording voices, mostly his own but sometimes those of others, and in processing the tapes in various ways, Chopin managed to disassemble and analyze vocal matter, disclosing to the listener some of its hidden layers and facets. Thus, listening to Chopin's work potentially alters the perception of voice similar to the way in which a contemporary artist such as Douglas Gordon, in his slowed-down version of Alfred Hitchcock's film in the video installation *24 Hour Psycho* (1993), forces viewers to observe and reflect on not only overlooked elements in the visual field of the film but also visual experience itself.

The practice of composing sound poetry with the tape recorder during the postwar decades was by no means an exclusively French affair. Similar sonic work was pursued in a number of countries and languages. Apart from Austria and Brazil, which have already been mentioned, one might make a list of poets from Canada (Steve McCaffery, bpNichol), England (Bob Cobbing, Lily Greenham), Germany (Franz Mon, Oskar Pastior), the Netherlands (Paul de Vree), Sweden (Sten Hanson, Bengt Emil Johnson), and the United States (Charles Amirkhanian, Jerome Rothenberg, Charles Bernstein), among other countries, while still only presenting a tiny fragment of the work performed.

However, the important point is that sound recording and, more specifically, the tape recorder took part in *shaping* the genre of sound poetry, and that use of the technology came to highlight hitherto undetected aspects of voice, writing, reading, and listening. The practice also prompted a reconsideration of certain notions such as presence, intimacy, and authenticity that were associated with recorded voices. On the one hand, such notions were technically and semiotically supported by the understanding of recorded voice and sound as indexes or traces of the real *and*, of course, by the immersive effects and physiological intrusiveness of sounds. But, on the other hand, they were also deferred and even undermined in poetic practice, which not only manipulated and disfigured potential traces of the real but also manifested the voice as a plastic entity submitted to editorial interventions, as a time-based live event hypostasized into an object, which would only later on, in the act of playback, return as the simulation of a living voice present to the body and mind of a listener.

TALKING, TELLING, AND CUTTING

One of the traditional functions of voice has been its role in shaping subjectivity and personal identity, especially if one takes into account the inner voice of silent reading and thought. That the inner voice differs awkwardly from one's externally transmitted voice was one of the lessons of the phonographic apparatus during the last century, and this lesson was repeated with higher frequency when tape recorders made it possible for more people to encounter their voices through an exterior source.[25] But if this seemed to install a gap in the experience of identity, it also opened up the possibility of actively constructing identities through the use of recorded voice and sound. Most notably, this was manifested in the documentary use of tape recorders in literature, journalism, ethnography, and oral history. Here the tape recorder could be used, for example, to bring forth voices that had earlier been marginalized or ventriloquized by a dominant discourse. The tape recorder gave a voice to these people, letting them tell their own stories.[26]

Fiction sometimes addressed similar kinds of tape-based identity production as poetry, and sometimes with a more sinister twist. In Paul Bowles's *Up Above the Sky* (1966), one of the main characters, Grove Soto, a young man who combines an appearance of charm with a violent and unpredictable personality, keeps in his house a recording machine employed to rehearse and record imagined events, thus at once processing memories and traumatic experiences of the past and, more importantly, trying to control and organize the future with the support of technology. Even though it is a minor presence in the novel, the tape recorder and the cluster of associations it generates are disseminated throughout the text, where they hook up with related topics, such as cybernetics, and thus acquire an allegorical function in relation to the construction of selves and narratives. Once again, it is the machine's capacity to transform time and events into objects susceptible to manipulation that is crucial—and manipulation and control are, for sure, major themes in Bowles's novel.

As a composer, Bowles was probably acquainted with the impact of magnetic tape, and he was good friends with William S. Burroughs, whose tape experiments were among the most famous literary experiments with the technology during the postwar period. Since the Beats (Jack Kerouac, Neal Cassady, Allen Ginsberg) were among the first writers to incorporate tape recorders into compositional practice—a practice that had an impact on their development of a spontaneous, speech-based poetics—Burroughs had probably, as a close associate, been aware for some time of the machine's aesthetic potential.[27] But it was not until 1960 that he began using it. From one viewpoint this was logical: in 1959 Brion Gysin had introduced him to the cut-up method (on paper), an operation of cutting and pasting congenial to the medium of tape. And in retrospect Burroughs himself saw this as an "obvious step": "The first tape recorder cut-ups were a simple extension of cut-ups on paper," he wrote in the essay "It Belongs

68   *Jesper Olsson*

to the Cucumbers." But the new practice allowed for a variety of interventions and editorial operations:

> We went on to exploit the potentials of the tape recorder: cut up, slow down, speed up, run backwards, inch the tape, play several tracks at once, cut back and forth between two recorders. As soon as you start experimenting with slowdowns, speedups, overlays, etc., you will get new words that were not on the original recordings.[28]

Burroughs observes a generative capacity here in the fact that the manipulation of tape can produce new words and sentences. This observation stems in part from the context of his essay, which was a series of books from the period conjuring up paranormal forces in tape recordings.[29] However, as Robin Lydenberg observes, even more important was the political potential of tape to scramble the "prerecordings" of that societal "control machine" that, in Burroughs's view, regulated our lives and programmed our identities.[30]

In the tapes that Burroughs produced with Gysin and Ian Sommerville in the 1960s, one finds several affinities with the research into the materiality of voice that animated sound poetry, and Burroughs was familiar with the work of Chopin and others, just as he was acknowledged by them as an important contributor to the movement of *poésie sonore*.[31] This connection is obvious in early pieces such as "Recalling All Active Agents" or "The Silver Smoke of Dreams," in which cuts and splices, layering, and similar techniques are used to disfigure the verbal output, and thus the vocal identity, of the author and his companions.[32]

Lydenberg traces the features of this voicescape in her essay on Burroughs, which takes as its starting point Joan Didion's marvelous remark that Burroughs "is less a writer than a 'sound.'"[33] However, one thing that distinguishes Burroughs's work with tape from most recordings of sound poetry is the recurrent elaboration on narrative.[34] Burroughs was, after all, very much a storyteller, but the stories he tells into the microphone are often subjected to technical interventions, which will dismantle the narrative and instead confront the reader with frictional juxtapositions of voices and words. For example, in a short piece from the mid-1960s titled "23 Skidoo," one story narrated by Burroughs is interlaced with and refracted by another story, also told by him, but in a different vocal register; and in a few passages noise from the street intrudes on the reading, thus disturbing but also expanding the listener's experience.[35] "Are You Tracking Me?" another recording from the same period, reveals how Burroughs varied the use of other sounds.[36] The piece starts with a recorded broadcast (picked up from radio to judge by the talker's speed), which is interrupted by a cut-in fragment of orchestral music before the reading of Burroughs begins with a generically recognizable cue—"My name is Clem Snyder, and I'm a private eye"—the beginning of a narrative further modified by disruptive and divertive operations.

The Audiographic Impulse 69

If the articulating voice—the vocal shape of a speaking subject as a kind of anchoring point for post-Romantic poetry—is challenged in tape-based sound poetry, then narrative as a privileged cultural form is similarly distorted in the tape experiments by Burroughs, which is also characteristic of his printed works from the period and especially evident in his cut-up trilogy of novels.[37] Certainly, this kind of distortion was the motivating force as well as the logic of the cut-up method in general. And as Burroughs acknowledged in his first essay on the subject, "The Cut-Up Method of Brion Gysin" (1961), the technique has, through the collage and the montage, a prominent genealogy within twentieth-century artistic practice.[38] However, one might assume that the manipulative possibilities of the postwar tape recorder heightened the awareness of the productivity of such aesthetic operations—even, perhaps, their specific significance in an expanding information society, where a flood of mass-mediated images and stories seemed to demand new forms of critical intervention from the composer, the artist, and the writer.

EDITORIAL POETICS, DISTRIBUTION, RECEPTION

The tape recorder was thus a tangible presence in literary practices of the postwar decades.[39] If many poets continued the investigation of voice in the wake of sound poetry, there were others who also furthered the transformation of narrative in the vicinity of sound recording. One example of the latter is the American poet and art critic David Antin's talk poems, which he began to perform in the early 1970s and has continued to perform ever since. Antin's talk poems are improvised performances in which the tape recorder plays the role of storage medium, giving the poet the possibility to return to his talks, to transcribe the stories and the reflections he has verbalized, and then to insert them into the print culture of literature.[40] However, there is no straight line from tape to print, and the talks, shaped by their different performance contexts, are always edited in the transposition between media. Thus Antin's pieces come with a reminder of the editorial poetics always at play in tape recorder poetics, as we saw in sound poetry and in the work of Burroughs as well.

Antin's talk poems also remind us that tape was not really considered a viable medium in the literary "business" of this time. The book or rather print was still, of course, the dominant venue. Yet sound recording also found its way into the distributive networks of literature and at least suggests alternative ways of reaching an audience. Burroughs, for example, released his first LP in 1965, *Call Me Burroughs*, containing readings of excerpts from his novels, and the sound poets in different countries followed the same trajectory and put out records (or more rarely tapes) with readings and performances of their works. For instance, as early as 1959, German poet Hans G. Helms published a record of his *Fa:m' Ahniesgwow*,

70   *Jesper Olsson*

and Swedish concrete poet Bengt Emil Johnson's voice collage *Gubbdrunk-ningar* (Old man's drownings) (1965) came with both a record and a book which could function as a kind of score for the reader.[41]

This combination of record and book introduced a mode of reading of literature quite rare in history—what German scholar Reinhart Meyer-Kalkus has called *Hörlesen* ("hear-reading"), listening to the words and sounds of a poem while also reading them silently to oneself.[42] On the one hand, such reading engages the reader to a higher degree than ordinary reading because he or she has to employ a wider register of motor functions and perceptual acts as well as cerebral faculties; on the other hand, it gives the writer further control over the reception of the work by offering not only the writing but also a singular vocal interpretation of it. This is distinct from recorded literature without an accompanying text, which on the contrary tends to make reception more indeterminate because we always try to find a visual correlate (whether a text or something else) to stabilize the fluid sonic sensations.[43] Surely the listener of the record or the tape can—just as can the reader of the book—stop, rewind, relisten, or even skip passages that are blurred or tedious. But this will hardly adjust the inescapable imbalance between the eye and the ear.

If the output of records and tapes by individual authors tended to be irregular and a little random, there were other publishing ventures taking shape that, on the contrary, manifested a remarkable persistence. Perhaps the first continuous output of recorded literature is to be found in the magazine that Henri Chopin edited from the late 1950s onward, *Cinquième saison*, which in 1964 added to its name the two letters *OU*, and from then on was to publish recordings of poetry regularly for ten years. It was not the first journal to exploit sound recording, but it was definitely one of the first *literary* magazines to do it.[44] In the age of McLuhan, this seemed like a reasonable choice, and, as Nicholas Zurbrugg has claimed, *OU* was "one of the truly—and most authentically—'contemporary' publications of its time."[45] Chopin himself wrote in 1964 that the recordings were "necessary" in order to "illustrate the published poems" and "to augment the range of the revue," and he would, in retrospect and without false modesty, declare: "I know that no publication since the Futurists can be compared to it."[46]

Without doubt, *OU* was a pioneer project, and it found followers in the years to come. The late 1960s and especially the 1970s witnessed the launch of several publications of recorded art and literature such as John Giorno's famous series of records, *Giorno Poetry Systems*.[47] An important technological event in this context was the invention of the cassette recorder. Artists, writers, and editors soon discovered the durability and flexibility of cassettes as a medium for distribution. In 1973 British artist William Furlong launched the cassette journal *Audio Arts*, one of the most long-lived projects of this kind in continuing until 2006, far beyond the death throes of the analog tape recorder.[48] And quite soon a dynamic and multiform cassette culture emerged that would include everything from mail art with

The Audiographic Impulse 71

tapes to poetry, sound experiments, and alternative rock music.[49] This heterogeneous outlet can be considered as the subcultural terrain surrounding the mainstream cassette book of the time, usually nurtured by material from the upper echelons of the bestseller lists.

An obvious difference between the output of cassette books from the 1980s onward and the underground cassette culture is that the latter was focused primarily on tape technology, which was basically a supplement to the book for the former. On the one hand, the transposition of a novel into another medium, despite changing the mode of reception, did not have any radical repercussions on literary work as such; on the other hand, artists, musicians, and writers involved in the making of cassettes tried to forge *media-specific* products. Thus cassette enthusiasts Rich Jensen and Robin James, for example, prophesied a "new form of literature, beyond the illusion of theater and into reality" in the form of "a novel contained entirely on cassettes" without a written master text.[50]

It is interesting to observe here how the idea of a tape recording as a trace of the real comes up in the artistic production of cassettes. This notion also marks the *Audio Arts* project of Furlong, which was based on the idea that "sound is a primary medium" and that "in listening to the recorded voice we hear what was (and inserted into our real time, still is) the thing itself," as Mel Gooding writes in the introduction to a book sampler of Furlong's work.[51] Such a view presupposes, on the one hand, that we close our eyes and ears to the transduction of soundwave to electric signal—and the deferral and deformation that this process entails—and, on the other hand, that we ignore the fact that an editing of the tapes took place in the "selecting, splicing, synthesizing" of *Audio Arts*, to quote the source above.[52] Thus the longing for the real invoked by recorded voice and sound is, once again, contaminated by an editorial poetics that seem to haunt the medium.

Or, should one say, is part of sound-recording technology's functioning as such? The editing of tape is an operation "extremely easy to perform," as manuals for the tape recorder once preached. In the practice of poets and artists, this potential for manipulation was definitely one of the most suggestive aspects of the machine, and it cast a shadow over the tape recorder's apparent capacity to store and retrieve the actual voices of men and women. If most recorded literature seems to take voice reproduction as an unquestioned condition, charging the literary works with the living presence of a voice that smoothly enters the reader's inner world, early experiments with tape recording were more ambiguous on this point. This ambiguity left its mark on the material and formal imagination of artists working with sound as well as on the piecemeal distribution of a fascinating body of literature and art.

NOTES

1. *Trådnytt* 1 (1951): 6; my translation.

72 *Jesper Olsson*

2. For a history of magnetic recording, see, for example, David L. Morton, *Sound Recording: The Life Story of a Technology* (Baltimore: Johns Hopkins University Press, 2004).

3. Jacques Lacan's famous ontologic tripartition *the imaginary, the symbolic,* and *the real* has been linked by Friedrich A. Kittler to the three media technologies of film, typewriter, and phonograph, which I allude to here. See Kittler, *Gramophone, Film, Typewriter,* trans. Geoffrey Winthrop-Young and Michael Wutz (Stanford, Calif.: Stanford University Press, 1999).

4. Nicholas Zurbrugg, "Regarding Recorded Literature," in *Aural Literature Criticism,* ed. Richard Kostelanetz, a special issue of the journal *Precisely* 10–12 (1980): 61–74.

5. Edison's phonographic book was primarily intended for the blind. See his article in *Phonogram* 1 (1891–1893): 1–3, quoted in Jacques Attali, *Noise: The Political Economy of Music,* trans. Brian Massumi (Minneapolis: University of Minnesota Press, 1985), 93.

6. C. G. Nijsen, *The Tape Recorder: A Guide to Magnetic Recording for the Nontechnical Amateur,* 2d ed. (New York: Drake Publishers, 1972 [1964]), 97.

7. Lists of potential applications of the tape recorder can be found in almost all manuals; see, for example, Nijsen, *The Tape Recorder,* 115–119. On the hobby of sound hunting, see Karin Bijsterveld, "'What Do I Do with My Tape Recorder . . . ?': Sound Hunting and the Sound of Everyday Dutch Life in the 1950s and 1960s," *Historical Journal of Film, Radio, and Television* 24, no. 4 (2004): 614–634. The mention of twelve hundred applications can be found in Harold D. Weiler, *Tape Recorders and Tape Recordings,* Audio Library vol. II (Mineola, N.Y.: Radio Magazines, Inc., 1956), 5.

8. While writing his play, Beckett consulted a manual on recording sent to him by Donald McWhinnie. See James Knowlson, *Damned to Fame: The Life of Samuel Beckett* (New York: Grove Press, 1996), 399.

9. The anthology *Audioculture: Readings in Modern Music,* ed. Christoph Cox and Daniel Warner (New York: Continuum, 2008) is a good source book here.

10. See Pierre Schaeffer's comments on his early work in *A la recherche d'une musique concrète* (Paris: Editions du Seuil, 1952).

11. See especially *Traité des objets musicaux* (Paris: Editions du Seuil, 1966).

12. Actually, this objectification had already begun with a range of prephonographic practices that turned *sound* into an object of study and knowledge—a process thoroughly presented and analyzed in Jonathan Sterne's *The Audible Past: Cultural Origins of Sound Reproduction* (Durham, N.C.: Duke University Press, 2003). But, with the tape recorder this transformation became part of cultural practices on a wider scale, and it was, as we shall see, incorporated into an evolving aesthetics.

13. Richard Kostelanetz, ed., *Conversing with Cage,* 2d ed. (London: Routledge, 2003), 170.

14. This was a topos in manuals and pamphlets. See Bijsterveld, "'What Do I Do,'" 614–634.

15. On Blackburn's presence in the Manhattan poetry scene in the 1960s, see Daniel Kane, *All Poets Welcome* (Berkeley and Los Angeles: University of California Press, 2003); and Michael Davidson, "Technologies of Presence: Orality and the Tapevoice of Contemporary American Poetry," in *Ghostlier Demarcations: Poetry and the Material Word* (Berkeley and Los Angeles: University of California Press, 1997), which discusses the impact of the tape recorder on the work of several postwar American poets.

16. A speculative hypothesis might forge a link between the emergence of tape recording and a host of different poetic projects from the 1960s using tape or paper strips as the carrier for poetic language, from Raymond Queneau's

The Audiographic Impulse 73

Cent mille milliard des poèmes (Paris: Gallimard, 1961) to A. A. Ammons's Tape for the Turn of the Year (Ithaca: Cornell University Press, 1965).

17. Henri Chopin, "Open Letter to Aphonic Musicians," originally published as "Lettre ouverte aux musiciens aphones," in OU 33 (1968), reprinted in the collection Revue OU (Alga Marghen, 2002), 35–41; bold print in original. The reprinted edition contains four CDs with material from issues 20–44 of OU, including broadsides and a booklet with material from and on Chopin's journal, most of it rendered in English as well. Quotes in the text are from the latter, hereafter abbreviated as ROU.

18. Paul Valéry, "Rhumbs," Œuvres complètes (Paris: Gallimard, 1960), 637.

19. See Mladen Dolar, A Voice and Nothing More (Cambridge: MIT Press, 2006), 23–24, where he underlines the significance of coughs and other sounds in the definition of the "linguistic" voice.

20. See, for example, Walter J. Ong, Orality and Literacy: The Technologizing of the Word (New York: Methuen, 1982), 133.

21. Chopin, "Open Letter," in ROU, 38.

22. One of the most suggestive and inventive readings of Chopin's poetry can be found in Steve McCaffery, "Voice in Extremis," in Prior to Meaning: The Protosemantic and Poetics (Evanston, Ill.: Northwestern University Press, 2001), 161–186.

23. Henri Chopin, comments on his own poems, in ROU, 18. The poem is available on one of the CDs included with the publication.

24. Chopin, in ROU, 18.

25. Even though phonographic voices were naturalized during the last century, it is difficult to deny the alienating effect that hearing your own voice from another source has had, and still has, for most of us today. For a discussion of this, see, for example, Steven Connor, Dumbstruck: A History of Ventriloquism (Oxford: Oxford University Press, 2000).

26. An example of this kind of oral history is the well known work of Studs Terkel in books such as Division Street: America (1967) or Working: People Talk about What They Do All Day and How They Feel about What They Do (1974).

27. In 1951–1952 Neal Cassady and Jack Kerouac began recording conversations and readings that were to be used as material for transcription. The tapes have now disappeared, but the most famous result of this work persists in the chapter "Frisco: The Tape" in Kerouac's posthumously published novel Visions of Cody (1973). For an account of this, see, for example, Paul Maher, Jr., Kerouac: The Definitive Biography (Lanham, N.Y.: Taylor Trade Publications, 2004). For an analysis of the recordings, see John Shapcott, "'I Didn't Punctuate It . . . ': Locating the Tape and Text of Jack Kerouac's Visions of Cody and Doctor Sax in a Culture of Spontaneous Improvisation," Journal of American Studies 36 (2002): 231–248.

28. William S. Burroughs, "It Belongs to the Cucumbers," in The Adding Machine: Selected Essays (New York: Arcade Publishing, 1993), 53.

29. The most well known names in this context are Friedrich Jürgenson and Konstantin Raudive. Raudive published the book Breakthrough: An Amazing Experiment in Electronic Communication with the Dead (London: Colin Smythe, 1971), which received quite a lot of attention at the time. For a discussion of these experiments, see, for example, Jeffrey Sconce, "The Voice from the Void," in Haunted Media: Electronic Presence from Telegraphy to Television (Durham, N.C.: Duke University Press, 2000), 59–91.

30. Robin Lydenberg, "Sound Identity Fading Out: William Burroughs' Tape Experiments," in Wireless Imagination: Sound, Radio, and the Avant-Garde, ed. Douglas Kahn and Gregory Whitehead (Cambridge: MIT Press,

74   *Jesper Olsson*

1994), 409–437. Other essays have been devoted to Burroughs's tape works, but Lydenberg's text is one of the most thorough discussions.

31. See, for example, Chopin's account of modern sound poetry in *Poesie sonore internationale* (Paris: Jean-Michel Place Éditeur, 1979), which was prefaced by none other than Burroughs.

32. Both pieces are accessible at UbuWeb, http://www.ubu.com.

33. Lydenberg, "Sound Identity Fading Out," 409.

34. Of course, one also finds sound poetry elaborating on narrative in, for example, some of the works by French poet Bernard Heidsieck. On his ouevre, see Jean-Pierre Bobillot, *Bernard Heidsieck: Poésie action* (Paris: Éditions Jean-Michel Place, 1996).

35. See the triple CD, *Real English Tea Made Here* (Audio Research Editions, 2007).

36. *Real English Tea Made Here.*

37. The trilogy consists of *The Soft Machine* (1961), *The Ticket That Exploded* (1962), and *Nova Express* (1964).

38. Burroughs's essay was first published in *A Case Book of The Beat* (1961), reprinted in William S. Burroughs and Brion Gysin, *The Third Mind* (London: John Calder, 1979), 29–38.

39. The full weight of such a proposition is, unfortunately, difficult to corroborate since the tape was often no more than a vehicle in the production of writing and thus discarded after use, or at least not properly archived. While printed books subsist in libraries, sound recordings are harder to track down. However, with the emergence of digital archives for poetry such as PennSound, http://writing.upenn.edu/pennsound/, at which tapes by a number of poets have been made accessible, new possibilities are opened up to investigate this history.

40. For a discussion of the tape recorder in Antin's work, see Davidson, "Technologies of Presence."

41. A tentative discography of sound poetry can be found in Chopin, *Poesie sonore internationale*, 295–296.

42. Reinhart Meyer-Kalkus, "Literatur für Stimme und Ohr," in *Phonorama: Eine Kulturgeschichte der STIMME als Medium* (Berlin: Matthes & Seitz, 2004), 179.

43. This correlation is one of the basic assumptions of Connor's *Dumbstruck*. As Connor writes, "Sound, and especially the sound of the human voice, is experienced as enigmatic or anxiously incomplete until its source can be identified, which is usually to say, visualized" (20).

44. One example is the French news journal *Sonorama: Le magazine sonore de l'actualité*, which began its run in the 1950s and which distributed news stories of various kinds on flexidisc. See Birgitte Felderer, "Die Stimme. Eine Ausstellung," in *Phonorama* (2004), 15–16.

45. Nicholas Zurbrugg, "Living with the Twentieth Century," in *ROU*, 3.

46. Chopin, "About OU—Cinquieme saison," in *ROU*, 9.

47. See Michael Hennessey's essay "Poetry by Phone and Phonograph: Tracing the Influence of Giorno Poetry Systems," chapter 4 in this collection.

48. The actual *Audio Arts* archive can be found at the Tate Gallery in London. A presentation of the project and a selection of transcribed interviews are offered in William Furlong, *Audio Arts: Discourse and Practice in Contemporary Art* (London: Academy Group, 1994). Recently published is also the new selection of transcribed interviews, William Furlong, *Speaking of Art: Four Decades of Art in Conversation* (London: Phaidon, 2010). Another art magazine on cassette, *Voicespondence*, was launched the year after *Audio Arts*, in 1974, by artist Clive Robertson in Vancouver. The most famous art

magazine using the medium was probably *Tellus*, which began publication in 1983; all of its issues are available at UbuWeb.

49. See *Cassette Mythos*, ed. Robin James (New York: Autonomedia, 1992) for a presentation of the underground cassette culture from the 1970s and 1980s.

50. Rich Jensen and Robin James, "A Sound Mind," in *Cassette Mythos*, 41.

51. Mel Gooding, "The Work," in *Audio Arts*, 6.

52. Gooding, "The Work," 8.

4 Poetry by Phone and Phonograph
Tracing the Influence of Giorno Poetry Systems

Michael S. Hennessey

> In 1965, the only venues for poetry were the book and the magazine, nothing else. Multimedia and performance didn't exist. I said to myself, if these artists can do it, why can't I do it for poetry? That was what started the whole thing. There actually were countless venues for poetry, the thing you did in your everyday life. You listened to rock'n'roll from a phonograph. The LP record and sitting in the living room became the venue.
>
> —John Giorno, 2002[1]

At present we find ourselves in a period of tremendous change in the field of poetry—greater perhaps than at any time since the invention of movable type—largely due to the fruitful interaction between poetry and technology. In the twenty-first century, new modes of access to poetry have emerged, as well as new venues for creative discourse, and these developments, along with our vastly increased daily hyperconnectivity, have given rise to both exciting and original forms of expression as well as a revitalized and democratized critical response to the work of previous generations.

Recalling that poetry is primarily rooted in a tradition of orality, a number of recent anthologies—including *Close Listening: Poetry and the Performed Word* (ed. Charles Bernstein, 1998), *The Sound of Poetry / The Poetry of Sound* (ed. Marjorie Perloff and Craig Dworkin, 2009), and, of course, this collection—have reasserted the centrality of sound to our understanding of poetry. Likewise, in the past dozen years, we've seen groundbreaking work addressing the means of poetic distribution, including Daniel Kane's *All Poets Welcome: The Lower East Side Poetry Scene in the 1960s* (which traces the histories of New York's germinal café reading series that paved the way for the Poetry Project at St. Mark's Church in the Bowery) and Steve Clay and Rodney Phillips's *A Secret Location on the Lower East Side: Adventures in Writing, 1960–1980* (an encyclopedic rumination on the phenomenon of small-press journals that emerged in the postwar era).

Despite this critical reorientation, the work of John Giorno has been criminally neglected by scholars. Initially inspired to seek innovative

Poetry by Phone and Phonograph 77

solutions for his own personal expression, he would eventually spend more than three decades sharing the work of a diverse, cross-generational array of poets with millions through various permutations of Giorno Poetry Systems. Giorno conceives of his work as "one continuous ever-changing development from 1962 to [the present]," and his ongoing experiments with emerging media—from his late-1960s performance environments through the Dial-A-Poem telephone exhibitions and radio broadcasts, culminating in Giorno Poetry Systems' record, CD, and video releases—not only serve as means of connecting with new audiences but also erase international boundaries, fostering a sense of aesthetic community.[2]

This last consideration is key to understanding how the output of Giorno Poetry Systems is both similar to and different from other forms of recorded literature including the audiobook. All of these media recognize the importance of sound to literature and seek to revivify the printed word, bringing it off the page and connecting with audiences through the power of the human voice (and if that voice is the author's, then the auratic bond is greater still). However, while the transmutation effected by traditional formats is passive and often one-dimensional (substituting listening for reading), as we shall see, the venues Giorno created, such as the Dial-A-Poem service or his GPS record releases, are not only democratic and highly participatory (encouraging the audience to make and distribute work through similar means, not unlike mimeograph magazines) but also function contextually, granting listeners admittance into social circles and regional scenes as they simultaneously celebrate those subcultures. Moreover, at the heart of Giorno's explorations, we find him grappling with issues—such as performance considerations, technological intervention, and means of dissemination—that prefigure the breakthroughs of twenty-first-century poetics contingent upon data and media, and in this era of rapidly evolving techno-aesthetics, Giorno's methods and perspectives are perhaps more illuminating than ever before.

ELECTRONIC SENSORY POETRY ENVIRONMENTS

"New York in the mid-1960s was in the middle of a major cultural renaissance, in which experimental electronic music, Pop art, dance, and performance came together in a profusion of happenings, installations, and multimedia events," observes Marcus Boon; however, despite all of this aesthetic cross-pollination, "[p]oetry was curiously and conspicuously absent."[3] Conversely, the poetry scene had fallen behind the times: "There was almost never any sound system," Giorno recalls. "Poets actually just performed . . . with no microphone and nobody could hear anything but the echo."[4] Having come to the realization that "poetry was 75 years behind painting and sculpture, dance and music," and believing that "[i]t was the poet's job to invent new venues and make fresh contact with the audience,"[5]

78   Michael S. Hennessey

Giorno sought to find novel and innovative ways "to connect with an audience using all the entertainments of ordinary life."[6] His first attempt to achieve this goal was a series of Electronic Sensory Poetry Environments, or ESPEs, taking place between 1967 and 1969 in New York City and elsewhere, which infused the poetry reading with the energy of both Fluxus-style happenings and the psychedelic rock experience.

The inaugural event, entitled *Raspberry*, would take place at NYU's Loeb Student Center on March 7, 1967. Participants mingled in the empty theater ringed by blacklights, creating an environment resembling "a fish tank of ultra-violet water," as they listened to tracks from *Raspberry & Pornographic Poem*, a twelve-inch LP Giorno released the same year.[7] Four months later, he would stage *Raspberry* once more at the Filmmakers Cinémathèque, and later that fall, at the School of Visual Arts, he launched *Chromosome*, during which seated audience members listened to four new stereo tape collaborations between Giorno and synthesizer pioneer Robert Moog—"Cycle," "Rose," "Flavor Grabber," and "Chrome"—as spotlights "with changing color gels were moved randomly over [them]."[8]

In her classic 1962 essay "Happenings: An Art of Radical Juxtaposition," Susan Sontag notes that "[t]he Happening takes place in what can best be called an 'environment,' and this environment typically is messy and disorderly and crowded in the extreme."[9] "What is primary in a Happening," she continues, "is materials—and their modulations."[10] From 1968 through to 1970, Giorno's ESPEs would grow increasingly elaborate, incorporating more and more gadgetry in an effort to engage the full range of human senses and drawing larger audiences in New York and throughout North America. His description of *Johnny Guitar*—undoubtedly the most lavish of these productions, taking place at the St. Mark's Poetry Project on April 2, 1969—merits reproduction in full:

> A stereo Moog tape of the poems *Johnny Guitar* and *Cunt* was played through 6 stereo speakers around the church. It is 40 minutes in length and was played continuously from 7:30 to 11:30 PM. An 8-foot double light column was lashed to the cross above the altar. The light column contained 30 150-watt bulbs (4,500 watts) of red, yellow, blue, green and was connected to a Light Organ which analyzes the light content of the sound from the recording tape. The light column responding in brightness to volume and color to pitch.
>
> The church pews in the front half of the church had been removed and 3 dozen votive candles were placed in that space with cushions to sit on. 3 Time-Mist aerosol dispensing units, which release odors at timed intervals, filled the church with the smell of chocolate candy. The church was flooded with 6 1,000-watt spotlights with amber gels.

Poetry by Phone and Phonograph   79

A pitcher of LSD punch was on a table at the side of the altar. The audience was invited to help themselves. Each cup contained ¼ of a trip. 5 gallons of punch were given away.

In the Parish Hall in the back of the church, a birthday party was given for Anne Waldman. There was rock music, food, wine, grass soup, grass birthday cake, and 600 joints were given away. The audience moved from the reading to the party, back to the reading and to the party.

The text of *Johnny Guitar* published by The Poetry Project at St. Mark's was given out at the entrance.[11]

Other ESPEs featured similar sound setups with wild variations in terms of their extrasensory garnishments. Giorno's lightshows would change from event to event, his spotlights augmented by different combinations of striplights, light panels, and electroluminescent tape, while the various scents—from strawberry and peeled oranges to Frankincense and Chanel No. 5—were delivered to the audience through aerosol, fog machines, bubble machines, and incense.[12]

Aside from the more general tradition of happenings, there are a number of more proximate precedents coming out of the Factory of Giorno's former lover, Andy Warhol, in the mid-1960s, most notably the Exploding Plastic Inevitable (also known as EPI), which ended its nationwide tour just as Giorno's ESPEs began. Warhol devised the EPI in early 1966 as accompaniment for a raucous band he'd started sponsoring, the Velvet Underground and Nico, creating "multimedia environments includ[ing] dancers, lights, filmmakers, colored and patterned slides, strobe lighting, and the projection of Warhol's films on walls around the auditorium and behind the performers on stage, usually on multiple screens and with sometimes as many as five projectors at once, some of them hand-held."[13] Later that spring, *Screen Test Poems*—organized by Gerard Malanga and making use of thirty-one of Warhol's *Screen Test* short films (many starring poets from New York's underground scene)—premiered at Cornell University. The two-hour multimedia event featured three-screen simultaneous projections, a nonstop soundtrack of pop music, and roving spotlights, while poet René Ricard read Malanga's poetry.[14]

Although Giorno's ESPEs bear some similarities to the endeavors of Warhol, they differ in terms of scale, integration, and intensity. The Exploding Plastic Inevitable is essentially a lavish, three-dimensional adornment for a rock concert, and while *Screen Test Poems* creates a more fruitful juxtaposition between its constituent media, it is ultimately an anemic poetry-reading-by-proxy. Despite the technologically enhanced nature of the ESPEs, Giorno still conceived of them primarily as readings, as evidenced by his

80   *Michael S. Hennessey*

handing out copies of the texts at many of the events. Contrary to Sontag's conception of happenings, their "emphasis on spectacle and sound" does not carry the cost of "disregard for the word," and rather than "assault the audience," Giorno's intricate preparations aim to cater to their every need, providing a nurturing (albeit overstimulating) environment that privileges a full sensory experience of his poetry.[15] This multifaceted focus to the written word would ultimately lead Giorno to Dial-A-Poem, which far surpasses any of these happenings in terms of immediacy and technological innovation, offering unprecedentedly large audiences the ability to connect with both individual poets and the scenes they inhabited.

DIAL-A-POEM AND RADIO FREE POETRY

"A new service, yoking the genius of the telephone company to the genius of living poets, now makes it possible for anyone with access to a dial to listen to ready-to-roll verse at any hour of the day or night." So begins a January 14, 1969, *New York Times* article by Richard F. Shepard celebrating the previous day's launch of John Giorno's Dial-A-Poem service at New York's Architectural League. "Thoroughly exhausted from the effort" of staging his ESPEs as well as a series of Central Park poetry readings (which drew audiences in the hundreds), Giorno claimed he was inspired to create the installation "while dialing the weather" a year prior: "I thought the telephone would be a way to reach a huge public. . . . Anyone anywhere in the world can telephone and hear a poem."[16] The Architectural League show would be the first of many incarnations of Dial-A-Poem, beginning rather modestly with a bank of ten phones and reel-to-reel tapes of thirteen poets each reading a dozen poems (all recorded by Giorno at his loft in the Bowery). Its reception, however, was anything but modest—Dial-A-Poem received widespread media attention (from the *Times* to *Junior Scholastic Magazine*), and in just five months 1,112,337 people called the service, all of whom were motivated by a desire to participate in a hip and modern cultural event, to hear some new and exciting poetic voices, or to get a scandalous earful.[17]

Whereas Daniel Kane situates much of Giorno's genius in "the simple discovery that if he drew media publicity to an arts project, he would receive a lot of attention," not all of this attention was conducive to Giorno's aims.[18] The first incarnation of Dial-A-Poem, by Giorno's admission, "was very sexual . . . [p]oems with sexual images, straight, or preferably gay, as I'm a gay man; and as political activism,"[19] and it was not long before "reactionary members of the community started hassling us, and The Board of Education put pressure on the Telephone Company."[20] Although Giorno had legal backing from the New York State Council on the Arts and the lines were reinstated, the museum soon ran out of funding and was unable to pay the bill.[21]

Poetry by Phone and Phonograph   81

After a six-week run at Chicago's Museum of Contemporary Art, Dial-A-Poem returned to New York for ten weeks in July 1970 as part of the Museum of Modern Art's "Information" show—its title a fitting comment upon the ways in which Giorno had moved beyond the printed page and conventional notions of textuality into a hypermodern data environment. "By '69 and '70, everything had completely changed," Giorno observes: "Naked people on Broadway in *Hair*, and on the cover of *Time*, and *Screw* magazine. There was no point doing it anymore."[22] Therefore, to keep the material timely, Giorno made sure that "half the content . . . was politically radical poetry . . . Bobby Seale, Eldridge Cleaver and The Black Panthers were well represented."[23] "At the time, with the war and repression and everything," Giorno explains, "we thought this was a good way for the Movement to reach people."[24] A September 3, 1970 *New York Times* article noted that while the show featured the work of "many radical figures and writers, many of them denouncing government policy and advocating violence . . . only one letter of complaint" had been received, and the article speculated that due to popular interest the program might be continued beyond the planned close of the "Information" show.[25] In a politically charged climate of Weather Underground violence, however (including the accidental destruction of a Greenwich Village townhouse and the June 1970 bombing of the New York City Police Headquarters), a condemnatory article less than two weeks later in *Time*—focusing on inflammatory selections by Diane DiPrima, Bernadine Dohrn, and Allen Ginsberg and concluding with the reactionary observation, "[f]or this public service, the museum is paying $284 a month for tapes and telephones. But is it art?"[26]—prompted an FBI investigation, the end of the show, and the firing of Museum of Modern Art director John Hightower, who had championed the experiment.[27]

Whereas the creative combination of literature and telephony seems in retrospect like a natural fit, Giorno was the first to consider its possibilities. In Marshall McLuhan's epochal *Understanding Media: The Extensions of Man* (1964), the chapter on the telephone is directly preceded by one on the typewriter that is largely concerned with the practice of poets such as Charles Olson and e e cummings who, in the author's view, realize the full potential of the instrument in ways largely untapped by common users. Summarizing Olson's concept of "projective verse," McLuhan enthusiastically declares that contemporary poets, embodying a spirit of "autonomy and independence," have become "eloquent in proclaiming the power of the typewriter to . . . indicate exactly the breath, the pauses, the suspension, even, of syllables, the juxtaposition, even, of parts of phrases which [they] intend, observing that, for the first time, the poet has the stave and the bar that the musician has had."[28] Not unlike "jazz musician[s]," poets "experience . . . performance as composition," they "command the resources of the printing press," they wield "a public-address system"; McLuhan goes so far as to speculate on the influence of the typewriter on the development of

82   *Michael S. Hennessey*

free verse.[29] When he turns his attention to the telephone, the poets are left behind—technological exploitation of text to approximate the vivid characteristics of speech or music is to be applauded, but a more direct mode of sonic access to language seems unimaginable. However, by the end of the decade, Giorno would facilitate that exact process through Dial-A-Poem.

Poetic potential aside, McLuhan notes that the telephone "fuses the functions of composition and publication" and "demands complete participation . . . of [the listener's] senses and faculties . . . unlike the written and printed page."[30] Moreover, this medium "demands a partner, with all the intensity of electric polarity"; thus, by embracing the telephone's unique characteristics, Dial-A-Poem builds on the advances of Giorno's ESPEs to create a multifocal environment of complete poetic investment, fostering, as we shall see, more intimate and immediate connections between individual listeners and poets.[31]

Of course, the marriage of poetry and telephony brings to mind Frank O'Hara's 1959 essay "Personism: A Manifesto," in which the author comes to the conclusion that he could "use the telephone instead of writing" a poem to the unnamed object of his affection.[32] This innovation, representing "the death of literature as we know it," situates the poem "between two persons instead of two pages," stressing immediacy and emotional communication as well as "correspondingly gratif[ying]" the work itself.[33] Marjorie Perloff, while warning us not to take O'Hara so seriously, concludes that "'Personism' means the *illusion* of intimate talk between an 'I' and a 'you' . . . giving us the sense that we are eavesdropping on an ongoing conversation, that we are *present*."[34] For O'Hara, this intimate presence is of vital importance, both personally and aesthetically. As Lytle Shaw points out, the notion of coterie is central to O'Hara's poetics, reaffirming the relationships that constitute both the New York School and a larger poetry scene sharing similar values—something as socially important as the poetry itself, or perhaps even more so, as this is a source of inspiration in and of itself. Thus, even if illusory, Dial-A-Poem, as well as Giorno Poetry Systems' subsequent audio and video projects, give listeners a fuller, realer sense of aura—a vital connection to the poets whose work is represented through the primal intimacy of the voice, the casual warmth of the recordings—granting listeners vicarious access to this social scene.

Giorno's clever adaptation and subversion of preexisting means of production is reminiscent of two other innovations taking place concurrently within the same circles. First, there's the subculture of coffeehouse readings, taking place at venues like Le Metro and Les Deux Mégots, which would find its fullest flourish with the 1966 establishment of the Poetry Project at St. Mark's Church in the Bowery. Giorno was a fixture in the Poetry Project scene, appearing in both its in-house journal, *The World* (Giorno even designed the typographic cover for issue number 22),[35] as well as the 1969 collection *The World Anthology: Poems from the St. Mark's Poetry Project*, and, alongside a number of "Release Benefits" curated between

Poetry by Phone and Phonograph 83

1969 and 1970, he also organized the Project's first New Year's marathon reading (running thirty-four hours)—a beloved tradition that continues to this day.[36] Many Poetry Project mainstays were also fervent proponents of the "mimeograph revolution," and Giorno's work would appear in a number of their journals, including "C" (whose editor, Ted Berrigan, gave Giorno his first reading in 1963)[37] and *Angel Hair* (edited by Anne Waldman and Lewis Warsh, who also published his 1971 book *Birds*),[38] while Peter Schjeldahl's *Mother* published his debut volume *Poems* in 1967.[39]

The empowering spirit of the times influenced Giorno greatly. "When you do it yourself," he observes, "a lot of energy arises, and enough money always comes in, designers and people to help, and distribution. And the energy and wisdom of the small group, and the interconnecting small groups, makes amazing things happen."[40] Moreover, Dial-A-Poem synthesizes the most integral characteristics of both of these innovations by delivering the vicarious emotional power of the poet's voice through a portable and readily accessible format similar to mimeography. And as Giorno's focus shifts from a technologically mediated presentation of the self (in the case of his ESPEs) to a venue for communal expression (starting with Dial-A-Poem), the potential benefits for a broader audience grow exponentially.

Although Dial-A-Poem would have numerous incarnations both domestic (in Philadelphia, Albany, Cambridge, Indianapolis, and Providence, among other cities) and international (in the Netherlands, Wales, England, Belgium, France, Switzerland, and West Germany) from the early 1970s into the mid-1980s, Giorno's frustrations with the controversies and censorship that followed it led him to explore other popular media, starting with radio, as a means of distributing poetry. Giorno's first venture into wireless poetics, christened "Radio Free Poetry," took place in 1969 at the Jewish Museum as part of a group show entitled "Software," in which he employed "a small radio transmitter which circulated signals via a simple plug which you stuck into an electrical socket,"[41] thus making the building's wiring one giant antenna with a range of "several hundred feet" that was capable of being "picked up by museum visitors on transistor radios."[42] His next incarnation—far more ambitious, but short-lived—corresponded with a benefit for Ron Gold at the Poetry Project and involved Giorno mounting his equipment in the belfry of St. Mark's Church, enabling him "to reach a big swathe of around ten blocks."[43] When word got out through a write-up in the *Village Voice*, Giorno was confronted by the FCC and threatened with arrest. "The last thing I wanted to do was go to jail, but I had already broadcast it that morning," he recalls. "I did it that afternoon anyway, just to do it. It was the sixties, after all."[44]

Giorno's next flirtation with radio took place in the spring of 1971, when, undeterred by threats of being arrested (or shot on sight) for treason, Giorno—together with Abbie Hoffman and Mayer Vishner—produced alternative musical and political programming for US forces in Vietnam, broadcast under the moniker WPAX over Radio Hanoi.[45] Later radio projects included

84   *Michael S. Hennessey*

"The Poetry Experiment" (1976–1979) and "Satellite Radio Poets" (1981) on New York City's WBAI-FM, and Giorno distributed hundreds of free copies of new GPS record releases to "FM and college radio stations across the country, where they are put in heavy rotation, and are played for decades," reaching, in his estimation, "[m]illions of people."[46]

In addition to these ambitious endeavors, the early output of Giorno Poetry Systems—as chronicled in the poet's 1994 collection *You Got to Burn to Shine*—also included silk-screened and lithographed "poem prints" as well as a wide array of "Consumer Product Poetry" projects from the late 1960s into the early 1970s, which "publish[ed] poetry on the surface of ordinary objects," resulting in "Matchbook Poems, T-Shirt Poems, Flag Poems, Chocolate Bar Poems, Window Curtain Poems, Cigarette Package Poems, and [poems] included in the design on commercial packaging."[47] It's clear that Giorno sought to revivify mundane existence by ensuring that poetry and art permeated every facet of the quotidian. Kenneth Goldsmith, who hails the poet as "a non-stop advocate for poetry," observes that "[Giorno] set out to connect with an audience using the entertainments of ordinary life—television, the telephone, record albums," and it is through this last medium that he would achieve his most widespread success.[48]

GIORNO POETRY SYSTEMS AND BEYOND

Giorno's movement from telephone-based poetry systems to the record album was largely influenced by political contingencies. "Dial-A-Poem received millions of phone calls, yet we were disconnected," he observes in the liner notes to 1974's *The Dial-A-Poem Poets: Disconnected*; therefore, conceiving of the record album as "a do-it-yourself Dial-A-Poem kit," he encourages listeners to take matters into their own hands: "Start your own Dial-A-Poem in your own hometown. Get hooked up to the telephones. Call your local telephone company business office; order a system and put on it these LP selections; put on your own local poets and we'll supply you with more poets."[49] Altogether, from *The Dial-A-Poem Poets* (1972) through to the 1993 compilation *Cash Cow: The Best of Giorno Poetry Systems, 1965–1993*, the label would release more than twenty records, many of them double albums, creating an indelible document of a thriving international poetry scene.

While Giorno Poetry Systems was not the first label to release recorded poetry, it nevertheless broke new ground in terms of democratic inclusiveness as well as a flashy rock-and-roll visual aesthetic. The clearest historical precedent for Giorno Poetry Systems is Caedmon Records, started in 1952 by Barbara Holdridge (then Cohen) and Marianne Roney—recent Hunter College graduates who had aspirations of a future in the record business despite limited opportunities for women in that field. The young women's persistent solicitation of Dylan Thomas during the final year of his life

Poetry by Phone and Phonograph 85

resulted in their debut release, *Dylan Thomas Reading, Volume 1* (1953), along with three subsequent volumes of the poet's work, and firmly established the label's credentials. Billing itself in early advertisements as "a Third Dimension for the Printed Page," Caedmon continues to this day, hundreds (if not thousands) of releases later, as a subsidiary of HarperCollins.

Asked to speak to her original intentions in a 2002 interview with NPR's Renee Montaigne, Holdridge explains, "We did not want to do a collection of great voices, or important literary voices—we wanted them to read as though they were recreating the moment of inspiration. They did exactly that: they read with a feeling, an inspiration, that came through. This is what we wanted . . . we wanted our authors to read to people in the same way that the bards of old read, a communication directly to receptive ears."[50] Whereas Caedmon's output included some adventurous selections from poets such as e e cummings, Walt Whitman, Charles Baudelaire, William Carlos Williams, and Gertrude Stein, much of their catalogue served to promulgate a polite Western canon, with titles such as *Wellsprings of Drama*, *Greek Prose and Poetry*, *Psalms and David*, and a five-volume *Cambridge Treasury of English Prose* recited by renowned Shakespearean actors appearing alongside recorded speeches and a wide array of children's recordings.

Although Caedmon served a more mainstream audience, by the early 1970s, there were also a number of landmark albums representing countercultural authors. Jack Kerouac released a trio of LPs—*Poetry for the Beat Generation* (with Steve Allen, Hanover Records, 1959), *Blues and Haikus* (with saxophonists Al Cohn and Zoot Sims, Hanover Records, 1959), and *Readings by Jack Kerouac on the Beat Generation* (Verve, 1960)—which capitalized on popular interest in the Beats and served as documents of the jazz/poetry hybrid pioneered by West Coast poets like Kenneth Rexroth and Lawrence Ferlinghetti, as well as Kenneth Patchen (who collaborated with such diverse talents as John Cage and Charles Mingus). These records were widely known by the generation of young poets who would, in turn, fill out the sides of Giorno Poetry Systems albums.

No individual poet embraced the tremendous communicative potential of the recorded word, however, as much as Allen Ginsberg. Starting with the albums *Allen Ginsberg Reads Howl and Other Poems* (1959, Fantasy Records) and *Allen Ginsberg Reads Kaddish: A 20th Century American Ecstatic Narrative Poem* (1966, Atlantic Records)—corresponding with his first two major poetry collections—Ginsberg would release a steady stream of records throughout his lifetime, including collaborations with Bob Dylan, Philip Glass, Paul McCartney, and the Clash. Ginsberg was also a fervent supporter of Giorno Poetry Systems, with more than a half-dozen recordings appearing on various releases, including 1976's *Totally Corrupt*, the cover of which depicts a board meeting featuring Ginsberg and Giorno alongside Cage, Waldman, and William S. Burroughs.

What differentiates these albums, or other contemporaneous examples such as the 1970 Harvest Records release *Listening to Richard Brautigan*,

86 *Michael S. Hennessey*

from the output of Giorno Poetry Systems is the stature of the artists involved—the Brautigan record, for example, started as a project for the Beatles' Zapple label, and by that point the author's countercultural classic *Trout Fishing in America* had sold millions of copies. Whereas iconic writers of similar stature appeared on early GPS records, Giorno's democratic editorial eye gave equal exposure to authors whose work might not have been known outside of London, San Francisco, or New York, let alone the small yet vibrant scene surrounding the St. Mark's Poetry Project.

Kenneth Goldsmith notes that "Giorno made no distinction between scenes, between gender, between sexual preference, between various ethnic groups,"[51] mirroring the poet's own observation in the liner notes to *The Dial-A-Poem Poets* that the album "represent[s] many aspects and different approaches to dealing with words and sound [including] the New York School, Bolinas and West Coast Schools, Concrete Poetry, Beat Poetry, Black Poetry and Movement Poetry."[52] Many of these geographic distinctions originate in Donald Allen's anthology *The New American Poetry: 1945–1960*, which effectively demarcates the territory of postwar, post-avant poetics. The Beat Generation is well-represented: Ginsberg and Burroughs appear often, alongside Gregory Corso, Amiri Baraka, Diane DiPrima, Peter Orlovsky, and others, and most of their San Francisco confreres, including Gary Snyder, Philip Whalen, and Michael McClure, also show up on Giorno Poetry Systems releases. Similarly, the major Black Mountain poets are present—Charles Olson, Robert Duncan, Robert Creeley, Paul Blackburn, Ed Dorn, and others—and the New York School, the group with which Giorno would most closely be affiliated, is a dominant force on all of the albums, with members from its first generation (O'Hara, John Ashbery, Kenneth Koch, Edwin Denby), second generation (Berrigan, Waldman, Ron Padgett, Joe Brainard, Bernadette Mayer) and beyond (Jim Carroll, Harris Schiff, Eileen Myles) appearing frequently. It is important to remember, however, that these groupings are somewhat arbitrary placeholders and that throughout the country, but especially in New York, there was a tremendous amount of aesthetic cross-pollination—a phenomenon evidenced by the iconoclastic juxtapositions of Giorno Poetry Systems' track listings.

More interesting still are the poets present on the various releases who serve as outliers to these prevailing groupings, starting with the decidedly non-countercultural poets Sylvia Plath and Robert Lowell—the latter of whom engaged in rather public feuding with both Ginsberg and O'Hara—who made appearances on Dial-A-Poem records. Major poets who don't tidily fit into one of the aforementioned groupings, such as William Carlos Williams, John Wieners, Jack Spicer, Charles Bukowski, and Helen Adam, show up, as do a number of figures from the Warhol coterie (Malanga, Taylor Mead, Jackie Curtis) and confrontational novelists (Terry Southern, Kathy Acker, Ishmael Reed). Then there are the political selections, including tracks from poet/activists John Sinclair and Heathcote Williams

Poetry by Phone and Phonograph 87

along with speeches from Bobby Seale and Kathleen Cleaver. Cage reads his poetry, while Brion Gysin, Charles Amirkhanian, and Clark Coolidge contribute sound and speech experiments, and Ed Sanders and Tuli Kupferberg's band, the Fugs, plays subversive rock and roll.

Given that the Giorno Poetry Systems albums mimic both the medium and the aesthetics of rock-and-roll releases, it is fitting that music of all sorts became more and more central to the label's releases. As Kenneth Goldsmith observes, "[A]t this point downtown, there was really no difference between rock and roll and poetry, as evidenced by Patti Smith and Anne Waldman, and John Giorno himself was somewhat of a rock star. Everybody could have their fifteen minutes in the downtown scene of John Giorno in the 60s and 70s.[53] New music stalwarts Philip Glass, Meredith Monk, and Robert Ashley, as well as pioneering underground bands such as Sonic Youth, Hüsker Dü, and the Butthole Surfers all contributed tracks, and the newly minted John Giorno Band released No Wave electro-punk tracks on split albums with Waldman, Laurie Anderson, and Glenn Branca.

Building upon Giorno's earlier solo performances, which featured a three-dimensional layered sound comprised of prerecorded tapes of the poems and live manipulation through delay devices, the later concert tours took his aesthetic priorities—"using breath and heat, pitch and volume, and the melodies inherent in the language, risking technology and music, and a deep connection with the audience, [to] fulfill [the] poem"—to the next level.[54] Giorno's notion of performance was not tied to "performance art" but rather entertainment: "Poetry is so boring that any entertaining qualities are a triumph! When I said 'entertainment,' I meant it in its most profound sense, which is play—the play of all phenomena, the display of all the realms—that's entertainment!"[55]

"I have a theory that from the '50s on," Giorno observes, "countless kids who were poets by nature were given electric guitars for Christmas. They fiddled around with the chords, and words arose in their minds— they experimented with words and music and the great ones became rock stars."[56] However, he notes that "[i]t's only die-hard poets, like me, who stayed true to the music inherent in the word," and, barring outliers such as Patti Smith and Lou Reed, "[o]ften, when poets go over to rock, the focus is on the rock song, not on the poetry."[57] It's worth noting once again that Giorno's conception of poetry is intimately connected to rock music, to energy and performance, and that traditional notions of poetry as text never enter into the discussion; moreover, it is only through electronic means that poets are capable of fully expressing their talents.

The 1980s and early 1990s saw the label's output slow down considerably with a handful of rock band-heavy CD releases—which served as benefit albums for Giorno's AIDS Treatment Project—leading up to its final project: 1998's four-disc box set, *The Best of William Burroughs: From Giorno Poetry Systems*, a fitting tribute to the poet's longtime friend and inspiration who had died the previous year.

88   Michael S. Hennessey

The final, inevitable frontier for Giorno was transitioning from audio into moving pictures, and the four "VideoPaks" GPS released between 1984 and 1990 combined the eye-catching spectacle that was a recurring theme in Giorno's work from the late-1960s ESPEs through to the John Giorno Band's punk and new wave-inspired concert tours with the vicarious portability of the label's record albums, seeking to canonize the previous generation's poetic heroes and reinvent poetry for a young generation in much the same way that the nascent MTV had radically altered the music industry. Alongside several compilation tapes, the series also included a pair of Beat Generation documentaries: Howard Brookner's *Burroughs, the Movie* (1985) and Maria Beatty's *Gang of Souls* (1990). Giorno Poetry Systems also distributed films, including Allen Ginsberg's *September on Jessore Road* (1971, which was also directed by Giorno) and perhaps most influentially Ron Mann's 1982 film *Poetry in Motion*, which received a considerable amount of mainstream exposure.[58] For example, Sheila Benson begins her enthusiastic *Los Angeles Times* review of the film—which showcases a characteristically diverse array of twenty-four poets including Helen Adam, Baraka, Berrigan, Cage, Jayne Cortez, Creeley, The Four Horsemen, Ginsberg, Michael Ondaatje, Sanders, Snyder, Tom Waits, and Waldman—by observing, "If the language that surrounds us every day seems flat and uninspiring, the antidote is 'Poetry in Motion' . . . a vial of smelling salts for those reeling from indifferent speech."[59]

CONCLUSION

In the twenty-first century, one could argue that poetry has come closer to the technologically augmented utopia that Giorno first envisioned a half-century ago. "This is a golden age of poetry," he acknowledges in a 2002 interview. "For the last forty years, poetry has flourished, as never before from the beginning of time. Endless venues connecting countless poets all over the world to vast audiences. The technologies have completely fulfilled my pathetic beginnings."[60] Whereas Giorno once felt "passively aggressive" about the Internet, admitting, "I don't have my own site, because I don't want to put in all the time making it great. For a site to be alive, it has to change everyday, a constant flow of new information," he has since had a change of heart and put together a modest homepage where visitors can interact with his work in methods both high-tech (YouTube videos documenting recent performances) and traditional (the typographically innovative "poem prints" he has been making since the 1960s), and he keeps in touch with his audience through Facebook.[61]

While Giorno Poetry Systems is no longer active, John Giorno—now in his early eighties—remains a tireless advocate for poetry, and his work, as well as that which he spent decades distributing, is still a vital presence in the cultural world. In 2008, Soft Skull Press released a career-spanning

Poetry by Phone and Phonograph   89

collection of the poet's work, *Subduing Demons in America: Selected Poems, 1962–2007,* that makes available a wide array of previously unreleased and long out-of-print texts, giving readers for the very first time a full sense of the aesthetic continuum that evolved from his early found poetry to ESPEs, Dial-A-Poem, numerous record releases, and beyond. "I always used to be first, and nobody ever remembered," Giorno lamented in 2002. "[N]ow, I just want to be best."[62] However, there are many who did remember, and through the endeavors of his ideological descendents, the trailblazing spirit of Giorno Poetry Systems continues to shape the development of contemporary poetics in the Internet age.

Kenneth Goldsmith, poet and founder of the online cultural depository UbuWeb,[63] goes so far as to claim that "John Giorno, in setting up the Giorno Poetry Systems was actually predicting the internet," and it's fitting that on UbuWeb visitors can browse through and download recordings from the vast majority of the label's releases.[64] UbuWeb follows in the tradition of online poetry multimedia archives such as the Electronic Poetry Center[65] and PennSound,[66] as well as SUNY-Buffalo's POETICS e-mail listserv, all cofounded by Charles Bernstein (himself a GPS alum, appearing on the 1980 album *Sugar, Alcohol, & Meat*), and all of which privilege connectivity, cross-genre communication, and advocacy of diverse perspectives as key facets of the poetic experience. It's practically inconceivable to imagine the existence of any of these entities without the groundbreaking example of Giorno Poetry Systems, and younger generations of poets, raised in a media-saturated environment, have gone further still, developing online reading series, blog journals, literary podcasts, Twitter poetry, collaborative writing environments, interactive textual games, and more.

At the heart of Giorno's innovation, buried beneath all of its technological augmentation, is the simple desire of a poet to connect with his audience, not just emotionally, but with full sensory involvement. In an era without boundaries, one in which poetry has flourished thanks to the free and easy exchange of information, understanding the development of John Giorno and Giorno Poetry Systems helps us to see not only how we have arrived at where we presently are but also the places to which we might still hope to go.

NOTES

1. John Giorno, interview by Hans Ulrich Obrist, *UnDo.net: Guide to the Contemporary Art in Italy,* July 22, 2002, http://www.undo.net/cgi-bin/openframe.pl?x=/cgi-bin/undo/features/features.pl%3Fa%3Di%26cod%3D42.
2. Quoted in Marcus Boon, "Introduction," in John Giorno, *Subduing Demons in America: Selected Poems, 1962–2007* (New York: Soft Skull Press, 2008), xxii.
3. Boon, "Introduction," xiii.
4. Quoted in Boon, "Introduction," xiii.
5. John Giorno, "Wisdom Is His Voice," (liner notes) in *The Best of William Burroughs from Giorno Poetry Systems* (New York: Mouth Almighty Records, 1998).

90 *Michael S. Hennessey*

6. John Giorno, "Giorno Poetry Systems," in *You Got to Burn to Shine: New & Selected Writings* (New York: High Risk Books, 1994), 182.
7. Giorno, *Subduing Demons in America*, 138.
8. Giorno, *Subduing Demons in America*, 138.
9. Susan Sontag, "Happenings: An Art of Radical Juxtaposition," in *Against Interpretation* (New York: Farrar, Straus & Giroux, 1964), 268.
10. Sontag, "Happenings," 268.
11. Giorno, *Subduing Demons in America*, 136–137.
12. Giorno, *Subduing Demons in America*, 135–137.
13. Callie Angell, *Andy Warhol Screen Tests: The Films of Andy Warhol Catalogue Raisonné* (New York: Abrams/Whitney Museum of American Art, 2006), 265.
14. Angell, *Andy Warhol Screen Tests*, 280.
15. Sontag, "Happenings," 273.
16. Richard F. Shepard, "Dial-A-Poem, or Even a Hindu Chant," *New York Times*, January 14, 1969, 34.
17. Giorno, "Dial-A-Poem Hype," (liner notes) in *The Dial-A-Poem Poets* (New York: Giorno Poetry Systems, 1972).
18. Daniel Kane, *All Poets Welcome: The Lower East Side Poetry Scene in the 1960s* (Berkeley and Los Angeles: University of California Press, 2003), 183.
19. Giorno, Obrist interview.
20. Giorno, "Dial-A-Poem Hype."
21. Giorno, "Dial-A-Poem Hype."
22. Giorno, Obrist interview.
23. Giorno, "Dial-A-Poem Hype."
24. Giorno, "Dial-A-Poem Hype."
25. "Museum May Keep Dial-A-Poem Phones," *New York Times*, September 30, 1970, 38.
26. "Nation: Dial-a-Radical," in *Time*, September 14, 1970, http://www.time.com/time/magazine/article/0,9171,902744,00.html.
27. Giorno, "Dial-A-Poem Hype."
28. Marshall McLuhan, *Understanding Media: The Extensions of Man* (Cambridge: MIT Press, 1994), 259.
29. McLuhan, *Understanding Media*, 260.
30. McLuhan, *Understanding Media*, 266, 267.
31. McLuhan, *Understanding Media*, 268.
32. Frank O'Hara, "Personism: A Manifesto," in *The Collected Poems of Frank O'Hara* (Berkeley and Los Angeles: University of California, 1995), 499.
33. O'Hara, "Personism: A Manifesto," 499.
34. Marjorie Perloff, *Frank O'Hara: Poet among Painters* (Chicago: University of Chicago Press, 1998), 26–27.
35. Steve Clay and Rodney Phillips, eds., *A Secret Location on the Lower East Side: Adventures in Writing, 1960–1980* (New York: Granary Books, 1998), 188.
36. Giorno, "Giorno Poetry Systems," 186–187.
37. Boon, "Introduction," xii.
38. Anne Waldman and Lewis Warsh, eds., *The Angel Hair Anthology* (New York: Granary Books, 2001), 130, 615.
39. Clay and Phillips, *A Secret Location*, 286.
40. Giorno, Obrist interview.
41. Kane, *All Poets Welcome*, 184.
42. Giorno, "Giorno Poetry Systems," 186.
43. Kane, *All Poets Welcome*, 267, 184.
44. Quoted in Kane, *All Poets Welcome*, 184.

Poetry by Phone and Phonograph 91

45. Larry Sloman, "Selections from the Author's Notes," *Boldtype*, 1998, http://www.randomhouse.com/boldtype/0798/sloman/notebook.html.
46. Giorno, "Giorno Poetry Systems," 185.
47. Giorno, "Giorno Poetry Systems," 186–187.
48. Kenneth Goldsmith, "What Did Patti Smith, Frank O'Hara, and Meredith Monk Have in Common?" *Avant-Garde All the Time* (podcast), December 5, 2007, http://www.poetryfoundation.org/journal/audioitem.html?id=237.
49. Giorno, "This Album Is a Do-It-Yourself Dial-A-Poem Kit," *The Dial-A-Poem Poets: Disconnected* (New York: Giorno Poetry Systems, 1974).
50. Barbara Holdridge, interview with Renee Montagne, "Caedmon: Recreating the Moment of Inspiration," *Morning Edition*, NPR, December 5, 2005, http://www.npr.org/templates/story/story.php?storyId=866406.
51. Goldsmith, *Avant-Garde All the Time*.
52. Giorno, "Dial-A-Poem Hype."
53. Goldsmith, *Avant-Garde All the Time*.
54. Giorno, "Epilogue," *You Got to Burn to Shine*, 191.
55. Giorno, quoted in Nicholas Zurbrugg, "Poetry, Entertainment, and the Mass Media: An Interview with John Giorno," *Chicago Review* 40, no. 2 (1994), 85.
56. Giorno, interview by Marcus Boon, *BOMB* 105 (Fall 2008), http://bombsite.com/issues/105/articles/3179.
57. Giorno, Boon interview.
58. Giorno, "Giorno Poetry Systems," 184, 186.
59. Sheila Benson, "'Poetry in Motion': Words That Leap," *Los Angeles Times*, May 13, 1986, J3.
60. Giorno, Obrist interview.
61. Giorno, Obrist interview.
62. Giorno, Obrist interview.
63. http://ubuweb.com.
64. Goldsmith, *Avant-Garde All the Time*.
65. http://epc.buffalo.edu.
66. http://writing.upenn.edu/pennsound/.

5 Soundtracking the Novel
Willy Vlautin's *Northline* as Filmic Audiobook

Justin St. Clair

In common parlance, the term "audiobook" often evokes a particular type of spoken-word recording: those 1980s-style books-on-tape, umpteen cassettes tightly packed inside a flimsy plastic binding and tucked away in some musty corner of the local public library.[1] Rapid and considerable changes in media technology over the past several decades, however, have not only rendered the traditional audiobook more portable (as cassette tapes gave way to compact discs, and CDs, in turn, to digital audio files), but those selfsame changes in recording technology have facilitated "hybrid audiobooks": literary works that necessitate multimodal engagement, requiring the audience to both read *and* listen. These experimental audiobooks often remediate extant forms, and film's "audio/visual" paradigm provides a compelling template for hybridizing the novel.[2]

The past decade, in fact, has seen a variety of attempts to acoustify the traditional print novel by way of a soundtrack or "book score."[3] The British folkie John Wesley Harding, for example, followed his print debut, *Misfortune: A Novel* (2005), with a CD soundtrack titled *Songs of Misfortune* (2005), performed by the nonce ensemble Love Hall Tryst. Mark Z. Danielewski's obsessively filmic *House of Leaves* (2000) is another recent novel that boasts a soundtrack, this one composed and performed by the pop singer Poe. Best known for her 1995 hit "Angry Johnny," Poe (born Annie Decatur Danielewski) crafted *Haunted* (2000) as a companion piece to her brother's labyrinthine novel (and, following the simultaneous release of *Haunted* and *House of Leaves*, the siblings took their multimedia show on the road, appearing together in a series of hybrid events). Elmore Leonard's *Tishomingo Blues* (2002) is yet another novel attempt at soundtracking print fiction. A hard-boiled detective yarn steeped in blues lore, *Tishomingo Blues* incorporates multiple references to a musician named "Marvin Pontiac," mysterious references that send many a reader searching for Pontiac outside the bounds of the novel. Persistent sleuths discover an album titled *The Legendary Marvin Pontiac—Greatest Hits* (2000), a rather intricate hoax perpetrated by legendary Lounge Lizard John Lurie.

Among these and other curious attempts to soundtrack the novel, Willy Vlautin's *Northline* (2008) stands out as particularly filmic.[4] The novel

Soundtracking the Novel 93

itself is a collection of forty-five short cinematic scenes and, in its first edition at least, comes bundled with an instrumental soundtrack featuring Willy Vlautin and Paul Brainard (both members of the critically acclaimed alt.country band Richmond Fontaine). The narrative follows Allison Johnson, a downtrodden character who also surfaces on Richmond Fontaine's album *Post to Wire* (2004), as she wends her way from Las Vegas to Reno, through abusive relationships, the misery of minimum wage, and a series of substandard accommodations.[5] Whereas the novel is a desperate, heart-wrenching portrait of America's underclass, it is the inclusion of sound that may be its most significant formal aspect. Not only does the CD soundtrack offer a prime example of the recent "book score" phenomenon, but the forty-five chapters are themselves insistently aural: they include an extensive system of musical references and allusions, a preponderance of offscreen (or off-page) sound, and even an extended imaginary exchange between Allison and the actor Paul Newman. *Northline* is, in short, an exemplary case study in the remediation of film sound, and this chapter considers both the possibilities and limitations of the book score, while simultaneously using Vlautin's novel to envisage a future for the hybrid audiobook.

THE FUNCTION OF SOUNDTRACKS

In her landmark book on film sound, *Unheard Melodies: Narrative Film Music* (1987), Claudia Gorbman opens with a series of questions concerning the function of film soundtracks:

> What is music doing in the movies, and how does it do it? . . . What and how does music signify in conjunction with the images and events of a story film? What can we learn from dramatic forms of the past that employed music—nineteenth-century theater and opera—and in what ways does cinema's particular technological and historical situation give a specific thrust to this inquiry into the interrelations among media? Why do we tend not to hear music consciously in watching a story film? What business does music have in a movie in the first place? . . . How does music in film narration create a *point of experience* (note the visual chauvinism of saying "point of view") for the spectator?[6]

I have quoted Gorbman at length here because I believe her approach is not only sound—pardon the pun—but also relevant to the nascent hybrid audiobook. Whereas the study of film sound has developed significantly in the decades since her study, the same implicit skepticism with which Gorbman had to contend is certainly applicable here, and in spades.[7] To rephrase but slightly: what business does music have in a book in the first place? The reaction of many readers is predictable, and, given that many recent hybrid audiobooks have been the work of musicians moonlighting as novelists, it

94 *Justin St. Clair*

is tempting to see such soundtracks as little more than marketing ploys.[8] In fairness, it is safe to assume that some Richmond Fontaine fans, for example, purchased *Northline* merely to get their hands on the band's latest music. Nevertheless, if we can withhold judgment for a few pages even while acknowledging that some book scores may be mere gimmickry, we are apt to conclude that the hybrid audiobook presents a unique set of possibilities to writers and readers alike.

To begin, I propose following Gorbman's lead in examining the "dramatic forms of the past that employed music"; in particular, I wish to use her own assessment of the cinematic soundtrack to appraise the "particular technological and historical situation" of the book score. In *Unheard Melodies*, Gorbman applies Gérard Genette's narrative theory to film sound, arguing that film music can be divided into three main categories: diegetic, nondiegetic, and metadiegetic. Diegetic music, she writes, is "music that (apparently) issues from a source within the narrative," whereas nondiegetic music is a "narrative intrusion upon the diegesis" (in other words, the film's musical score) (22). Metadiegetic music, meanwhile, "pertain[s] to narration by a secondary narrator" (in other words: this is music hallucinated or imagined by a character within the diegesis, but is nonetheless, by virtue of its "imaginary" qualities, inaccessible to most—if not all—of the other characters) (22). From Gorbman's perspective, "music enjoys a special status in filmic narration" (3):

> Music in film *mediates*. Its nonverbal and nondenotative status allows it to cross all varieties of "borders": between levels of narration (diegetic/ nondiegetic), between narrating agencies (objective/subjective narrators), between viewing time and psychological time, between points in diegetic space and time (as narrative transition). (30)

Ultimately, she concludes that background music in film is "utilitarian," that it is the equivalent of Muzak, functioning "to lull the spectator into being an *untroublesome* (less critical, less wary) *viewing subject*," much as Muzak functions to "lull the individual into being an *untroublesome social subject*" (58, 57). She grounds these observations in psychoanalytic theory, arguing that music "greases the wheels of the cinematic pleasure machine by easing the spectator's passage into subjectivity" (69).

REMEDIATING THE SCORE

Immediately our cross-medium analogy hits a snag: synchronicity. A film soundtrack is irrevocably synchronized with the image content, and, as a result, the auteur (or, as the case may be, the sound editor) knows precisely the narrative moment at which the audience will apprehend each audio stimulus. In many respects this gives a distinct advantage to the film's creators if, as Gorbman suggests, audience manipulation is the ultimate function of the soundtrack. The creator of a book score is unable to control how and when readers access the soundtrack.[9] The issue of synchronicity, as it pertains to soundtracking, thus recalls Roland Barthes's famous distinction between the "readerly" and the "writerly." A readerly text, in Barthes's estimation, renders the reader a passive consumer; the reader of such a text is "plunged into a kind of idleness—he is intransitive."[10] Writerly texts, meanwhile, require readers to participate actively in the production of meaning. Barthes, needless to say, privileges the writerly text, emphasizing that "the goal of literary work (of literature as work) is to make the reader no longer a consumer, but a producer of the text."[11]

We might assert, then, that a book score (at least in its present iterations) is inherently more writerly than a film score: readers of soundtracked fiction must actively juxtapose the book score and the printed text to construct composite significance. And whereas this writerly (or even composerly) activity may fail to address the ostensible slippage of our cross-medium analogy, it does seem an implicit endorsement of soundtracked fiction, insofar as the book score necessitates participative action on the part of the reader. Temporarily leaving the issue of synchronicity aside, however, I would like to examine how *Northline* internally remediates film sound—that is, how the book manages to hypostatize a soundtrack within the confines of the printed text, for even if Vlautin's novel had not included a score, it would remain, nonetheless, very much an "audiobook." Indeed, *Northline* incorporates each of the three categories of narrative sound—diegetic, nondiegetic, and metadiegetic—that Gorbman identifies within a filmic context; the subsections that follow treat each in turn.

Diegetic Sound

The first and most apparent way in which *Northline* remediates cinematic sound comes in the form of diegetic music—what film industry insiders refer to as "source music."[12] In typical Hollywood fare, this often takes the form of characters interacting with other media devices—a sort of remediated metamoment in which a source within the diegesis (a car radio, a jukebox, and so forth) provides film music. Alternately, some diegetic film music is the result of "live" performance and occurs when characters are either attending a concert or themselves performing music. *Northline* is replete with instances of all the aforementioned examples—from the band we encounter in the novel's second sentence to music issuing from cassette recorders, CD players, jukeboxes, and radios. Vlautin depicts a world awash in sound, and his aural inclusions occasionally recall Don DeLillo's *White Noise* (1985). Whereas DeLillo retransmits the sound of a comfortable middle class, however, Vlautin's soundscape is that of the markedly underprivileged, much of it seeping through thin tenement walls. Even trips to the supermarket, for example, rather than offering a transcendent

96   *Justin St. Clair*

portrait of American plenty, as they do in *White Noise*, depict the drunken reality of the disadvantaged, an irritative subsistence punctuated by a litany of impecunious options: "Under the fluorescent lights, she saw them, the people, the kids, the shoppers yelling and running around all talking and in a hurry. A lady on an intercom announced 'Fryer breasts on sale for $1.70 a pound. Betty Crocker cake mix on sale for $1.99 a box.'"[13]

It quickly becomes apparent, however, that much of the music in *Northline* serves not only as a character-shaping literary device, but also as something of an anodyne for those same characters.[14] When we first meet twenty-two-year-old Allison Johnson, she is a high school dropout who works as a waitress in Las Vegas. Her abusive boyfriend, Jimmy Bodie, is an unapologetic racist whose only animating raison d'être appears to be railing against Mexicans. In the novel's opening chapter, Allison passes out while they are having sex in a casino toilet; she falls and gashes her head, and Jimmy responds by kicking her "as hard as he could, with his steel-toed boots" (6). When Allison regains consciousness the next morning, bruised and bloodied, Jimmy promptly handcuffs her to a bed, naked, and leaves the house. In short, one would be hard pressed to imagine a more unsavory introduction to this abhorrent individual. The musical selections that accompany Jimmy are in keeping with his character: scattered near the bed are "[h]undreds of country and rockabilly records," including the legendary hard-living (and short-lived) Hank Williams and the once incarcerated (and always incendiary) David Allan Coe (8).

Vlautin has an uncanny knack, however, for humanizing even the most unlikable of his characters, and Jimmy, as detestable as he may be, is no exception. The novel never attempts to excuse or recuperate Jimmy or his behavior, but it does portray him not only as the victim of a horrific childhood but also as a character who actively grapples with his demons. The novel's diegetic music is instrumental in rendering Jimmy something more complicated than a gratuitously violent bigot. Several chapters in, for example, Jimmy "put[s] in a mixed tape of Johnny Cash" and the song "San Quentin" sends him spiraling into a reflective state (34). The musical choice is noteworthy, for the Man in Black famously cultivated an outlaw persona yet, as Jimmy himself notes, "never spent any real time in jail" (36). In fact, for all his hell-raising and bad behavior, Johnny Cash famously counterbalanced his outlawry with devotion to both faith and family. Equal parts prison ward and parson-bard, Cash died one of the most beloved figures in American music. This extratextual template for living outside the law and being honest, to paraphrase Bob Dylan, clearly appeals to Jimmy, whatever his issues, and he immediately launches into a pointed critique of several of his skinhead friends.

A connected diegetic selection appears in the chapter "Flying J." On their way to a skinhead rally in the desert, Jimmy and Allison stop at a truck stop for dinner. A band playing in the lounge catches Jimmy's attention: "'I like this song. It's an old Merle Haggard song,' Jimmy sa[ys]. His eyes

Soundtracking the Novel   97

beg[i]n to water. 'Music saved my ass so many times'" (30). Once again, the choice of music is a pointed allusion to a well-known country musician's real-life persona. Although never directly mentioned in the novel, Haggard was one of the prisoners in the audience during Johnny Cash's famous San Quentin concert. In later interviews, in fact, Haggard credited the show— to cop a phrase from Jimmy's vernacular—with saving his ass: Cash's concert convinced Haggard to pull his life together and repudiate his criminal past. Moments after hearing the Merle Haggard tune, Jimmy breaks down crying and recounts several heartbreaking episodes from his abusive childhood. This particular example of diegetic music operates on several levels simultaneously. Not only does it serve to flesh out Jimmy's character (both as a method of identity construction through association and as an internal device for the revelation of formative details), but it also functions as part of an allusive extratextual framework. Furthermore, the episode reveals the role of music both in Jimmy's life and in the novel: amidst desperate circumstances, music provides a comforting and reassuring palliative.

Music serves the other characters as something of an analgesic as well, and in a range of suggestive registers. Several of these inclusions are cursory, but throughout *Northline* diegetic music functions as a coping mechanism. When Jimmy and Allison finally arrive at the desert rally, for example, they are greeted by "a band playing on a makeshift pallet stage" (38). The lead singer, "his shirt off . . . tattoos covering his chest, arms, and neck," gives voice to the angry claque: "The music was fast and he was screaming as hard as he could while the rest of the band played" (38–39). Once again, Vlautin does not condone the racism implicit in the event, but he does offer a sympathetic portrait of disaffection. The musical performance is explicitly cathartic to both the band and its audience, and the novel thereby provides insight into underlying emotional issues rather than merely addressing their contemptible forms of expression. The novel's diegetic music, therefore, once again plays a dual role: it brings relief to the characters and, at the same time, serves as a formal method of complicating those characters.[15]

In the life of the novel's protagonist, Allison Johnson, diegetic music figures in much the same manner. She eventually slips Jimmy's orbit and hops a bus to Reno, but the escape is less than ideal. Pregnant, she enlists the help of an agency that both pairs her with a family looking to adopt and also provides her with financial support while she carries the child to term. Beyond this assistance, however, Allison must cope in an entirely new environment without any meaningful support system, and she quickly falls into self-recriminating despair. These anxiety attacks and episodes of self-loathing often lead Allison to the bathtub, where she turns to music to calm her nerves:

> She grabbed her walkman, undressed, and got in the tub. She started her tape player. Patti Page came on the headphones. She only had two tapes. Patti Page and Brenda Lee. She closed her eyes and tried to figure

98   *Justin St. Clair*

out what to do. She would keep herself busy and try not to think about the past anymore. (86)

That Allison should turn to music for solace comes as no surprise; what is more than a little unusual, however, is her choice in music. Patti Page may have been the bestselling female artist of the 1950s, but she is someone who, in popular consciousness at least, has slipped into relative obscurity. It is safe to assume that most twenty-somethings in the early-twenty-first century have no idea who Patti Page is, even if they might recognize her 1953 hit "(How Much Is) That Doggie in the Window?" Allison's musical selections, I would argue, are not altogether realistic representations of the musical predilections of someone in Allison's position; rather, they are nostalgic substitutions—idealized replacement "pasts" for the traumatic realities that Allison is trying to forget. As such, this diegetic music, while certainly part of the storyworld, has a predominantly literary function.

Such is also the case with Brenda Lee, Allison's other salvific chanteuse.[16] Brenda Lee, I would wager, has even less name recognition today than does Patti Page. However, in the late 1950s, Brenda Lee shot to fame as a child star; she was only thirteen, for example, when she recorded her enduring hit "Rockin' around the Christmas Tree" in 1958. Once again, Allison's choice of music (if slightly unrealistic) is telling: the 1950s, in the American imagination, is a rosily wholesome time of traditional order. The fictional idyll of the 1950s contrasts sharply with Allison's own upbringing, and the musical space into which Allison escapes is thereby an "other place" of tantalizing possibility. Brenda Lee's position as a child star only amplifies the effect, as does the fact that her best-known recording is a Christmas standard.[17] The contrast between Allison's "musical place" and the place in which she finds herself, moreover, is further underscored by her two aborted suicide attempts. On both occasions Allison is listening to her cassettes as she unsuccessfully tries to bring herself to slit her own wrists. During one of these episodes, the music continues to play as Allison's thoughts spiral toward her darkest moment: her own rape at the hands of two busboys outside the Horseshoe Casino where she once waitressed. The dissimilarity between the diegetic music and the suicide attempt is jarring in and of itself, but as the narrative lapses into analepsis, the incongruous musical selection amplifies the horror of Allison's violation.

Nondiegetic Sound

The second category of film sound Gorbman enumerates consists of music that does not originate in the diegesis but is part of the narrative structure external to the storyworld. In the case of film scores, this includes much of the music we are accustomed to hearing (or not hearing, as the case may be) while watching a film—from the foreboding minor chords that alert us to prepare for an inevitable disaster to the swelling symphonic strings

Soundtracking the Novel   99

that tug at our heartstrings during a film's more poignant moments. On the surface, it would seem that nondiegetic music would be the most difficult type of film sound to remediate in print fiction. And, indeed, it is difficult to conceive of print fiction directly remediating a nondiegetic score, save, perhaps, for a self-conscious narrator telling the readers to "cue the strings," or an experimental work providing parenthetical (and music-related) staging cues.

Vlautin, however, does include a distinct category of textual music and sound that I believe qualifies—at least provisionally—as nondiegetic. Throughout *Northline*, audio streams repeatedly drift onstage, as it were: sound and music that are not part of the immediate setting waft in from some nearby location.[18] Many of these moments involve Allison, who, isolated in her own apartment, can "hear her neighbors, the faint sound of a TV, of people talking, of running water" (80). Whereas adjacent living quarters, for example, are arguably part of the larger storyworld, they are not part of the immediate diegesis: neither Allison nor the reader is afforded the privilege of peering inside these spaces. Nevertheless, the sound leaks out and into Allison's world, although it remains on a distinctly different register than the diegetic inclusions discussed earlier.

Many of these instances serve to amplify Allison's sense of isolation and alienation. For example, on one representative occasion "[t]here was a show playing on the TV but she could only vaguely hear it" (75). "It felt miles away," the narrator sympathetically reports, "like she was disappearing down a long hole" (75). This telescoping effect recurs: on another occasion, "[a] band was playing in the carport and people were talking and yelling, but to her it was a thousand miles away" (158). As with the novel's diegetic music, which typically resonates on several levels simultaneously, the preponderance of aural offscreen (or off-page) references also signify in stereo. These audio streams not only augment the novel's pervasive sense of alienation and isolation, but they also serve as a constant gesture toward the outside world. As do Allison's curious cassettes, the nondiegetic music offers her the possibility of an "other space," albeit remote, and, at times, seemingly inaccessible.

Metadiegetic Sound

The third and final category of film sound Gorbman describes consists of music that originates in the diegesis but, given its figmental status, is only internally accessible to the character who imagines it (in other word, music that occurs in dreams, visions, and so forth). Whereas it cannot be said that *Northline* contains much—if any—music that falls into this category, the metadiegetic warrants mention here given the series of extended, imaginary conversations Allison has with the actor Paul Newman. In short, Allison depends upon these conversations for advice and support. He is, in the simplest of terms, both the child's imaginary friend and a stand-in for her

100 Justin St. Clair

absent father, hypothesized and conjured from years of movie marathons on cable television.

NORTHLINE'S SCORE

In the United States, *Northline* first appeared as a Harper Perennial "P. S. edition" in 2008. As the tagline of the imprint's series indicates—"Insights, Interviews & More"—novels designated "P. S. editions" include contextualizing appendices. *Northline* is no exception: it includes an eighteen-page postscript comprised of biographical information, an interview, and several short pieces on the novel's creation (in addition, of course, to the altogether atypical inclusion of a compact disc titled "The Exclusive Soundtrack to the Book"). In one of the short pieces appended to the novel, Vlautin reflects on the creation of the soundtrack and on his efforts to enlist the help of Paul Brainard (steel pedal guitarist and Vlautin's bandmate in Richmond Fontaine):

> I asked him if he would help me with it and he said yes. He didn't even give me a hard time about it. He never said, "Does an instrumental soundtrack to a book make any sense?" (I don't know.) "Has the publisher asked you to do this?" (No.) "Have they said they'll take it?" (No.) "Are they going to pay for it?" (No.)[19]

Beyond offering a bit of extra peritext—that is, paratextual elements such as prefaces, notes, dedications, and so forth, located within the same volume as the central text—it is doubtful that Harper Perennial's "P. S. editions" provide the critic with much useful content.[20] The postscript, it seems, is little more than a nod to contemporary readers' expectations— a bit of "behind-the-scenes" chatter for the DVD generation. Vlautin's remarks regarding the soundtrack, however, are noteworthy insofar as they acknowledge the proverbial elephant in the room: does a hybrid audiobook, which pairs an instrumental soundtrack with a traditional print novel, make any sense?

The score itself consists of fourteen instrumental tracks. The opening and closing tracks—"Northline Main Theme" and "Northline Reprise," respectively—are the only general inclusions; the other twelve tracks bear titles that direct the reader/listener to specific characters, episodes, or chapters within the novel. However, whereas the novel itself unfolds in fits and starts, repeatedly doubling back to fill in formative episodes, the sequencing of the soundtrack is very nearly chronological. As a result, synchronizing the textual episodes with their corresponding musical tracks is even more of a writerly endeavor than one might expect. The soundtrack's second selection, for example, "The Busboys from the Horseshoe," would seem to direct the reader to the novel's nineteenth chapter, "The Busboys at the

Horseshoe Casino," which is nearly halfway through the book. (And by the time the reader gets there, she has already read the episodes corresponding to tracks three, four, and five.)

Supposing, then, that our writerly reader takes the time to juxtapose the busboys' song with the appropriate chapter, what is she likely to discover? Namely, that Vlautin has composed an unsettling musical counterpoint to one of the novel's most disturbing scenes. In the text, Allison flashes back to an episode that occurred while she was waitressing in Las Vegas. After enduring ongoing sexual harassment at the restaurant, Allison finally reacts and tells the head cook what has occurred. As retribution, two of the busboys attack her one night as she is on the way to her car. The younger of the two pins her arms to the ground, while the older one begins to rape her. When Allison makes eye contact with the younger busboy, he pulls the other off her, and the boys run away; Allison is left lying in the street, traumatized. The soundtrack, however, contains none of this violence—it is sweeping, perhaps a touch elegiac, but devoid of any mimetic musical markers (in other words, speed, discord, rhythmic aggression, and so forth). Whereas the music is clearly an escapist "other space" representing Allison's psychological response to the trauma, and while readers unwilling or unable to hold both the textual episode and the musical track in their heads simultaneously might also find the instrumental a welcome escape from the disturbing narrative passage, it is nearly impossible to imagine the short piece (2m 36s) serving as background music to a comparable cinematic representation. The music seems more fitting for sweeping wide-screen shots of a rugged western landscape, picturesque and plaintive. In much the same fashion as music is internally juxtaposed with the scene (as previously discussed, either Patti Page or Brenda Lee plays on Allison's Walkman during the narrative flashback), the external score's incompatibility with the narrative action serves to intensify the horror of the episode.

A reader who pairs the track "Doc Holiday's" with the chapter of the same name is likely to be similarly disconcerted. In the novel, Allison enters a bar, despondent, and drinks five vodka 7UPs in quick succession. Meanwhile, the narrator announces, "There was a jukebox playing," the aside serving as something of a reminder to the reader to cue the novel's soundtrack (99). Debilitatingly inebriated, Allison is escorted from the bar by a pair of miscreants named Red and Marty, whose idea of a party appears to be gang-raping the incapacitated. Throughout the entire episode Allison is unresponsive, until that is, she begs Red to hit her. As with the previous busboy incident, the repulsiveness of this sordid scene is amplified by the incongruity of the musical score. The song on the soundtrack features the pleasant pizzicato of a six-string guitar over a steel pedal's moody moaning. Once again, by evacuating the violence from the musical accompaniment, Vlautin renders the textual episode doubly tragic. The vaguely melancholy strains of the instrumental track are almost comically understated and seem to suggest that Allison's trajectory is a fait accompli.

102 *Justin St. Clair*

As a whole, however, *Northline*'s soundtrack is not all ironic counterpoint. On several occasions, Vlautin offers musical accompaniment that is more purposefully mimetic. For example, at an early point in the novel, Allison's teenage sister runs off to Mexico with her boyfriend. The sister is entirely incommunicado until Allison receives a worrisome phone call: "It was the middle of the day and she was in bed asleep when the phone rang. Her sister was crying, but the connection was full of static and the line went dead within a minute" (114). The corresponding musical track, "Her Sister Calls from Mexico," sounds like an outtake from Bob Dylan's score to *Pat Garrett and Billy the Kid* (1973), all border guitar and high-pitched harmonica. Moreover, in a mimetic nod to the narrative account, the song clocks in at a mere thirty-three seconds—over, very nearly, before it has even begun.

THE FUTURE OF THE HYBRID AUDIOBOOK

In one of the supplemental pieces that appear in *Northline*'s "P. S. edition," Vlautin offers this explanation of the soundtrack's function:

> I guess in the end my hope is that the music reflects the feel of the book, the heart of the book, and that after you've finished the novel you'll listen to the music and once in a while think about Allison Johnson and TJ Watson, Penny Pearson and Dan Mahoney, Evelyn and Jimmy Bodie. Maybe the music will help the novel stay alive a bit longer.[21]

On the one hand, Vlautin's account is a bit disingenuous: as we saw in the previous section, *Northline*'s soundtrack is more than mere mood music. On the other hand, however, the response is accurate, for Vlautin could easily have undertaken a variety of additional measures to integrate the soundtrack more fully into the literary experience. I would like to close with a brief consideration of several ways this might have been accomplished. Whereas such speculative analysis may be critically presumptuous, the hybrid audiobook seems poised to become an established literary mode over the coming decade, and thus a brief interrogation of its possibilities seems constructive.

Creative Cueing

First and foremost, Vlautin might have done a more thoroughgoing job of signaling connections between the novel and the soundtrack. This is not a call for something less writerly, just an acknowledgment that a text can do more to integrate a soundtrack into the reading experience. For example, throughout *Northline*, characters repeatedly—and often inconsequentially—interact with media devices. Some of these less relevant "turned on the stereo"/"turned off the music" moments could easily have appeared at points of coincidence between the narrative episodes and the score, thereby reminding the reader

Soundtracking the Novel   103

to consult the soundtrack (177, 63). Whereas this arguably occurs on one or two occasions (such as the jukebox mentioned previously), it does not transpire with enough regularity to be relevant. Alternatively, Vlautin might have interwoven a particular word or phrase into the narrative to signal such cue points. These keywords—or *cuewords*, as the case may be—would not necessarily need to be overly obvious; in fact, subtly deployed, such cuewords would add a layer of complexity to the exegetical experience. One could also envision some sort of graphic marginalia—a CD symbol, for example, or a pair of musical notes—employed as a signal to the reader. Whatever the methodology, some sort of creative intratextual cueing would help hybridize the experience on a practical level, which would thereby allow for a range of higher-order interconnections. Similarly, Vlautin might have embedded cues in the music itself, creating, for example, musical phrases that correspond to specific characters or recurring situations.

Aural Outsourcing

Second, Vlautin might have relegated one of the modes of narrative sound discussed earlier—diegetic, nondiegetic, or metadiegetic—to the accompanying CD. For example, the various metadiegetic episodes in *Northline* during which Allison hallucinates Paul Newman might have been altogether removed from the printed text and placed solely on the soundtrack. Such "aural outsourcing" would raise the importance of the score, necessarily coercing readers into considering the global implications of the hybrid audiobook, rather than, as is often the case, prioritizing the printed text over the supplemental soundtrack. The novel's various diegetic inclusions—from Johnny Cash to Merle Haggard, Patti Page to Brenda Lee—might also have been offered as part of the bundled soundtrack to great effect. As we saw, the music of Patti Page and Brenda Lee (in particular) contrasts notably with the narrative thrust. If this music had been presented aurally rather than graphically, the rich allusive framework would have been slightly less elusive. Similarly, the off-page sound that I dubbed "provisionally nondiegetic"—the sounds and music that are not part of the immediate diegesis but that waft, nonetheless, into the storyworld—might have found articulation on the accompanying CD. As I suggested earlier, this off-page sound signals the existence of an "other space," or place of possibility just outside the characters' reach. Appending this soundscape to the novel would have emphasized its exteriority while enabling an even richer set of connections between the characters' immediate environment and the larger cultural milieu.

Choral Counterpoint

Finally, Vlautin might have used the accompanying CD as a formal method of undercutting, contradicting, or otherwise destabilizing the narrative

104   *Justin St. Clair*

perspective of the text. Whereas such a technique would have changed the overall tenor of *Northline*, the move would certainly have been a novel realization of narrative instability. Moreover, this approach seems to be a natural extension of the musical counterpoint discussed earlier; instead of merely unsettling the reader with an incongruous instrumental score, however, the tracks could lyrically offer an alternative narrative perspective. Regardless of whether this would serve to collectivize the narrative perspective (think William Faulkner's *As I Lay Dying*) or distance and further destabilize the primary narrative voice (think Vladimir Nabokov's *Lolita*), a soundtrack offering a "choral counterpoint" would necessitate the equal consideration of the book score, forcing the reader to consider the audio as an indispensable puzzle piece rather than an optional complement.

And this, ultimately, is one of the key roles that hybrid audiobooks can play: by pointedly foregrounding sound, they call attention to our acoustic environment, to our increasingly cluttered soundscape, and to our susceptibility to aural manipulation at the hands of sound-savvy filmmakers, advertisers, and employers. The aural has long been understood as secondary or complementary, the "ground" to visual culture's "figure." Fiction that formally compels an equal consideration of the aural realm necessarily addresses our cultural "sense-ism"; it makes us listen—actively, in a writerly fashion—and disallows our impulse to tune out much of our acoustic environment as mere background sound. By rendering subtexts audible, soundtracked novels open new registers of narrative possibility, allowing authors the freedom of multimodal presentation, while simultaneously encouraging audiences to attend to the ocular-centrism of contemporary consumer culture.

NOTES

1. I would like to thank Michael Mason, my research assistant at the University of South Alabama, for all his help. Thanks go as well to Heidi LaVine for her feedback and suggestions.
2. For more on the concept of "remediation"—that is, the way in which new media forms borrow techniques of presentation from extant media—see Jay David Bolter and Richard Grusin, *Remediation: Understanding New Media* (Cambridge: MIT Press, 1999).
3. There were, of course, forerunners in the field of soundtracked fiction. Three prominent precursors include one-time Monkee Michael Nesmith, who released an LP/novella in 1974 titled *The Prison: A Book with a Soundtrack*; Ursula K. Le Guin, whose 1986 novel *Always Coming Home* was accompanied—at least in one edition—by a cassette titled *Music and Poetry of the Kesh*; and Kathy Acker, whose 1996 novel *Pussy, King of the Pirates* had its release synchronized with an eponymous Mekons album.
4. Other recent efforts to soundtrack the novel include Joe Pernice's *It Feels So Good When I Stop* (2009), Thomas Pynchon's *Inherent Vice* (2009), and Nick Cave's *The Death of Bunny Munro* (2009). Pernice, the principal songwriter in the 1990s alt.country act the Scud Mountain Boys and the brains behind the indie outfit the Pernice Brothers, supplemented his print debut

Soundtracking the Novel 105

with an album of corresponding songs—both actual (covers) and fictional (allegedly written by the novel's characters). In a similar vein, Pynchon followed his "book trailer" for *Inherent Vice* (which is, purportedly, narrated by the reclusive author himself) with an Amazon.com posting titled "Thomas Pynchon's Soundtrack to Inherent Vice," a hot-linked, forty-two-item list of real and imagined songs referenced in the novel. Cave, meanwhile, not only served as the reader for the audiobook version of his novel but scored an accompanying soundtrack, which was recorded in experimental "3D audio."

5. Also of note is the Richmond Fontaine song "Northline," which appears on the album *Winnemucca* (2002).

6. Claudia Gorbman, *Unheard Melodies: Narrative Film Music* (Bloomington: Indiana University Press, 1987), 2. Hereafter cited parenthetically by page number.

7. Recent noteworthy studies of film sound include Michel Chion, *Un art sonore, le cinéma: histoire, esthétique, poétique* (Paris: Cahiers du Cinéma, 2003), translated into English—by Claudia Gorbman, incidentally—as *Film, a Sound Art* (New York: Columbia University Press, 2009); Rick Altman, *Silent Film Sound* (New York: Columbia University Press, 2004); and Jay Beck and Tony Grajeda, eds., *Lowering the Boom: Critical Studies in Film Sound* (Urbana: University of Illinois Press, 2008).

8. Indeed, some "book scores" *are* merely marketing ploys. See John Jurgensen, "Reading, Writing—and Rocking Out," *Wall Street Journal*, August 19, 2006, retrieved via ProQuest, April 1, 2010. To promote *Maximum Ride: School's Out Forever* (2006), for example, James Patterson commissioned a soundtrack "designed to appeal to young readers' tastes" (Jurgensen). The soundtrack reportedly cost someone—Little, Brown and Company, one would imagine—$100,000 (Jurgensen). Another noteworthy example of the book-score-as-marketing-ploy phenomenon can be found on the well-trafficked music blog *Largehearted Boy*, http://www.largeheartedboy.com. Since 2005 the blog has featured a section titled "Book Notes," to which authors may submit short essays and playlists to promote their publications. As of April 2010, the blog has archived more than five hundred such playlists, and contributors have ranged from musicians moonlighting as memoirists (for example, Juliana Hatfield and Janis Ian) to contemporary fiction's avant-garde (for example, Jonathan Baumbach, Curtis White, and Ken Kalfus).

9. Of course, one can envision a future in which hybrid audiobooks have synchronous, or near synchronous, soundtracks. Today's e-readers provide a platform that enables hybrid presentation, and should future iterations of the technology include, for example, infrared eye-tracking to monitor readers' progress, the possibilities for synchronous soundtracking would expand considerably.

10. Roland Barthes, *S/Z: An Essay* (New York: Hill and Wang, 1975), 4.

11. Barthes, *S/Z: An Essay*, 4.

12. Gorbman, *Unheard Melodies*, 3.

13. Willy Vlautin, *Northline* (New York: Harper Perennial, 2008), 15. Hereafter cited parenthetically by page number. Compare Vlautin's supermarket in *Northline* to the one described in *White Noise*: "I was suddenly aware of the dense environmental texture. The automatic doors opened and closed, breathing abruptly. Colors and odors seemed sharper. The sound of gliding feet emerged from a dozen other noises, from the sublittoral drone of maintenance systems, from the rustle of newsprint as shoppers scanned their horoscopes in the tabloids up front, from the whispers of elderly women with talcumed faces, from the steady rattle of cars going over a loose manhole

106   *Justin St. Clair*

cover just outside the entrance. Gliding feet. I heard them clearly, a sad numb shuffle in every aisle" (Don DeLillo, *White Noise*, New York: Penguin, 1986, 168–169). As Vlautin does, DeLillo emphasizes the auditory elements of the supermarket experience; however, the tones here are muted and hushed—"cultured," in a word (if depressive). This is a middle-class cathedral of commerce, not a bustling, blue-collar storehouse. Moreover, the high-end product descriptions we find in *White Noise* contrast dramatically with the fryer breasts and cake mixes of *Northline*: "Unpackaged meat, fresh bread . . . Exotic fruits, rare cheeses. Products from twenty countries. It's like being at some crossroads of the ancient world, a Persian bazaar or boom town on the Tigris" (Don DeLillo, 169).

14. While beyond the scope of this essay, it should be noted that "diegetic sound" has been employed as a narrative device since the novel's inception.
15. Similarly, in one of the novel's later scenes, we encounter Penny, an obese and unhappy friend of Allison's, who binges on Neil Diamond songs as she does Camel Lights and Baskin-Robbins. The music, however, with its attendant extratextual connotations, serves as a far more resonant device than either cigarettes or ice cream.
16. Allison takes Brenda Lee to the tub as well: "She shut all the curtains and found her tape player and listened to Brenda Lee while she sat in the darkness in the warm water" (Vlautin, *Northline*, 103).
17. Note as well that Patti Page's best-known song—"(How Much Is) That Doggie in the Window?"—is also what one might call a "happy childhood" classic.
18. One is reminded of the "blue piano" refrain from Tennessee Williams's *A Streetcar Named Desire* (1947), which is, for all intents and purposes, non-diegetic music that occasionally seems to issue from a diegetic location.
19. Willy Vlautin, "The *Northline* Soundtrack," in *Northline* postscript, 16.
20. For more on the uses of peritext, see Gérard Genette's *Paratexts: Thresholds of Interpretation* (New York: Cambridge University Press, 1997).
21. Vlautin, "The *Northline* Soundtrack," 17.

Part II
Close Listenings

6 Novelist as "Sound-Thief"
The Audiobooks of John le Carré

Garrett Stewart

I well remember my first revelatory encounter with the audiobook phenomenon. I was gently proselytizing Dickens for the sake of my teenage daughter on a long car trip to Chicago when, although I had read and taught the novel several times, I for the first time heard, actually heard, Dickens's sly anticipation of his famous second-chapter set piece from *Hard Times*—the drudge Bitzer's definition of a horse in bite-sized categorical increments: "Quadruped. Graminivorous. Forty teeth," and so forth, including a double emphasis on hoofs: "Sheds coat in spring; in marshy countries, sheds hoofs, too. Hoofs hard, but requiring to be shod with iron. . . . Thus (and much more) Bitzer."[1] Every lover of Dickens remembers this passage, one that might have gone over well on the lecture circuit in his famous readings just before the days of the phonograph. But what I had never noticed before is the pun that sees this satiric turn coming, when the pedant Gradgrind fails to browbeat Sissy Jupe, the circus girl who lives and breathes horses, into becoming abstract about them—and humiliates her instead in front of the class. It takes the expert, unctuous delivery of Frederick Davidson on the CD to let Gradgrind's bombast contaminate even the inflated phonetic irony of indirect discourse: "'Girl number twenty unable to define a horse!' said Mr. Gradgrind, for the general *behoof*"—with three double *oo*'s at least—of the assembled students (called "pitchers" in their waiting ful(l)-fill-ment by fact).[2] My car swerved dangerously under impact from this exhalation of hot air in "behoof."

A gifted stylist and hugely popular novelist following in the Dickensian tradition, and the multiple beneficiary of sound technology a century later than Boz's uncaptured star turns, the undercover spy novelist John Cornwell, code name John le Carré, doesn't just grant the rights for, but actually writes, "audiobooks" (by any other name). He accomplishes this like Dickens before him, in whose fiction, for example, by delegation from the Master, an enterprising newspaper reader in *Our Mutual Friend* is said to "do the Police in different voices" even before any novelist takes to the lectern, as le Carré follows Dickens in doing.[3] Then, too, le Carré's "audial" books, well before their transfer to magnetic tape or digital files, are ventures in

110   *Garrett Stewart*

narrated audition frequently obsessed with sound recording in the form of covert surveillance and its invasions of privacy.

There is, of course, an opposite mode of disinterested voice recording. On the other end of the textual spectrum from both commercial recordings and surreptitious sound capture, a recent instance comes to mind, albeit fictional. Before eventually sending his own personally recorded cassettes of book recitations to his former lover and illiterate auditor in prison, the protagonist of Bernhard Schlink's 1995 novel *The Reader* admits what any parent falling asleep over his child's favorite book well remembers: that oral delivery, at least until mastered as a discipline, typically impedes comprehension for the enunciating agent rather than maximizing it.[4] The commercial audiobook can be seen—that is, heard—as an end run around this dilemma. Instead of having to read out loud to glean the cadence and sonority of toned writing even at the risk of its escaped inference, we delegate that sounding board—so that, in the audiotape or its digital upgrade, the textual voice of the other can be lent full ear.

But how—the question may appear odd at first—how might the seemingly contingent and ancillary function of recorded books enter into the so-called hermeneutic spiral of the narratives they render? This question leads me to my chosen case in point. Ubiquitous on the audiobook shelves for over a quarter century, le Carré doesn't just write for the voice, his books widely contracted for audiotape versions from early on. He also, it bears repeating, inscribes the voice, netting its intonations but also its subterranean channels of intent, transcribing not just diversely accented dialogue but also the paths of covert speech in everything from the stenographic record of wiretapped phone lines to stored radio decryptions—including, in his more recent work, voice tracks imprinted from satellite sound feeds and cell phone intercepts. I'm interested in what happens when this thematic is, so to say, recirculated out loud by professional readers.

The audiosphere of le Carré's fiction is a world of already secondary vocal record thus given tertiary dramatic life in the books-on-disc mode. In the greatest performances in this vein, by the renowned Frank Muller for Recorded Books, the novels are not said to be "read by" or "performed by" but actually "narrated by" the elocutionary artist, after which, by a framing and deliberately tinny commercial voice, each user is thanked not for listening but for "being a Recorded Books reader." In these paired terminological anomalies, narration is given voice even while audition is returned to the zone of the page: a twofold gesture toward the phenomenology of borrowed presence in the thick of everyday reading. The suggestion is clear. The audiobook is only a better way of reading—more intimate and vivid, yes, but familiar.

It is almost as if Recorded Books had commissioned analytic philosopher Peter Kivy to package their materials for them, given his emphasis on even silent reading as a performance, always in part interpretive.[5] Kivy's purpose is to level the unnecessary distinction, in Nelson Goodman's philosophy of art, between works of notation-plus-instance like dance or music—or call it score-plus-execution—and the supposed self-containment of literary textuality, in which notation is all. On the contrary, the only activation of a text Kivy would rule out of the performance category is a totally unthinking one, as in the phonetic mouthing of a language barely understood or in the automatized computer-voicing, for instance, of books-for-the-blind software. This would also make Kivy a good defense witness if called to the stand in the recent copyright law suits against digitized versions of otherwise performed books, for which software engineers claim to be doing very different work from that of interpretive reading. In short, prosthetics versus aesthetics.

HISTORICAL REWIND

The technological history in question is easy to summarize. Before its CD incarnation, the audiobook was the last commercial innovation in the long march of an analogue tape technology whose initial reel-to-reel format derived from the kind of military precursors for mainstream media that Friedrich Kittler is so assiduous at smoking out.[6] He might have put it this way: postphonographic portable recording technology had to be miniaturized—and its functions in other ways economized—for more tactical use before its further commercial development in playback modes, first in cassette, then in compact disc, and now in digital forms. Long before the wireless downloads dear to joggers and terrorists alike, the vest-pocket tape recorders of Cold War spying evolved into the freeway commuter's audio deck—including of course, for long-distance transit, the time-killing book-on-tape, later on-disc, where at times, in one of the most popular candidates for this format, namely le Carré's novels, the very logic of privileged transmission returns from within the content of certain tape-conscious espionage plots.

What follows will locate a specific cluster of narrative motifs and techniques from the surveillance thematic of le Carré's fiction within the history of tape-recording and transmission technology that evolved into the audiobook—and in the process come to discover that very history inserted within those same narrative operations, whose generic bearings le Carré has pointedly lifted to the metanarrative level by claiming that all novelists are not only "fakes" but "spies."[7] Which means eavesdroppers. Which means hidden portable recorders. Or in the explicit terms of his 2006 novel *The Mission Song*, not just sequestered cameras but "sound-thieves," each operating as an "ear-witness" to the unseen.[8]

Apart from technological paradigms of voice transcription, there are in le Carré's novels also strictly oral models that precipitate in-jokes ratcheted one notch further into reflexivity by their audiobook execution. In *Tinker, Tailor, Soldier, Spy* (1974), a once betrayed and nearly slain agent—and

112   *Garrett Stewart*

now, in forced retirement from the service, a teacher at the prep-school breeding ground of all such spies—is "pledged" by the dormitory students "to finish a story by John Buchan," none other than le Carré's own predecessor in the British espionage genre.[9] It's an unexpected chore: "Reading aloud, he noticed that there were certain sounds he had trouble pronouncing; they caught somewhere in his throat."[10] His bullet injuries, combined with the aftereffects of torture, are affecting his jaw muscles; but that's only part of it, we are to infer. Reading from an early phase of the genre steeped in nationalist moral certainty, after having been double-crossed by one of his own, this betrayed agent should not be surprised that certain complacent ethical sureties do stick in the craw. Certainly when read aloud by Frank Muller with the full acidic bite of le Carré's irony, the right pitch of skeptical distance is achieved in the clenched timbres of orality.[11]

And technological history is even more often replayed by le Carré's irony than is literary history. Its emphases at times congeal into a different kind of in-joke, as when, in the 1986 novel *A Perfect Spy*, written during the earliest commercial deployment of compact disc recording but backdated to an earlier scene in Cold War Berlin, a female functionary is handed an antiquarian book by the hero and asked to "put a CD into the binding."[12] Flirting with him, she pretends that she "hadn't heard of CDs except on diplomatic cars," and he dutifully explains that it means a "concealment device"—in this case a pouch to be inserted under the endpaper with just space enough for "one standard sheet of coding cloth," an encrypted text-within-the-text. More, perhaps, is being flirted with here than the hero. Whereas inside the novel, a CD is bound into a book format, it is also the case that the whole long novel itself will soon be contained within a CD format.

The digital intertext aside, the evolving forms of le Carré's military-industrial surveillance and transmission technology rehearse the large arc of media advance theorized by Kittler and itself anticipated by nineteenth-century literary models, including what amounts to the international espionage text of *Dracula*. Beyond the cutting-edge high-tech Victorian dictagraph in Stoker's novel (whose wax cylinders, as we find in Chapter 27, can be slowed down, like tape, in order to be transcribed by the secretarial labors of Mina Harker, whose resulting pages thus provide in turn a searchable although no longer phonic data bank), what explicitly interests Kittler is a scene in *Dracula* in which surveillance and intercept technologies are not just reflected but their future anticipated. This is the climactic episode of Mina the typist's uncanny telepathy, in which, under the count's spell, but also Van Helsing's counterhypnosis, Mina's unconscious body becomes a radar antenna for the submarine detection of the count in his coffin beneath the waterline of his Baltic escape route.[13] Next stop, for Kittler, the sonar technologies of the First World War.

Even before Stoker in the annals of a prophesied media culture, and intersecting the history of commercial recording technology rather than its military-surveillance counterpart, there is actually a nineteenth-century

Novelist as "Sound-Thief" 113

literary fantasy—missed as precursor by Kittler—that leapfrogs over the storage limitations of the gramophone mechanism to imagine audiobooks themselves—recorded narratives composed, so it would seem, of untold numbers of phonographic cylinders. Almost a decade before *Dracula*'s appearance in 1896, with those unchaptered dictagraph rolls and their outstripping only by an indexical thought-transference that records all its traces in the searchable brainwaves of Mina as mesmerized remote witness, American futurist Edward Bellamy predicted in 1889 the actual recorded text in popular dissemination. His futurist short story "With the Eyes Shut" is narrated by a man ordinarily excluded from the unmentioned (and hereby outmoded) "railway novel" mass marketed to passengers like him.[14] Because he can't read on moving vehicles, he dreads the three-hour journey that awaits him as the story opens—until roused from a doze by a train-car attendant offering one of the "new-fashioned phonographed books and magazines" (153). A list of titles is recited, and when he perks up at the mention of a novel about which he's heard promising things, he is told that "[h]alf the train's on it this trip" (154)—the technological vernacular compounding the fact of being "on" the train in the first place and further borrowed from something like "on the telephone" (rather than the unidiomatic "on the gramophone"). Although, technically, the chosen text can be started at any point in the phonographic sequence, in order to begin at the beginning the narrator must wait a few minutes until "the batch that's on now gets through"—a prescient anticipation, in its way, of in-flight movies and, until very recently, their full-length time-delays before respooling (154).

The prognostications continue with giddy precision. With a forking ear-plug apparatus "in the similitude of a chicken's wishbone," Bellamy's narrator spends most of the next three hours enthralled, as he punningly puts it, "by my novel experience" (154). After a brief summary of the labored linguistic decoding by which one ordinarily activates a text—"the roundabout means of spelling out the signs that stand for the words, and imagining them uttered, and then imagining what they would mean if uttered"—our up-to-the-minute hero revels instead in the incomparable "delight of sitting at one's ease, with closed eyes, listening to the same story poured into one's ears in the strong, sweet, musical tones of a perfect mistress of the art of story-telling" (154). Not Amtrak's electronic "Julie" but a real female voice, a quintessential woman reader facilitating the primal, almost infantine pleasure of being read to: here is Kittler's "mother's mouth" (the origin of phonetic pedagogy in the age of Goethe) revisited by technology.[15] Later in the story, among the other newfangled phonographic innovations the astonished narrator encounters, is not just the "phonographic annunciator" of the various station stops while he's still on the train, or the promise soon of an audio guidebook perfectly synchronized with the passing landscape and its featured sights, but, in addition to these, the latest phenomenon of a "phonographic clock" (156). Among the most popular innovations in this

114   *Garrett Stewart*

line are the "Dickens clocks" which, beyond speaking out loud the hour, include "sayings" of the writer transcribed on audial "cylinders" that can be inserted and varied at will, all of which contribute, in another play on idiom, to helping one "improve the time" (161, 160).

INTERMEDIAL FEEDBACK

But leaving aside unwitting nineteenth-century forecasts, like Bellamy's, of the recorded book trade, or Stoker's of radar and sonar, I will be concentrating on novels, audiobook phenomena in themselves, that point by name to such paramilitary media advances while folding them into the structuring functions—what we might call the narrative technology—of their own circumscribed discourse networks as genre plots. What kind of feedback loop—so the question might go—can contemporary spy fiction install with the media it actually reports upon rather than fantasizes in futuristic disguise? One answer begins to take shape when noting that the reigning triad of Kittler's book *Gramophone, Film, Typewriter* is actually traversed and ghosted by a fourth medium (certainly not escaping Kittler's notice) that is in an unsaid way supplemental to all three: the reel-to-reel tape-recorder that, first of all, evolved from the gramophone in time for portable military use; that, second in Kittler's media triad, was discovered in the form of confiscated German equipment and rapidly adapted across the Atlantic to commercial uses in sound recording for film, then later for television; and that, third, has a storage capacity serving to enhance, in its first military use, the typewriter's distance-spanning alternative in nonalphabetic telegraphy, the signals of which could now be audially intercepted and logged.[16] And the tape recorder made its contribution to Morse encoding at sending as well as receiving ends, not only allowing for the automatic record of the audio signal but also, in a way not fully explored by Kittler, replacing, at point of origin, the impress time of typescript, for instance, by the recording of arbitrary codes for fast-forward transmission as well as playback detection—all this until the serial dots and dashes of the Morse signal evolved into the 1–0s not of typescript printouts but of the tape-based earliest computers, first via paper spools, then wire, then acetate.

As augmented in his audiobook treatments, le Carré's prose encompasses this complex interplay between voice and other modes of sonic rather than phonic transcription. The plot of *The Looking Glass War*, for instance, concerns the gearing up of a former wartime unit for a new mission in East Germany—suspected flashpoint for another Cuban-style missile crisis (when Soviet rockets are supposedly photographed in an East German warehouse). A related photomechanical process is then enlisted in a military training film through which the apprentice spy is submitted to a montage of discrepant points of view from cars and trains, or optically "taken on a walk through a town," until "a vehicle or a face reappeared."[17]

Novelist as "Sound-Thief" 115

Complementing this cinematic regimen, prewar "gramophone records"—similarly designed to test memory and pattern recognition through arbitrary repetitions—have been transferred to newer reel-to-reel technology and are played repeatedly for the trainee to boost his recall skills, even while, in their tape-deck remediation, a single scratch on of the original Victrola disc is automatically retained, slicing across the arbitrary variations of the track in a nagging continuity of pure noise (151).

Beyond the audiovisual calisthenics of the training devices, *The Looking Glass War* takes up the newer microrecorders that can capture a Morse message and then send it out in a matter of seconds in encrypted high-speed form. Stressed by Kittler instead is another use of tape technology by the Germans, who were able to store samples of the Morse-code mannerisms of the agents not for voice identification, of course, but for what we might call rhythm recognition, the clinching testimony quoted by Kittler—with his usual deadpan fanfare—being that "operators swear they can tell the individual sending-hands."[18]

Late in *The Looking Glass War*, in fact, such a signature effect of that audiovisually schooled agent, trained as we have seen by tape and film, is detected by enemy spies in his second intercepted and taped transmission from behind East German lines: "Different call sign but the same handwriting. Quicker than yesterday; better" (266). Yesterday, as we know, he was tormented by thoughts of the boy he had just killed, a young border guard: thoughts weighing heavily on his mind—and hand. It was as if the voice of conscience was getting in the way, and this from a naturalized Polish operative whose spoken English, with its obvious challenge to the audiobook performer, lacks, we have been told, as well as heard for ourselves on disc, "the slur and elision which escapes even gifted imitators" (125). So, too, with his overwrought articulation of the Morse alphabet. The automaticity of transcoding has been encumbered by moral distraction. Although "his lips were spelling out the letters . . . his hand wouldn't follow, it was a kind of stammer that got worse the more he spoke, and always the boy in his mind, only the boy" (242). Propelled by a run-on, comma-spliced grammar, the vocabulary of enunciation ("stammer") has itself figuratively invaded the missteps of nonphonetic transmission in ways that the audiobook treatment of this scene (by Frank Muller) intensifies in its staccato delivery. Only when arriving at this late crisis do we realize, that is, the point of the novel's colorless epigraph from F. Tait's *Complete Morse Instructor*, from which we have learned that "the carrying of a very heavy weight such as a large suitcase or trunk immediately before sending practice, renders the muscles of the forearm, wrist, and fingers too insensitive to produce good Morse." The onerous weight in this case is, by unspoken cliché, the burden of a guilt whose manual traces give his hand away.

As a result, the East German mission is aborted and the abandoned Polish telegrapher's latest messages ignored by his British handlers in their cabin hideout just on the other side of the border. He is deserted in his guilt and left

116   *Garrett Stewart*

in a now futile and mute ether. The winter air alone speaks back, but only in a depersonified dumb noise caught with absolute flatness in the sardonic monotone of the Frank Muller reading—in other words, "narration"—of le Carré's great last sentence: "They had gone, leaving nothing behind but tyre tacks in the hardening mud, a twist of wire, and the sleepless tapping of the north wind," where the British spelling of *tyre* doesn't succeed in blunting, even on the page, the verbal torque by which it is stretched and rebent phonetically into "t(wist of w)ire," last dying echo of the wiretapping on which the plot has pivoted (271).[19] In terms of Kittler's post-Romantic devolution (Goethe to Stoker) of voice into mediation on the way from maternal orality through modern warfare to audiophile marketing, we find here the unpunctual signal without code or operator, nature itself as a mute discourse network, closed on itself in inaudible short circuit.

A decade and a half later, the protagonist and would-be novelist of le Carré's masterpiece *A Perfect Spy* opens the book by willing himself before his suicide to draft a series of disjunctive, expiating texts whose shifts in time and space are as much like the spliced tape dear to his trade as they are like film flashbacks. In their scattered, manic shifts of temporality, they recall further the title character's secret radio transmissions with his former Czech counterpart, contacts carried out in treasonously exchanged fragments over "matched handsets that hopped like bedbugs between the frequencies and must have sent the listeners just as frantic."[20] As the British get wise to their traitor, however, tape comes more explicitly into play, trapping the signals for later analysis. As a technician explains: "We use all tape, no handwriting. . . . Accelerated Morse, we unroll it both ends." The operator's own clipped language continues to mimic breathless economy: "Transmission takes maybe one and a half minutes, two. Unroll and decode takes maybe five" (389).

Live by interception, die by it. For the autobiographer-spy, writing now as if from beyond the grave, has been a surveillance machine in his own person since before the beginning. A passing metaphor for the charming hero when a young man, a "diplomat in embryo," carries us back to the primal scene of surveillance in utero, where the unborn narrator begins his first flashback from the womb of his as yet unmarried mother, where he rests latent as a "deaf microphone" (167, 33). Himself a seditious plant rather than a genetic implant, even here his biological latency seems seeded with his professional destiny as Secret Service eavesdropper, in the role of which he will again finally penetrate the veil of the Iron Curtain to take refuge in a "secret womb" (526). Then, too, the specifically audial image of a "deaf microphone" returns later at linked turning points when the narrator will in fact go deaf twice over to the life his father had a way of smothering for him in advance, once at his marriage, once at his suicide. First, the father barges in uninvited to his son's wedding ceremony to steal the show. All was going well on this ritual day "until somebody switched off the soundtrack . . . and the faces of his audience turned mysteriously

Novelist as "Sound-Thief"   117

away" from the groom, "looking for the cause of the breakdown" (520). His death, although deeply continuous with this public effacement, must wait awhile yet.

The audiobook treatment of the wedding scene cannot imitate the silence, of course, just enunciate the suspended animation of this castrating paternal intrusion. Beyond this conceit of the world as if everywhere tracked and taped—and suddenly gone blank—rather than lived in the moment, there are actual techniques of audiophonic operation that structure the narrative drive. We have been present, for instance, at a brief, unsatisfactory interrogation of the defector hero's old school chum, which, when over, is replayed in the fuller form of its secret recording (hidden from us too, until now) on the investigating agent's "pocket tape-recorder," the agent himself now "Jotting as he listened" and "forwarding" in replay to double-check details we ourselves never heard when present at the scene (406). Audial technology is the narrative's own figured interface with elapsed dialogue.

Soon now, for a second and final time, the novel's own audio switch is thrown to off. Alone in hiding at the end, a dragnet closing in, our turncoat protagonist, whose treachery has been confirmed by the taped record at headquarters of secret radio signals, "held the gun to where his right ear was"—that oddly dissociative subordinate clause, as if the ear is no longer his in the moment of doing so (589). Updating Madame Bovary's deathbed mirror, the perfected spy has found, in the ultimate self-betrayal of suicide, the only true and ultimate stand-off in the looking-glass war of mutually assured destruction. Scanning his image in the bathroom glass, impersonally, "he noticed how he was leaning: not away from the gun, but into it, like someone a little deaf, straining for a sound." A new paragraph follows, taking up his once wife's, now widow's, position in a surveillance car outside: "Mary never heard the shot" (589). Thus has the prenatal "deaf microphone" been returned not to the womb but to a final negation. A paragraph later, the ensuing silence of the audiobook is deafening.

This is all brilliantly done by Frank Muller, but I have since discovered a partially abridged "edition" of the reading by le Carré himself on predigital cassette tapes, in which he puts a marked emphasis, unexpected by me in my silent reading, and different from Muller's inflection, on "heard" rather than "shot" in "She never heard the shot." The author's own reading is less melodramatic than any attempt to fill in a mortal blank with the foregone conclusion of retort, as displaced from the suicide's own self-deafening.[21] Rather, le Carré's unexpected inflection opens up the instantaneous sense that his wife inferred the worst from the immediate police action it precipitates in the rapid plot denouement to follow.

Beyond this shift in intonational stress, le Carré's performance of the novel makes two additional and arresting changes at the beginning and end of this frame tale, first when the hero takes up his pen to write, later as he takes up a gun when all is done by being said. Where the novel has "With a bump, he sat down at the desk," on the tape you hear a revision that serves

118   *Garrett Stewart*

to evoke a preexistent audial space, recasting the described agitation as an interrogative—"The bump?"—as if we were there to hear it with le Carré just as his hero, in inadvertently budging his desk, sits down to write. Cued by the abridger's compressions or not, the novelist's reading aloud translates his book on the spot into a kind of radio play.

Then, at the end, we hear le Carré in a further phrasal liberty with his printed text, adjusting another of his breath-catching minimalist finales: in this case the deliberately flat-footed and affectless last eighteen words about the hero's landlady, who shows no sign, one way or the other, of recognizing the tragic end of the boarder she had so admired. Without ceremony at the last, in the midst of reconnaissance and chaos, "everyone was watching a dignified little lady in a dressing-gown coming down the steps of her house" (590). Brilliant enough, in its understatement. On tape, however, and in the flickering opposite of "abridgment," le Carré enhances the stair-stepped falling cadence of this dramatic comedown as letdown, not just through his clipped vocalizing but with the extra metrical insertion of "and shawl" after "dressing-gown," the neo-Dickensian prose stylist waxing yet more iambic and metrical at the microphone than on the printed page.

DIGITAL TRACKING AND THE SURVEILLANT EAR

Two decades after this novel, complot is again indistinguishable from the machinations of the narrative masterplot. So perhaps the keenest irony in the audiophonic imaginary of *A Most Wanted Man* (2008) comes with the offhand and completely elliptical explanation of a digital tape recorder hidden in a fountain pen: "It looks like a pen, writes like a pen, listens like a pen. If they take it apart, it's still an ordinary fountain pen."[22] No one can tell by looking that transcription happens without human hand, that in fact the pen will later talk. More resonant even than the "whisper" of that felt tip pen wielded by the traitor-novelist of *A Perfect Spy*, here is the implement of inscription as the machine of its own eavesdropping: a celebration of le Carré's art under the auspices of all it anatomizes in invaded privacy (143). Again, the novelist as audiovisual spy.

So we can look aside as well, for models of omniscience, to the prehistory of covert digital recording in the evolution of wiretapping. Long after the earliest modes of telegraphic interception, the later sophistications of telephone surveillance were only legalized in America for FBI and police use in the late 1920s, where for the next half decade this technology contributed to the tracking down of such criminals as John Dillinger and other "public enemies." As we know from Michael Mann's recent film of that name, this wiretapping involved not just listening in on conversations but recording them phonographically, as shown by Mann in several close-up shots of the transcribing needle tracing its rings on the dusted wax platter. Still a decade and a half before the invention of the LP, the storage capacity of such intercepts was woefully limited. Only with the invention of voice-activated wire tape players in the 1940s was such covert technology rendered feasible for continuous monitoring.

This wartime innovation in the start-stop economies of covert sound surveillance not only leads to the commercial dictation machine and the telephone answering device but, in the climax of *Tinker, Sailor, Soldier, Spy*, is used for the incrimination of a Cold War double agent lured to one of the mole's own safe houses, whose dummy light switches have been turned upside down by his would-be captors and rewired to fool him into engaging rather than turning off a set of voice-triggered tape decks and their emergency backups. When, in muffled conversation with a Soviet diplomat, the undercover villain's well-known intonations are finally, although intermittently, recognized by the hero from an adjoining room—audible in live if muffled space, in real rather than taped time—we may suspect that voice-activated recording has become another name for the bridged discontinuities of fictional dialogue itself, let alone its audiobook renditions, in the spaces between which plot is often momentarily disengaged.

So one more book as example, one more installment in le Carré's meta-history of the tape recorder. As flagged in the title of this chapter, the term "sound thief" is originally coined by le Carré to describe just the sort of hidden microphone involved in such scenes of entrapment as in *Tinker, Tailor, Soldier, Spy*. Decades later, in *The Mission Song*, the term has drifted from personification to an actual job description for the hero himself, Bruno Salvador. As an orphaned Congolese boy, this eventual "ear witness" was already a repository of polyglot sounds even before he immigrated for a British doctorate in African language and became a valued government translator enlisted into the British Secret Service for work in their clandestine "chat room" (52). Yet again a novel recorded on disc, as *The Mission Song* was within the first year of its publication, is a novel devoted in part to a reading of recording technology's place in a culture of surveillance, information analysis, and potential coercion, to say nothing of narrative omniscience.

Never before, however, has le Carré probed so deeply into the knotted linguistic roots of literature and sound technology together, their interlinked manifestation of voice. Bruno the translator is so fluent in his chameleon shifts between French, Swahili, and dozens of other sub-Saharan dialects, and his English so unmarked, that people always ask him, "Hey, Salvo . . . What's your mother tongue?" (19). The question is imponderable because he had no mother to speak of, or at least to speak from, no mother whose voice he has ever heard or could internalize—in Kittler's terms, no Mother's Mouth from which to stabilize the accents of his desire. He is the illegitimate son of an Irish missionary and a Congolese girl who died in massacre of her entire tribe months after giving birth to and abandoning him to the safety of a Carmelite convent. No maternal pedagogy, as in Kittler's vision of Europe during the epoch of Romanticism, has drawn him into the discourse network of a thoroughly alphabetized consciousness.

120 *Garrett Stewart*

Yet even as a child, Bruno's interest in stories was inextricable from a fascination with their voicing. He always listened in on itinerate narratives in that way station of a convent, very much a live microphone rather than a "deaf" one. His thirst for the cadences of story is inflected even in recall by the lilt of his own retrospective (belling) assonance: "I listened spellbound to the tales of itinerant witch doctors, spell-sellers, warriors, and elders" (11). With his maternally deprived ear, he develops an "ever growing love for the Eastern Congo's many languages and dialects." He was always "pestering native and missionary alike for a nugget of vernacular or a turn of phrase" (12). And through it all, fantasmatically, in the flux and timbre of these languages, conjuring as they do "legend, history, fable and poetry," he hears as well "the voice of my imagined mother regaling me with spirit-tales" (17).

Such, then, in a variant of Kittler's terms, is an only imagined mother—the pure Imaginary—eked out from speech sounds in the real. Bruno's recapture of a strictly fictive sound (from a nurturing voice he never heard) is merely the orphaned exception that proves the rule. In him and his expertise the unknown mother, unlike the real one, is not dead, just as in him the fate of an orality without literacy is suspended and forestalled: "Every language was precious to me, not only the heavyweights but the little ones that were condemned to die for want of written forms" (16). Voicing alone is their reprieve. The irony of the plot is that the boy's native gifts—couched at first in natural (nay, zoological) terms as "my mynah-bird ear and jackdaw memory"—are co-opted into the spy trade in his role as larcenous "ear witness" (16).

The 2006 audiobook of *The Mission Song* is read by a British stage and screen actor of Nigerian descent, David Oyelowo, with the perfectly unmarked middle pitch on which the autobiographical narrator preens himself, discriminated here with an all-purpose metaphor interchanged between the British class system and its equivalent railway hierarchies, from high class to coach.[23] Here's the textual narrator about the voice and accent in which we might imagine ourselves hearing his words: "It isn't upper, middle, or coach. It isn't faux royale, neither is it the Received Pronunciation derided by the British Left. It is, in anything at all, aggressively neuter, pitched at the extreme centre of Anglophone society"—a final phrase which Oyelowo reads so "aggressively" in his turn that the throw of "pitch" gets an apt snarl associated with combative gesture rather than mere tonal register (16). Motherless, such a voice betrays no origin: "It's not the sort of English where people say, 'Ah, that's where he was dragged up, that's who he's trying to be, that's who his parents were, poor chap, and that's where he went to school'" (16). His anglophonics bear no involuntary trace of African origin, nor any discernible British coordinates: "It's not regional, it's not your Blairite wannabe-classless slur or your high-Tory curdled cockney or your Caribbean melody" (19). This tour de force passage is of course a hurdle and a springboard at once for any audiobook performer, and Oyelowo hits his even vocal stride in its delivery.

Bruno's is a voice that might have been computer-generated, as machinic as the gears of translation as he describes them, one in which something like linguistic "cognition" is itself played on by metaphor. "Your top interpreter," Bruno explains, is at his best "if he doesn't think at all, but orders the spinning *cogs* on both sides of his head to mesh together, then sits back and waits to see what pours out of his mouth" (18; emphasis added). This vocal transcoding is almost involuntary, and thus nearly preternatural, in its immediacy. Electronically abetted in the "chat room," it is a kind of teleportation by electronic transmit: "One minute I'm listening to a top-ranking Acholi-speaking member of the Lord's Resistance Army in Uganda plotting by satellite phone to set up a base across the border in East Congo, and the next sweating it out"—that telling phrase of immaterial labor doing double duty for phenomenological identification and the work of translation at once—"sweating it out in Dar-es-Salaam docks with the chatter of shipping in the background . . . as a murderous bunch of Islamist sympathisers conspire to import an arsenal of anti-aircraft missiles in the guise of heavy machinery," while "the very same afternoon being sole ear-witness to a trio of corrupt Rwandan army officers haggling with a Chinese delegate over of the sale of plundered Congolese minerals" (52). The somatic charge being not just adrenal but literally transporting, it's as if he's there in the scenes into which he is plugged. And we too, on disc or page, are transmitted there under the typical sign, in le Carré's prose, of medial eavesdropping.

Soon Bruno is dispatched as an aboveboard French and Swahili translator (his other language kept "below the waterline") to a top-secret conference of politicos and mercenaries on an island in the North Sea, plotting a lucrative coup in the Congo instigated in part by British intelligence operatives (111). In his simultaneous translations, almost emitting the words as they occur, Bruno allows how "I become what I render" (169). This, as he explains, is the "psychology of your multi-linguist," who is, in effect, not just a vocal chameleon but an inevitably dispersed subject (168). And an automaton as well, malfunctioning when he fails to "change track" in his shifting of linguistic gears (207). Whenever an "oversized voice descends to the confiding depths," Bruno's voice "clambers down after it in French"— the verb clamber-with-a-b reverberating with the bellowing—or homophonic clamor—it tracks (172). Calling to mind not just a translator's work but the vocal performance of the audiobook to which we may well be listening, this is the kind of oral cue noted when Bruno pushes "my voice to the back of my throat to achieve the extra breath and husky tone required" (168).

And when Bruno goes into the hidden basement chambers for secret intercepts, he sometimes finds himself "stealing sound from three separate mikes in three separate languages in one sentence," as "my right hand skips across the page" in rendering the tape: stenography as audial choreography (233, 123). By such means, not just Bruno, but I, the reader, "am there beside them," the plotters, feeling the beat of their scheming interlocution (123). In all this, Bruno's linguistic recognition scrolls forward "the way

122   *Garrett Stewart*

a news flash rolls along the bottom of a television screen while the main action continues up above" (180). And sometimes there are mismatches caught quite effectively in the audiobook rendition, with signifier and signified temporarily out of sync, as when, on Bruno's replayed tapes, the recurrent sound of the French phonemes "a-k" (ahk) in proximity to the syllable and potential suffix "a-i-r-e"—suspected at first of indicating *attaque militaire*—is eventually fine-tuned by the tape technicians as the less threatening plural place name for some African "lacs" near Minière (242).

Plot eventually thickens along with the layers of transcribed discourse. The liberationist excuse for this fomented ousting of the present corrupt government in his home country goes sour for Bruno the more he translates in person the conference-room rhetoric—and especially as he takes part in the wiretapping and surveillance bugging in a high-tech basement lair. There his role as "sound thief" grows exponentially disillusioning as he is privy to secret torturings and shady payoffs above ground. Then, too, his own position is growing suspect. When asked by a dubious superior about his illegible annotations, his "Babylonian cuneiform," and especially about the "twiddly bits in the margins," he explains them as "notes to self" (296). The next question follows inevitably: "And what do they *say* to self?" (296). Things in fact like that last italics on *say*. What Bruno glosses are inflections not carried by diction and grammar alone: "Style Points. Innuendo. Things to pick up on when I'm rendering," including most of all "[s]arcasm. You can't do much with sarcasm, not when you're rendering. It doesn't come over" (296). Not unless you're a novelist and have given it unmistakable context, or have given it over to the commissioned nuance of an expert professional reader with an audiobook contract.

Mission control is right to be wary, however. For Bruno has been violating the first rule of the "sound thief." His work is by fiat "[a]rchival, not operational. We record but we don't listen" (247). Inadvertently, however, Bruno has heard too much, and the final stage of his disenchantment comes with the taped intercept of a satellite call from a high-placed British power broker and supposed pro-African humanitarian authoring a bribe to facilitate the self-serving coup. It is at this point, thieving earwitness to this final hypocrisy, that Bruno decides actually to steal the evidence—including the notebooks full of his own "cuneiform" elucidations—along with the backup of the whole conference, overt and covert, in the compact format of "digital tape" (411).

True to form, however, in a paranoid thriller like *The Mission Song*, and quite apart from any allegory of the passing of such reel-based recording, the medium disappears along with its cautionary message. The pirated and incriminating tapes—as in Francis Ford Coppola's *The Conversation* (1974), like the photographs before them in Michelangelo Antonioni's *Blow-Up* (1966)—are stolen in turn from the absconding hero, in this case landing him in a British prison in wait for trial and a now longed-for extradition back to Africa: a prison house identified only in retrospect as the

Novelist as "Sound-Thief" 123

prolonged scene of language as inscription. For the whole autobiographical first-person narrative is now revealed to be a kind of epistolary novel written behind bars to his adopted son Noah in Africa, child of the Congolese nurse for whom, in the intricacies of an early subplot, Bruno has left his indifferent and ambitious British wife.

The narrator writes, in other words, for posterity, telling the story straight at least once—and sending it back to whom, on site in the Congo, it most nearly concerns: "An interpreter, Noah, even a top one, when he has nothing to interpret except himself, is a man adrift. Which is how I've come to write all this down without quite knowing whom I was writing to" (439). In so doing, Bruno looks forward to more verbal intimacy yet, hoping one day to read aloud to the boy, not the chronicle we ourselves may be listening to at this very moment on disc, but that great prototype of the political prisoner novel, Alexandre Dumas's *The Count of Monte Cristo*. In the meantime, we're listening our way through the generic future of such fiction.

And so we've seen how the quite specific practice of recorded books, as inserted into the longer history of tape and now digital technology, can, in the case of a given narrative system like le Carré's, also highlight the way that same course of technical development has been enfolded to begin with, at the level of espionage plotting, into his inscribed, then later performed and recorded, stories. What we find is an exemplary instance, for the engineering rather than the biological sciences, of ontogeny recapitulating phylogeny—or, in other words, a case of narrative recitation emplotting the archaeology of its own medium. It is a history that has included its Kittlerian paramilitary archive of innovative signal technology on the way to eventual commercial patents, the Recorded Books trademark not least.

Part of the technical innovation, as always for Kittler, involves those military interceptions provided by signal jamming and related interference devices. These machinations of counterintelligence take a uniquely 180-degree turn in le Carré. Three years after that ambiguous "CD" is sewn into a book in *A Perfect Spy*, the in-joke on the new commercial technology is no longer so current, and narrative reverts in *The Russia House* (1989) to the full spelling of "concealment device"—yet does so in an even more suggestive twist of narrative transmission. Two books are readied for a top-secret rendezvous at the novel's climax, one a popular novel into which a highly classified paper is tucked, "the other a fatter volume, leather-bound, which was a concealment device containing a sound-baffler to be activated by pulling open the front cover."[24] What else is new? Open a book, and the world goes quiet. But the technology operates this time, anomalously, from the outside in. The hero's intended espionage can continue uninterrupted, even as he confounds those who would spy in turn on him: "His body microphones were tuned to defeat the impulses of the device, but normal wall microphones were not" (440).

Once such a book is opened, as is the case on the inside of all books, literal hearing is of course baffled, inhibited, by the standard operating

124   *Garrett Stewart*

procedures of subvocal audition. But that's only part of what this particular high-tech decoy book seems stationed to reflect upon. It further serves to measure the difference, as well as the abiding link, between reading and mechanical eavesdropping. For although this Book of Books is designed to rebuff external surveillance, it is still as if you, the reader of le Carré's book, will really be there in the audial surround of the covert meeting place along with that facilitating device, absorbing with it (although in a different sense) the unhindered dialogue it permits—rather than being walled out and plugged in only at an impalpable distance like a mere spy. That the awaited episode never in fact transpires—that the mission is subverted by the double-agent hero who defects before he reaches his foreseen assignation—only secures the point by a roundabout parable. The scene that never happens is so fully expected as to be prototypical, our own "earwitness" primed by the norms of narrative in a baroque and finally irrelevant technological exaggeration.

Any such emblematic impedance of audible voicing would of course be overridden when the novel itself is actually recorded. And to confirm the relevance of such literary dissemination not just to this particular novel from the late 1980s, when books-on-tape were still flourishing, but to all of le Carré's fictional manifestations in whatever media, there has been a more marked clue yet in *The Russia House*. The story begins with the publisher-hero having fallen on hard times—and thus made vulnerable to Secret Service recruitment. Inheriting a lackluster "romantic list" from his father, with sales steadily languishing, he has tried to branch out but is nipped in the bud (84). Asked by British interrogators why he cancelled his plans for the Moscow "audio fair," he explains: "I thought I'd take the firm into audio cassettes. The family found out and thought I wouldn't. End of story" (85). End, certainly, of any marketable story he might have recorded. But not the end to le Carré's novel, nor to its own enterprise in remediation, whereby it arrived on cassette within a year of publication—and again read by the author himself, going public twice over in the relay of his own clandestine verbal exchanges.

But in looking ahead to *The Mission Song* over a decade later, we find one last question hanging over the audial reflexes of le Carré's narrative transmission in that novel. Long before any reading aloud to the narrator's son from Dumas may or may not take place, the present epistolary text of the story, if it ever arrives at its intended destination, might be subject to another reading aloud, this time from a real maternal source, the mouth of Noah's own mother. But in what language has Bruno, the motherless African, the former translator turned self-interpreter, been writing "all this down"? In French, perhaps, or in one of the Congolese dialects legible to a mother and son? That's a question not exactly meant to be asked, a question of le Carré's fictive license. Yet it yields a certain kind of answer. Above and beyond plot, of course, the text is initially in English because it is a British novel, written down first of all for us. But the fact that it could pass as if unmediated into the eyes, and perhaps in turn ears, of Third World reception seems a final escape from the prison house not of language but of its technological capture and manipulation, whether in ink, magnetic signal, or binary trace.

Phrased positively rather than negatively, what escapes is the voice of the other, not so much lost to us as put beyond appropriation, gone private, vulnerable to no theft but that of the novelist who invents it. When read to us in the cool neutral intonation of the David Oyelowo performance, with Bruno's lost digital tape replaced as narrative evidence by our digital book, we come to its end—in allusion to *Heart of Darkness*, but with more potent uncertainty than futility in the offing, more possibility looming than gloom—with the view of a distant sliver of sea from the prison window, where, in the symmetrical hinge of the last seven words, "their England ends and my Africa begins" (449).

Then silence; just as, on the page, blankness. For conjured there at the novel's geopolitical vanishing point is a prospect of which there is nothing more, because nothing yet, to say, whether to write or to speak. Not in any language—and least of all in English. Yet beyond merely encountering this novel in Anglophone print, our entertaining its story in voiced form can seem to rehearse in advance the hero's fantasy of intimate vocal delivery, albeit in translation, a fantasy on which we eavesdrop by displacement. Which is only to say again that, in their aural witness, John le Carré's books, even in unplugged form, are in themselves audiobooks: ventures of sound theft, or call it lent voice as well as espied event, well before any contract is signed—except the fundamental narrative one—with any reader more professional than you or me.

NOTES

1. Charles Dickens, *Hard Times* (Oxford: Oxford University Press, 1955), 5.
2. Charles Dickens, *Hard Times*, read by Frederick Davidson (Ashland, Ore.: Blackstone Audiobooks, 1993; Prince Frederick, Md.: Audio Adventures and Landmark Audiobooks, 2007). Davidson has also been a frequent audiobook narrator of le Carré's novels.
3. Charles Dickens, *Our Mutual Friend*, ed. Michael Cotsell (New York: Oxford University Press, 1989), I.198.
4. Bernhard Schlink, *The Reader*, trans. Elizabeth Brown Janeway (New York: Random House, 1997), 184.
5. Peter Kivy, *The Performance of Reading: An Essay in the Philosophy of Literature* (Oxford: Blackwell, 2006).
6. The argument is most fully laid out in Friedrich A. Kittler, *Gramophone, Film, Typewriter*, trans. Geoffrey Winthrop-Young and Michael Wutz (Stanford, Calif.: Stanford University Press, 1999).
7. See "From the Author," http://www.johnlecarre.com/biography.html, where the comparison with espionage is rounded out as follows: "Artists, in my experience, have very little centre. They fake. They are not the real thing. They are spies. I am no exception."

8. These crucial terms are in adjacent paragraphs of John le Carré, *The Mission Song* (New York: Little, Brown, 2008), 52. Hereafter cited parenthetically by page number.
9. John le Carré, *Tinker, Tailor, Soldier, Spy* (New York: Knopf, 1974), 265.
10. le Carré, *Tinker, Tailor, Soldier, Spy*, 265.
11. John le Carré, *Tinker, Tailor, Soldier, Spy*, read by Frank Muller (Prince Frederick, Md.: Recorded Books, 1988).
12. John le Carré, *A Perfect Spy* (New York: Scribner, 1986), 399.
13. The Stoker novel is first discussed by Kittler in *Discourse Networks, 1800/1900*, trans. Michael Metter with Chris Cullens (Stanford, Calif.: Stanford University Press, 1990), 353–356, after which this one key scene of psychomagnetic telepathy is returned to in Kittler, *Gramophone, Film, Typewriter*, 103, with preliminary remarks on Seward's dictaphone recording, 87.
14. Edward Bellamy, "With the Eyes Shut," in *Apparitions of Things to Come: Tales of Mystery and Imagination* (Chicago: Charles H. Kerr, 1990), 153–171. Hereafter cited parenthetically by page number.
15. See Kittler, "Learning to Read in 1800," in *Discourse Networks, 1800/1900*, 27–52, in a chapter called "The Mother's Mouth."
16. See the main discussion of tape technology in Kittler, *Gramophone, Film, Typewriter*, 105–114.
17. John le Carré, *The Looking-Glass War* (New York: Scribner, 2009), 154. Hereafter cited parenthetically by page number.
18. Kittler, *Gramophone, Film, Typewriter*, 107.
19. *The Looking-Glass War*, read by Frank Muller (Prince Frederick, Md.: Recorded Books, 1988).
20. le Carré, *A Perfect Spy*, 155. Hereafter cited parenthetically by page number.
21. John le Carré, *A Perfect Spy*, read by John le Carré, abridged by Sue Dawson (Ontario, Canada: Listen for Pleasure, 1986). The unabridged version is *A Perfect Spy*, read by Frank Muller (Prince Frederick, Md.: Recorded Books, 1987).
22. John le Carré, *A Most Wanted Man* (New York: Scribner, 2008), 265.
23. John le Carré, *The Mission Song*, read by David Oyelowo (Westminster, Md.: Books on Tape, 2006).
24. John le Carré, *The Russia House* (London: Hodder and Stoughton, 1989), 439. Hereafter cited parenthetically by page number.

7 Hearing Hardy, Talking Tolstoy
The Audiobook Narrator's Voice and Reader Experience

Sara Knox

> Listen, says a voice: some being is giving voice.
>
> —Steven Connor, *Dumbstruck*

INTRODUCTION: SOUNDS OFF

As Hillel Schwartz points out, the ear is a vulnerable organ and "our true bodily *avant garde*, in all senses of the term—military, psychological, cultural."[1] That the "indefensible ear" is at the mercy of loud sounds, or of sounds that cannot be switched off, is borne out by techniques of interrogation and torture currently undergoing a renaissance thanks to "no-touch torture" protocols.[2] Whereas music is the more typical weapon of choice, voice and address have also been used to control, subdue, or demoralize.[3] The soothing female voices of the propagandists broadcasting from Japanese-controlled radio stations during the Second World War evoked such antipathy and rage in Allied troops that they aggregated the different female voices under a single identity ("Tokyo Rose"). That act of incorporation—the giving of a body to the voices of their enemies—is a vivid example of what Steven Connor terms "compensatory substance": the "indeterminate force" of sound "given an imaginary but determinate form."[4] "If sound suggests the idea of the exercise of power," writes Connor, "this may be because it more fundamentally involves the subjection to it."[5]

Connor's "gestalt of force" is the flip side to what Michael Bull terms "we-ness."[6] If sound "appears to perform a largely utopian function in this desire for proximity and connectedness," then so too is it invested with the power to terrorize and dispossess.[7] What this points up, and what other theorists of aural culture have already noted, is that sound has a powerful relationship to affect[8] and that the voice has "deep laid associations . . . with various kinds of corporeal intensity, with suffering, love, and pleasure."[9]

As a species of sound, the voice has particularly strong capacities for affect. The implications of this for understanding narrator presence in the audiobook were flagged early in the development of scholarship on the audiobook:

128 *Sara Knox*

audio books are predicted [sic] upon *direct address.* We are not over-hearing, or eavesdropping; the narrating voice is explicitly addressing the listener. In fact, "envoicing" the narrator creates a sense of connection stronger than reading impersonal printed pages: the communicative paradigm—storyteller to listener—that underlies printed texts has again become flesh.[10]

More recently, Matthew Rubery has described the vestigial but powerful presence of voice in an otherwise decorporealizing digital age: "the portable player does not present an actual person before you; there is no body movement, no facial expression, and no eye contact. The difference here lies in what might be called ear contact, the unbroken link between voice and ear."[11] The "umbilical continuity of the voice," in Connor's phrase, binds listener to narrator, a binding that may—if listener reviews are any indication—be felt as pleasure or as irritation.[12]

Elsewhere in this volume James Jesson notes that audiobooks, like the radio treatments that are its precursor, complicate authorial identity by instituting a doubling of authorship. As Jesson points out, a narrator like Orson Welles arrogated to himself the status, and presence, of the literary author whose work he was treating: becoming, in effect, its "duplicate author" (chapter 2, this volume). Elaborating on Jesson's insight, I suggest that the movement of a novel from the printed page to pageless audio might best be understood as both a remediation of form and a translation of the *voice* of the text. Jason Camlot has argued that the fact that the "talking book necessarily entails a concrete 'envoicing' narrator" is a significant departure where "one of the primary values attributed to the act of reading literature" has been the readers' "process of constructing the author's voice."[13] Camlot's logic tends to support the idea (still hotly contested by audiobook critics and listeners alike) that listening is a more passive interpretive activity than reading, precisely because the interpretive act of voicing has already been surrendered by the listener. But the doubling of authorship implies something more than the sacrifice of one voice for another.

The present chapter examines the implications of the voicing narrator's presence in the audio text and, more broadly, of affect and audiobook listening. I will be focusing the conceptual work around a discussion of unabridged audio treatments of the novels of Thomas Hardy and Leo Tolstoy: very different figures in the nineteenth-century literary canon, but both writers credited for their capacity to evoke the world of sound. According to musicologist Murray Schafer, it is the "special talent of novelists like Tolstoy, Thomas Hardy and Thomas Mann" to "have captured the soundscapes of their own places and times."[14] Although having less of the "latent aurality" of Dickens's novels, Hardy's Wessex stories and novels lend themselves to audio performance.[15] His use of the vernacular of the rural workers of Dorset calls on a narrator's skills of characterization and voicing—markedly so in *Under the Greenwood Tree*. Tolstoy presents challenges of quite another order to production teams and voice actors, particularly when the length (and thus duration) of the work is concerned. The cast of characters in *War and Peace*—a cast so large that it has traditionally presented problems to translators needing to bring to the English language the idiosyncratic argot, vernacular, and diverse characteristics of speech of a wide variety of stations and classes of persons—presents, by corollary, an almost overwhelming challenge to a performer doing a voice performance of the work. Thus whereas listeners to the audiobook productions of the unabridged *War and Peace* embrace the translation of form for its capacity to clarify action, and distinguish to the ear one character from another, the defrayed labor of listening is gained at the expense of the phenomenal amount of work involved in voicing the performance. But the labor of performance gives body to voice and is instrumental in shaping the presence of the narrator.

"VOCALIC BODIES"

That the work of solo narration of an unabridged literary work is arduous physical labor—the whole body being brought to bear to give affective force to the work—is evidenced by narrators' descriptions of how they work. Martin Jarvis tells of getting "up to all kinds of weird physicality" during recording—whatever it takes to get the story "from the brain, to the mouth, to the microphone." For the duration, he'd "live inside the story."[16] Another narrator noted that one reading (of a Michael Connelly thriller) made him feel as if he was "doing King Lear in a closet. Sometimes I banged on the table. Sometimes I got up and started to rant."[17] When journalist Richard Johnson met Jarvis at the studio, engaged in the labor of reading, Jarvis explained that he was "conducting a séance."[18] Jarvis's allusion to the "weird physicality" of voicing suggests that, like the medium in the grip of a trance, the narrator is channeling the characters: embodying them, and giving body to their voices.[19]

Given this invisible physical work of the narration—the gestures, the table-thumping, the mugged expressions—how well narrators have done the work of performance can be measured by how exhausted they are at the end of recording:

> To ask Paula Radcliffe, after a marathon, "Did you enjoy that?" would be rather inappropriate [but to] ask her the next day: "Do you feel really satisfied to have done that? Do you feel you achieved the targets that you set yourself? Do you think that you gave of your best?" would be more appropriate. I'm pretty sure that, when we've finished recording an audiobook, that's how we all feel.[20]

130 *Sara Knox*

This language of targets and measures; of marathon effort; of the inability to reflect on the task until "the next day"; of giving one's best is more like the language of heroic sacrifice than of work. It speaks of emotional as well as physical exhaustion. Having run the full gamut of human emotions, the reader has given her all. But what is given is not simply gone: the effort, the emotion, the "weird physicality" are translated as vocal presence.

A TOLERABLE PRESENCE

Having given up on Frederick Davidson's reading of *War and Peace* after no small time investment (the halfway point of fifty-six hours), one listener complained that the speaker's English accent was "so affected" that he could put up with it no longer: "I couldn't listen to the story for the words."[21] A similar formulation, and one just as rueful, can be heard from the mouth of one of the choristers of Mellstock, Hardy's comic chorus in *Under the Greenwood Tree*. The members of the Mellstock "quire," philosophers all, seem fond of speculation: they wonder what's to become of the choir when the church organ arrives, or debate what makes a tolerable parson. Of the troubling Parson Maybold it is observed that the poor man's sermon of the previous Sunday had been "well enough, a very good guessable sermon, only he couldn't put it into words and speak it."[22] The line is a delightful working of paradox, but it is also an apt description, in the negative, of the doubling of authorship in the audiobook.

I first encountered that line as voiced by English actor Robert Hardy. *Under the Greenwood Tree* was Thomas Hardy's concerted attempt to put down on paper the dialect of his home country, to make audible the voices of Higher and Lower Bockhampton, of Stinsford—his "Mellstock"—and of the "dwellers in the wood" of Thorncoombe. Robert Hardy's singsong rendition of the intonations and accents of the rural folk of Dorset brings the choristers of Mellstock so close to the surface of the text that they seem to be elbowing distance away; they are taking up all the good air and cannot be made to shut up. He voices the Dorset folk peopling the novel with exuberance and fancy, whether it is the foghorn voice of Tranter Dewey or the squeak of Thomas Leaf. Given the prosody of Robert Hardy's reading, a line that is wry to the eye positively tickles the ear. Old Dewey need only say, "Where's Dick?" and the vigor of those two words, sung up sung down, cues the author's whimsy: "every man looked round on every other man as if Dick might have been transmuted into one or the other."[23] In Robert Hardy's voicing, the "where" is high and the "Dick" low and long, as if the two words are a transliteration of the night landscape in which the boy has gone and lost himself. The villagers are whimsical vocal variations on a theme, whereas the voice of the Vicar—a man "outwith" and of a station far beyond the villagers' own—echoes the poise and measure of the narrator's voice, the voice of action and authorial interpretation, and a voice doubly authoritative for being that of *two* Hardys. The voicing narrator puts spit and blood and muscle to his master's dialogue: truncating one word and drawing the following out very long, squashing the third, and making the fourth wander, and so on and so on, until wrapping up the line of dialogue with a rising intonation.

The labor of voicing a literary work for an audiobook is precisely to put "it into words and speak it," and with such a force of presence that the "voice" previously to the fore in the reader's encounter with the printed text is dropped to the rear.[24] That this risks an over-the-top performance is duly recognized by listeners, narrators, and audiobook producers. On its Web site the Wayne June Voice Talent agency warns that "a fine balance must be maintained to deliver the necessary emotion, characterization and tone without overshadowing the story. . . . The narrator must be able to serve the needs of the role while remaining 'transparent.'"[25] Writer David Sedaris puts it even more strongly. Sedaris has a particular stake in balancing the voice of author and narrator: he performs his own books for commercial audio formats. "The problem with audiobooks," writes Sedaris, "is that they're so often imbalanced. That is to say that the narrator is better than his material. Just as often, the situation is reversed, and a so-so actor will ruin a good book."[26] The performance of a work transforms it, and decisively. When Sedaris says to "ruin a good book," he means to ruin the experience of hearing it. The source itself remains unchanged. Hardy on the page is Hardy on the page: the text cannot be further transformed, except by the craft of abridger or literary translator. The question then becomes phenomenological. Is the nature of that transformation in the voicing or in the ear of the active listener? Or is it in some intermediary space: transformation as an artifact of production?

Which returns me to the Mellstock choir, and to Tranter Dewy on the virtues of Parson Maybold. In my 1925 pocket edition of *Under the Greenwood Tree*, Tranter calls the sermon of the Sunday before "excellent."[27] There is no "very good guessable sermon" on the page. Thomas Hardy's body of work is notorious for the variety of printed editions, and in that compass this disagreement of textual versions is a small thing, hardly worth mentioning. Robert Hardy reads the 1912 Macmillan edition for the Chivers audiobook production, the edition that is also on Project Gutenberg. But the fact that I find this out from reading the printed page before me, while listening to the audiobook version, and comparing both with the HTML version on the twenty-one-inch LCD monitor in front of me is a telling indication of the contextual vacuum in which the audio text operates.[28] The translation of form that foregrounds the voicing narrator, drops the author into the shade, and sends the translator—should there be one—into an unfathomable outer darkness also works more subtle changes on the text, changes that derive, in part, from the nature of the container technologies that deliver audio content.

132   *Sara Knox*

Where the commercial audiobook is concerned, the translation of form involves a translation of format: from cassette to compact disc and then to MP3 (or its proprietary equivalents). Jonathan Sterne argues that the MP3 is a container technology that "at the psychoacoustic level as well as the industrial level . . . is designed for promiscuity."[29] That is, it is designed for "free, easy and large-scale exchange."[30] Sterne's discussion of the technicalities of sound compression that work to identify and strip deadweight data—sound that is not within the range of human hearing—suggests that stripping mimics the processes of human hearing itself. In a sense, the MP3 *prehears* the sound for us, and it does so by reconstructing the conditions for hearing where other noises compete.[31] The MP3 is, therefore, designed for "casual listening," for those "moments when listeners may or may not attend directly to the music—and are therefore even less likely to attend to the sound of the music."[32] Like much of the best theoretical work on aural culture, Sterne's argument does not discriminate between the *kinds* of sound contained. Whether the sound that is stripped and promiscuously delivered to its distracted, casual listeners is music or spoken word is not relevant to his analysis. But his argument is nevertheless useful here. The idea of a promiscuous technology, of downloadability gained by the digital stripping of data that would in any case not be naturally heard, can be usefully repurposed to describe the audiobook. In an online discussion about the success of auditory as opposed to visual learning techniques, one post argues that reading is a better intellectual workout than listening for the reason that "the data rate is lower with audiobooks—typically you read a lot slower than someone speaks. So if you just look at how much information your brain has to deal with per minute, it's higher for reading."[33] By this logic even an unabridged audiobook is a stripped-down version of the printed text in regard to both form and content.

In the translations of format, one of the first things to have been jettisoned is provenance: the bibliographic identity of the work in question. What glassy-eyed confusion must library cataloguers suffer when faced with a digital audio file: front matter, back matter, *no matter.* But where provenance disappears, the narrator's presence comes to the fore.

TRANSLATION AND THE DOUBLING OF AUTHORSHIP

Whereas there are fewer choices to be made between different unabridged audio treatments of *War and Peace* than there are between English translations of the printed text, there is sufficient choice that the "translation wars"[34] have an equivalent in the argy-bargy of listener reviews on Audible, one of the largest online suppliers of audiobooks.[35] Listeners' postings on the virtues, respectively, of performances by Frederick Davidson, or Neville Jason, or "the droning" Walter Zimmerman are analytically useful because their preoccupations are with the success of the latest translation *from text to audio*, a preoccupation that wholly displaces anxieties about the fidelity of English translations to the work in its original language.[36]

The "doubling of authorship" is a shared characteristic of the production of unabridged literary works for audio as well as of literary translation. The role and presence of the voicing narrator looms as large for listeners as does the presence of the translator for readers of literary works in translation. In a posting on the Audible review blog for the Neville Jason reading of *War and Peace*, one listener writes that she had "loved W&P since college. . . . But never . . . quite so much as in this splendid reading. Neville Jason is a genius. (And, duh, so is Tolstoy)."[37] Glossed by this conflation is the presence of the literary translator, or even the question of which translation of *War and Peace* this is: the doubling of authorship does not allow for a trebling. The doubling of authorship means that provenance—the bibliographic wherewithals of a text in translation—quite rapidly vanish. It takes some searching to discover that Neville Jason is "carefully" enunciating "each syllable of Leo Tolstoy's 560,000-word epic"[38] as translated by Louise Maude and Aylmer Maude: few are the listener reviews that give a nod to the translator, a presence overshadowed by that more close-pressing "translation" by the reader's voice.[39]

The narrator voicing a commercial audiobook is a palpable presence. As Camlot has pointed out, the narrator's "envoicing" is the very stuff of the experience of "reading" an audio text.[40] The literary translator is, by contrast, a self-effacing and distant presence, but in no sense a negligible one. The doubling of the presence of the author with that of voicing narrator/translator is also underpinned by the context of the encounter of the listener/reader with the text. Whereas some listener reviews of the novels of Hardy and *War and Peace* on Audible and Amazon indicate that they've previously read printed versions of the audiobooks they are rating, more of them imply that the recorded performance is their first contact with the text.[41] They listen because they have not read—or have not been able to get through—the novel on the page.[42] Likewise, the majority of readers of literature in translation encounter the work as translation because they cannot read the work in its original language. It is the reader versed in the language of the translation *and* the original text who experiences the doubling of authorship as discomfort—even as tyranny or betrayal: witness Vladimir Nabokov calling Constance Garnett's translations of the work of Gogol "dry shit" or Joseph Brodsky's rage at the inabilities of English readers to distinguish Tolstoy's prose from Dostoevsky's prose: "How could they, when they're reading Garnett?"[43]

My first audiobook experience was with the Garnett translation of *War and Peace*—62 hours and 18 minutes' worth in Walter Zimmerman's reading. As a relatively early production and one predating the data-stripping habits of digital audio, this Books on Tape production includes Zimmerman's reading of the publication details from the title page at the recording's start. The sound engineering is parlous, a result of the evolution of the work from

134   *Sara Knox*

audiocassette to digital audio file with no stops between, and for the first few hours of reading, Zimmerman sounded to me as if he'd been recorded in a duck shooter's blind. The quality of voice was reedy, to say the least. Nor was the pace reliable. At one moment the narrator might be speeding along at a clip and then, midsentence, the pitch would drop, the end of a sentence might be clipped, or the hiss of white noise intrude. It was as if I was being read to by members of the family Zimmerman: sometimes Zimmerman the elder, sometimes Zimmerman the younger; at other times it seemed to be Madame or Mademoiselle Zimmerman performing the work. But three or four hours into the recording the differences between slow and fast Zimmerman, high and low Zimmerman became suddenly moot; I heard them as part and parcel of the texture of the work, its cadence—as native to the narration as the deliberate shifts of voicing the narrator employed in shaping the characters for the ear. (The need for this process of acclimatization to the narrator's voice is evidenced elsewhere, as noted by listeners to the less-maligned Davidson reading of *War and Peace* and to the Jill Masters reading of Hardy's *Far from the Madding Crowd*.[44])

It wasn't long after warming to the voice of the narrator that I discovered a section of the MP3 audio file was missing. No amount of my rewinding or fast-forwarding could make the vanished section of the book appear. So I took myself off to the library, borrowed the only translation on offer—the one by Louise Maude and Aylmer Maude—and retired to an easy chair to pick up my place in the reading where I'd left off. But where before had been that bright chorus of the family Zimmerman, I was now met with an arch silence from the page. My apprehension of that silence was the first shock, one immeasurably deepened by my sense of the difference between the Maude and Garnett translations. (Suddenly I had a "Prince Andrew" to contend with—looming up before my mind's eye was a heavy-jawed Royal, in flight suit, the open door of a Chinook helicopter behind him.) I missed Garnett's finesse, her ironing out of Tolstoy's gloriously wrinkled prose.

In 1917 Joseph Conrad wrote disparagingly of the version of *War and Peace* popular then with middle-class readers in his adopted nation. What did they know about Russian literature when it reached them secondhand, so prettily packaged? In Conrad's words, "Turgeniev for me is Constance Garnett and Constance Garnett is Turgeniev."[45] Tolstoy is Garnett, and Garnett Tolstoy: the author's art inseparable from the translator's treatment. In the logic of Brodsky's or Conrad's carping, the novel before translation is pure and of the novelist's making, a purity progressively degraded by the *personality* of the translation. Garnett's critics chafe at the presence of the translator, her mark on the work, as if she is the character to whom the reader is first introduced in the novel and is the last one to leave it. But if we accept that it is the doubling of authorship that is being balked at here, then the presence—the personality—of the translator is a constituent part of the text and shapes the reading encounter. Thus, on moving from the Garnett to the Maude translation I had the impression of having left the

Hearing Hardy, Talking Tolstoy   135

company of an intimate for that of an acquaintance; felt the cooling of the encounter; the entry of a creeping restraint. What I was suffering was two distinct losses: the loss of Garnett the translator and Zimmerman the narrator. They had disappeared as persons are apt to disappear, and I missed them while I sat doggedly turning the pages of the missing section, sounding the voices of the characters in my head.

It was after being stung by this experience that I invested in a subscription to Audible. Their servers keep a copy of every book downloaded to a subscriber's "library," so I could be content about what I was getting: no more scratched CDs, no more computer-generated voices, no more mislabeled, out-of-order MP3 files. The most basic subscription is for one free "credit" per month, and the value of that credit is more elastic than any currency on earth: one buys Jack London's short story "To Build a Fire," all forty-nine minutes of it, or the whole of Dickens's *Bleak House*. But the hours and minutes of an audiobook's runtime are not set. Proprietary audiobook formats, in their marriage to the MP3 player, allow listeners to set an audiobook at fast or slow to correct, say, "the speed of a droll or hyper reader."[46] As the critics of his reading of *War and Peace* make plain, Frederick Davidson is (in)famously droll, and his performance of the title character in *David Copperfield* is so laconic that a listener might think that it's David rather than dear (dying) Dora who's taken to bed.

Only once have I resorted to the "fast" setting for an audiobook: when I was deep in despair at (or during?) the Flo Gibson narration of Hardy's *Tess of the d'Urbervilles*. Not that I wanted to hurry the suffering Tess on to her death on the gallows—quite the opposite. I'd once or twice pleaded with the MP3 player as if it was the ear of an innocent Tess. "Oh, don't . . . !" I'd say. Don't . . . accept the offer of the ride home with Alec d'Urberville; don't . . . tell Angel; don't . . . go back up the stairs of that hotel in Sandbourne— protestations as pointless as the horror fan's chafing at "the last girl" going out into the dark, where the killer is. Whether Tess's end came fast or slow, it was coming, and neither Flo Gibson nor I could do anything about it.

My desire to tinker was prompted by the quaver in Flo Gibson's voice, those eloquent cracks and dips and warbles that—like the voice of the actress Thora Hird in the audio version of Alan Bennett's "A Cream Cracker under the Settee"—are the remonstration of the text outside of the text, letting you know that you are listening to the main character and the voice talent teeter on the brink of death; reminding you that what you are hearing is time passing. The implicit body—the body behind the voice, the body laboring in the reading—was what prompted me to reach for a technical fix. If the narrator's voice was too old for the winsome Tess, might I not *make* it the voice of a breathless young girl? For Gibson's age is one of the things a listener quickly identifies in her voice, and during those first few hours of listening to *Tess* it seemed the thing most amenable to change. So I put Gibson on double-time when the car was parked at a petrol pump at the service lay-by of the Sydney M4, westbound. The setting thus changed, and

136 *Sara Knox*

with the reading on pause, I drove off down the feeder road, merged like a zipper, and hit the "play" button. The result was Flo Gibson on helium. All the menace had gone out of Alec d'Urberville: he might have been calling a race rather than initiating a seduction, and Tess—oh, Tess!—what had she become?

I endured *Tess of the d'Urbervilles* on the fast setting through the scene of Tess's introduction to Alec d'Urberville:

"I came, Sir, to tell you that we are of the same family as you. . . ."

"Ho! Poor relations!"[47]

It was a ride as rough as it was brusque, and it was not long before I hit the pause button and turned the car stereo off, leaving nothing but road noise. That the critical scene had raced past me was galling: Tess at a merry clip, and none the younger for it.

My experiment with play-speed reconciled me to Flo Gibson's *Tess*: Tess the character and *Tess* the novel, "as read by." By the time Tess and Angel are spending their last night on the Salisbury Plains, among the "blackly defined" monoliths and trilithons of Stonehenge, the narrator's tone struck me as perfect for the book: world-worn and weary to the point of being used up. I reached that scene while walking the paths of the decommissioned asylum in Rozelle on the inshore waterfront of Sydney's inner West. The road winds past the old Convalescent cottages, the roofs of which are home to a tribe of stray cats, and down past Rose Cottage and Foundation House. At the bottom of the hill there is a path beaten by dog walkers shortcutting down from the main road above.

When the exhausted Tess lies down on the oblong stone, I had arrived at the dog path, and was within shouting distance of a woman throwing a stick for her schnauzer. And when Angel tells her that he thinks she is lying on an altar, and Tess replies that she "likes very much" to be there, where it is "so solemn and lonely after my great happiness, with nothing but the sky above my face. It seems as if there were no folk in the world but we two, and I wish there were not," the woman coming down the path toward me turned pointedly away to call the dog heeling, in any case, close by.[48] A street—even one in the grounds of Rozelle Hospital—is a public place, and weeping is an activity both more obvious and less acceptable in walkers out for a Sunday stroll than it is for drivers in the privacy of their own car. I was pole-axed by misery and no longer in control of myself: my lungs squeezed closed and I had to sit on the curb. Perhaps the woman with the schnauzer thought my earphones were connected to a mobile phone: that I'd had bad news or an argument with a lover; that I was in the grip of some actual— rather than textual—tragedy.

My listening to the penultimate chapter of *Tess of the d'Urbervilles* on the road beside Rose Cottage is the only time in my life that a work of literature has given me hysterical asthma. I've since wondered how much of the extremity of my response could be put down to Hardy: his unremitting unkindness in shaping the fates of his characters in the later novels,

Hearing Hardy, Talking Tolstoy   137

his bleak view of the world—that "blighted star." But holding Hardy to account, even if we give the author his due, is to miss what cultural historians would call the discrete context of the reading experience: in this case, the culmination of hours spent listening to a familiar, trusted, vulnerable human voice—the voice of the narrator—telling the story.

The power of the narrator's voice to amplify the affective power of a work has been attested to by other listeners, including one who admits to laughing "out loud at audio books. . . . [M]y reactions are actually stronger to them than the books that I read."[49] One listener writes appreciatively of the Pamela Garelick recording of *The Mayor of Casterbridge*: "The work is slow but its drama effects one directly. I find it hard to listen to a work of this sort without becoming personally invested." Indicating the depth and degree of this identification, he adds, "I am going to be upset about the book ending because I have taken sides," while another listener directly credits the author—Hardy—with the success of having made him "literally angry with the characters in the book for what they did," but only does so after praising the narrator for putting "emotion into the story."[50] The qualifier "literally" is a telling redundancy, for it indicates the listener's surprise at how thoroughgoing that affective implication has been.

PERSONALITY AND VOCAL PRESENCE

That major audiobook distributors like Audible offer alternative recordings of canonical works now in the public domain follows the basic commodity logic of the provision of buyer choice: voices and performance styles for a listener to choose from. Certainly the "narrator wars" of the listener reviews of *War and Peace* attest to this: there's a definite pattern of buyer-beware advice and shopper self-castigation about the perils of making the wrong choice (Davidson over Neville, for instance). And satisfied listeners rebut critics of their choice with variations on the if-you-don't-like-him-select-another-reader theme.

Audiobook producers are also mindful that they must compete with other productions of a work to catch a listener's ear. Explaining the Naxos production of the unabridged *Tess of the d'Urbervilles*, the producer Roy Macmillan invokes the altruism of service to excellence ("Tess . . . is one of the great English novels, and that would have been reason enough for Naxos audiobooks to record it"), then moves to the nitty-gritty: the need to compete: "Even if other publishers have recorded it in the past, or will do so again, it was important to [the managing director] of Naxos Audio-books, to have the title in bookshops, record stores and on their virtual shelves." Macmillan then returns to the subject of the book's demand that it be produced: even given the dubious balance of costs to profits it "mattered" that Tess should be made "available to Naxos Audiobooks audience." But the bulk of Macmillan's article is devoted to showing the amount

138 *Sara Knox*

and complexity of the work involved in a recording, and most particularly the narrator's labor. First there is Anna Bentinck's reading and annotating ("the script is peppered with instructions . . . like 'cheer up here'"), then it is dramaturgical research to get "a deeper sense of the atmosphere that pervades the scenery, the language, the characters, the setting." Bentinck peers into the nitrate prints of photographic exhibitions of farm machinery to get "a sense of what it must be like for Tess to wear those gloves or work on that machine." And "meanwhile," writes Macmillan (in a sympathetic doubling of Alec d'Urberville's fantasizing about Tess), Bentinck "was imagining herself as Tess; inside Tess's body, feeling the physical weight of the clothes and the emotional weight of her experiences."[51]

Such descriptions of the labor of the narrator make me want to look harder at that otherwise perfectly ordinary phrasing of Macmillan's: "it mattered that *Tess of the d'Urbervilles* was available to Naxos Audiobooks' audience." The novel, the narrator, and the central character merge into one another and take form: as if Naxos is giving Tess bodily to its listening audience. That impression is further underpinned by the rationale for the choice of narrator: whereas Naxos generally followed the rule that "if a man wrote it" then "the book should be read by a man," with *Tess*, "giving the whole book a female voice" seemed the only way to proceed.[52] "Giving the whole book . . . voice" suggests an act of transmutation, but also a kind of political or ethical representation: the enfranchisement of literary character. The phrase recognizes the overriding presence of character, not of the "old misery" Hardy. To "capture the essence" of the book is to give it a body, and to give that body voice.

The doubling of authorship, and the investiture of the presence of the narrator in the voice-body of the text, has some odd ancillary effects. One of these is the implicit invitation to readers to listen to different audio productions of the same work. That there is such a variety of unabridged recordings of a single work (particularly of those no longer under copyright) facilitates the consumption of multiple productions of a work, even if it does not assume it. Of the major Hardy novels, unabridged, Audible offers four versions of *Far from the Madding Crowd* and *Return of the Native*, three of *The Mayor of Casterbridge*, two of *Under the Greenwood Tree*, and no fewer than seven versions of *Tess of the d'Urbervilles*. There are elsewhere available other unabridged versions of all of these novels (and the underserved *Jude the Obscure*, available only in the Stephen Thorne reading on Audible), and on Audible a listener can choose from a variety of abridged versions of them too.

It was not as research for the writing of this chapter that I chose to listen to three versions of *Tess*, and two of *The Return of the Native* and *Under the Greenwood Tree*. The "hear-over" is something the audiobook listening experience implicitly invites. It is not simply (like the "comb-over") a cosmetic cover-up to a built-in deficiency: those lapses of concentration that make a catch-up necessary. If, as I've argued above, the narrator assumes a

Hearing Hardy, Talking Tolstoy 139

significant presence—is the body as well as the soul of the reading— then a listener discovers not only a new text but forms the (one-sided, admittedly) acquaintanceship with the new speaker. If Bull's concept of "accompanied solitude" holds true, then part of what it implies is that that the narrator's presence is—for a period—that of companion, and one accordingly meets a new reader of the same text with interest.[53] "An audio book is not a book," writes one listener. "When you curl up with an audio book, *there's another person there* while you drive to work or walk the dog."[54] And, unlike the doubling of authorship as it applies to literary works in translation, audiobook listening brings with it another kind of doubling—one altogether native to the technology and its use. That is, the doubling of authorship is mirrored by what Caroline Bassett, in a different context (that of the mobile phone user) pictures as the divided consciousness of *listening* in one space while *being* in another. There is a second "auditory space" into which the listener directs her "emotions" and "intellectual attention" while "walking here but listening there."[55]

Audiobook listening creates an auditory space in which things happen that are both present to the listener affectively and present as a doubling of their actual physical location and emotional state. That doubling is an effect of patterns of use (that audiobooks are more often than not consumed as adjuncts to other activities, most notably driving) and of the technologies for delivery that create "a praxeology of listening that emphasizes distraction over attention."[56] My own experience of the uncomfortable convergence of the space of listening and the space of walking in my encounter with Flo Gibson's *Tess* is but one example of that divided consciousness in action. Reflecting on his experience of Philip Pullman's *Dark Materials* trilogy, one listener recalls how "Lyra entered the underworld as I turned from Atwater onto Lapeer Rd."[57] The otherwise banal activity of negotiating an intersection becomes significant here because it marks for the listener a successful negotiation of the greater "difficulty of existing in two world [sic] at once."[58]

To return, then, to the question I posed earlier about the nature of the transformation of literary text into the voice performance of that text by a solo narrator. I had asked whether the transformation occurred in the voicing or in the ear of the active listener. The answer might be that a transformation occurs in both places, and that it does so in response to (at the risk of contorted phrasing) a doubled doubling: the doubling of authorship and the divided consciousness of listening. A listener meets each reading as a distinct textual encounter, both in terms of the personality of the reader and the auditory space of listening.

For myself, hearing Hardy, each reading and each reading-encounter has been distinctive—the punch of affect coming at different places in the text. In Flo Gibson's reading of *Tess* I felt that winding blow at the end, but in Anna Bentinck's I experienced it in the to and fro of Angel and Tess's discussions the night after she has told him about her seduction by

140   *Sara Knox*

Alec. Each narrator's voicing was so idiosyncratic that I came to feel that it was not *one* Tess suffering betrayal, disappointment, and ruination—instead it was three distinct Tess Durbeyfields being destroyed, in series. Feeling the vicissitudes of the Gibson Tess only made worse what had to be borne by Bentinck's Tess, or Steven Jack's—even if Jack played his Alec d'Urberville like a moustache-twisting vaudeville villain, and Tess like the villain's counterpart, the girl whose fate it is to be tied to the railway tracks so that she might scream her little heart out. I did not so much like Jack's interpretation, but his Tess, like the Tess before her, was in the worst of trouble, and I was bound to hear it.

NOTES

1. Hillel Schwartz, "The Indefensible Ear," in *Hearing History: A Reader*, ed. Mark M. Smith (Athens: University of Georgia Press, 2004), 488.
2. Suzanne G. Cusick, "Music as Torture/Music as Weapon," *Transcultural Music Review* 10 (2006), http://www.sibetrans.com/trans/trans10/cusick_eng.htm. (Accessed 2 July 2010).
3. Just one example predating the current war on terror: the Federal Bureau of Investigation used "acoustic bombardment" during the siege at Waco, Texas, booming out Nancy Sinatra's "These Boots Are Made for Walking" around the clock, an assault to which the Branch Davidians could find no answer.
4. Steven Connor, "Edison's Teeth: Touching Hearing," in *Hearing Cultures: Essays on Sound, Listening and Modernity*, ed. Veit Erlmann (Oxford: Berg, 2004), 157.
5. Steven Connor, *Dumbstruck: A Cultural History of Ventriloquism* (Oxford: Oxford University Press, 2004), 26.
6. Connor, "Edison's Teeth," 162.
7. Michael Bull, "Soundscapes of the Car: A Critical Study of Automobile Habitation," in Erlmann, *Hearing Cultures*, 177.
8. See Connor's "Sound and the Self," in Smith, *Hearing History*, 54–66; see also Erlmann's discussion of "sound as a medium through which we feel," in "But What of the Ethnographic Ear," in *Hearing Cultures*, 10; and Caroline Bassett on "affective priority" in "How Many Movements?" in *Hearing Cultures*, 349. On audience emotion and musical affect, see James Johnson, "Listening and Silence and Eighteenth Century France," in *Hearing History*, 170–174.
9. Connor, *Dumbstruck*, 411.
10. Sarah Kozloff, "Audio Books in a Visual Culture," *Journal of American Culture* 18, no. 4 (1995): 92.
11. Matthew Rubery, "Play It Again, Sam Weller: New Digital Audiobooks and Old Ways of Reading," *Journal of Victorian Culture* 13, no. 1 (Spring 2008): 72.
12. Connor, "Edison's Teeth," 158.
13. Jason Camlot, "Early Talking Books: Spoken Recordings and Recitation Anthologies, 1880–1920," *Book History* 6 (2003): 167.
14. R. Murray Schafer, "Soundscapes and Earwitnesses," in *Hearing History*, 7.
15. Rubery, "Play It Again," 58.
16. See Richard Johnson, "Audiobook Confidential: The Art of Reading Aloud," *Daily Telegraph*, February 11, 2010, http://www.telegraph.co.uk/culture/7188438/Audiobook-confidential-the-art-of-reading-aloud.html. (Accessed 2 July 2010).
17. Johnson, "Audiobook Confidential."

Hearing Hardy, Talking Tolstoy 141

18. Johnson, "Audiobook Confidential."
19. See Connor's work in *Dumbstruck* on the preoccupations of nineteenth-and early-twentieth-century spiritualists and their pundits with the physical mechanisms, and the labor, of the medium's transmission to the living of messages from the dead. See also Jonathan Sterne's work on the relationship between changing nineteenth-century attitudes to death and practices for the preservation of the body on attitudes to, expectations around, and the uses of, early sound-reproduction technologies, in "Preserving Sound in Modern America," in *Hearing History*, 295–318.
20. Johnson, "Audiobook Confidential."
21. Filiep, "War and Peace," online review, November 14, 2005, http://www.audible.com. (Accessed 2 July 2010).
22. Thomas Hardy, *Under the Greenwood Tree*, read by Robert Hardy (Bath: BBC Audiobooks/Chivers Audio Books, 1989), 1:50:06.
23. Hardy, *Under the Greenwood Tree*, 50:36.
24. Hardy, *Under the Greenwood Tree*, 1:50:06.
25. Wayne June Voice Talent, http://www.waynejune.com/audiobook_production_and_narration.htm. (Accessed 2 July 2010).
26. David Sedaris, "What David Sedaris Read this Year," *New Yorker*, December 11, 2009, http://www.newyorker.com/online/blogs/books/2009/12/what-david-sedaris-read-this-year.html.
27. Thomas Hardy, *Under the Greenwood Tree* (London: Macmillan and Co., 1925), 89.
28. See Deborah Philips for a contra view on decontextualization. Philips argues that "although the voice speaking is intrinsic to the text," the status of the narrator is more or less invisible on distributors' Web sites and in publishers' catalogues. Phillips, "Talking Books: The Encounter of Literature and Technology in the Audio Book," *Convergence* 13 (2007): 301–303.
29. Jonathan Sterne, "The MP3 as Cultural Artifact," *New Media Society* 8, no. 5 (2006): 836. (Accessed 2 July 2010).
30. Sterne, "The MP3 as Cultural Artifact," 831.
31. Sterne, "The MP3 as Cultural Artifact," 834–835.
32. Sterne, "The MP3 as Cultural Artifact," 835.
33. "Chuckforthought.com," December 19, 2005, posting to http://ask.metafilter.com/29270/Is-listening-to-an-audiobook-less-intellectually-stimulating-than-reading-the-same-book. (Accessed 2 July 2010).
34. David Remnick, "The Translation Wars," *New Yorker* 81, no. 35 (November 7, 2005), 98.
35. The Audible website is at http://www.audible.com. (Accessed 2 July 2010).
36. As characterized in a review by "James E" posted on February 16, 2005, to the listener reviews blog on Audible.
37. "Stanley," posting August 14, 2009, Audible.
38. Review of *War and Peace*, read by Neville Jason, posted by "Bentley," October 11, 2007, on Amazon, http://www.amazon.com.
39. Only one out of forty-three listener reviews on Audible of the Frederick Davidson reading of the unabridged *War and Peace* indicates awareness that they are listening to the Garnett translation. And not one of the twenty reviews of the Neville Jason reading mention the Maudes. There is a better ratio for the reviews of the Jason version on Amazon (the content of which is, in any case, Audible's catalogue): one out of the three reviewers is aware that he is listening to the Maude's translation.
40. Camlot, "Early Talking Books," 167.
41. In reviews on Audible of *War and Peace*, read by Neville Jason, "John" writes that he had read the book three times before hearing it, but that the reading "added a new dimension to the experience" (June 7, 2008); "Emily" likewise

142 *Sara Knox*

posts that she'd "felt the desire" to read *War and Peace* again and had opted for audio for "a little variety" (May 15, 2008).

42. "Lisa" posts a listener review on Audible of *War and Peace*, read by Neville Jason, saying that she had "tried a couple of times to read *War and Peace* and always got mired in Part Two," but that "thanks to this talented narrator and a relaxing 40 minute commute," she'd finally "made it through Part Two" and was "totally engrossed"—so much so that she'd been nerved to "go back and read the book" (February 17, 2008).
43. Quoted in Remnick, "The Translation Wars," 99.
44. For example, one listener got over Davidson's peculiar "intonations . . . quite easily" and even learned to "appreciate them . . . but they did take getting over first" ("Antony," September 22, 2008).
45. Quoted in Orlando Figes, "Tolstoy's Real Hero," *New York Review of Books* 54 (November 22, 2007), http://www.nybooks.com/articles/archives/2007/nov/22/tolstoys-real-hero/. (Accessed 4 July 2010).
46. Kirk McElhearn, "The Complete Guide to iPod Audiobooks," http://www.ilounge.com/index.php/articles/comments/the-complete-guide-to-iPod-audio books/. (Accessed 5 July 2010).
47. Thomas Hardy, *Tess of the d'Urbervilles*, read by Flo Gibson (Washington, D.C.: Audio Book Contractors, 1991), pt. 1, 1:15:01.
48. Hardy, *Tess of the d'Urbervilles*, pt. 2, 6:25:20–34.
49. "Onshi," posting to http://ask.metafilter.com/29270/Is-listening-to-an-audiobook-less-intellectually-stimulating-than-reading-the-same-book (December 19, 2005). (Accessed 2 July 2010).
50. "Patrick," reviewing the Pamela Garelick reading of the unabridged The *Mayor of Casterbridge* on Audible (January 6, 2005); "Tim," reviewing the Pamela Garelick reading of the unabridged *The Mayor of Casterbridge* on Audible (August 27, 2005).
51. Roy Macmillan, "Off the Page, On the Ear: Recording Tess," *Hardy Society Journal* (Spring 2008), http://www.hardysociety.org/ . . . /Off%20The%20Page,%20On%20The%20Ear.pdf. (Accessed 2 July 2010).
52. Macmillan, "Off the Page."
53. Bull, "Soundscapes of the Car," 364.
54. Nate Dimeo, "When Audio Books Jar the Ear" (transcript, National Public Radio News, September 26, 2008), http://www.npr.org/templates/story/story.php?storyId=95090092. (Accessed 2 July 2010).
55. Bassett, "How Many Movements?" 342–343.
56. Sterne, "The MP3 as Cultural Artifact," 828.
57. Lisa Maruca, "What Do Audiobooks Say?" blog posting February 8, 2010, http://hotbookwsu.wordpress.com/2010/02/08/audiobooks/. (Accessed 2 July 2010).
58. Maruca, "What Do Audiobooks Say?"

8 Talking Books, Toni Morrison, and the Transformation of Narrative Authority
Two Frameworks

K. C. Harrison

Twenty-eight percent of Americans have listened to an audiobook in the last year, according to a 2008 survey conducted for the Audio Publishers Association.[1] In a population where only 7 to 12 percent of adults report reading literature, this indicates that audiobooks may constitute the most vibrant site of literary activity in a population in which extended, book-length reading has been overtaken by other forms of media engagement, most notably television and Internet use.[2] This chapter began as a defense of the literary value of the recorded book; a dearth of scholarly literature on the medium seemed to show that a widely popular form was not being taken seriously by the academic establishment. Whereas it is true that a volume addressing the medium is long overdue, my research tends to show that, on the contrary, academics and avid readers happily avow their enjoyment and appreciation of recorded books. These readers may not take advantage of the pedagogical potential of recordings, but they take for granted that recorded books have an important place in contemporary culture that augments, rather than impoverishes, literary life.[3] Given the widely acknowledged popularity of audiobooks, therefore, what are the appropriate frameworks for assessing the stakes of the transition from print to audio? This chapter proposes that reception studies complement ongoing discussions in African American studies considering the relationship between oral expression and the technologies of print and sound. Rather than identify meaning with an ideal reading that resides within the fixed pages of the book, understanding how meanings arise from the varying conditions of performance and reception in the case of the audiobook illuminates avenues for interpreting print literature that include a diverse range of audience responses.

I began my own inquiry into the practices and attitudes surrounding audiobooks by formalizing a series of casual conversations on the topic, distributing surveys in August and September 2009. I collected results from

144   *K. C. Harrison*

approximately forty surveys, the number returned from hundreds dispersed via e-mail to acquaintances nationwide, including volunteers at the Women's Prison Book Project in Minneapolis and colleagues in English departments at the University of Minnesota and the University of St. Thomas in the Twin Cities, and at Yale University in New Haven, Connecticut. The bias of the sample in favor of individuals with a professed commitment to literature has the advantage of garnering strong opinions on the medium from those with clear allegiances to print and the limitation of representing only an especially literate segment of the overall number of audiobook listeners.[4] Whereas such survey results do not carry statistical weight, they initiate an inquiry into the qualitative, affective aspects of audiobook listening for users and indicate a role for further quantitative research on listeners and their habits. The first aim of this chapter is to inspire interest in assessing the cultural impact of audiobooks with recourse to readers' and listeners' reports. This empirical data can help us answer questions that the critical conversation cannot, such as: Where and when do people listen to audiobooks? For how long do they do so? Do audiobook listeners read more or less than print readers? Do they buy audiobooks, if they do, instead of or as well as their print originals?[5]

The second aim of this chapter is to put the emerging discussion of audiobooks within sound and media studies into conversation with the significant corpus of African American criticism that attends to the relationship among bodies, voices, and technology. In his study of sound art, *Noise, Water, Meat*, Douglas Kahn argues that by removing sound from source, voice from physical presence, recording provokes anxiety that "permanence outside the subject invites greater mutability, where the primacy and purity of voice are subjected to the machinations and imaginations of culture and politics."[6] Considering the effects of recording technology in an African American context both highlights some particular "machinations and imaginations" and shows how Kahn's distinction between natural and recorded voice relies on an oversimplified notion of authenticity. The long history of the appropriation and exploitation of black voices for commercial profit, as well as the creative and defiant responses of black artists working within these limitations, has generated a body of criticism addressing the transformations oral expressions undergo through their representation in media—print, visual, or aural. This criticism begins, chronologically, with the Talking Book trope that appears in early transatlantic slave narratives as a figure for the alien encounter between spoken and written language.[7]

As Michael Chaney suggests in his article about Vocoder voice-alteration software in contemporary R&B music, media theorists stand to benefit by drawing on this existing discourse that considers what freedoms and constraints new formats offer.[8] Below I discuss Toni Morrison's literal and figurative use of sound in her works to posit how the Talking Book may frame questions for contemporary "talking books," such as: How do voices propagated over the airwaves maintain and abdicate narrative authority?

Talking Books, Toni Morrison, and Narrative Authority 145

One of the most common responses to my survey, and a theme that emerges in the scant criticism on the topic, regards the "orality" of recorded books. "What is better than having someone read to you?" asks one respondent (Surveys). Others aver their nostalgia for a time—in childhood, or in the historical past—when reading aloud was more commonplace and therefore experience "hearing a story" as "a little more ethereal, a little more of a luxury." They cite precedents from Charles Dickens to workers in Cuban cigar factories for the value of public readings.[9] Audiobooks, whereas neither "live" nor "public" in the sense of these examples, nevertheless conjure scenes of shared storytelling that stir listeners' emotions. Sarah Kozloff has argued that audiobooks create a stronger bond than printed books between storyteller and listener by "envoicing" the narrator; indeed, many listeners particularly enjoy hearing authors perform their own works.[10] (David Sedaris was frequently cited in the surveys as an author whose physical voice enhanced appreciation for his narrative "voice.") Whereas audiobooks summon powerful associations with human presence, however, this prerecorded orality differs in several respects from "primary" orality. Media theorist Walter Ong, an associate of Marshall McLuhan, groups telephone, radio, television, and various kinds of sound tape and electronic technology under the category of "secondary" orality. Whereas secondary orality can partake of qualities of preliterate culture such as "its participatory mystique, its fostering of a communal sense, its concentration on the present moment," according to Ong, technology enables "essentially a more deliberate and self-conscious orality, based permanently on the use of writing and print."[11]

Under the heading "How to Read (?) a Book-on-Tape" in an article on Oprah Winfrey and Toni Morrison, John Young argues, against Ong, that audiobooks are not just derivative versions but "importantly new textual forms . . . a distinct medium that changes the public nature and reception of the text."[12] Extending Young's suggestions about Morrison, I wish to interrogate the nature of audiobooks' "orality," including their capacity to promote antiphony (call-and-response) among communities of listeners despite the seeming unidirectionality of playback and often solitary scene of listening. The audiobook listeners I surveyed commented on the immersive quality of the sound medium and showed evidence of audiobooks' "participatory mystique." Different listeners—and at times the same respondents— shift between referring to a recording as a derivative version tied closely to the text and calling it "an interpretation," "closer to theater," or "once removed from the author's intent" (Surveys). Discussions of the audiobook should avoid drawing too strict a dichotomy between the supposed stability of the textual artifact and the flexibility of the audio performance, however. Rather, the variety of audiobook listening experiences highlights the ways in which the text is always subject to vicissitudes of reception.

There has been a growing movement toward considering the active process of meaning-making, rather than the fixed art form, as the object

146   *K. C. Harrison*

of study of the humanities. Nathaniel Mackey's "othering"; Houston Baker's "sounding"; Christopher Small's "musicking": African American scholars have led this shift away from the isolated, self-contained work described by Walter Benjamin, toward a more contextual and responsive model.[13] Small summarizes:

> The presumed anonymous "thingness" of works of music is, of course, only part of the prevailing modern philosophy of art in general. What is valued is not the action of art, not the act of creating, and even less that of perceiving and responding, but the created art object itself.[14]

Small coins the term "musicking" to defy the static quality of music as a "thing" or an abstraction. Instead he argues for a dynamic understanding of music as "activity," with meanings inherent not in some nonexistent performance defined by the score but constantly changing according to different circumstances of production and listening.

Small's understanding of sound versus score, his privileging of performance over text, presents a useful rubric for conceiving the relationship between an audiobook and its textual "original." Meanings that arise around a particular listening experience—say, the association between the landscape of a particular road trip and the audiobook heard while driving—could thus be treated as interpretive possibilities rather than departures or adulterations of an imaginary ideal reader's experience. Simon Stow, in his essay "The Way We Read Now: Oprah Winfrey, Intellectuals, and Democracy," takes to task critics like Martha Nussbaum and Richard Rorty, who claim to champion "democracies of reading" but instead, she argues, overstep their literary authority in dictating the terms of interpretation.[15] He does so in the context of defending "the book club model" for exemplifying intellectual honesty because of the ways that "[l]ay readers instinctively seem to understand that, when they are talking about the novels they have read, they are talking about their own moral and political reactions."[16] Oprah's Book Club has drawn fire for its support of a "therapeutic" model of reading in which book club participants baldly assert the ways that personal experience influences interpretations.[17] In studying the responses of audiobook listeners to literature on tape, CD, and digital formats, I became convinced of the relevance of considering readers' responses in critical evaluations of literature in all formats.

Toni Morrison's literary corpus provides exemplary cases for evaluating the stakes of the transition from print to audio in several respects. First, her works display a commitment to oral history, storytelling, and song that particularly lend themselves to audio formats. Although the survey respondent who said that "I often listen to books I have read and find that I 'hear' things I didn't 'see'" did not refer specifically to Morrison, the comment shows how, for authors who engage the auditory sense, listening enriches reading.[18] Second, as Young has argued, Morrison's media presence merges

Talking Books, Toni Morrison, and Narrative Authority   147

the gravitas of the Nobel-winning author with the commercial clout of a wide readership. The popular appeal of audiobooks may in part explain their neglect from scholars who have tended to view the relationship between quality and popularity in inverse proportions. But Morrison epitomizes the trend of literary studies in general to challenge this traditional elitist divide, a divide that sometimes persists in critical evaluations pitting the cultural impoverishment of new formats against the purported purity of the old.[19] Finally, Morrison's involvement in the recording of her own works and her commitment to the public discourse in Oprah's Book Club, among other forums, attempt to forge a wider community of readerly interpretation and thus to revive the participatory qualities of oral literature.

In discussing her novels, Morrison invokes the situation of primary orality that Ong attributes to preliterature cultures: "There was an articulate literature before there was print. There were griots. They memorized it. People heard it. It is important that there is sound in my books. That you can hear it, that I can hear it."[20] Independent of her involvement in audiobooks, Morrison uses sound on the page to tie the work of literature to living speech and to the significant oral history of the African diaspora. According to Houston Baker, Morrison's novels undertake traditional "spirit work" that relies on the power of human voices to heal and empower groups of listeners.[21] In Morrison's 1987 novel *Beloved*, a community of women coheres around the "long notes held until the four-part harmony was perfect enough for their deeply-loved flesh."[22] Roxanne Reed, in her article "The Restorative Power of Sound," demonstrates how shared music transforms the women's bodies from the "despise[d]" flesh of the victimized and wounded into that which is "deeply-loved."[23] Throughout the novel, sound returns as a means of connection among fragmented bodies and minds, as an immersive, inclusive medium: "In the beginning was the sound, and they all knew what that sound sounded like."[24]

The celebration of oral traditions in African American communities inspires a heated critical discussion that addresses the dangers, as well as the strengths, of an oral aesthetic like Morrison's. Nathaniel Mackey warns against a "too easy infatuation with the oral that ethnopoetics might lapse into."[25] We see this easy infatuation in the romanticized and condescending tone that Ong takes toward so-called preliterate cultures when he refers to their "dynamic, magical power of spoken language" but denies their capacity to achieve the "fuller potentials" of human consciousness without writing.[26] As Aldon Lynn Nielsen argues in his introduction to *BLACK CHANT*, the "contours of 'black orality' are too often taken for granted."[27] Alexander Weheliye's work on sound and black identity joins others in highlighting how orality bears a "vexed relationship to authenticity," and Haryette Mullen warns that the "commodification of black expressiveness" renders "black interiority not only comprehensible but directly accessible to white consumers."[28] Farrah Jasmine Griffin's critique resonates with Mullen's discussion of the commercial uses of symbolic blackness; in "When

148   *K. C. Harrison*

Malindy Sings: A Meditation on Black Women's Vocality," Griffin demonstrates how black women's voices command market power even as they are used to "nurture and heal the family they are in but not of."[29] These discussions reveal the stakes of viewing audiobooks in a continuum with oral traditions not only for authors of color but for all writers concerned with maintaining a nuanced view of the relation between orality and print.

Whereas Morrison's resonant prose has made her one of the most respected and widely read living authors, it has also drawn critique for the way that it idealizes a premodern, communal, agrarian past regarded by some as a retreat from the realities of the black urban present.[30] Critics like Madhu Dubey rightly point out the ways that Morrison's oral communities "do not reckon with the print-literary medium through which oral communities are constructed," but I am not convinced that this limitation therefore "thwart[s] the project of community building," as Dubey argues.[31] Morrison's career in publishing would in fact suggest an acute awareness of the mediated nature of print. Reading Morrison's orality in a broader context that includes her activities as a publisher and a public author allows us to see how she navigates the media of print, sound, and television to foster forms of community that are only possible in the technological present. As I have suggested, one important way that Morrison embodies and shares the voices of her written work is by recording audiobooks. Whereas many of the pleasures of audio derive from an illusion of unmediated sound, acknowledging the technological format is important for authors and listeners, particularly (as Griffin has shown) for women of color whose relationship to the technological medium is underplayed to bolster illusions of authenticity.

Although Morrison has not commented on her involvement in audiobooks, interviews relate countless instances when Morrison describes her books as "talking," as well as the "talking life" of books, "a discourse that follows" the solitary act of reading.[32] Morrison uses the term "talking" to describe her process of composition, her work's relation to readers, and the conversations readers propagate: "talking" pervades the past, present, and future of Morrison's books. We've seen earlier in this chapter some of the ways that the sounds of voices function for Morrison, and I've provided a few touchstones for the discourse surrounding orality in her works and in others. Can we extrapolate from Morrison's deployment of the "talking life" of "talking books" a way that the audiobook medium supports this work? And, if the audio format does support certain roles for literature's oral life among readers, is this "talking life" a feature of audiobooks in general?

Many authors describe the way that characters "speak" to them during the composition process. In a recent National Public Radio broadcast, for example, Barbara Kingsolver explained how she enjoyed recording her audiobook, *The Lacuna*, because it allowed her to "channel" the voice of Frida Kahlo, a central character in the novel.[33] When Toni Morrison describes the voice of her work, however, she makes a notable distinction:

Talking Books, Toni Morrison, and Narrative Authority 149

"The thing is, I could not think of the voice of a person. . . . The voice is the voice of a talking book."[34] In her formulation, the book is not a channel for the voices of its characters but is itself an entity independent of author, character, or reader. Rather than imbue the textual object with the ephemeral quality of voices, calling it a "talking book" in this sense emphasizes its material presence. Morrison elaborates on the relation between "talking book" and reader:

> So when the voice says, "I know what it's like to be left standing when someone promises," it talks to the reader. It sounds like a very erotic, sensual love song of a person who loves you. This is a love song of a book talking to the reader. . . . It was interesting to me how the whole act of reading, holding, surrendering to the book, is part of that beautiful intimacy of reading. When it's tactile, your emotions are deeply involved. . . . I deliberately restricted myself using an "I" that was only connected to the artifact of the book as an active participant in the invention of the story of the book, as though the book were talking, writing itself, in a sense.[35]

Morrison here explains her use of the first-person "I" in *Jazz* not as a character but as the book itself. There are parts of the narrative, for example, that address the reader directly: "Make me, remake me. . . . Look where your hands are. Now."[36] They have the effect of removing Morrison from the scene of intimacy between the book and the reader, abdicating her authority as writer, and placing herself in a more equal relationship with the reader, both of whom are subject to the "active participa[tion]" of the book "itself."

It seems intuitive that the audio format would complement the orality of Morrison's novels, certainly in the case of *Beloved*, which she describes as having a "non-book quality . . . something I felt was spoken and more oral and less print."[37] But in *Jazz*, a book that, despite its musical theme, relies on its material presence to create a sensual relationship with readers, how does the aural medium change the book's meaning? Audio theorists from Walter Ong to Sarah Kozloff argue that sound is more intimately experienced than sight. But what about the feel of books? Listeners must experience cognitive dissonance upon hearing a book-on-tape instruct us to "look where your hands are" when their hands are in fact on the steering wheel or in a pan of dishes.

This dissonance arises from the distinction between the materiality of the book and of the audiobook. We encounter them as physical objects—whether paper, tape, or a digital audio player with headphones—as well as intangible experiences. When reading a book or listening to an audiobook, the medium can seem to disappear; we may feel as if the words enter our imaginations directly. The audio medium, as well as other new literary formats like e-books, invites us to consider whether our yoking of the book to its physical presence on the page was not always somewhat inaccurate. Does

150 *K. C. Harrison*

the book exist in ideal editorial perfection somewhere in the interstices of its different editions, or in the author's mind? Or does it exist as the aggregate of readers' experiences and conversations? Does a recorded book take shape in the vocal impressions on magnetic tape or the strokes of computer code, or does it achieve materiality at the moment its vibrations strike the inner ear?

In both cases—the healing power of sound, a "non-book quality," in *Beloved* and the "talking book" of *Jazz*—Morrison aims to transform the relationships that link author, reader, and text into something more reciprocal and improvisatory. She abdicates her authority, as author, to determine what readers take from a text, and in so doing empowers her readers to actively consider their roles in constructing all texts. This challenge to a hierarchical notion of the relationship between author/expert and passive reader/receiver recalls the trope of the talking book in early transatlantic slave narratives. John Young has already suggested that there are compelling connections to be traced among Morrison's description of her books as "talking," the audiobook medium which began as so-called talking books for the blind in the 1930s, and the figure that Henry Louis Gates, Jr., identifies as a feature of early African American literature. Young argues that Morrison literalizes the African American trope of the talking book and "subverts [a] history of bodily commodification by overtly taking control of the process herself."[38] We have seen earlier in this chapter how Morrison uses the term "talking book" in a way that emphasizes the materiality of the physical artifact rather than correlating it with the oral or spoken quality of her work. Does the trope of the Talking Book, as described by Gates, provide a similarly misleading analogy or can Morrison's work, and in particular her audiobooks, extend this metaphor from its origins into the present-day media ecology? Does Gates's Talking Book trope provide a useful framework for assessing the role of audiobooks in contemporary African American literature and literature in general?

The Talking Book began at the intersection of oral and written language in scenes of cultural contact that resulted from the Atlantic slave trade. Transatlantic slave narratives written in the 1770s and 1780s by Ukawsaw Gronniosaw, Ottobah Cugoano, and Olaudah Equiano feature scenes of reading in which the master's book will not "talk" to the enslaved: Equiano, after seeing his master reading, holds the book up to his ear and wonders why it will not "speak" to him. Literacy is thus powerfully aligned with freedom and mastery, and the enigma of the "talking book" inspires these narrators to acquire the facility with language that eventually leads to their freedom and the ability to "speak" for themselves through published narratives. Literature becomes the primary arena for establishing the humanity of the black speaking subject, argues Gates.[39] The reappearance and adaptation of the trope becomes proof for an early intertextual African American literature in which authors adapt and implicitly comment on the Talking Book, calling attention to the quandary that requires them to submit to the white, Western system of written language as the prerequisite for

Talking Books, Toni Morrison, and Narrative Authority   151

reasoned discourse—and thus humanity—in order to overcome the inhumane conditions of the slave trade.

Like Morrison's use of the term "talking book" in her personification of *Jazz*, the Talking Book trope in slave narratives in fact demotes the oral in favor of the power of the textual. Gates himself discerns this tendency in noting that the Talking Book disappears, to be replaced in the nineteenth century by Frederick Douglass, Linda Brent (Harriet Jacobs), and others with metaphors of writing rather than speaking. Other scholars like Alessandro Portelli and Houston Baker, conversely, argue for the continuing significance of speech in Douglass's *Narrative of the Life of Frederick Douglass, an American Slave*, a "story of the arduous conquest of writing" that nevertheless "ends at the moment in which he begins to speak as a preacher and an orator."[40]

Much contemporary discussion of the relationship between oral and written language rests on the claim, stated perhaps most influentially by Jacques Derrida, that Western linguistics is founded on a demotion of the written as derivative and secondary, an ex post facto record of the oral. Derrida challenges this hierarchy by claiming that oral utterance in fact cannot exist without a conception of language as written—if not in actuality, then as a structure to which spoken language refers. Ong offers a critique of Derrida's position by citing primary oral cultures that converse without a concept of the written. Whereas Derrideans might counter that a concept of linguistic structure equivalent to writing nonetheless exists in theory if not in name, Ong argues that oral cultures have "no sense of language as a 'structure'" and instead view words as "occurrences" or "events."[41] With his romanticization of primary oral culture, Ong performs precisely the attitude that Derrida critiques, but he shares with Derrida the assumption that systems of logic and reason are unimaginable in the absence of written language.[42]

This bias toward writing as the prerequisite for critical thinking appeared in survey responses as well, with comments such as "I would speak of a[n audio]book as having 'read' it, but I wouldn't assume the same mastery." Other readers reported: "Generally I pick 'light' stories, knowing that I won't have the same experience as reading a book at home" and "I wouldn't listen to any 'serious' literature on audiobook" (Surveys). But listeners also reported an increased aural acuity ("Sometimes it's easier to listen to classics that I might not make it through in print") and pointed out that "one can be distracted in any circumstance" (while reading print just as much as while listening). One even described audio as a spur to sustained reading in an increasingly competitive media environment: "The nature of internet reading (shortened bits) has definitely changed my reading habits, and I rarely read for hours at a time anymore. I miss that coziness. Audiobooks let me 'read' good, long books, digest them slowly, and get a feel for both the author and performer" (Surveys). If one effect of audiobooks is to train hearers to become more acute listeners, then perhaps audiobooks contribute

152   *K. C. Harrison*

to a valuing of oral culture in less ethnocentric and more nuanced ways than are acknowledged by either Ong or Derrida. Listeners may experience audiobooks first as "derivative versions," but they also practice engaging their senses as an audience to storytelling in ways that have broader implications for a revival of oral culture.

Cultural critics from Ong to Benjamin lament having lost a culture of storytelling. Benjamin writes of a society that no longer coheres around stories shared among a community of listeners. For Benjamin, the technological means of shared listening such as radio and records hold no hope for reversing this decline (although his German radio broadcasts suggest a personal affinity that belies his professional stance).[43] Whereas it is certainly true that listening to records or radio may isolate listeners from one another, and thus stifle discourse, this view takes for granted a conception of electronic media as acting unilaterally on listeners, transmitting the same unexamined messages into homes across a vast geographical span. When Morrison uses the figure of the "talking book" to reimagine her work's relationship to readers, or when we critics value listeners' accounts of their experience of the audio as an "interpretive layer," however, we see how the audio—as metaphor or material reality—may transform notions of narrative authority and offer alternatives to the unidirectional broadcast model.

I first encountered Lynne Thigpen's rendering of Morrison's *Jazz* under the imprint Griot Audio, a division of Recorded Books. The griot has been a central figure in African American letters for the reasons that Morrison herself describes, as discussed earlier in this chapter, as a means of valuing the way that diasporic communities retained vibrant traditions in the New World through shared stories and songs: "there was articulate literature before there was print."[44] Claudia Brown identifies antiphony as the key component of the griot analogy and argues that Morrison continues this call-and-response tradition by inviting readers to participate in the narrative process.[45] Morrison hopes for the relation between reader and writer to be more improvisational and democratic, thereby departing from models of textual authority that pit the integrity of the printed word against the submission of the reader. The antiphonal model of literary production takes on added political meaning in an American historical context in which literary authority was equated with freedom and orality with the illiterate and enslaved. Valorizing the vernacular, ephemeral sounds of human communities as a form of authority and self-definition makes the "talking life" of a book "talk back" to would-be arbiters of the literary in a way that is valuable for all readers, and listeners, to consider, even as critics like bell hooks stress its specifically African American significance: "for us, true speaking is not solely an expression of creative power; it is an act of resistance, a political gesture that challenges politics of domination that would render us nameless and voiceless."[46]

Can audiobooks take on this political meaning, by nature of their medium, content, or the fruitful combination of the two? The audiobook

Talking Books, Toni Morrison, and Narrative Authority   153

medium tends to valorize the spoken (except in extreme cases where listeners report repugnant, flat, "mechanical" sounding readers) but how antiphonal are audiobooks? One survey respondent astutely observes: "Actual books have no 'pace' other than the one you're reading at, but audiobooks have a pace of their own" (Surveys). For some listeners this unrelenting pace is a source of enjoyment, a spur to sustained concentration and immersion in a tale. But for the respondent quoted, the preset pace is a hindrance; it oversteps the bounds of textual authority to determine an aspect of her reading that she prefers to control herself.

Ong argues that "despite their cultivated air of spontaneity, these [electronic] media are totally dominated by a sense of closure."[47] Indeed, despite the sound of living speech, an audiobook is prerecorded from a textual artifact; the only way for the audience to participate is by turning the audio player on or off, or by skipping forward or backward in the narrative (although one could argue that this is not far removed from the experience of print). Ian Baucom offers a corrective to this unidirectional model of listening when he charts audience responses to Algerian radio broadcasts in "Franz Fanon's Radio."[48] Demonstrating the rich and varied dialogue that nationalistic programs inspired among communities of listeners, Baucom crucially highlights how the life of a narrative is hardly contained by the medium of its transmission but rather proliferates and mutates in the minds of its audience and in their continuing conversations. In opposition to a model in which the speaker/author is authoritarian, the participatory model credits the audience with agency and media-savvy similarly confirmed by my surveys. Multiple respondents compared the audiobook experience to theater, noticing how "being read to, by an author or an actor, can completely change your interpretation of a story." One spoke of the reader/actor precisely as "a mediator, an interpretive layer, between author and listener" (Surveys).

Ong unfavorably compares the solitary act of reading with the storytelling situation of primary oral culture: "To think of readers as a united group, we have to fall back on calling them an 'audience,' as though they were in fact listeners. 'Readership' is an abstraction. Print isolates."[49] Institutions like Oprah's Book Club represent an attempt to overcome this isolation; whereas the television show necessarily limits itself to presenting the interactions of a few readers, it fosters a powerful imagined community among fellow viewers and readers.[50] The tremendous sales of the books Oprah endorses as well as participation in the considerable online resources the club offers suggest that the on-air proceedings of the club are a catalyst for significant off-the-air involvement, varying in degrees from reading the book or watching the show only to participating in Web forums or local book clubs to connect with other readers. Listening to an audio recording in this context of support for shared reading would certainly seem to promote a sense of the storytelling community. It remains to be seen whether listeners in other contexts find that audio promotes shared literary culture.

The usual scene of audiobook listening—while commuting or performing housework—would seem to oppose the potential for audiobooks to foster communities of readers. But it may be precisely the fact of isolated listening that makes an aurally imagined community so appealing. Again and again in the surveys I conducted, audiobooks presented a cherished escape from the demands of domestic labor. As one respondent reports: "[Audiobooks] have proved to be essential in performing the tasks of a mother, that is, chauffeuring long distances to sports events and back, etc." Another says, "I've listened to many books while ironing, washing dishes, cooking—mindless activities that I'd otherwise be impatient with. I enjoy music, but audiobooks are much more engaging" (Surveys). Particularly for those whose primary occupation consists of domestic labor, audiobooks provide not only an escape from monotonous housework but also a sense of intellectual engagement that they may miss from professional life. The contact with another adult voice gestures outward toward the broader world, whereas the interiority of the privately heard sound creates a sense of personal time and space that sociologists Eileen Green and Alison Adam argue is necessary to identity formation. In their essay collection *Virtual Gender: Technology, Consumption, and Identity*, Green and Adam stress the importance of everyday practice and "household uses of technology" in assessments of technological effects.[51] This chapter has indicated some ways that new media discussions could benefit from an African American critical corpus invested in the relationship between bodies and technology. A critical conversation about the meanings of audiobooks would similarly profit from the awareness, imported from feminist sociology, of the ways that liberatory listening occurs not only in the theoretical implications of technology but especially in its uses.

The potential for audiobooks to create an imagined community was demonstrated to me recently by the experience of listening to eight different women read sections of Kate Chopin's *The Awakening* via LibriVox. org, a site that allows volunteers to create free downloadable recordings of books in the public domain. The effect of Chopin's 1899 tale of a woman's struggle for identity amid the demands of domesticity and motherhood was heightened by the knowledge that eight women had collaborated from afar to create a shared recording. Roxanne Reed argues that Toni Morrison's "need to provide a 'non-book quality . . . a sound' . . . pleads the case for a womanist understanding of 'voice,'" that values the lived experience of men and women of color, "in direct contrast to word and text."[52] As downloadable formats make audiobooks more accessible to listeners and platforms such as LibriVox.org allow listeners to become readers and producers, the opportunities multiply for audiobooks to engage audiences as active participants in the antiphonal play of performance and interpretation. For criticism to be relevant in this context, it needs to keep pace with the adaptability and innovation of a diverse range of readers and reading practices.

NOTES

1. Audio Publishers Association 2008 Sales and Consumer Survey, available at http://www.audiopub.org/resources-industry-data.asp.
2. Nicholas Zill and Marianne Winglee, *Who Reads Literature? The Future of the United States as a Nation of Readers*, Research Division Report #22, National Endowment for the Arts (Cabin John, Md.: Seven Locks Press, 1990). APA Survey shows fiction represented 73 percent of audiobook sales in 2008.
3. Professors surveyed were most concerned that audiobooks prevent rereading and marking passages for study but acknowledged that audiobooks "have a place in the study of literature and teaching of literacy" and that "different people learn best through different means. For some people taking in information through their ears is most powerful." K. C. Harrison, "Audiobooks" Survey, August–September 2009. Survey reports are anonymous and will be cited hereafter as "Surveys." Concerns regarding abridgment are belied by APA data, which shows 85 percent of audiobooks sold in 2008 were unabridged, up from 78 percent in 2007.
4. Janice Radway's *Reading the Romance* (Chapel Hill: University of North Carolina Press, 1984) and Amy Johnson Frykholm's *Rapture Culture* (New York: Oxford University Press, 2004) serve as models for the attempt to forge new territory in the field of reader reception, working within the constraints of one researcher's ability to survey and assess a limited group of consumers. Both Radway and Frykholm demonstrate the value of qualitative, as opposed to quantitative, reception studies, emphasizing the insights to be gained from attending to the particularity of individual readers and the ways that they construct meaning in their communities and activities.
5. In addition to surveying audiobook listeners, I interviewed publishers from Brilliance Audio (a division of Amazon), podiobooks.com (which provides an online platform for self-published recorded books), and Recorded Books. All reported that industry data regarding audiobooks users is virtually nonexistent and that audiobook publishing decisions are made based on statistical consumer interest in print books by the same author. The only publicly available data on audiobooks shows that CDs account for 72 percent of sales in 2008, with sales of downloadable audiobooks rising to 21 percent, up from 17 percent in 2007. Measured by publisher revenue, retail is the audio industry's strongest channel, at 36 percent, followed closely by the library channel at 32 percent (APA 2008 Survey). My survey results came from avid readers whose audiobook listening augmented their considerable consumption of print literature. Most listened via free downloads and library loans. The most common scene of audio listening was in the car or during a bus commute, followed closely by being at home, doing housework.
6. Douglas Kahn, *Noise, Water, Meat: A History of Sound in the Arts* (Cambridge: MIT Press, 1999), 8.
7. See Henry Louis Gates, Jr., "Introduction: The Talking Book," in *Pioneers of the Black Atlantic: Five Slave Narratives from the Enlightenment*, ed. Henry Louis Gates, Jr., and William Andrews (Washington, D.C.: Counterpoint, 1998), 1–29.
8. Michael Chaney notes the "alarming scarcity of critical work on the intersection of race and technology in contemporary literature" in "Slave Cyborgs and the Black Infovirus: Ishmael Reed's Cybernetic Aesthetics," *Modern Fiction Studies* 49, no. 2 (2003): 261.
9. See, for instance, Alberto Manguel, *A History of Reading* (New York: Penguin, 1997).

156   K. C. Harrison

10. Sarah Kozloff, "Audio Books in a Visual Culture," *Journal of American Culture* 18, no. 4 (1995): 83–95.
11. Walter Ong, *Orality and Literacy: The Technologizing of the Word* (New York, Routledge, 1982), 136.
12. John Young, "Toni Morrison, Oprah Winfrey, and Postmodern Popular Audiences," *African American Review* 35, no. 2 (Summer 2001): 196.
13. See Christopher Small, *Musicking: The Meanings of Performances and Listening* (Hanover, N.H.: Wesleyan University Press, 1998). Sounding is Houston Baker's term for the nonlinguistic sounds of black vernaculars that signify both the pain of past oppression and a strategy of expressive resistance. See *Blues, Ideology, and Afro-American Literature: A Vernacular Theory* (Chicago: University of Chicago Press, 1984). Nate Mackey identifies "othering practices" in black speaking, writing, and music making that "accent variance [and] variability" and "implicitly react against and reflect critically upon the different sort of othering to which their practitioners, denied agency in a society by which they are designated other, have been subjected" ("Other: From Noun to Verb," in *Discrepant Engagement: Dissonance, Cross-Culturality, and Experimental Writing* [New York: Cambridge University Press, 1993], 266). Walter Benjamin, "The Work of Art in the Age of Mechanical Reproduction," in *Illuminations*, trans. Harry Zohn (New York: Schocken Books, 1968), 217–252.
14. Small, *Musicking*, 5.
15. Simon Stow, "The Way We Read Now: Oprah Winfrey, Intellectuals, and Democracy," in *The Oprah Affect: Critical Essays on Oprah's Book Club,* ed. Cecilia Konchar Farr and Jaime Harker (Albany: State University of New York Press, 2008), 284.
16. Stow, "The Way We Read Now," 284.
17. For specific objections to the so-called therapeutic model of reader response, see Cecilia Konchar Farr and Jaime Harker, eds., *The Oprah Affect: Critical Essays on Oprah's Book Club* (Albany: State University of New York Press, 2008).
18. A recent survey by librarian Teri Lesesne found that audiobooks used in conjunction with print aided elementary school students' reading comprehension and fluency. She cites a study by Mitchell Levine that found a 34 percent edge in comprehension scores, 65 percent fluency gain, and 77 percent more pages read by students using audiobooks versus the control group. Teri Lesesne, "Audiobooks: How and Why," Powerpoint presentation, Sam Houston State University Department of Library Science, 2009.
19. Kathleen Fitzpatrick explores the stakes behind protective attitudes toward print in *The Anxiety of Obsolescence: The American Novel in the Age of Television* (Nashville: Vanderbilt University Press, 2006).
20. Nellie McKay, "An Interview with Toni Morrison," in *Toni Morrison: Critical Perspectives Past and Present*, ed. Henry Louis Gates, Jr., and Kwame Anthony Appiah (New York: Amistad, 1993), 408.
21. Houston A. Baker, Jr., *Working of the Spirit: The Poetics of Afro-American Women's Writing* (Chicago: University of Chicago Press, 1991).
22. Toni Morrison, *Beloved* (New York: Knopf, 1987), 89.
23. Morrison, *Beloved*, 89; Roxanne R. Reed, "The Restorative Power of Sound: A Case for Communal Catharsis in Toni Morrison's *Beloved,*" *Journal of Feminist Studies in Religion* 23, no. 1 (Spring 2007): 55–71.
24. Morrison, *Beloved*, 259.
25. Mackey, *Discrepant Engagement*, 122.
26. Walter Ong, *Orality and Literacy: The Technologizing of the Word* (New York, Routledge, 1982), 32, 14–15.

Talking Books, Toni Morrison, and Narrative Authority   157

27. Aldon Lynn Nielsen, *BLACK CHANT: Languages of African-American Postmodernism* (New York: Cambridge University Press, 1997), 19.
28. Alexander G. Weheliye, *Phonographies: Grooves in Sonic Afro-Modernity* (Durham, N.C.: Duke University Press, 2005); Harryette Mullen, "Optic White," cited in Thomas Foster, *The Souls of Cyberfolk: Posthumanism as Vernacular Theory* (Minneapolis: University of Minnesota Press, 2005), xxiii.
29. Farrah Jasmine Griffin, "When Malindy Sings: A Meditation on Black Women's Vocality," in *Uptown Conversation: The New Jazz Studies*, ed. Robert G. O'Meally, Brent Hayes Edwards, and Farah Jasmine Griffin (New York: Columbia University Press, 2004), 102–125.
30. Madhu Dubey, *Signs and Cities: Black Literary Postmodernism* (Chicago: University of Chicago Press, 2003). The chapter "Reading as Listening: The Southern Folk Aesthetic" charts the literary uses of the rural South for imaginative resolutions to the problems of urban literary representation that follow the failed promise of modernity, "retreat[ing] from a century-long history of urbanization that has belied the hopes fueling northern urban migrations . . . [authors] disavow the dream of full national integration and imaginatively recover the coherent black community that seems increasingly inaccessible in the postmodern urban present" (145).
31. Dubey, *Signs and Cities*, 171.
32. Farr, *The Oprah Affect*, 121.
33. NPR Books podcast, Barbara Kingsolver, November 26, 2009.
34. Interview with Angels Carabi for *Belles Lettres* 10, no.2 (1995): 40–43. Cited in Caroline Brown, "Golden Gray and the Talking Book: Identity as a Site of Artful Construction in Toni Morrison's *Jazz*," *African American Review* 36, no. 4 (Winter 2002): 641.
35. Cited in Brown, "Golden Gray and the Talking Book," 641.
36. Toni Morrison, *Jazz* (New York: Knopf, 1992), 229.
37. Toni Morrison, interview by Kay Bonetti, 1983, quoted in Cheryl Hall, "Beyond the 'Literary Habit': Oral Tradition and Jazz in *Beloved*," *MELUS* (Spring 1994): 89.
38. Young, "Toni Morrison," 196.
39. Gates, "Introduction: The Talking Book," 2.
40. Alessandro Portelli, "The Sign of the Voice: Orality and Writing in the United States," in *The Novel*, vol. 1, *History, Geography and Culture*, ed. Franco Moretti (Princeton: Princeton University Press, 2006), 545. The Talking Book continues to appear as a figure among black "folk" preachers sermonizing with the Bible before them but upside down. A recent work by Allen Dwight Callahan, *The Talking Book: African Americans and the Bible* (New Haven: Yale University Press, 2006), treats this topic in depth.
41. Ong, *Orality and Literacy*, 169, 31.
42. Ong writes, "[L]iteracy [is] absolutely necessary for the development not only of science but also of history, philosophy, explicative understanding of literature and of any art, and indeed for the explanation of language (including oral speech) itself" (*Orality and Literacy*, 15).
43. Walter Benjamin, "The Storyteller," in *Illuminations*, 83–110.
44. McKay, "An Interview with Toni Morrison," 408.
45. Call-and-response has been an important rubric for understanding the African American literary tradition in general, as Robert Stepto explores in *From Behind the Veil: A Study of Afro-American Narrative* (Champaign: University of Illinois Press, 1991). Paul Gilroy argues in *The Black Atlantic* (Cambridge: Harvard University Press, 1993), "there is a democratic, communitarian moment enshrined in the practice of antiphony which symbolizes and anticipates (but does not guarantee) new, non-dominating social relationships" (79).

158 K. C. Harrison

46. bell hooks, *Talking Back: Thinking Feminist, Thinking Black* (Cambridge, Mass.: South End Press, 1989), 8.
47. Ong, *Orality and Literacy*, 137.
48. Ian Baucom, "Frantz Fanon's Radio: Solidarity, Diaspora, and the Tactics of Listening," *Contemporary Literature* 42, no. 1 (Spring 2001), 15–49.
49. Ong, *Orality and Literacy*, 74.
50. I use the term "imagined communities" from Benedict Anderson's seminal work on nationalism to reflect the ways that individuals cohere around a mental image of their affinity, as opposed to face-to-face interactions. See Anderson, *Imagined Communities: Reflections on the Origins and Spread of Nationalism*, rev. ed. (London: Verso, 1991).
51. Eileen Green and Alison Adam, eds., *Virtual Gender: Technology, Consumption, and Identity* (New York: Routledge, 2001).
52. Reed, "The Restorative Power of Sound," 64. It is important to note, however, that Chopin's work has been claimed as a foundational text for the white feminist movement that Alice Walker and Delores Williams react against with their founding of womanism. Kimberly Chabot Davis investigates the possibility of cross-racial identification through reading, versus the threat of identification as hostile erasure, in "Oprah's Book Club and the Politics of Cross-Racial Empathy," in Farr, *The Oprah Affect*, 141–162.

9 Obama's Voices
Performance and Politics on the *Dreams from My Father* Audiobook

Jeffrey Severs

During the eight years of the George W. Bush administration, the major literary news from the White House concerned antiwar poets rejecting the First Lady's invitations to join her symposium and the president engaging in year-long reading contests with adviser Karl Rove. Rove won 2006 with 110 books read to Bush's 94; newspapers that August reported that one of Bush's reads at his ranch in Crawford, Texas, was Albert Camus's *The Stranger*, but, as Rove later confessed to Rush Limbaugh, they also both racked up many John D. MacDonald mysteries before mutually deciding to "get back to the serious stuff."[1] American literati thus had many reasons to warmly greet Senator Barack Obama's candidacy in 2008 as the possible advent of a president who not only read "the serious stuff" but could write it too. Although his 2006 campaign book, *The Audacity of Hope*, has its merits, Obama's literary reputation rests on the memoir he published in 1995, *Dreams from My Father: A Story of Race and Inheritance*, a book contracted based on the fame he acquired as the first black editor of the *Harvard Law Review* and predating his entry into Illinois state politics. As Obama's star rose with his celebrated 2004 Democratic National Convention speech, the book appeared in two new editions (2004, with a new preface, and 2007, with an excerpt from *The Audacity of Hope*) and has been a long-term best-seller.[2] It also garnered the attention of critics, academic and otherwise, keen to appreciate the book not so much for its prehistory of a political career as for its play of genres and the long lines of its influences, from the bildungsroman and American autobiography to the black authors Obama reports reading as a teen—W. E. B. DuBois, Langston Hughes, Ralph Ellison, Richard Wright, James Baldwin, Malcolm X.[3]

I know that I, as one of those literary critics, felt elated at the prospect of a president who was a real writer ("a writer . . . in my high esteem," as Toni Morrison put it) when I first read *Dreams from My Father*—or more precisely, heard the author read it to me on my car stereo as I drove across Arizona, New Mexico, and West Texas in the summer of 2008.[4] On this audiobook, first released by Random House Audio in 2005 and winner of the 2006 Grammy for Spoken Word Album, some wondrous combination of the written and the auditory—the "voice" and the voice—accounted for

160 *Jeffrey Severs*

my delight over those seven and a half hours of desert landscape. Although *Dreams* does in part tell the story of the growth of a political leader and orator, and the packagers of the audiobook had included Obama's 2004 Convention keynote as a coda underscoring that destination, the effect of that address, once the legendary embodiment of Obama-speak in my mind, paled next to the longer romance with Obama's voice—a different sort of romance—that I had just experienced. It was not really the purposiveness of oratorical skill that suffused the audio *Dreams* but an actor's gifts, those of an amateur but gifts nonetheless: the sustained, intimate mimicry of the voices of others, known so well as to be embodied, and a sly enactment of the acceptance of a sonic legacy of black identity and diasporic consciousness that Obama had already woven into the written text's metaphors. The broad humor of his Kansan grandfather, the fiery diatribes of a Muslim black nationalist in Chicago, the sharp complaints of the working-class women he served in Chicago, the varying accents of the Kenyan English of his father, his half-brother Roy, and his half-sister Auma—these are just a few of the dozens of examples of Obama's evocative character work on *Dreams*, by turns tender and ironic. Although the audiobook's abridgment omits what I estimate to be about 30 percent of the written text, from lines on almost every page to entire sections, these performances made me glad to have encountered Obama's memories for the first time in audio form.[5]

Here I attempt to raise that intuitive response to the level of analysis by examining the *Dreams* audiobook as it articulates Obama's struggle to take up the inheritance, figured sonically, of his absent father and black manhood more generally (although also with crucial engagement with female and feminist voices). I also examine the audiobook's role in popular media portrayals of black anger during the presidential campaign and beyond and turn, finally, to the question of what kind of political pluralism *Dreams* centers on voice. In doing so I hope to resolve what it is that compels Obama the audiobook narrator to give so many spirited performances of the people in his autobiography and what larger meaning to grant those performances.

The audiobook offers an opportunity to investigate the vocal Obama in ways that go beyond the many invocations of his voice as the essential element of his vaunted charisma. Frank Browning, in an unscientific consultation with opera-singing coaches about the instinctively felt appeal of Obama's voice during the primary season in 2008, suggested that baritones like Obama tend to be associated with authority in listeners' minds, in contrast to his then-opponent, "all too often labeled Hillary the Shrill, including all the gendered codes buried beneath the word 'shrill.'"[6] How to describe Obama's baritone in any rigorous way, though, beyond the litany of obvious adjectives that often turn up: rich, soothing, lovely, authoritative? As Roland Barthes writes in "The Grain of the Voice" (an essay Browning also cites), when music and voices are translated into language, "the adjective"—"the poorest of linguistic categories"—"is inevitable," when what is needed is "the impossible account of an individual thrill" produced by voice.[7]

Likewise, the *Dreams* audiobook affords a chance to counter and complicate cynical readings of Obama's vocal code-switching in less artificial moments, as when a conservative blogger accused Obama of practicing "dog whistle politics" while paying for his chili dog at a noted black eatery in Washington, D.C., shortly after his inauguration in 2009. Telling the cashier to keep the change, had Obama said, "No, we're straight," as news reporters had written it, or "Nah, we straight," as the tape, replayed often on YouTube, revealed? The vernacular "Nah, we straight" was a synecdoche for Obama's intention to appeal to black constituents in a divisive way, this blogger insinuated, and one could infer her desire to monitor the secret messages carried in the vocal cords of this first black president—as though forty-three white presidents had not been performing multiple American identities, depending on context, for centuries.[8] Pitch, cadence, melodicness, his pointed echoing of Abraham Lincoln and Martin Luther King, his considerable involvement in the speech-writing process—all of these can be cited as what make Obama a master of the podium and inspire business books with titles such as *Say It Like Obama*.[9] But in what does the elusive "grain" of Obama's voice consist? In search of it I turn to the less-discussed topic of Obama the intimate vocal portraitist, sometimes glimpsed on the podium or in press coverage of his words, but rarely in a sustained way.

I take the *Dreams* audiobook to be a distinct artifact, not a subsidiary growth on Obama's written text—an artifact requiring its own analysis and theorization, although also one that must be read in dialogical conjunction with the *Dreams* book. Here I follow John Young, who, in his examination of the cultural impact, Oprah-driven and otherwise, of Toni Morrison, writes of her audiobooks not as commercial add-ons or lesser (abridged) versions of the novels but as, in many ways, the best artistic vehicles for her themes. Morrison, relatively rare among novelists, reads her audiobooks herself, and Young argues that her decision heightens the effects of her direct reader addresses and places Morrison's work yet more firmly in the African American tradition Henry Louis Gates has identified with "the trope of the talking book."[10] Gates's influential idea is based on a recurring scene in late-eighteenth- and early-nineteenth-century slave narratives of slaves regarding acts of reading from a book as evidence of the book "talking," and it claims that these roots of African American literary consciousness result in a twentieth-century proliferation of "speakerly texts," works that use the patterns of actual speech to produce the illusion of oral narration.[11] Elements of Gates's category certainly apply to both the audio and written *Dreams*.

But in suggesting that aspects of Obama's speakerly text become most compellingly visible when placed in the new(er) technological form of the audiobook, I also employ more recent scholarship by Alexander Weheliye.

162   *Jeffrey Severs*

In *Phonographies: Grooves in Sonic Afro-Modernity*, Weheliye writes against the implication of many descriptions of black sound—the idea that black cultural production exists as an outside or other to Western modernity's deep relationship to the technological. The history of sonic Afro-modernity should be centered instead, Weheliye argues, on the phonograph's appearance in the late-nineteenth century. Weheliye does not treat any audiobooks, although they would seem to fit into his definition of "sonic Afro-modernity" as the "open totality" of "cultural practices" that arise out of the "complex interfacing of modern black culture and sound technologies." [12] Moreover, Weheliye draws lengthy readings from Ellison's use of sound technology in his work, as my readings will show Obama, inspired by Ellison, doing in his own. By "phonograph" Weheliye does not mean simply the record player. Etymologically, phono-graph—"sound-writer" or "sound-writing"—implies the second-class status of sound; whereas "alphabetic script is construed as a natural extension of the human body" and naturally leaves a record without reproduction or duplication, speech and sound "have to be reiterated and imagined as writing"—phonograph—"in order to operate as recordings." [13] I take from these complex formulations an authorization to break down an intuitive understanding of the audiobook as simply a faithful record of a written book rather than a record all its own, operating as a separate text and, as in Weheliye's description of a CD or MP3, an "event[ ] in [its] own right." [14]

The *Dreams* audiobook may even deserve, from a cultural studies perspective, greater scrutiny than the *Dreams* book because the former is so widely traversed and sampled, so readily misappropriated for political and other ends. Those who will never read (in the traditional sense) a word of the *Dreams* text can encounter, on YouTube online videos, several user-generated collections of samples from the audiobook. One of these, a conservative attack appearing during the presidential election campaign, framed quotations from the book's probing and multifarious treatments of black-white relations and radical black politics with the header "Shocking Words from Obama's Mouth: His Own Words, His Own Voice." [15] The excerpts appear on a black screen as Obama's voice reads them aloud. As that header suggests, through its intensification of "His Own Words" with "His Own Voice," the voice of the author, however inflected, tends to overwhelm distinctions that the writer, a first-person narrator of a large ensemble of remembered figures, sought to make. Obscured (if not erased) by the author's voice are the distancing effects of prefaces like "Ray assured me . . ." that appear on the screen and, of course, the critical assessments that frequently follow these attacks on whites in the book. This particular video also interweaves parts of the infamous, often replayed Fox News footage from Reverend Jeremiah Wright's sermons with quotes from *Dreams*, *The Audacity of Hope*, and television interviews of Obama about his attendance at Trinity United Church of Christ. The general goal of this ten-minute collection is to create an air of self-contradiction and deceit around Obama, and his voicing of all

Obama's Voices 163

the racial viewpoints taken up by *Dreams* is integral to that goal—but so, it should be noted, is that voice's absence. Some quotes appear silently on the screen with the note "left out of audiobook."

The joke of other YouTube clips, more sympathetic to Obama, is that, as the title of one recording puts it, "Obama Swears (Funny Stuff!)"; such clips loop and reloop, often against a dance or rap beat, some assortment of six or seven sentences from *Dreams* uttered by Obama in a tone laced with insolence:

"'Your shit's getting way too complicated for me'" (74).

"'"Sure you can have my number, baby"'" (73).

"'You ain't my bitch, nigger'" (73).

"'[B]uy your own damn fries'" (73).

"'Now you know that guy ain't shit'" (73).

"'Sorry-assed motherfucker got nothing on me'" (73).

"'There are white folks, and then there are ignorant motherfuckers like you'" (81).[16]

Most of these lines—although, importantly, as we will see, not all—are said by Obama's outspoken high school friend Ray, convinced of the racism of potential white dates, in chapter 4, which covers the narrator's experiences around age fifteen. This chapter goes on to give an ultimately quite tempered treatment of sentiments like Ray's, spurred by another of the often remixed lines—"That's just how white folks will do you"—which, along with the italicized phrase "*White folks*," Obama uses in the chapter's later pages as a kind of refrain while probing various aspects and degrees of white racism (including the attitudes he perceives in his grandparents) and black responses to that racism (80, 81).

Ray is the youngest and most callow of the many ardently political black men Obama shows himself encountering in *Dreams*, from former Black Panther and radical poet Frank (in real life, Frank Marshall Davis) and college friend Marcus (in real life, Earl Chew) to Chicago black nationalist Rafiq al Shabbaz (in real life, Salim al Nurridin) and Wright.[17] In chapter 4, what at first seems like a counterpoint between hot-headed Ray and level-headed Barry, as well as a play for what Obama must know will be a few laughs, eventually suggests something more like vocal merger. "'There are white folks, and then there are ignorant motherfuckers like you,'" a line used often in the YouTube remixes, certainly "sounds," in isolation, as though it would be Ray, in its profane, combative content. But this line is

164 *Jeffrey Severs*

actually the teenage Obama himself, using profane attack to greater purpose, responding late in this chapter to a white assistant basketball coach who, after losing a pickup game to a team of blacks, says, "[W]e shouldn't have lost to a bunch of niggers." When Obama tells him to shut up, the coach responds that "there are black people, and there are niggers. Those guys were niggers" (80). Obama's table-turning retort follows.

Individually, the anonymous YouTube appropriations are not to be taken very seriously. At most, the "Obama Swears" clips provide fodder for those invested in simplistic understandings of the already simplistic (and racially coded) debate that developed around the issues of Obama's "elitism" and "street cred" during the campaign.[18] But considered alongside similar acts in more powerful media outlets, these clips attest to the ability of voices speaking on race—particularly voices of a certain pitch and timbre—to overwhelm discursive distinctions in the American political and social imagination. Higher up the media power ladder, Obama's recordings of his own audiobooks have been a means by which conservatives, through further decontextualization, get "Obama" to say what they want, to vocally provide the associative bridge that the cable news caption of "Obama's Pastor" added to video clips of Wright. For instance, Sean Hannity on his radio show in August 2008 said, "I don't think Barack Obama ought to be hurling around words like 'bigot' given the things he's said himself"—followed immediately by a very short clip from the *Dreams* audiobook, "'White folks' greed runs a world in need.'"[19] In context, the line is part of Obama's extended quotations from Wright's "The Audacity of Hope" sermon, after which he would title his campaign vision. Never mind the compelling nature of several of Wright's arguments, reasonably considered, or that Wright's (and Obama's) lead-in to those eight words is the rather apt proof that "'cruise ships throw away more food in a day than most residents of Port-au-Prince see in a year'" (293). Obama the vocal performer and potential candidate, anticipating such misappropriations (as he certainly could have when he recorded the audiobook in 2005), was in a bind: give no actor's inflection to such lines, and it seems like "Obama" is saying it; attempt to imitate the faster paced and impassioned voice of Wright, and the opponent's association of Obama with a stereotypical sound of black anger becomes all the easier.

In terms of reading *Dreams*, restoring "Obama's" lines to their proper speaker attribution does more than simply shed further light on the writer's marshaling of the characters in his drama, for an almost obsessive thematic concern in *Dreams* is the mysterious means by which the voices and sounds of others—their sonic materiality, rather than their semantic content—impress the listener and compel changes in behavior and consciousness. Listening is the great leitmotif of *Dreams*, and Obama asks repeatedly how the listener incorporates into himself and makes use of heard voices—that is, the very process he went through in producing the one-man performance of the audiobook. Consider this seminal scene of listening and dancing to

Obama's Voices 165

music at the end of chapter 3, from the last day Obama, then ten years old, ever spent with his father. In it, the quest for the father at the heart of the book becomes an act of discerning sounds:

> The day of his departure, as my mother and I helped him pack his bags, he unearthed two records, forty-fives, in dull brown dust jackets.
>
> "Barry! Look here—I forgot that I had brought these for you. The sounds of your continent."
>
> It took him a while to puzzle out my grandparents' old stereo, but finally the disk began to turn, and he gingerly placed the needle on the groove. A tinny guitar lick opened, then the sharp horns, the thump of drums, then the guitar again, and then the voices, clean and joyful as they rode up the back beat, urging us on.
>
> "Come, Barry," my father said. "You will learn from the master." And suddenly his slender body was swaying back and forth, the lush sound was rising, his arms were swinging as they cast an invisible net, his feet wove over the floor in off-beats, his bad leg stiff but his rump high, his head back, his hips moving in a tight circle. The rhythm quickened, the horns sounded, and his eyes closed to follow his pleasure, and then one eye opened to peek down at me and his solemn face spread into a silly grin. . . . I took my first tentative steps with my eyes closed, down, up, my arms swinging, the voices lifting. And I hear him still: As I follow my father into the sound, he lets out a quick shout, bright and high, a shout that leaves much behind and reaches out for more, a shout that cries for laughter. (71)

Obama here is working through the globally scattered subjectivity, the diasporic consciousness, that he tried to come to terms with as a child. The music on this record, fleetingly described, supposedly holds "the sounds of [his] continent"—a continent he has at this point never even visited. What may seem a solid example of modern African culture devolves into sonic contradiction when his father adds his own voice, the "shout that leaves much behind and reaches out for more, a shout that cries for laughter"; and such contradictions are easily scripted onto both the falsely positive image the young Obama receives of his father and the confusing hyphenations of the boy's identity—an absent African father, a sometimes absent white American mother, white American grandparents who do much of the work of raising him, and an Indonesian stepfather he lives with in his home country for four years. When it is heard on the audiobook, the phonograph moment at age ten serves as a bridge between modes of elaborating the sonic: Obama follows his romanticization of sound by working with voice in the more varied, less monumental mode of performance. The audiobook does not announce chapter numbers, and so after a brief pause we abruptly hear a line of unattributed dialogue: "'Man, I'm not going to any more of these bullshit Punahou parties'" (72). This is Ray, the speaker of the much-quoted

166 *Jeffrey Severs*

lines of profanity. Young Obama answers him with his muted, weary reply, "'Yeah, that's what you said the last time,'" establishing this chapter—and larger swaths of the audio *Dreams* to come—as a counterpointing of the maturing Obama's performed racial identities (72).[20]

Anticipating the journey to his father's continent that will occupy him in part 3, Obama spatializes sound at the phonograph in part 1. He "follow[s] [his] father into the sound," suggesting an active listening. With this image Obama may have in mind similar rhetorical maneuvers from Ellison's *Invisible Man*, which provides, as David Samuels emphasizes, the foil for *Dreams*' racial politics but also Obama's narrative- and scene-making template.[21] Obama makes his early organizing career resemble the Invisible Man's struggles with the Brotherhood, and he builds scenes of oratorical self-consciousness and growth—such as his antiapartheid speech at Occidental College—that owe their basic structure to Ellison. The Invisible Man's phonograph moment occurs in his prologue, in which, in his basement room lit by 1369 light bulbs and their stolen electricity, he also powers the spinning on his record player of Louis Armstrong's "What Did I Do to Be So Black and Blue?" He wishes for five records playing all at once. "[W]hat you hear vaguely in Louis' music," Ellison writes, is invisibility's "slightly different sense of time. . . . Instead of the swift and imperceptible flowing of time, you are aware of its nodes, those points where time stands still or from which it leaps ahead. And you slip into the breaks and look around."[22] His own moment with a record also allows Obama to overcome boundaries of time, to secure the making-present of the past on which memoir depends; note the ending shift into present tense with "And I hear him still."

Obama is working out the book's primary pattern of metaphor here, so let me elaborate on the scene further still. An entry into the intersection of familial and Kenyan history that will obsess the mature Obama, this is also a rebirthing scene in which the biracial American boy seems like a toddler taking his "first tentative steps," launching his ego on a dogged quest to reconcile with his ungraspable African origins. Obama threads this emblematic tottering into many moments in which his youthful persona encounters surrogate versions of his father; and he aligns the mental toddler's lack of agency with images of vibration and sound that are destabilizing, literally earth shattering. One such surrogate father is Frank, former Black Panther, radical poet, and friend of Obama's grandfather, Stanley Dunham, in Hawaii. Davis marks a transition in Obama's embrace of his multiracial heritage when he gives the confused teen a new way of seeing the racism in his grandfather that Obama has suspected without being able to pinpoint, along with a consciousness of unbridgeable gaps in black and white knowledge. Stanley is "basically a good man," Frank tells Barry. "But he doesn't *know* me. . . . He *can't* know me, not the way I know him. Maybe some of these Hawaiians can, or the Indians on the reservation. They've seen their fathers humiliated. Their mothers desecrated.

Obama's Voices 167

But your grandfather will never know what that feels like" (90). After this seismically disturbing discourse, Obama, once more a tottering youth in search of a true father, closes the chapter thus: "The earth shook under my feet, ready to crack open at any moment. I stopped, trying to steady myself, and knew for the first time that I was utterly alone" (91).[23] Frank's thoughts on essential racial difference, inspired by his black cultural nationalism, are the "sounds of [Obama's] continent" translated into an American context; and the idea that such a voice can rend a subjectivity is confirmed when, nearly three hundred pages later, in Kenya, after hearing stories of his paternal grandfather, nicknamed "the Terror" for the fear he inspired in his children and grandchildren, Obama has a nightmare. In it he is pursued by "a giant figure looming as tall as the trees, wearing only a loincloth and a ghostly mask. . . . I heard a thunderous voice saying only that it was time, and my entire body began to shake violently with the sound, as if I were breaking apart" (372). With the terrain of "his" continent now seemingly secure beneath his feet, the chaos of Obama's racial subjectivity—handed down through various fathers and figured sonically—now targets his body, his self. In my reading, Obama's assured performances of many voices throughout the audiobook function as a continual implied opposite to this sonic trauma—on the one hand, monumental voices with the power to tear the individual apart and leave him "utterly alone," and on the other, the individual's power to successfully embody many voices, as part of a community, while still remaining whole.

In achieving the latter state, Obama follows many other important figures "into the sound," often crediting inexplicable life transformations (particularly those of political consciousness) to sounds or voices exercising agency outside of their signifying content. In 1983, a twenty-two-year-old Obama is in New York, hoping to start a career in community organizing and meanwhile working as a financial writer. A bad phone connection with his Kenyan half-sister Auma decides his fate for him: "For a few moments I couldn't understand the words, only the sound [of Auma's voice], a sound that seemed to have always been there, misplaced but not forgotten" (137). Later he notes: "I still wonder sometimes how that first contact with Auma altered my life. . . . Maybe by this time I was already committed to organizing and Auma's voice"—not what she said, but her voice—"simply served to remind me that I still had wounds to heal, and could not heal myself" (138). This association of his African family in particular with the sonic never devolves into a fetishization of drumbeats or a characterization of diasporic mysteries as something beyond linguistic explication. And it seems that it must at least in part be this respect—awe, really—for the indissolubility of the twin powers of meaning and vocality that compels Obama the audiobook narrator to give so many strong performances of the people in his autobiography. When Auma visits the US, she gives in Obama's kitchen a lengthy monologue on "the Old Man"—all about their father's revolutionary politics, but also his abusiveness and drinking, his

168   *Jeffrey Severs*

marital, professional, and personal failings—that Obama the audiobook narrator faithfully presents in her British-accented speech, the first of many such stories he will deliver, each in a distinctive voice, when he meets other relatives in Kenya (212–218).[24] The phonographic romance of the dead has thus met a living, articulate, African voice here in nearly the memoir's exact center. "[M]y father's voice had . . . remained . . . inspiring, rebuking, granting or withholding approval," Obama writes. "Now he was dead, truly. He could no longer tell me how to live" (220–221).

The gendering of these new, living voices does matter. Important men in *Dreams* tend to be advisers and rhetoricians; women, while they often advise, do so more often through the power of storytelling. While Barbara Foley calls *Dreams* "distinctly gendered—unabashedly Oedipal in its focus on fathers and sons," and Obama himself writes in his 2004 preface that, had he known his mother's death from cancer was imminent while writing, he might have composed "a different book—less a meditation on the absent parent, more a celebration of the one who was the single constant in my life," *Dreams* does in fact have important feminist undertones, especially in identifying what forces can overcome the sonic/Oedipal chaos (xii).[25] In chapter 5 the text begins preparing for Auma's decisive voice by showing women shaping the racial consciousness that Obama's various fathers failed to solidify. The literary apprentice returns to the phonograph image perhaps too soon, framing the chapter's many memories of his college days with a scene of him sitting awake at 3:00 A.M. after a party, drinking and listening to Billie Holiday sing "I'm a Fool to Want You" on yet another record player. The chapter discusses some powerful voices who attempt to draw the dissolute Obama—focused on drugs and partying, no longer in touch with his father—toward racial politics, especially that of Regina, a black female friend at Occidental who urges him, partly through stories of her grandmother's suffering, to continue his involvement in the campus movement for divestment from South Africa. "[A]fter what seemed like a long absence," Obama writes when he decides to become more political, "I had felt my voice returning to me [during a conversation] with Regina. It remained shaky afterward, subject to distortion," but grew "stronger, sturdier, that constant, honest portion of myself, a bridge between my future and my past" (105). The image counters those of tottering and being overwhelmed by (male) voices; and at the chapter's end, Obama completes the transfer of phonograph images by singing along with the last song on the Holiday record, resolving to "make music that wasn't there before" (112).

Here, the interplay between the book Obama wrote and the abridgment for audio comes to the interpretive fore. For this framing scene with the record is left out of the audiobook, which delivers only the background memories. The book and the abridgment follow the same pattern in chapter 10, when Obama, now a community organizer, again finds himself skeptical of a discourse strongly associated with black women: the importance of "self-esteem" in the mid-1980s (193). And again, he becomes attuned to the vocal lessons of women by the end of the chapter, this time by attending a feminist theater performance by local black women with a constituent, Ruby, with whom he becomes close. "[A] chorus of many shades and shapes, mahogany and cream, round and slender, young and not so young," the women (to quote one of their lines) *"sing a black girl's song,"* telling musical stories of aging, rape, abortion, and murdered children (205–206). Their singing, dancing, and forthright storytelling undo the cryptic, monolithic memory of Obama's dancing father. This entire scene is cut from the audiobook as well. The standard line on the back of the *Dreams* audiobook package, "This abridgment has been approved by the author," of course tells us nothing particular about Obama's actual involvement in the cuts or, more importantly, the principles behind them. But if my argument is right, Obama's performances throughout (especially when we hear him going well outside himself to play women) effectively *replace* these framing metaphors of listening, singing along, and vocal incorporation. The audiobook need not metaphorize the influence the voices of others have on Obama's own; it *is* the constant display of that influence.

Obama will draw his quest to a close in the book's third and final part, "Kenya," with a long monologue by another Kenyan woman—his paternal grandmother's answer to his request to tell him his heritage "from the beginning" (394).[26] We learn about "the Terror," Hussein Onyango Obama, as well as the youth and first marriage of Barack Senior; and Obama, listening, prefaces her story with his major motif, suggesting that the thunderous voices of dead patriarchs have been softened and mediated by female survivors: "I heard all our voices begin to run together, the sound of three generations tumbling over each other like the currents of a slow-moving stream, my questions like rocks roiling the water . . . but always the voices returning to that single course" (394). The image of an earth smoothly and slowly changed by water supersedes the earlier earthquake imagery. After so many stirring performances, minutes from the end of his many hours on tape, Obama records this story in his own voice because it is translated from Swahili for him by Auma. Especially since the monologue is saturated with proper names, though, which Obama renders in proper Kenyan accents that remind us of the real storyteller, the audiobook listener has a heightened sense of vocal merger at this three-person act of storytelling—indeed, "all our voices begin to run together."

Onyango draws this tale of a conflicted identity seeking a stable origin to an appropriately rough, interracial close: as a young man he scandalizes his family by disappearing for many months from their village and returning from a traders' settlement nearby wearing the "strange skin" of "the trousers of a white man, and a shirt like a white man, and shoes that covered his feet"—in contrast to his family's goatskin loincloths (398). He learns English at a young age, works as a cook and translator for white travelers and colonists, fights for the British in the First World War, and is later also tried in a British magistrates' court for political sedition, leading to

170 *Jeffrey Severs*

six months of imprisonment and torture. Tellingly, Onyango brings back a gramophone from his world travels as a cook for the British military during the Second World War. "[O]n his gramophone he played strange music late into the night," the text notes in an offhand way (410). But Obama brings the phonograph image full circle as a sign of the patriarchal past when, quite oddly, he includes it in a list of the elements of African modernization in his stirring valedictory address, at his father's grave, about Barack Senior's "confusion" over his African and Western experiences. The passage suggests that what has seemed all along like a search for the father's voice has really been a confrontation with his "silence," a desperate projection onto blank space:

> Oh, Father, I cried. There was no shame in your confusion. Just as there had been no shame in your father's before you. No shame in the fear, or in the fear of his father before him. There was only shame in the silence fear had produced. It was the silence that betrayed us. If it weren't for the silence, your grandfather might have told your father that he could never escape himself, or re-create himself alone. Your father might have taught those same lessons to you. And you, the son, might have taught your father that this new world that was beckoning all of you involved more than just railroads and indoor toilets and irrigation ditches and gramophones, lifeless instruments that could be absorbed into the old ways. (429)

By including the gramophone alongside railroads and modern plumbing as another "lifeless instrument[ ]," Obama suggests that the riven subjectivity of Kenyan men trying to fight toward a postcolonial age has had alienating effects in the familial sphere as well: the grandfather who came home in white man's clothes sat alone with his sound machine rather than engaging with the living voices of his large family. Such moments of solitary listening are not so sound-filled as they seem; they are rife with the "silence" of the Obamas' alienated black manhood, entrapping sons like the "invisible net" Barack Senior's dancing created in the first phonograph scene as he commanded his son to "learn from the master." Obama thus reaches to connect his forebears' struggle to his own, to make the phonograph a postcolonial emblem. For while he has not endured his ancestors' dramatic history, Obama has, we have seen, sat drinking and listening to his own phonograph during college—skeptical of racial politics, alienated from the women in his life, remembering his distance from his mother in high school, seeming (we see in retrospect) to follow momentarily in his elder's substance-abusing footsteps. If *Dreams* is, then, a story of men shedding the "lifeless" phonograph, then Obama's performance of the audiobook—vocally mediating many identities, becoming, in essence, his own phonograph—underscores the theme of vocal mastery and merger, of connecting with others.

Obama's Voices 171

Is a politics implied in all these metaphors of voice? Naturally, yes. And the skill with which the writer turns this literary trope into a political term needs to be heeded. The best and most rigorous readers thus far of the mediation of the political by the literary in *Dreams* have, while remaining basically sympathetic with Obama's views, focused on how his skill with narrative construction, allusion, metaphor, and perspective actually undergird or help paper over his disowning of both epistemological and political radicalisms. For instance, Samuels admiringly illustrates the intertext Obama creates between his story and *Invisible Man* but then disparages *Dreams* for departing from Ellison to embrace, in Obama's questioning of his white grandparents' motives and obsession with a father who is a "bona fide monster," an "old-fashioned, unabashedly romantic, and quite weird idea of racial authenticity."[27] Yet more thoroughly damning is an impressively researched article by Barbara Foley that now stands as the most provocative literary-political interpretation of *Dreams*. A Marxist employing Pierre Macherey's notion of "structured silences," Foley compares Obama's reconstructions of his life to the historical record in order to expose the memoir's "argument by innuendo and dismissal by marginalization" of left-wing politics in many forms: his ignoring of the contribution made by Marxism to Davis's racial politics, his caricaturing of the political savvy of the Altgeld Gardens residents he organized in Chicago, and, most shockingly, his omission of key details about Hussein Onyango Obama's imprisonment by the British and about Barack Senior's socialist writings.[28] Foley also finds Obama employing a "ventriloquistic device" that steps inside the minds of white characters, his grandfather and mother in particular, and condescendingly invents and distorts their opinions about race in America, fascism in Indonesia, and other topics.[29] All this Foley reads as the play of Obama's memoir for the political middle and a broad base for a political career, and thus as a prelude, planned out or not, to a presidential administration in which far-left viewpoints are not heard.[30]

To Foley, the metaphorical apparatus of vocal merger I have revealed in *Dreams* may seem like another of the text's political mystifications—an authorization to "hear" but ultimately neglect real differences in people's politics in favor of the leveling harmony of "liberal pluralism," constituted by what is in the end a single voice, Obama's, bidding for representative status.[31] Yet rather than remaining silent (Foley's key term) on issues of broad political representation, the text and audiobook actually speak in a loud voice. To see the achievement of liberal pluralism in *Dreams* as simply or primarily an effect of ideology-laden silences or suppression of political divisions is to miss the self-consciousness and artistry with which Obama constructs his belief in himself as a Whitmanian representative of the many. This is a highly mediated and (if my readings are followed) clearly constructed belief, responsive at numerous points to accusations about the text's unerring drive toward, as Foley puts it, "metonymic inclusion—to 'contain multitudes,' in Walt Whitman's phrase."[32]

172 *Jeffrey Severs*

Acknowledging readings like Foley's, though, does expose the poetics of voice Obama creates, amid the wealth of such examples in the African American literary canon, as a rather order-making, optimistic, and recuperative sort. Nathaniel Mackey, for instance, claims that black literary texts that incorporate vocal and musical effects (what he aptly terms their "will to song") are attempting to reconcile with the "wounded kinship" of African American lives, and thus in reading such texts one must make a "[d]iscrepant engagement," "remain[ing] open" to "dissonance, noise," and other symbols of ongoing social conflict.[33] *Dreams* is certainly a story of "wounded kinship," even though its familial disruptions arise from outside the context of slavery in the Americas that Mackey examines; but the "will to song" of *Dreams*, a traditional realist narrative far from the experimentalism Mackey surveys, is a will toward a well-ordered polity. Dissonance remains in the domain of Obama's psychological battles; as he increasingly assumes political leadership on Chicago's South Side in part 2, the chorus line of women and the church congregation—and not the deep sonic variety of, say, jazz—are the musical forms through which he illustrates his development.

Part 2 projects part 1's and part 3's familial racial quests onto the wider issue of constructing a racial polity. "You're starting to listen," says Marty, Obama's organizing mentor (in real life, Jerry Kellman), about his interviews to learn about residents' needs as he starts the job; but Obama is "too abstract," Marty notes, "like you're taking a survey or something" (158). When Obama says a page later he "still had no idea how I might translate what I was hearing into action," he summarizes the political branch of the text's ongoing question about voices and persons. Obama makes the somewhat predictable rhetorical maneuver (often used in his presidential speeches as well) of presenting a catalogue of people he talks with at meetings, including Mrs. Crenshaw, whose lawyer son has become a housebound schizophrenic. Voice again is a seat of strength, regardless of what suffering it signifies: "As she spoke, [Mrs. Crenshaw's] voice never wavered; it was the voice of someone who has forced a larger meaning out of tragedy" (189). A minipolity is taking shape before our ears through what Obama calls "[s]acred stories," people's "central explanation of themselves," "studded with events that still haunted or inspired them"—in other words, stories much like Obama's memoir, making him the articulate narrator-leader at the head of them all (and eventually, the memoir seems to imply, an even wider polity). Illustrating this logic of his own cohesive representativeness, Obama writes in the space of two sentences that the stories were "a knot to bind *our* experiences together" and something that "helped me bind *my* world together, that . . . gave me the sense of place and purpose I'd been looking for" (190; emphasis added). The sacred story motif thus gives greater ballast, greater detail, to the association of individuals with voices—a deepening of the text's embrace of pluralism that, while no doubt

Obama's Voices 173

insufficient from Foley's Marxist perspective, clearly seems to Obama a heeding of Marty's warning about being "too abstract."

The proper site for the ultimate merger of sacred stories is a church, of course, and Obama ends this political part 2 in Trinity United by transforming sacred stories back into the more pliable materials of voice and song, bringing all his writerly powers to bear on an invocation of ritual vocal concord as he listens, in tears, to Wright's sermon on "hope" and the congregation's response. The scene of an ecstatic communal moment in a black church has clear roots in the turbulent work of Ellison or Baldwin; but Obama's elaboration of this vocal crescendo seems to come straight out of high Modernist poetry, ignoring, for instance, the ironizing and dissonant effects Ellison brings to bear on Homer Barbee's soaring, unifying eulogy on the suffering of "the Founder" in *Invisible Man*.[34] "[A]ll the notes from the past three years swirl" about Obama. "The courage and fear of Ruby . . . The race pride and anger of men like Rafiq"—all merge in Wright's "single note—hope!" along with "the stories of ordinary black people" in "thousands of churches," stories of biblical survival, "our story, my story" (note the conjunction of those possessives again), "at once unique and universal" (294). On the audiobook, the moment is uniquely stirring and textured. In the clearest evocation of the audiobook's "will to song," Obama gives a full-throated enactment of Wright's sermon, going so far as to imitate the pastor's rendition of his parents' prayerful singing when Wright was arrested as a youth: "Thank you, Jesus / Thank you, Jesus / Thank you, Je-sus / Thank you, Lo-ord" (295). True to his focalizing methods, a half-page later Obama gives the final line in part 2 to the elderly woman next to him in church, who echoes Wright echoing his parents (while all, of course, are echoed by Obama). "'Oh, Jesus . . . Thank you for carrying us this far,'" she "whisper[s] softly"—suggesting that it has been Obama's role as memoirist and narrator/performer to amplify such unheard speech even as he gives voice to his own (295).

Ultimately, the distinctiveness of *Dreams'* vocal poetics may lie in the act that, once a text has been written and recorded, only its consumers can perform, not its creator: the act of listening. Ellison is on Obama's mind as a model when he constructs so many chapters around vocal performances; but comparison to the masculinist master brings out just how often his disciple's invisible man is an auditor, learning to listen to speeches rather than making them (for now at least), engaged constantly in the listening campaign Marty urges on him. Perhaps listening to you, rather than speaking for you, allows the Obama of *Dreams* to not end up alienated and underground: where Ellison's narrator, from his phonograph-furnished hole, writes of his representativeness with trademark Whitmanian hubris—"Who knows but that, on the lower frequencies, I speak for you?"—his disciple's persona is innately more humble, more open.[35] As Obama says when a woman comes to him for help with the neighborhood, a woman whose

174   *Jeffrey Severs*

motivations he will misread before, upon developing a closer relationship, getting right: "My ears perked up" (159).[36]

NOTES

1. On Bush's reading of Camus, see Maureen Dowd, "Camus Comes to Crawford," *New York Times*, August 16, 2006, 12. For Rove's remarks, see "Rush Interviews Karl Rove" (transcript), August 15, 2007, http://www.rushlimbaugh.com/home/daily/site_081507/content/01125106.guest.html.

2. The *Washington Post* reports that Obama's royalty income from *Dreams from My Father* was about $3.3 million for 2009, while *Dreams* and *The Audacity of Hope* together earned him $2.6 million in 2008. See Michael D. Shear and David S. Hilzenrath, "Book Royalties Fuel Obamas' Millionaire Status, Tax Return Shows," *Washington Post*, April 16, 2010, A04. For an argument on the different political teleologies suggested by the additions made to later editions, see Barbara Foley, "Rhetoric and Silence in Barack Obama's *Dreams from My Father*," *Cultural Logic* (2009): 5–10, http://clogic.eserver.org/2009/2009.html.

3. Representative of the laudatory writing on Obama the author by literary journalists during and after his presidential candidacy are Darryl Pinckney, "Dreams from Obama," *New York Review of Books*, March 6, 2008, 41–45 (Pinckney calls the book "beautifully written" and likens one passage to the work of Hughes [41–42]); David Samuels, "Invisible Man: How Ralph Ellison Explains Barack Obama," *New Republic*, October 22, 2008, 22–27 ("a terrific book—an insightful, well-written, cunningly organized black male bildungsroman that also serves as a kind of autobiographical rejoinder to one of my favorite American novels, Ralph Ellison's *Invisible Man*" [22]); Michiko Kakutani, "From Books, New President Found Voice," *New York Times*, January 18, 2009, A1 ("the most evocative, lyrical and candid autobiography [ever] written by a future president" [A1]). Among academics, Marjorie Perloff, addressing the 2008 Modern Language Association convention in San Francisco on the topic "Why Teach Literature Anyway?" used impassioned close readings of *Dreams* to answer that question. See the text of her remarks, "The Centrality of Literary Study," January 5, 2009, http://pressblog.uchicago.edu/2009/01/05/audacity_of_literary_studies.html. For Obama's account of his reading, see *Dreams from My Father: A Story of Race and Inheritance* (1995; New York: Three Rivers Press, 2007), 85–87. Subsequent references are given with page numbers in parentheses.

4. Morrison goes on to praise Obama's "ability to reflect on this extraordinary mesh of experiences" and "to set up scenes," "all of these things that you don't often see, obviously, in the routine political memoir biography. . . . [I]t's unique. It's his." "Toni Morrison on Bondage and a Post-Racial Age" (transcript), interview by Michel Martin, NPR, December 10, 2008, http://www.npr.org/templates/story/story.php?storyId=98072491.

5. See Barack Obama, *Dreams from My Father: A Story of Race and Inheritance*, read by Barack Obama (New York: Random House Audio, 2005), six discs. I refer to this edition in later notes with "Obama, *Dreams* audiobook" and a track number. Also available is the eleven-disc *The Essential Barack Obama*, which includes the audio *Dreams* and *The Audacity of Hope*, both read by Obama (New York: Random House Audio, 2008).

6. Frank Browning, "Does Obama's Baritone Give Him an Edge?" *Salon*, February 28, 2008, http://www.salon.com/news/opinion/feature/2008/02/28/obama_clinton_voices.

Obama's Voices 175

7. Roland Barthes, "The Grain of the Voice," in *Image, Music, Text*, trans. Stephen Heath (New York: Hill and Wang, 1977), 179, 181.

8. Nia-Malika Henderson, "Blacks, Whites Hear Obama Differently," *Politico.com*, March 3, 2009, http://www.politico.com/news/stories/0309/19538.html.

9. Shel Leanne, *Say It Like Obama: The Power of Speaking with Purpose and Vision* (New York: McGraw-Hill, 2008). Jon Favreau, who wrote the daily stump speeches during the campaign, is now President Obama's chief speechwriter. Ed Pilkington, after quoting Obama calling Favreau his "mind reader," notes, "Obama is an accomplished writer in his own right, and the process of drafting with his mind reader is collaborative. The inaugural speech has shuttled between them four or five times, following an initial hour-long meeting in which the president-elect spoke about his vision for the address, and Favreau took notes on his computer." See "Obama Inaguration: Words of History . . . Crafted by 27-Year-Old in Starbucks," *Guardian*, January 20, 2009, 2. Interestingly, this article also notes that Favreau, in addition to memorizing Obama's 2004 Convention keynote, "is said to carry . . . *Dreams From My Father*, wherever he goes. As a result, last November when Favreau sat down to write the first draft of the inaugural address, he could conjure up his master's voice as if an accomplished impersonator" (2). It is well known that Obama wrote the first draft himself of the highly personal "A More Perfect Union," his March 2008 speech on race widely thought to be his oratorical masterpiece.

10. John Young, "Toni Morrison, Oprah Winfrey, and Postmodern Popular Audiences," *African American Review* 35, no. 2 (2001): 198–199.

11. Henry Louis Gates, Jr., *The Signifying Monkey: A Theory of Afro-American Literary Criticism* (New York: Oxford University Press, 1988), 127–169.

12. Alexander G. Weheliye, *Phonographies: Grooves in Sonic Afro-Modernity* (Durham, N.C.: Duke University Press, 2005), 19.

13. Weheliye, *Phonographies*, 24, 25.

14. Weheliye, *Phonographies*, 33.

15. Didyoulisiten [sic], "Barack Obama—Dreams of [sic] My Father," www.youtube.com/watch?v=oYnle2q16Rk.

16. I have taken these example lines from three of the several very similar videos posted on YouTube: ServetheBeaver, "Obama Swears (Funny Stuff!)," http://www.youtube.com/watch?v=3FG41mdEx3M; RealHeadz, "Obama Cusses OFFICIAL REMIX," http://www.youtube.com/watch?v=H-46VL4kFQY; BeachesKT, "Obama Mashup: Sure you can have my number, baby!" http://www.youtube.com/watch?v=1hOg83QjmVE. Some of these videos include elaborate animations (featuring caricatures of the likes of Bill O'Reilly in time with certain words) and infamous photos (Obama with a cigarette dangling from his mouth, Obama shirtless in the surf in Hawaii). For the quoted audiobook clips, see Obama, *Dreams* audiobook, disc 2, tracks 12 and 14.

17. Here and throughout, in identifying these real-life counterparts, I have depended on the list (sourced to various news articles) provided in the Wikipedia entry for *Dreams*, http://en.wikipedia.org/wiki/Dreams_from_My_Father#cite_ref-15.

18. Considering the vast amount of writing on the topic of Obama's perceived elitism, I will only note that Obama invoked these memes himself in April 2008 comments on the campaign trail, when questioned about his clothing and his bowling abilities: "I don't want to go out of my way to sort of prove my street cred as a down-to-earth guy." See Maureen Dowd, "Desperately Seeking Street Cred," *New York Times*, April 27, 2008, 12.

19. See "Misrepresenting Obama's audiobook, Hannity claimed Obama said, 'White folks' greed runs a world in need,'" *Media Matters*, August 21, 2008,

176 *Jeffrey Severs*

http://mediamatters.org/research/200808210006. With "bigot" Hannity was referring to Obama's remarks about Jerome Corsi (author of *The Obama Nation: Leftist Politics and the Cult of Personality* [New York: Simon and Schuster, 2008]) and his anti-Catholic writings. The clip Hannity uses is from disc 5, track 1. The text of *Dreams* has of course provided many other conservative commentators with fodder, most of it based on distortion and misinterpretation of the book, little of it worth taking seriously, especially in a literary forum: Ann Coulter, in the most egregious example, called the book Obama's "Mein Kampf"; see "Obama's Dimestore 'Mein Kampf,'" *Human Events*, April 7, 2008, 286. For overviews of such right-wing attacks, see Foley, "Rhetoric and Silence," 3–4, n. 4; 43, n. 27.

20. Obama, *Dreams* audiobook, disc 2, track 12.
21. See Samuels, "Invisible Man," 22–25.
22. Ralph Ellison, *Invisible Man* (New York: Vintage, 1995), 8.
23. Davis's words here and Obama's reaction have drawn much attention from readers critical of the attitudes toward whites and radicalism espoused in *Dreams*. Foley, for example, sees Davis as Obama's "most fully novelized character," a figure Obama unduly characterizes as a "biological essentialist" while giving little to no attention to the Marxist politics backing his views. See Foley, "Rhetoric and Silence," 33–35. Samuels, "Invisible Man," writes disapprovingly, "Obama quotes Davis's sentiments without a shadow of dissent: The logic of the narrative gives the author permission to show his white family members in a bad light because, as Davis suggests, he is more closely related to other black people than he is to the white-skinned members of his family" (24).
24. Obama, *Dreams* audiobook, disc 4, tracks 5 and 6.
25. Foley, "Rhetoric and Silence," 5.
26. Obama, *Dreams* audiobook, disc 6, tracks 1–7.
27. See Samuels, "Invisible Man," 22.
28. On Macherey, see Foley, "Rhetoric and Silence," 3, n. 3; for "argument by . . . ," 19; on Davis, 33–35; on Altgeld Gardens, 28–31; and on Barack Senior's status as "not primarily an ambitious careerist" (as Obama portrays him) "but instead a distinctly leftist voice in the mid-1960s debates over the direction that post-independence Kenya should take," 42–45. Foley cites news reports that, quoting Obama's grandmother, contradict the account of Onyango his grandson shows her giving in *Dreams*: Onyango's actual prison term lasted two years and involved repeated acts of torture, as well as his stoic resistance to betraying political comrades. This, Foley argues, gives the lie to Obama's suggestion that he may have been an "Uncle Tom. Collaborator. House nigger," given his service of whites (406).
29. Foley, "Rhetoric and Silence," 20–24.
30. Foley, "Rhetoric and Silence," 5.
31. Foley, "Rhetoric and Silence," 4.
32. Foley, "Rhetoric and Silence," 40.
33. For an overview of "wounded kinship," see Nathaniel Mackey, *Discrepant Engagement: Dissonance, Cross-Culturality, and Experimental Writing* (New York: Cambridge University Press, 1993), 231–236. For other quotes, see Mackey, 240, 20.
34. Ellison, *Invisible Man*, 121–131. In a similar vein, Samuels chides Obama for being devoid of Ellison's biting humor and for giving an irony-free depiction of Wright: "One can only imagine what Ellison would have done with . . . the incredibly juicy character of Dr. Jeremiah Wright—a religious con man who spread racist and anti-Semitic poison while having an alleged sexual affair

with a white church secretary and milking his congregation for millions of dollars" ("Invisible Man," 23).

35. Ellison, *Invisible Man*, 581.

36. My thanks for feedback on an early draft of this article to participants in the Department of English Faculty Research Colloquium at the University of British Columbia.

10 Bedtime Storytelling Revisited
Le Père Castor and Children's Audiobooks

Brigitte Ouvry-Vial

Whereas audiobooks in Britain and the United States have been popular for a long time, they are newcomers in France, having developed in the last decade of the twentieth century. As is the case with their English counterparts, audiobook production in France consists of classic or contemporary texts recorded by their authors or by actors in order to be listened to at home, in cars, or elsewhere. A quick overview of the target market shows that, in France, audiobooks were initially intended for young people, then developed for language instruction and for visually impaired people. The latest target market of the audiobook industry is women, who represent 75 percent of printed book readers. Yet so far in a country that propounds its "cultural exception" and literary tradition, the total number of audiobooks hardly matches one-tenth of the total in the United States. This is partly because the audiobook in France is still linked with the tradition of children's narratives dating back to Charles Perrault's *Le petit chaperon rouge* (in *Contes de ma mère Loye*), first published in 1695, in which a comment in the margins of the manuscript indicates the intended oral recitation of the tale for young people: "On prononce ces mots d'une voix forte pour faire peur à l'enfant comme si le loup l'allait manger" (These words are to be spoken in a loud voice in order to scare the child as if the wolf was about to eat him).[1]

The status of today's French audiobooks suggests how innovative the *Père Castor* audiobook collection was when it came out in the late 1970s. *Les albums du Père Castor* first came out in 1931, and it was based on the innovative educational movement "Education nouvelle" introduced in France by Paul Faucher after his encounter with the Czech pedagogue Frantisek Bakulé. The first hundred titles were conceived, tested, and published by a group called Les Ateliers du Père Castor founded by Faucher in 1931, followed and implemented by Le Centre de recherche biblio-pédagogique de l'Atelier du Père Castor in 1946 and L'Ecole du Père Castor in 1947: by 1966, 320 titles had been published.[2] After Paul Faucher's death in 1967, his son François Faucher took over the center, sticking to his father's dedicated approach, intellectual legacy, and educational values while inventing new forms through which to transmit them: as François Faucher had an interest in popular, mass market formats, he launched the paperback and then audiobook versions of the Père Castor's classics, thereby allowing a number of renowned stories—many of them translated into several languages, as was the case with the story *Michka*, which had sold 250,000 copies by 1951—to reach a third generation of readers in audible versions almost sixty years after the same titles of *Albums du Père Castor* were released in print. François Faucher retired in 1996, and the publishing house, commercially hosted and distributed by Flammarion, is now under the direction of Hélène Wadoswki. New reprints of the classic *Albums du Père Castor* in the original format—a soft-cover brochure to ensure easy handling by children and affordable prices for parents—are periodically released along with new collections of albums, short stories, and novels in paperback editions.

CLASSICS IN AUDIBLE EDITIONS

The collective workshop first recorded audio versions of nineteen titles from Les Classiques du Père on vinyl, then tapes at François Faucher's initiative, and later progressively released them on CDs. These titles are currently marketed by Livraphone online bookshop as "Le livre qui parle" ("The book that talks").[3] Whereas some titles are periodically out of print and must be reprinted, several titles are continuous bestsellers: *La sieste des mamans* (The mummies' nap), *Les trois petits cochons* (The three little pigs), *La grande Panthère noire* (The big black panther), and *Epaminondas*. The most famous of them are *Marlaguette*, *Michka*, *La vache orange* (The orange cow), and *Roule galette* (Roll pie/cookie). Some of the texts are adapted into English versions as language learning tools, including *Les bons amis*, translated as "Good friends," and *Petit chat perdu*, translated as "Little lost kitten."

The publication of Les Classiques du Père Castor and new Père Castor titles in paperback formats was a major change in editorial policy, reflecting an effort to adapt to new reading practices. The move was even more daring in the case of Père Castor audiobooks as the production of tapes was scattered among various publishers, some of whom aimed at entertainment rather than literary or educational fiction, and the balance between narrative and music was neither clearly identified nor thought through. Thus Père Castor's audiobooks were the first book collection in France to be, as a whole, transferred into audible versions.

This change led to the reformatting of Père Castor's classics: square-shaped albums, in Italian format, were altered into smaller rectangular booklets, in French format, encased with the matching tape in a plastic cover. These audiobooks looked like printed books. The text remained identical, but pictures were altered to captions or restricted to only one page rather than spread across the double-page as in the original. In several cases new illustrations, requested from a different illustrator than the original, were deemed necessary to aid consumers in adjusting to the new product, so that the appeal of the booklet in the packaging of taped audiobooks resembled that of the contemporary paperback. The "notebook" touch of the original albums on thick off-white paper that had made classics unpretentious, familiar, and attractive to children was lost: the booklet inside was thinner and cheap-looking with its glossy white paper. Yet the added sound, voice, and music supplemented the loss, and the narrative experience was not affected by the changes. As tapes became outdated, Père Castor audiobooks restored the album to its original format in paper and the illustrations to their original designs, only slitting a CD (duplicated from the tape or identically rerecorded without any change in style or settings) into the inside of the back cover.

Transferring albums into audiobooks was not meant to be a new editorial line as it was open neither to future titles nor to titles directly composed and conceived of as "talking books." Rather, republication was meant as an adaptation and revival of previous titles wherein the acoustic profile is

Figure 10.1a Sample audiobook covers from the series Albums-disques, Les classiques du Père Castor (Paris: Flammarion, 1976–2002) (Courtesy of Editions Père Castor-Flammarion).

Bedtime Storytelling Revisited 181

Figure 10.1b Sample audiobook cover.

Figure 10.1c Sample audiobook cover.

182 *Brigitte Ouvry-Vial*

Figure 10.1d   Sample audiobook cover.

Figure 10.1e   Sample audiobook cover.

Bedtime Storytelling Revisited   183

strictly consistent with the narrative pattern of the printed version. The acoustic profile in this way meets Philipp Schweighauser's definition of an "audiograph": "a characterization technique that endows fictional bodies with a set of distinctive acoustic properties."[4]

PÈRE CASTOR'S AUDIOGRAPH

The same voice, usually adult and female, tells the story and slightly varies in tone and pitch for the different characters among Père Castor's audiobooks. The voice carefully follows the text; it is clear, rather slow and expressive, and it is distinctly the voice of a reader, not an actor or comedian playing a part. In contrast to Charles Perrault's suggestion, Père Castor's audiobooks do not give auditors a full sense of reality but convey a vague realism, an illusion of reality that sets the story at a distance.

The stories include encounters between a central character, a child (Marlaguette, Epaminondas, Zohio); a childlike animal (a mouse, a cow); childlike vegetation (lilies); natural objects (water drops); or even inanimate objects (toys, pies) and other figures, situations, or realities considered to be adult because they are big or unusual or powerful (bears, crocodiles, mountains, sun, wind, independence, solitude, and so forth). Thus the main narrative voice is eventually relayed by alternate voices representing various characters and simulating animals or natural objects speaking the language of humans.

Such secondary voices—adult male voices or children's voices—match the various pitches of fictitious voices. Audiobooks convey textual suggestions by selecting an adapted voice for the replies: the capricious cow in *La vache orange* and the loyal wolf in *Marlaguette* are voiced in a masculine voice, for instance, while the good helping fox in *La vache orange* is voiced by a child. Yet secondary voices are restricted to nonfrightening characters as the storytelling must not have too big of an impact on young listeners. As a result, all of the voices convey a sense of reassurance, and variations depend on the characters depicted and on the indications given in the text.

The character's tone or manner of speaking may be indicated by the narrator: "Now Marlaguette was looking at the wolf and her anger was soon over. Poor little wolf! She said. He is really injured!"[5] It can be specified as a stage direction in the clause following a reply: "Good night, said the Cow with a deep low voice";[6] it can be stylistically suggested by the wording, as in the Fox's naïve speech ("Oh! oh! oh! cried the Fox, you have eaten far too much grass! You must change a little")[7] or as in Marlaguette's easy, childish playground talk ("Well done! Too bad for you! Marlaguette shouted while mocking the wolf").[8] Animal talk can also be mimicked through alliteration, onomatopoeia, and assonance acting as onomatopoeia: "*Si, Si, Si,* cria l'Oiseau-Moqueur" (*Si, Si, Si,* whistled the mockingbird);[9] "*Hou là! Hou!* Cria-t-il [le loup]" (*Hou là! Hou!* He [the wolf] cried);[10] "*Cra! Cra!*

184　*Brigitte Ouvry-Vial*

Cria le geai" (*Cra! Cra! Cried* the jay).[11] Or the animal's cry may require no specific code or alteration from conventional transcriptions: "The cow sat down and replied: '*Moo . . . Moo . . .* I feel very sick'"[12] or "And the poor cow started crying: *Moo . . . oo . . . Moo . . . oo . . .*"[13] In each case, the dialogue alternates between simulation of an animal's speech and illusory human language, both of which translate the hybrid childlike or animal-like speech and thoughts.

The mere pitch of the voice is enough to distinguish characters without further interpretation. The audio version does not overcharacterize the narrative pattern or dialogues, nor does it erase introductions or conclusions of replies. Although characters' separate identities are easily deciphered through the intervention of a secondary voice pronouncing speech in a direct style, the main narrative voice refrains from suppressing interpolated clauses, instead reporting and describing speech such as "The fox shouted" or "The cow answered." The reader's voice does not detract from the original score, just as one's own voice does not when reading aloud a story to a child after having read the printed book.

STORYTELLING AND SOUND EFFECTS

Throughout each story, a short musical line, generally a simple combination of a few instruments chosen from among clavichord, drums, flute, guitar, trumpet, and xylophone, is repeated identically. This line instantly punctuates the storytelling, as when a storyteller takes a breath, and signals for a fresh page: music discreetly marks blank spaces or transitions between actions, and it indicates to children when to turn the page while giving them the time to do so. During narrative phases of the story, melodies either stop or accompany the voice as musical backing, barely audible in the background. Although tunes are simple, with a binary tempo (1, 2, 1, 2) as in circus music or a brass band march, they are not easily graspable as a refrain or chorus, which means that they work as jingles and not as musical speech. Jingles vary from one audiobook to another in Père Castor's *Classiques*, easing the storytelling and listening process in equal measures like a beatbox.

There are also "noises" which, as in any professional recording, are intentionally part of the soundtrack. They comply with Schweighauser's communicational approach conceptualizing noise not as a disturbance interfering with communication but as a signal that increases information: noises such as knock–knock or rat-tat-tat or the rustling of crumpled fabric are sound effects added to the audible version.[14] Because the narrative is self-sufficient, sound effects are not necessary to complete it or to supplement its meaning. In *La vache orange*, for example, the central scene between the big sick orange cow and the little gray fox who nurses him is rhythmically punctuated by sounds: chewing plastic when the cow sucks

Bedtime Storytelling Revisited   185

a baby bottle; huffing and puffing to suggest the cow's sickness; running water when the fox fills the hot water bottle; the exclamation "atishoo" when the cow sneezes; rumbling and whistling for the train in the cow's dream, and so forth.

Sounds follow and duplicate the narration, mimicking the character's actions, and yet one cannot speak of redundancy. As sound effects use a different language or communicative system, one that is acoustic instead of verbal, they appear as part of a special language brought up by the audible version to enhance the original story. As in live narration, they function as resonances introducing another level of communication to the tale. The effect is playful. Indeed, indexical, recognizable sounds do not introduce a conflict or counterpoint to the narrative as they are neither synchronized with nor as loud as the voice. They echo the narrative in a low key and seem to confirm the tale by giving it an aura of reality, albeit in comical fashion. Studies of readers' responses to children's audiobooks—whether to those of Père Castor or the popular yet lowbrow narrator Marlène Jobert—show that children's listening to an audiobook recording to which a genuine book is attached consists of a combination of hearing, watching, reading words, and looking at pictures.[15] In the minds of young listeners, a proper narrative tone is one that follows the ups and downs of the sentence and marks the dots, commas, exclamation points, and question marks of the text. Their pleasure relies on respect for the written narrative—especially the written sentence and its punctuation—and conveyance of its intended meaning.

As opposed to noises in the "simultaneous poem" described by Douglas Kahn, which "represent the background—the inarticulate, the disastrous, the decisive, [showing] in a typically compressed way . . . the conflict of the *vox humana* with a world that threatens, ensnares, and destroys it," noises in Père Castor's audiobooks are a reassuring means of reconstruction.[16] Superfluous, they slow the narrative process, assessing its verbal statements as gestures acting out speech and thus empowering the three-dimensional audiobook. If picture books can be seen as "iconotexts" wherein meaningful effects rely on the interaction between text, pictures, and the material support of their transmission, then Père Castor's audio picture books are iconotexts (a mixed composition of written and graphic narratives) with an acoustic dimension.[17]

Yet Père Castor's audiobooks take only limited advantage of the possibilities presented by phonography and acoustic tools. Deliberately, rather than for a lack of know-how, they resort to sound effects to emphasize narration to the extent that it does not interfere with the storytelling. Utterly distinct from the voice that they accompany and from musical lines, these sounds have the effect of setting the listener within a specific frame of mediation: the process of storytelling is underscored through artificial sound effects, obvious imitations, and unrealistic mimicry that stage the representation process itself; in freely adding unwritten, nonverbal lines, the audiobook

186 *Brigitte Ouvry-Vial*

theatrically emphasizes the communication process and the acoustic tools on which it relies.

Cries and noises also create an attractive acoustic presence that seduces children and may induce them to laugh or add credibility to the scene. As actual adults reading aloud draw, catch, and keep the attention of children through the power of their physical bodies and intonation, sound effects act alongside alternate voices and music to sensuously enhance the narrative. The impact of Père Castor's audiobooks and other children's audiobooks consists not so much in re-creating bedtime storytelling as in creating an aural setting that reflects previous experiences of stories being passed on to the child through the mediation of an adult voice.

AN EDUCATIONAL APPROACH TO CHILDREN'S LITERATURE

François Faucher had to consider how to adapt to changing times after the political events of 1968 and the start of the modern era in children's literature. In 1975 he declared:

> Sur le fond, je reste fidèle à la pensée de Bakulé et de mon père, pensée fondée sur l'observation, le sens de l'humain, l'éducation de l'imagination, du caractère et du jugement, l'invitation à la création, plutôt que sur l'acquisition de connaissances par trop éloignées des besoins immédiats.

> [I remain true to the theory of [my godfather Frantisek] Bakulé and my father [Paul Faucher], based on observation, sense of humankind, education of the imagination, of the attitude and judgment, on the incentive to create rather than the acquisition of notions way too far from immediate needs.][18]

Thus, he asked, which specific, intrinsic aspects of Les Classiques du Père Castor made it possible, worthwhile, logical, or even necessary to turn these albums from the 1930s to the 1950s into audiobooks? And to which "immediate needs" of the child do the audible versions of Père Castor's classics respond?

Whether as a printed book alone or as a book accompanied by CD, Père Castor's classics are "albums," books in which pictures equally share the space of the page with the written text or in which pictures outweigh the words in the manner of the English picture book. The word "album" (derived from the Latin *albus*, white space for inscriptions and listings) is used in French for multiple objects including photography book, music book, song book, and musical record. In French albums at the turn of the twentieth century, text is secondary; easily readable pictures and visual typography essentially convey the narrative, displaying soft colors to promote good taste and to provide an idealized vision of childhood.[19] Paul Faucher may have inherited his notion of the album from nineteenth-century examples such as Louis Hachette's "Albums Trim pour les enfants de trois à six ans" (1861) and Jules Hetzel's "Albums Stahl" (1866). But he is considered to be the pioneer of the type in France: he conducted a systematic study and invented a radically innovative approach to its format involving a deep understanding of children's personal development and reading practices. Père Castor's classics are original compositions, not fairy tales or legends originating from an oral tradition. They respond to a natural perception of events as a dramatic script, yet one that is written to be read aloud by parents to children: Paul Faucher published them under the pseudonym "Père Castor," literally "Father Beaver," where the beaver is a reading beaver or (in later versions including DVD adaptations of the albums) an anthropomorphic bespectacled figure, half-animal and half-grandfather. As suggested by the "Father Beaver" brand name and logo, in which the beaver alternately stands as the young reader/listener or the adult reading to him, Père Castor's classics belong to a moral and educational outlook favoring a positive, constructive approach to life as well as the transmission to the younger generation of a deeply rooted, unwritten wisdom based on the observation of nature, animals, and the countryside.

Père Castor's primary albums, whether children's activities, tales, or documentaries on animals, all responded to children's narrative intelligence, as the psychologist Jerome Bruner would later put it, an intelligence that enables them to decipher other people's intentions and states of mind, to put themselves at a distance in order to look at the world from another point of view, and to understand someone else's behavior as that of an alter ego, at once similar and different.[20] Before the age of four years old, children are not able to decenter themselves in order to attribute to people beliefs different from their own. Yet developing this skill allows them to construct themselves and others as characters. Thus narratives are a fundamental way through which we give meaning both to our lives and those of others.[21]

According to Paul and François Faucher's way of thinking, the album is not a preformatted object. Instead, it is meant for multiple purposes: speaking, playing, discovering, learning, imagining. The album addresses young children with little or even no reading ability.[22] It must be brief in accordance with the child's capacity for concentration and include simple stories accompanied by pictures to sustain the understanding process. Texts and pictures alike are thoughtfully conceived and produced. Paul Faucher carefully chooses writers and artists from the avant-garde and from Eastern European graphic schools (for instance, Nathalie Parrain and Gerda Müller). It takes about a year to publish a printed book of fewer than twenty pages or an audiobook of comparable length through an essentially

Figure 10.2 Reading Beaver: the current company logo printed on the last page of all titles from the Secondes lectures series, Les Classiques du Père Castor (Paris: Flammarion, 1934–) (Courtesy of Editions Père Castor-Flammarion).

collective process. Similar to the way in which recurring authors and illustrators often sign several titles on paper (Paul François, Natacha, Gerda Müller), the same voices or storytellers consistently record multiple audio titles (Catherine Le Bars and Franca di Rienzo for female voices; Yves Barsacq and Marco Perrin for male voices and as jingle composers); children, only mentioned by their first name (Sebastien, Mathilde, Chantal, Élodie, Fred, Julien, Kathy, Loïc, Marion, Natacha, Régine, Sylvia, François), are often made use of in the recorded versions of several stories. Hence paperback editions and audiobooks result from a mixed team including illustrators and writers; the graphic design, publishing, and printing production group; musicians, composers and the audio design group; and pedagogues, educators, and psychologists sharing an interest in the child's welfare.

Bedtime Storytelling Revisited 189

Discussions of the books with children about their reactions to various drafts influence the decisions made by the group.

Père Castor's albums reflect an educational approach to the material. As stated in an address to the adult mediator at the beginning of particular albums that are strictly "picture books" without text, the objective is to induce children spontaneously and orally to articulate their reactions to the story. With the help of an adult, the child will:

> have the pleasure to recognize, and name objects he knows; identify and attach specifics to characters; analyze and explain, picture by picture, actions, movements and gestures; interpret expressions, looks; compare pictures and establish by deduction the chain of events. Once he has appropriated the various elements of a story, he will build it, add to it as he wishes and will tell it in his own way with the ease he will have acquired during your common "walks" through these pictures.[23]

An analogous educational objective is assigned to the "illustrated" book, designed as "Secondes lectures" or "second readings" following the child's physical and mental development. When the child masters the three first phases of picture reading—enumerating or naming, describing, and interpreting—as well as the differentiation and comparison of the fourth phase, the child is ready to learn how to read. Thus, Faucher states, whereas a more elaborated and focused type of reading appears, illustration becomes a substitute for pictures; it conveys the general context, describes the atmosphere, announces an action to come, and completes the written narrative, but the text narrates the main part of the story. Whatever the age of the child, the album, whether it is a picture book or an illustrated book, is the means to answer children's needs, to connect children through its reliance on applied pedagogy, psychology, literature, graphic art, and editorial techniques.

In accordance with this line of thought, Père Castor's audiobooks must respond to similar needs and concerns. Père Castor's albums on paper were meant to be the basis for verbal and oral narration, a verbalization of pictures initiated by the adult, possibly even imitated and rehearsed with him, and then ultimately carried out by the child alone: while induced to read aloud to himself a book open in front of him, the child reader stands as both the listener and the independent producer, the "voicer" of a home-made, self-produced, and unrecorded audiobook.

CHILDREN'S AUDIOBOOKS AND READING PRACTICES

Books in general are the means of mental representations transmitted by an author to a reader through a set of signs. As reader-response theory has shown, a text gains meaning by the purposeful act of a reader reading and interpreting it.[24] This suggests that texts do not exist without readers,

190   *Brigitte Ouvry-Vial*

and it implies that reading is not a one-way, top-down process from the book and implied author to the reader; rather, reading is also a bottom-up process, as readers themselves produce mental representations of their own based on experience or personal context, thus imposing or superimposing their responses onto the author's message. In other words, reading can be viewed as an individual process of reconstruction within the constraints of a written text.

This is especially true for children's reading, not because we may see it as an interpretive community but because of the child's cognitive style of reading: a physical, practical, functional, unconventional gesture of handling or relating to a book that implies deciphering, decoding words and pictures, and many other operations such as touching, laughing, jumping, imagining, extrapolating, identifying with characters, and playing a part in the narrative. Reading for a child is a means of self-construction, of building one's identity through a variety of methods among which consciously focusing in order to understand a specific story, an author's message, or a book's meaning is a secondary issue. At the same time, repetition or rereading is a typical pattern and the means of self-construction, as Père Castor's audiobooks acknowledge.

As Italo Calvino states in *Why Read the Classics?*, "The classics are those books about which you usually hear people saying: 'I'm rereading . . . ', never 'I'm reading . . . '"[25] Calvino elaborates by adding: "A classic is a book which with each rereading offers as much of a sense of discovery as the first reading" and "A classic is a book which has never exhausted all it has to say to its reader."[26] Père Castor classics are classics according to Calvino's definition because they shape children's future experiences, providing examples, role models, terms of comparison, and many other elements that remain active and influential throughout one's life, even when adults have forgotten a book read during childhood. They are also classics because they are never read once and for all but always read, told, narrated, thumbed, leafed through, flicked through, and glanced at again and again in addition to being transmitted from one generation to the other. Reading a favorite story for a child is a repetitive process of rereading it or, prior to the mastery of reading skills, a process of rehearing it again and again from a familiar voice—a feature indulged by Père Castor's audiobooks. The most obvious proof of the fact is that at L'Heure Joyeuse, the first children's library in France, copies of Père Castor audiobooks are renewed after every ten borrowers because listeners use the audiobooks so intensively. Just as one likes to replay a favorite tune, young audiobook listeners like to replay a favorite story. Each hearing adds to the previous one in order to build not only the child's general literacy but also an "imaginary text" that becomes an intrinsic part of the child's life and educational experience: this imaginary text consists in the basic story itself as it is progressively supplemented, superseded, enriched, and transformed by the diversity of private or personal listening sessions to which it has been submitted.[27]

A COMMUNICATIONAL APPROACH TO BOOKS

Altogether audiobooks demonstrate an interest in developing the child's linguistic skills and need for security; they also enhance children's ability to think freely and by themselves, to express tastes and judgments of their own. Thus, audiobooks comply with a communicational approach to books for children, that is to say an approach based not only on a practical subject-to-object relationship but also on a pragmatic subject-to-subject relationship.[28] In the case of a child's reading, the pragmatic, subject-to-subject relationship offered by the book is duplicated by the adult's intervention or mediation: for nonreading infants, books are identified as objects voiced out by their parents or surrounding adults; they first learn how to read by imitation, holding the book upright (even if upside down), following the black lines with their fingers, and producing accompanying sounds, from burbles to phrases.[29] Moreover, children attach the book to the voice that propels it, sometimes touching the adult's throat as an intrinsic part of the device. Were it not for pictures, the album would appear as a record requiring a human player to be heard.

Oddly enough, as Daniel Bougnoux has noticed,[30] at a time when the era of printed books or "graphosphere" is being replaced by the new order of videosphere, many fear the separation of culture from print.[31] Yet the printed book, inky black on white paper, with its regular, justified lines of typesettings and block letters, is among the most severe modes of representation, one that retains little of the sensory aspects of oral speech. The reader is isolated and, because *less is more,* as Nicholas Negroponte used to say, the typographic austerity of the book is the means of a mental, if not spiritual, liberation: the reader's consciousness focuses on the inner message of the book, enticing him or her to develop an individual analysis, a critical approach to knowledge, an ability to imagine, extract, and recompose a world from the black and white symbols.

Obviously children's books tend to alleviate this sense of isolation and lack of external seductiveness: attractive, colorful covers and pictures break the linear, rigid succession of words and allow a free, random, multidirectional circulation of the eye on the visible space of the page. Texts and pictures congregate and combine with each other in children's books to sustain the child's mental representations. Pictures and illustrations also compensate for the relative dryness of the printed text. As the impact of images is stronger and their potential danger or impact greater than text for a young, sensitive mind, pictures also tend to represent situations and characters in a milder or metaphoric way. Whereas the third meaning thus created may be specific to each individual reader, the general purpose is to convey a sense of security, to relate the child to a circumscribed world wherein one feels at home and where reality only enters drop by drop.

Children's audiobooks operate accordingly. One could take for granted that taste, time, or a reduction in reading abilities factor among the

192   *Brigitte Ouvry-Vial*

specific conditions attached to the success of contemporary audiobooks; yet children's reading, when considered in relation to its real or imagined environment and goals, brings forward unexpected findings about the circumstances in which young readers resort to audiobooks rather than to print, or to both audiobooks and print.

First, similarly to other new technologies of transmission, children's audiobooks operate as a filter: they create an intermediary reality, neither inside nor outside.[32] Second, audiobooks relay and supplement traditional printed works: the voice is an indicator of the transmitter's body that pilots the message and counteracts abstraction; the illusion of a presence, of direct, albeit deferred oral speech, adds to the seductive, soothing effect of the pictures on the attached booklet.

Third, audiobooks exercise the "auditory imagination" by restoring or replicating a communicational experience that is intrinsic to the child's primary or acquired narrative experience in which knowledge, culture, and imagination are relayed and transmitted by way of the book.[33] Studies tend to show that reading aloud is not practiced as often in the second half of the twentieth century as it used to be in previous eras; one reason for the decline is children's access to diverse listening, watching, and interactive recreational devices.[34] Yet technical objects are nevertheless social connections, albeit surrogate ones, and social relationships are shaped and conducted by technology. As is shown by Père Castor's Classiques albums in audible versions, audiobooks enhance rather than diminish the relational function and purpose of the album despite the lack of a real body voicing the story.[35] As Matthew Rubery suggests, hearing an audiobook has to do with the "perpetual immediacy" recommended by voice actor Barbara Rosenblat as a way "to recreate as far as possible the childhood experience of hearing stories read aloud," a phenomenon "described in synaesthetic terms through an aphorism formulated by Murray Schafer: 'hearing is a way of touching at a distance.'"[36]

Fourth, resorting to audiobooks is not the way in which, as Marshall McLuhan suggests, "our age translates itself back into the oral and auditory modes because of the electronic pressure of simultaneity."[37] On the contrary, it is precisely the electronic pressure of simultaneity that sustains the turn toward audiobooks for children: reading a printed book is an activity of its own that excludes doing other activities (except listening to music in the background); listening to an audiobook can be done alongside other tasks or endeavors, from traveling, walking, drawing, cooking, or playing to . . . reading another book! Although this takes us far from Père Castor Classiques, which are short "minutes" albums (from five to eight minutes at most) for younger children dedicated to story-time and intense listening, a study by a leading French documentation center, La Joie par les livres, and children's library, L'Heure Joyeuse, suggests that many heavy audiobook consumers tend to read a printed book or rather a comic book while simultaneously listening to an unrelated story on audiobook.[38]

Fifth, as Joy Alexander finds in her survey of Northern Irish pupils, 39 percent of 120 first- and second-year students, 12 percent of 65 third- and fourth-year students, and 22 percent of 125 sixth-form students said that they currently listened to audiobooks, whereas respectively 38 percent and 48 percent of the two latter groups said they had done so in the past and preferred print.[39] Asked about the merits and limits of specific titles (for instance, H. G. Wells's *The War of the Worlds* and Lee Hall's *Spoonface Steinberg*) as well as what they liked or disliked about the experience, the students gave answers showing a strong interest in the acoustic medium: "It is like other people reading for me"; "I liked the way it sounded so realistic"; "I liked it because it sounded so believable"; "I enjoyed it because it seemed very real and even though it was on the radio you could picture nearly everything"; "I liked it very much. I thought it was very life-like and very interesting to listen to it"; "It was fun to listen to."

Yet the students point to an equal and reverse preference for reading print because of negative aspects of the audible version: "I don't really enjoy it because they don't sound the way I think they do"; "I like to read in my mind and create my own voices for characters; "I would prefer reading a book at your own speed"; "I listened to them in primary school and I found them boring. It is much better to read it yourself." Some answers illustrate the listening practices of new generations—"You can just concentrate on listening"—or the current sense that reading print requires too much effort—"I don't like reading—only if it's a good book. Listening was better." They also point to a different, weaker experience: "I feel listening to a story you need a good imagination. I probably would like reading better." In the latter, "listening," understood as a skill of comprehension acquired over time and requiring concentration, could solely mean "hearing," the mere ability to perceive sound and one of the traditional five senses that may impair children's imaginary skills. Thus today's audiobooks still exercise the auditory imagination by inducing the transient state of mind and distant approach to reality that was brought about in the past solely by printed books.

THE GAME OF READING

Alexander's findings point to a distinctive purpose of reading—especially children's reading—to which both audiobooks and printed books attend: books as play. For children reading is not just leisure but a game. For adults too, reading may replace recreational activities such as cards, crosswords, or handcrafts. It is a game with literary effect, as has been suggested by several critics,[40] and yet no one had attempted a scientific approach of this game until Michel Picard's *La lecture comme jeu.*[41] Picard observes that children often associate reading with writing and drawing, but his analysis goes beyond the case of children; he resorts to various theories to present

194 Brigitte Ouvry-Vial

reading as a game obeying a set of rules and to outline the effects of reading experiences seen as playful. Although it would be interesting to apply Picard's ideas to specific cases of audiobooks and children's audiobooks in particular, there is insufficient space to do so in this chapter. Instead, let us simply lay out its guiding principles after Johan Huizinga's well-known essay on play. Trying to understand play as a cultural factor in life, Huizinga observes that "the great archetypal activities of human society are all permeated with play from the start" (notably language, which is playing with the wondrous nominative faculty, playing on words). He also observes that "although [play] is a non materialistic activity it has no moral function," and yet it cannot altogether be included in the realms of the aesthetic despite close links to beauty: thus Huizinga concludes that "play is a function of the living, but is not susceptible of exact definition either logically, biologically or aesthetically."[42]

Significantly enough, Huizinga approaches the notion of play by stating that one should "take play as the player himself takes it: in its primary significance" and gives an example: "If we find that play is based on the manipulation of certain images, on a certain 'imagination' of reality (i.e. its conversion into images), then our main concern will be to grasp the value and significance of these images and their 'imagination.'"[43] It seems appropriate to apply Huizinga's definition of play to the story-hearing experience—a free act that is felt as "fictitious" and remote from daily life, able to fully absorb the player, in accordance with fixed rules, generative of group relationships, and surrounded with mystery.

According to Huizinga's line of reasoning, children's audiobooks as middle- or lowbrow cultural objects (despite the highbrow quality of the texts recorded) belong to the game-play category. They consist of a voluntary activity done during one's free time. Whether or not they are considered educational by adults who provide them to nurture necessary faculties, audiobooks are not bound up with notions of obligation. They imply "stepping out of 'real' life into a temporary sphere of activity with a disposition of its own": all children, says Huizinga, know perfectly well that they are "only" pretending, as the conjuring effect of technology emitting and receiving a recorded voice sustains the pretense. For audiobooks, as for play, this pretense "doesn't prevent it from proceeding with the utmost seriousness with an absorption, a devotion, that passes into rapture and, temporarily at least, completely abolishes that troublesome 'only' feeling." Most of all, listening to an audiobook as play is free and thus enjoyable: "Play is superfluous. The need for it is only urgent to the extent that the enjoyment of it makes it a need."[44]

What then is the value of Père Castor's audiobooks? They remain special editions, as they are restricted to the Classiques Albums series. With the passing of time, they have become literary and historical landmarks. In today's urban societies they recall a rural life with which children are no longer familiar. Seemingly old-fashioned, audiobooks remain plausible;

they exercise a reader's ability to imagine; they provide a reassuring visual narrative along with an acoustic context; and ultimately they convey a message of hope and a sense of responsibility for children's life and endeavor. The naïve point of view adopted by the audiobooks of Père Castor strongly contrasts with that of today's series in which young readers are confronted with harsh contemporary issues. The idea that books should allow children to grow up in a protected environment, one that is adapted to their scale, size, and needs, is a distinctive feature of Père Castor's approach; it distinguishes him from other major publishers of quality literature for children, even François Ruy-Vidal and Harlin Quist, who appeared as distant followers in the 1970s and 1980s. Yet despite—or possibly because of—the sense of affective security and the old-fashioned social and psychological setting of the stories which contradict experiences of twenty-first-century children, Père Castor's fiction still offers a window to the world. How little the world in Père Castor's audiobooks resembles the world portrayed in today's media

Figure 10.3 Beaver reading over child's shoulder. From the cover to a promotional document for Paul Faucher, *A L'enseigne du Père Castor* (Paris: Flammarion, 1982) (Courtesy of Editions Père Castor-Flammarion).

196   *Brigitte Ouvry-Vial*

remains relevant: it is an accurate understanding of children's lasting exposure to adult surroundings, and it retains a philosophical value in strengthening children while suggesting resistance and enthusiasm.

Père Castor audiobooks derive from educational theories they subsequently broadcast. They relay an affective ritual of bedtime storytelling revisited by technical tools but not disembodied—in fact, the series' leading title *Michka* displays Père Castor's founding father Paul Faucher's very own voice.[45] The pictures in the print albums have aged, but the voices in the audiobooks update the stories. These audiobooks are regenerating the cultural phenomenon of storytelling for later generations of listeners.

NOTES

1. Marc Soriano, *Les contes de Perrault, culture savante et traditions populaires* (Paris: Gallimard, 1977), 153.
2. The full list is available at Le Père Castor: La liste des albums, http://www.pour-enfants.fr/pere-castor/albums-9.htm.
3. The full list of audiobook titles is available in the Catalogue des bibliothèques municipales spécialisées, http://bspe-p-pub.paris.fr, and at Livraphone online bookshop, http://www.livraphone.com/.
4. Philipp Schweighauser, *The Noises of American Literature, 1890–1985: Toward a History of Literary Acoustics* (Gainesville: University Press of Florida, 2006), 71.
5. Marie Colmont, *Marlaguette* (Paris: Père Castor, Flammarion, 1955), 11. Audiobook (Enregistrement sonore) read by Sylvia et François; illustrated by Gerda; music by Hugues Le Bars (Paris: Père Castor, Flammarion, [1984]). References for the following quotations will indicate page number in the printed book rather than minutes in the audiobook. The emphasis in italicized phrases is my own.
6. Nathan Hale, *La vache orange* (Paris: Flammarion, Les petits Père Castor, 12, 1942), 5. Audiobook read by Lucile Butel [s.d.].
7. Hale, *La vache orange*, 4.
8. Colmont, *Marlaguette*, 11.
9. Marie Colmont, *Histoire de Zo'hio,* illustrated by Gérard de Sainte-Croix (Paris: Père Castor-Flammarion, 1943), 6.
10. Colmont, *Marlaguette*, 10. The comic wailing sound "Hou là! Hou!" which suggests that the wolf has hurt himself, as in the interjection "ouille"/"ouch," is a slight distortion of the conventional frightening howl of the wolf: "houuuu."
11. Colmont, *Marlaguette*, 5.
12. Hale, *La vache orange*, 4.
13. Hale, *La vache orange,* 20.
14. See Schweighauser's discussion of Claude E. Shannon's work on information theory in relation to noise, in *The Noises of American Literature*, 6–8.
15. A former film actress, Marlène Jobert has recorded numerous stories for the Hachette audiobook series. Popular among children, her recordings are less favored by parents who find the style of her narratives to be lowbrow entertainment.
16. Douglas Kahn, *Noise, Water, Meat: A History of Sound in the Arts* (Cambridge: MIT Press, 2001), 49.
17. See Isabelle Nières-Chevrel, *Introduction à la littérature de jeunesse* (Paris: Didier Jeunesse, 2009), 118.

18. Quoted in Marc Soriano, *Guide de la littérature de jeunesse* (Paris: Flammarion, 1975), 241. My translation.
19. See Annie Renonciat, "BnF, Babar, Harry Potter et cie: Livres d'enfants d'hier et d'aujourd'hui." http://expositions.bnf.fr/livres-enfants/
20. Bruner made a detailed study of the child's cognitive development based on the principle that one understands and builds one's world in terms of differences and resemblances. See Jerome Bruner, *The Process of Education* (Cambridge: Harvard University Press, 1960); *Toward a Theory of Instruction* (Cambridge: Harvard University Press, 1966); and *Child's Talk: Learning to Use Language* (New York: W. W. Norton, 1983).
21. Jean Molino and Raphaël Lafhail-Molino, "Le récit, un mécanisme universel: Contes et récits: pourquoi aimons-nous les histoires?" *Sciences humaines* 148 (2004): 22–25.
22. See the three stages "Enactive Action," "Iconic Image," and "Symbolic Word" identified by Bruner in his research on children. John Bruner, *Toward a Theory of Instruction* (Cambridge: Harvard University Press, 1966).
23. Paul Faucher, *A l'enseigne du Père Castor* (Paris, Flammarion: 1982), 34.
24. For more on this approach, see the essays in Jane P. Tompkins, ed., *Reader-Response Criticism: From Formalism to Post-Structuralism* (Baltimore: Johns Hopkins University Press, 1980).
25. Italo Calvino, *Why Read the Classics?* trans. Martin McLaughlin (London: Vintage, 2000), 3.
26. Italo Calvino, *Why Read the Classics?* 5.
27. Quoted in Matthew Rubery, "Play It Again, Sam Weller: New Digital Audiobooks and Old Ways of Reading," *Journal of Victorian Culture* 13 no. 1 (2008), 61.
28. I use this term as defined by Daniel Bougnoux, *Introduction aux sciences de la communication* (Paris: La Découverte, 2001), 9.
29. Rolande Causse, ed., *L'enfant lecteur* (Paris: Autrement, 1988), 71
30. Bougnoux, *Introduction*, 92–93.
31. Régis Debray, *Cours de médiologie générale* (Paris: Gallimard, 1991), 51. Debray distinguishes three mediaspheres: "logosphere," dominated by scripture; "graphosphere," dominated by print; and "videosphere," dominated by audiovisual technologies.
32. Bougnoux, *Introduction*, 70.
33. The expression is borrowed from Joy Alexander, "Audio Books and Young People: Exercising the Auditory Imagination," paper presented at The Irish Society for the Study of Children's Literature Conference "Sound Image Text," Trinity College, Dublin, March 5–6, 2010.
34. See Anne H. Bustarret, *La fureur d'écouter, l'enfant, ses cassettes et ses disques* (Paris: L'Ecole des Parents-Syros alternatives, 1992) and Françoise Tenier, http://enfantsalecoute.blogspirit.com/.
35. Bougnoux, *Introduction*, 70.
36. Quoted in Rubery, "Play It Again," 72.
37. Marshall McLuhan, *The Gutenberg Galaxy* (London: Routledge and Kegan Paul, 1962), 72.
38. La joie par les livres, professional and educational documentation center on children's literature online review and Web site, http://lajoieparleslivres. bnf.fr/. See La revue des livres pour enfants: Caroline Rives, "L'audiovisuel à la bibliothèque," *Cinéma et lectures de jeunesse* 140 (1991) and "Dossier jeunes lecteurs et multimedia," *Cinéma et lectures de jeunesse* 195 (2000).
39. Joy Alexander, "Audio Books." Subsequent quotations are all taken from Alexander's survey, which was conducted in 2009.

40. See, for example, Roland Barthes, *Plaisir du texte* (Paris: Seuil/Points, 1982), 11; Norman N. Holland, *The Dynamics of Literary Response* (New York: Oxford University Press, 1968); and Jacques Ehrmann, "Game, Play, Literature," special issue of *Yale French Studies* 41 (1968).
41. Michel Picard, *La lecture comme jeu* (Paris: Minuit, 1986).
42. Johan Huizinga, *Homo Ludens: A Study of the Play-Element in Culture*, trans. R. F. C. Hull (London: Routledge and Kegan Paul, 2002), 6, 4, 7. Picard himself recalls Huizinga as a starting point of his essay.
43. Huizinga, *Homo Ludens*, 7.
44. Huizinga, *Homo Ludens*, 8.
45. Probably recorded as part of the tests conducted in l'Atelier du Père Castor before Faucher's death in 1967.

11 Learning from LibriVox

Michael Hancher

Founded in August 2005, the LibriVox international collective of readers-aloud[1] has posted more than three thousand audiobooks online, gratis, which have been downloaded, in whole or in part, more than five million times.[2] In the process it has begun to release poems and novels, histories and treatises from the abstraction of the page and to give them voice, renewing some of the popular protocols for articulate reading that were formalized, disciplined, and finally extinguished by Elocution a century ago.[3]

The LibriVox phenomenon can partly be recognized for what it is not: it is not the result of special training, although all of its participants have been schooled in one way or another; and, with few exceptions, it is not the product of professional skills. The range of accomplishment that different readers bring to their task is remarkable and often impressive—as is the global and social range of English accents. As one volunteer commented in an online LibriVox forum, "We love accents; we love variety; we love books and voices. We embrace American Southerners who read Jane Austen and Scot Highlanders who read Zane Grey equally. All are welcome."[4] (Most LibriVox readings are in English, although the archive of readings in other languages is rapidly growing.)[5] International accents aside, the range of reading skills may approximate what many listeners were accustomed to hearing in the eighteenth and nineteenth centuries, when reading aloud was a common social activity.

Otherwise, the LibriVox product resembles the more established commodity of the audiobook, which found a growing audience as cassette tapes gave way to CDs and then to MP3 files. Both LibriVox recordings and audiobooks embody a dramatic performance that is barely traced when a reader confronts the page alone. Also, the listening experience usually remains as private as the silent-reading experience: neither LibriVox nor a commercial audiobook restores the world in which persons, viva voce, customarily shared the same social space.

In 1880 a reviewer for the London weekly journal *Literary World* noticed, and regretted, the decline of communal reading that was already taking place:

> Reading aloud has fallen into disuse in families and in the social circle, because we read so much. The newspaper and the cheap novel have

200   *Michael Hancher*

> combined to bring this about. We rise from the table, we seize each of us a newspaper or a new paper-covered novel, and we plunge into their pages, and sit unsociably silent. We even resent the reading of anything aloud to us, because it interrupts our own selfish solitary pleasure, and because we think that we could have read the passage so much more quickly by ourselves. The pleasure of a common enjoyment is disregarded in favour of our own greedy devouring of our solitary mental meal; the charm of the sound of the human voice, conveying to us shades of meaning and points of emphasis, is undervalued, and seems to be passing away as one of the delights of life.[6]

An audiobook reading, whether published by LibriVox or another agency, restores something of that "charm of the sound of the human voice," at least partly "conveying to us shades of meaning, and points of emphasis"— if not actually freeing us from our solitariness and restoring the pleasures of "the social circle."

Like other audiobooks, LibriVox audio files also enable access to the printed word for millions of people who have a print disability of some kind. A LibriVox Web page for teachers mentions that function, and the topic is occasionally addressed by volunteers in LibriVox forum postings.[7]

In such ways LibriVox reading resembles the reading of other audiobooks. In other ways it will be different. As has already been suggested, a typical LibriVox recording will be an amateur project, in both senses of the word; not professional, but earnest. It will also be less shaped to market constraints. Especially when published on tape or compact disc, commercial audiobooks have often been abridged for economic reasons, but LibriVox readings are generously complete. (Read aloud, it turns out, a typical Victorian three-decker novel will last more than thirty hours.) A commercial audiobook may punch up the emotion with music, like the movies, but a LibriVox reading will rely on words alone.

Furthermore, as a Web 2.0 community the participants in LibriVox are distinctive, behaving in ways that an audiobook publisher (like any commercial publisher) could not, and expressing information about their interests as readers like that previously shown by the volunteers for Project Gutenberg.[8] That online text-publication project, years older than Google Books and now cast in its shadow, has so far supplied the source texts for most LibriVox readings. Like Project Gutenberg, LibriVox constrains the literary tastes of its participants to just what the law of copyright permits: that is, to books published before 1923.[9] The canon that its readers construct will necessarily be an old canon. But not necessarily *the* old canon: that is, not just the canon constructed by the schools up to the recent past. The choices made by this new collectivity of readers, although constrained by a chronological limit, range more widely than any syllabus and are open to inspection at a time when many scholars seek to recognize the experience of real (rather than ideal) readers.[10] Upwards of thirty-five hundred volunteers contribute to this construction of taste,[11] although the influence of a small set of those volunteers has been disproportionate, as has been the case with Wikipedia and other collaborative online projects.[12] This chapter will register the literary values constructed or expressed by LibriVox readers and also by their listeners, who give voice to their own values by deciding what to listen to and whose decisions are counted. The analysis will concentrate on statistical information derived from the main depository for LibriVox recordings, the noncommercial Internet Archive.[13]

The assertively noncommercial aspect of the LibriVox project is important. The economics of LibriVox, poised between what has been called "free riding" on the one hand and "sharecropping" on the other, are devoted to "acoustical liberation of books in the public domain"—which is the slogan that literally underscores the LibriVox logo.[14] "LibriVox" is a genitive construction in Latin—although compounded as one word in the style of contemporary media—which literally means "Voice of the Book." The Latin homonym *liber* (free), although etymologically unrelated to *liber* (book), is too good a pun to ignore, one worthy of Abbie Hoffman, author of *Steal This Book* (1971). With LibriVox, the liberation in question is equivocally liberation *from* the page and *of* the page (as in "information wants to be free").[15] Like Wikipedia, if on a smaller scale, LibriVox is a loosely organized community of ardent volunteers, anarchists of the free market. Not for nothing was the first LibriVox production a collective reading of Joseph Conrad's disruptive novel *The Secret Agent*.[16] How does LibriVox meet utopian expectations for the world of Web 2.0?

Ideally a LibriVox reading would be anechoic: only the voice of the reader enunciating the voice of the text. But an actual LibriVox recording may reveal noise that is made in the world or in the recording system. And each LibriVox reading, as only one reading, summons complementary or supplementary readings to the echo chamber. The quality that characterizes the modern novel, according to Mikhail Bakhtin—"the social diversity of speech types," or "heteroglossia" (*raznorečie*)—is the implicit norm for all the texts in all the genres at LibriVox.[17] Every LibriVox reading is an invitation to another reading. All voices are different; some are adequate or better; more are welcome.

LibriVox recordings are published in several digital formats: MP3 files, at 64Kbps and 128Kbps, and also Ogg Vorbis; in separate chapter files and in zip files containing a whole book. The LibriVox Web site and the Internet Archive Web site together make up the main portal for access; the popular Apple iTunes Web site is another. Most if not all of the LibriVox collection is also mirrored at Project Gutenberg in a greater variety of audio formats.[18] Because LibriVox recordings are based upon public-domain texts, and, furthermore, because they are deliberately released into the public domain, they can be repackaged commercially (for example, published on CDs) and sold.[19] As of April 2010, several dozen such LibriVox titles, identified as such, were offered for sale at eBay.com. A value-added format called Text

202　*Michael Hancher*

Synchronized Audio is also used by a company called AppSessions LLC to produce iClassix brand digital files, which coordinate LibriVox readings with a screen display of the text for presentation on iPhones; selected titles are available online at various sites for prices ranging upwards from ninety-nine cents each. LibriVox files can also be shared informally, or through BitTorrent applications, which, as the name implies, can generate considerable activity.

The advanced search engine at the Internet Archive allows for keyword searching on the term "LibriVox" and for downloading, in spreadsheet format, thirty fields of data; these include the date of posting and total number of copies that have been downloaded since the file was posted.[20] Because there are also other points of access, these local data give an understated measure of the absolute popularity of LibriVox files; but as an index of relative popularity they may be broadly reliable.[21]

The Internet Archive database records both the choices made by the producers of a LibriVox file and choices that are made by the consumers. The choices made by the producers are relatively easy to grasp: they are legible in the titles of the texts that they have bothered to record and see through the production process. But those titles vary in content from a single poem to a collection of stories or even a collection of books, like the Bible. The Bible is the book of books in more than one sense, and most books in the Bible have been separately recorded for LibriVox, often read from more than one edition or in more than one language. Altogether some 3,500 LibriVox titles were separately catalogued by the Internet Archive on March 22, 2010;[22] of these some 138, or almost 5 percent, were books or collections of books of the Bible. The most popular of these, as measured by the total number of downloads, has been Genesis, read in Hebrew by Israel Radvinsky (83,017). The second most popular was Genesis read by various readers in English from the American Standard Version (ASV) of the Bible (41,446); the next was Paul's first epistle to the Corinthians, also from the ASV (21,551). If measured in terms not of total downloads (for some files were posted long before others, skewing the results) but of download rate (that is, average number of downloads per day since a file was posted), the Hebrew and ASV versions of Genesis were closely matched (58.3 and 59.4, respectively), and the ASV versions of Matthew and First Corinthians were virtually tied for third place (23.5 and 23.1). Note that the statistics cited here and below are international; there is no regional information.

Taken together, there were a total of 581,021 downloads of books of the Bible at a rate of 649.6 downloads per day. These are high figures for LibriVox: the second-highest number in each case. Given the ancient and continuing preeminence of the Bible as *the* book, its popularity in LibriVox is no surprise. The consequential spread of literacy in Protestant Europe in the eighteenth and nineteenth centuries was spurred in large part by the importance of being able to read the Bible for oneself, or aloud to one's family. In British Evangelical culture, reading aloud from the Bible was

Learning from LibriVox 203

central to "Victorian domestic routine."[23] Although most LibriVox auditions of the Word will be private and interior rather than domestic, they relate implicitly to past social practice.

Two LibriVox titles have surpassed the Bible in popularity, and they are oddly sorted. The highest per diem download rate was claimed by Boccaccio's *Decameron* (translated by J. M. Rigg) at almost a thousand downloads per day, totaling 367,741. The highest total number of downloads was earned by one of the oldest titles in the LibriVox catalogue, Thomas Hardy's novel *The Return of the Native* (725,062).[24] The *Decameron* is available in 122 separate audio files (all in various formats), as well as in three entire versions; the Hardy novel in 44 files, as well as three entire versions. Despite their separate claims to classic status, the exceptional popularity of the *Decameron* and *The Return of the Native* is not easy to fathom. Do these high numbers result from robotic iteration or some other statistical problem that would discredit them as outliers? Perhaps. Neither work has benefited from recent film treatment, which might boost its popularity.

Certainly some nineteenth-century writers have thrived on the attention of modern media producers: Jane Austen, Emily Brontë, Charles Dickens, Arthur Conan Doyle, Bram Stoker. It makes sense that recordings of *Jane Eyre, Pride and Prejudice, Sense and Sensibility, The Return of Sherlock Holmes, Oliver Twist, Emma, David Copperfield*, and *Dracula* rank among the top-twenty downloads, along with such other classics as *Moby Dick, Huckleberry Finn*, and *Tom Sawyer*.

The last two books would be labeled "Young Adult Fiction" if published today. Other titles in the top twenty that would fall into the same category include *The Swiss Family Robinson* by Johann David Wyss and *Anne of Green Gables* by Lucy Maud Montgomery, each popular in its day. The remaining titles in the top twenty include *Pollyanna* by Eleanor H. Porter; two volumes of Aesop's *Fables*, stories now commonly marketed for children; and another book for children, the first volume of *The Junior Classics* (1912), which collects dozens of classic children's stories and fairy tales. As an anthology for children it resembles *Poems Every Child Should Know* (1904), an Edwardian American collection of poems for recitation that ranked number twenty-three—two places above Lewis Carroll's much-better-known children's book *Alice's Adventures in Wonderland*. The collection's poems are read with sympathy and finesse by Kara Shallenberg, one of the first and most loyal volunteers for LibriVox. Having engaged the attention of her son with children's audiobooks borrowed from the local library, she supplemented them with recordings that she had made herself and was regrettably prevented by copyright from sharing more widely. When Shallenberg heard of the LibriVox public-domain project, she was glad to volunteer, and many of the books that she has read for LibriVox have been books for children.[25] Like reading aloud from the Bible, reading aloud to children is one of the few customs that still survives from the wide range of social-reading practices

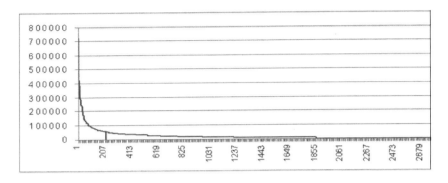

Figure 11.1 LibriVox downloads from Internet Archive by March 22, 2010: copies (complete or partial) plotted against titles.

that enlivened the nineteenth century; therefore it is fitting that LibriVox should be valued as a resource for children's literature. In this respect LibriVox differs from its mute textual resource Project Gutenberg, from which books addressed to children and young adults are in much less demand—save for Mark Twain's famous pair. The other children's books mentioned here depend for their popularity on the human embodiment that they are given by the LibriVox reader's voice.[26]

The top 20 or 25 titles in a list of 3,500 is not, of course, where all the action is. And yet download data does chart a classic "long tail": that is, half of the downloads are accounted for by a mere 210 titles—and the remaining 3,291 divide the rest (see figure 11.1).[27] The boundary is straddled by Aesop (*Fables,* vol. 7) and Milton (*Paradise Lost*). To its right are all the files not in English, some canonical in world literature (for example, Goethe, *Wilhelm Meister's Wanderjahre*), many of them unfamiliar to readers of English at least. The far end of the curve houses many distinctive works that cater to special interests; for instance, Leopold von Sacher-Masoch, *Venus in Furs* (3,023 downloads); Charlotte Smith, *Elegiac Sonnets and Other Poems* (823); John Bunyan, *Pilgrim's Progress,* in French translation (809)—matched by an English translation of Pierre Abelard's *Histoire de mes malheurs* (also 809); and G. E. Moore's *Principia Ethica* (41). The long-tail distribution for downloads per day is somewhat less dramatically compressed to the left, encompassing more than 300 titles on that side. The three titles that happen to straddle the median (37.4 downloads per day) exemplify the variousness of LibriVox: Anatole France, *Penguin Island*; Florence Louisa Barclay, *The Rosary*; and Guy Wetmore Carryl, *Fables for the Frivolous.*

The home page for LibriVox proclaims, "LibriVox volunteers record chapters of books in the public domain and publish the audio files on the

Internet. Our goal is to record all the books in the public domain." Not *some* such books, but *all* of them: the long tail will extend well beyond the horizon. That will take some time: in an interview in November 2008, Hugh McGuire, LibriVox's founder and chief spokesperson, estimated that it might take 550 years for the LibriVox collective to record only the 25,000 books already archived by Project Gutenberg.[28] In the short term, selection will be practiced by the volunteers who commit their time and skill to record, edit, and post each audio file. Eventually, however, nothing will be selected, because everything will be included. LibriVox has far fewer assets than Google (it does not sell files or advertising),[29] but its totalizing ambition is remarkably similar to Google's stated mission "to organize the world's information."[30]

LibriVox is catholic regarding not only the titles that it publishes but also the merits of its recordings. It does not discriminate in terms of the quality of readings aside from editing out intrusive noise and correcting outright mistakes. (Volunteers do proof-audit the files before they are released.) As one volunteer puts it, "Everyone is welcome to volunteer regardless of language, accent, country, age, or vocal ability."[31] Listeners may sense that some LibriVox readers are not as good as others; variation in quality may be especially apparent when the chapters of a book are distributed to a mixed group of volunteers. Some listeners have asked LibriVox to assign a quality grade to each file. LibriVox founder Hugh McGuire resists such calls for critical interference. Instead he offers the hospitality of the free market: if a reader is unhappy with a recording of a text, that reader can supplement it with a reading of his or her own, which LibriVox will gladly host.[32] Let a hundred flowers bloom. Not only will LibriVox provide recordings of "all the books in the public domain": it will provide an indefinite number of recordings of each those books.

The question of the quality of reading aloud is framed by several contradictory truths or truisms. Sometimes a reading will give the illusion of being *the* ideal reading of the text, perfectly realizing what the author wrote. For example, David Barnes's reading of Mr. Fairlie's narrative in *The Woman in White* seems (to me) to be exactly, preternaturally, what Wilkie Collins had in mind when he wrote that section. Opposed to this is the belief that only the text is adequate to its meaning: restricting it to an oral performance must diminish it. (Aristotle glanced in that idealist direction, remarking that tragedy can achieve its effect "even without a dramatic performance and actors"; that is, "simply through reading.")[33] Between these fantastic extremes of perfect embodiment and perfect abstraction is the commonsensical belief that skill in reading aloud is unevenly distributed and that some people are better at it than others.

Certainly the challenges of oral interpretation, as it used to be called, have long been documented. Manuals have cautioned against myriad ways of mangling a text,[34] and ordinary readers, or rather listeners, have found that their appreciation of a text depended on the skill of another reader.

206 *Michael Hancher*

"Papa reads beautifully, and I am sure if I had only read it to myself, I should not have entered into it half so much," Emily Shore noted in her diary in the 1830s. Later she complained that "'Ivanhoe' lost much of its beauty by being badly read." Reporting these remarks, Stephen Colclough and David Vincent comment that "[r]eaders with sophisticated reading skills must often have found listening to a poor reader frustrating."[35]

If a reading disappoints, offer a better one, McGuire recommends; LibriVox will publish it also. And readers have indeed made multiple readings, although not necessarily out of dissatisfaction with what is available: enthusiasm for an author or a book may be enough to motivate the extra effort. There are several dozen books that volunteers have read more than once for LibriVox, either as solo readers or in groups. These tend to track the profile of popularity reported above, and Twain, Brontë, Austen, and Montgomery all have drawn repeated efforts from LibriVox volunteers. Montgomery's *Anne of Green Gables* and Austen's *Persuasion* share the honor of being the most-recorded novel: five times each. Austen takes the prize overall: five of her six complete novels have been recorded two, three, four, or five times apiece. LibriVox volunteers have been as loyal to Austen as have producers for televison and the movies.

Another kind of iterative rereading is less obvious in the LibriVox catalogue (which offers limited search options) but more suggestive: that is, the weekly collection of multiple readings of the same lyric poem, usually performed by at least half a dozen readers and sometimes by more than a dozen. The Weekly Poetry Project, as it is called, was designed to introduce new volunteers to the LibriVox experience, including practice in the various LibriVox protocols for recording, processing, and uploading sound files. A similar function is served by readers periodically assembling a collection of short stories, but the result in that case is different: the prose collections are additive, one story after another, whereas the poetry collections are iterative—the same poem, again and again. Or *is* it the same poem when read in different voices? So, too, for novels: is *Persuasion* the same book in each of its five LibriVox readings?

By March 2010 a total of 163 poems had been selected for the Weekly Poem Project.[36] Many, although not all, are standard anthology pieces; indeed, ten of them figure in *The Classic Hundred Poems: All-Time Favorites*, the quintessential anthology of English and American poetry compiled by William Harmon of the poems that had been most often included in other anthologies.[37] These LibriVox favorites were, in Harmon order: John Keats, "Ode: To Autumn" (according to Harmon, *the* most anthologized poem); Samuel Taylor Coleridge, "Kubla Khan"; John Donne, "Death Be Not Proud"; Matthew Arnold, "Dover Beach"; William Blake, "The Tiger"; Gerard Manley Hopkins, "Spring and Fall"; Percy Bysshe Shelley, "Ozymandias"; Shakespeare, Sonnet 116 ("Let me not to the marriage of true minds"); Robert Browning, "Home Thoughts from Abroad"; and Elizabeth Barrett Browning, Sonnet 43 ("How do I love thee?"). Three had even appeared in F. T. Palgrave's bellwether anthology *The Golden Treasury of the Best Songs and Lyrical Poems in English*[38]: that is, Shakespeare's sonnet 116; Shelley's "Ozymandias"; and Keats's autumn ode.

Probably the most conspicuous, yet most explicable, omission from this list is Milton's "Lycidas," despite its plausible claim to be the best lyric poem in English.[39] Aside from the well-known reasons that Samuel Johnson gave for deprecating it, "Lycidas" is long and littered with unfamiliar words and names, a challenge for any contemporary reader, especially a reader aloud. The rival claimant, Keats's autumn ode, is more compact, less prickly, and easier to say; fifteen volunteers gave it a reading for LibriVox. The best is James Gladwin's reading. For one thing, he respects the enjambments; too many contemporary readers of verse rest at the end of each line, no matter what the syntax is doing.

Despite the endorsements accumulated from Palgrave and other anthologists, the autumn ode did not attract much attention from LibriVox listeners, generating hardly a dozen downloads per day. The two most popular selections proved to be Lewis Carroll's "Jabberwocky" and Rudyard Kipling's "If"—two resonant, if differently positioned, Victorian accounts of the will to prevail over insuperable difficulties. It is tempting to read the first poem as a deconstruction of the second, which "was voted Britain's favourite poem in a BBC opinion poll in 1995."[40] "Jabberwocky" ranked second in the number of total downloads (49,474) and second highest in the number of downloads per day (43.1); also second highest in the number of participating readers (34). The quality range is wide here, but listeners will do well to track the readings by several LibriVox veterans, Lizzie Driver, Kara Shallenberg, David Barnes, and Justin Brett—with Brett capturing just the right note of danger. Martin Clifton's reading of "If" has the merit of making the poem sound perfectly reasonable.

Robert Frost's "Good Hours" attracted 41 readers, more than any other poem in the series; but it proved less popular with listeners. James Gladwin, recording at Exeter, England, is one of the few to register the apologetic function of the phrase "by your leave." Lee Ann Howlett also does a good job of signaling the implications of what is said. Another poem that attracted many readers (29) but relatively few auditors, perhaps because of its title, was W. B. Yeats's "When You Are Old." Here the question of "correct pronunciation" is forced at the outset, with many readers identifying the author as "Yeets." Ernst Pattynama and Ruth Golding give this poem particularly effective readings. Other lyrics that attracted many readers but still lodge toward the end of the long tail include "Snow-flakes" by Henry Wadsworth Longfellow (21 readers); "Velvet Shoes" by Elinor Wylie (24); and "Life's Tragedy" by Paul Laurence Dunbar (27). Eleven readers recorded George Ellis's "The Twelve Months"—twelve words long, a trial for expressive reading—which was downloaded an average of 2.5 times a day.

One might have hoped for thirteen readers to read Wallace Stevens's "Thirteen Ways of Looking at a Blackbird." As it is, Alan Davis-Drake

208   *Michael Hancher*

gives it a thoroughly convincing reading in his collection of the poems that Stevens published before 1923. Two stanzas in particular seem to speak to the LibriVox multiplex:

> V
> I do not know which to prefer,
> The beauty of inflections
> Or the beauty of innuendoes,
> The blackbird whistling
> Or just after.

And especially:

> VIII
> I know noble accents
> And lucid, inescapable rhythms;
> But I know, too,
> That the blackbird is involved
> In what I know.

The ultimate test of LibriVox heteroglossia must be T. S. Eliot's *The Waste Land*, that ruined monument of high Modernism. Eliot had tentatively titled the manuscript "He Do the Police in Different Voices," echoing a remark by Betty Higden, the kind old woman in Dickens's *Our Mutual Friend* who cared for the orphan boy named Sloppy.[41] Less skilled at reading than her ward, she benefited from his dramatized readings-aloud from police reports: "You mightn't think it, but Sloppy is a beautiful reader of a newspaper. He do the Police in different voices."[42] Many LibriVox readers of Victorian novels have comparable ventriloquistic skill, shifting voice to distinguish the many characters conjured up by Dickens or Anthony Trollope. Mil Nicholson's performances of the multitudinous voices that inhabit *Dombey and Son* are exemplary.[43]

The Waste Land is an echo chamber of different voices in different languages, some quoting, some improvising. The multiplicity of LibriVox recordings of the "same" text compounds these voices exponentially. Although the challenges of reading *The Waste Land* surely exceed those of reading "Lycidas"—its many languages themselves being an impediment— six LibriVox volunteers have accepted the quest, one on his own and five in a Weekly Poetry Project. Basil Munroe Godevenos's reading of the poem is not error-free, but it gives the poem an urgency that it can lack on the page and even in the well-known recording that Eliot made for the Library of Congress in 1946. (Eliot's recently discovered recording from 1935 is better than either.)[44] Godevenos also ventures the Latin and Greek epigraph, which is more than Eliot did. Other notable readings are by Michael Balling and Greg Bathon, who also takes on the epigraph.[45] No one reads aloud in *The Waste Land* (except, perhaps, Madame Sosostris, who reads the Tarot cards that she deals), but many of the poem's voices recite from memory the literature of the past.

In 2005 Annie Coleman Rothenberg encouraged a reluctant LibriVox recruit to read Goethe's *Faust* by reporting her own project to read *The Waste Land* despite the authoritative reading on record by Eliot himself (apparently the 1935 version):

> [Y]ou should never worry about trying to live up to some standard. I'm psyching myself up to read T. S. Eliot's "The Waste Land." I've listened to the recording of Eliot reading it himself several times but I realized it wasn't good for me and I deleted my bookmark and am giving myself time to distance from that before I record. Why? I can't read it like Eliot can. NO ONE can read it like Eliot can. And it would be ridiculous if I *tried* to read it like Eliot did. All I can do is read it like Annie, with my life, my experiences, my emotions, my voice.[46]

Readers' anxieties or assurances about the acceptability of LibriVox readings have played themselves out in a dialogue of voices across several LibriVox forums, rehearsing controversies about pedagogy and literary interpretation that preoccupied the academy throughout the last half century. Questions of value are relative and should be set aside. No, questions of value are crucial and must be addressed: "there should be a basic principle applied that the reading should not do a disservice to the work's author or to the subject matter." It is impossible "to define what should or should not qualify as 'disservice' to any one author or his/her work. Even if said author left a voluminous treatise on the subject for future readers, I might be inclined to disagree with his/her interpretation of his/her own work! . . . That *we allow for infinite interpretations/recordings/performances of a single text* renders the point moot" (emphasis added). Poor readings risk misleading listeners "as to sense, through misplaced stresses, pauses and intonation." On the contrary, "there will be no 'better' recording of anything . . . there will only be different recordings."[47]

That there may indeed be "infinite interpretations/recordings/performances of a single text" returns us to the silent, textual echo chamber of Borges's infinite Library of Babel, in which printed books proliferate because one may differ from its neighbor on the shelf by but a single character.[48] Or, to vary the text (but not by much), it returns us to Gayatri Spivak's classic exposition of Derridean difference:

> Ferdinand de Saussure had remarked that the "same" phoneme pronounced twice or by two different people is . . . not identical with itself. Its only identity is in its difference from all other phonemes. . . . So do two readings of the "same" book share an identity that can only be defined as difference. The book is not repeatable in its "identity": each

210   *Michael Hancher*

> reading of the book produces a simulacrum of an "original" that is itself the mark of the shifting and unstable subject . . . using and being used by a language that is also shifting and unstable.[49]

"Different strokes, different folks," as we came to say in those days; or "Choice of voice," as an official LibriVox policy now has it. For several justifications of that policy, eloquently stated in several different voices, listen online to LibriVox Community Podcast number 105.[50]

In 2002 a computer engineer named Mike Eschman, then chief executive officer of Enigma Technologies in New Orleans, began to process selected Project Gutenberg texts through Emacspeak software, which he broadcast online under the title "Radio Gutenberg."[51] For a year or so these audio files were periodically replaced and then archived on the Project Gutenberg Web site. (It was dissatisfaction with the quality of these computer-generated readings that initially prompted McGuire to produce better alternatives for his own enjoyment and the enjoyment of others.)[52] Many dozens of these files remain available in the category "Audiobook: computer-generated," which complements the larger category called "Audiobook: human-read"— most of which files record readings by LibriVox volunteers.[53] By June 16, 2006, if not earlier, notice was given that no additions would be made to the computer-read archive because there were plans to generate such files "on demand."[54] Those plans have evidently been overtaken by technological progress. Increasingly sophisticated text-to-speech (TTS) synthesizer programs are now common features on computers and a variety of portable devices. Notably the Adobe Reader program for PDF files includes a "Read Out Loud" feature that mobilizes available hardware resources. Those resources have improved in recent years: the distinctly robotic voice of "Microsoft Sam" has given way to the somewhat more suasive voices of "Microsoft Mike" and now "Microsoft Anna"—and all of these personae are outclassed by a score of vocal pretenders merchandised by AT&T and other corporations. As of this writing the best of these mechanical readers are expensive (for example, several cents per word at NeoSpeech.com); but it is reasonable to expect that open-source TTS programs will improve rapidly, or that Google will stake its ad-supported claim to a large share of what will surely be a very large realm. Soon, that is, the LibriVox volunteers will be in serious competition with machines. Computers already defeat chess masters, and LibriVox readers may be outclassed by some combination of hardware and software.

Unsurprisingly, the crusty old Emacspeak-generated files that Eschman devised for Project Gutenberg include relatively few poems: some delicate lyrics by Thomas Hardy, which do not fare well, and, more plausibly, Edgar Allan Poe's "The Raven." (Even a crudely robotic reading of that poem is not irrelevant.) But most poems pose prosodic challenges for humans, which will challenge computer programmers in the next few years. The current frontier for such pathbreaking research is said to be the representation of "expression" in computer-generated speech—a term that quickly blends with the even less subtle term "emotion." A recent account of the state of the art concludes with the observation: "We are only in the very early stages of research into emotion in speech in general and speech synthesis in particular. Thus much current interest involves database collection and analysis . . . and ways to describe and control emotion . . . The study of emotion and expression in speech synthesis will certainly grow into a rich and exciting major topic of research."[55] Well, yes. "Human-read" audio-books may hold the field for a decade or more; but, sooner or later, the promised Babel of different human readings of all texts will give way to an even more Borgesian soundscape.

Or maybe not. When sympathetic text-to-speech readings can be generated on the fly by any (non)reader, there will be no need to preserve them with the curatorial attention that was given to Project Gutenberg's early archive of computer-generated audiobooks. Future computerized readings-on-demand will be as various and, in the aggregate, as vertiginous as Borges's sublime library, but they will exist only potentially. That is, they will be like any array of texts that wait to be read and to be understood.

NOTES

1. See http://LibriVox.org.
2. LibriVox files are deposited at the Internet Archive (http://www.archive. org), which provides statistical data. As is noted below, these files are also available at many other Web sites without statistical control, which means that the download information reported here (gathered March 22, 2010) is understated. The count of the number of titles (about 3,500) is more accurate, however. Each book usually occupies a set of files. Coincidentally the total number of titles closely approximates the number of LibriVox volunteers as of March 9, 2010 (http://purl.org/net/goal); it also happens to be of the same order of magnitude as the number of printed books that a reader might expect to read in a lifetime. In March 2010 the LibriVox archive added up to more than twenty-five months of recordings—enough to listen to for an hour a day, every day for half a century.
3. For a rude dismissal of Elocution personified see William Riley Parker, "Where Do English Departments Come From?" *College English* 28 (1967): 340. For searching accounts of the rise and fall of elocution as an academic study in England and the United States see Mark Morrison, "Performing the Pure Voice: Elocution, Verse Recitation, and Modernist Poetry in Prewar London," *Modernism/Modernity* 3 (1996): 25–50; Dwight Conquergood, "Rethinking Elocution: The Trope of the Talking Book and Other Figures of Speech," *Text and Performance Quarterly* (2000): 325–41; and Andrew Elfenbein, *Romanticism and the Rise of English* (Stanford, Calif.: Stanford University Press, 2009), 193–205. The exile of elocution, already secured by the New Criticism, was prolonged by Jacques Derrida's celebrated rejection of "phonocentrism" along with "logocentrism" in *Of Grammatology*, trans. Gayatri Spivak (Baltimore: Johns Hopkins University Press, 1976), 12.
4. Posting by "Steampunk (LibriVox Admin Team)," April 13, 2008 (http:// purl.org/net/steam).

212 *Michael Hancher*

5. As of April 28, 2010, the following numbers of works (complete or in progress) were reported by the LibriVox catalogue for thirty-nine languages: English (10,052), German (762), Chinese (516), French (440), Italian (256), Spanish (163), Dutch (75), Portuguese (55), Danish (49), Urdu (36), Javanese (23), Russian (18), Hebrew (14), Latin (14), Finnish (13), Romanian (11), Greek (10), Hungarian (10), Yiddish (10), Polish (9), Church Slavonic (8), Indonesian (7), Swedish (7), Afrikaans (6), Esperanto (6), Tamil (5), Arabic (4), Bulgarian (4), Japanese (4), Latvian (4), Old English (3), Ancient Greek (2), Irish (2), Tagalog (2), Turkish (2), Czech (1), Korean (1), Middle English (1), Welsh (1).

6. Unsigned review of Richard Grant White, *Every-Day English,* in *Literary World,* October 1, 1880, 210.

7. "Teachers and LibriVox" (http://purl.org/net/teachers). It has been estimated that as many as 10 percent of Canadians have a print disability. Turner Riggs, *Audiobook and eBook Publishing in Canada,* a report prepared for Library and Archives Canada, October 2008 (http://purl.org/Net/Canada). See also Matthew Rubery, "Play It Again, Sam Weller: New Digital Audiobooks and Old Ways of Reading,"*Journal of Victorian Culture* 13 (2008): 62–63.

8. http://www.gutenberg.org.

9. The law admits of some exceptions after 1923. However, the LibriVox administrative team finds it expedient to draw the line at that year "in general" (http://LibriVox.org/public-domain).

10. See, for example, Christine Pawley, "Seeking 'Significance': Actual Readers, Specific Reading Communities," *Book History* 5 (2002): 143–160.

11. On March 9, 2010, Hugh McGuire reported that LibriVox had enrolled 3,549 readers and that 3,347 had "completed something" (http://purl.org/net/goal). As of April 29, 2010, more than 22,000 persons had registered to contribute to the LibriVox forum discussions.

12. In November 2008 McGuire remarked, "As with Wikipedia, a huge portion of our recordings are done by a small number of readers. The 20 most prolific readers have read 30 percent of the sections in our catalog (!)." Mac Slocum, "Open Source, Community and Audiobooks: Q&A with LibriVox Founder Hugh McGuire," in *O'Reilly TOC: Tools of Change for Publishing,* November 5, 2008 (http://purl.org/net/Slocum). That steep asymmetry may slacken with time as more and more volunteers participate, but it will not vanish altogether; see Reid Priedhorsky et al., "Creating, Destroying, and Restoring Value in Wikipedia," in *Proceedings of the 2007 International ACM Conference on Supporting Group Work* (New York: Association for Computing Machinery, 2007), 260.

13. See note 2 above. Many LibriVox recordings are also available through iTunes (http://itunes.apple.com), as well as elsewhere, but the iTunes site does not publish statistical information.

14. Taly Weiss, "Free Riding Is Taking Place at Web 2.0," *TrendsSpotting,* December 27, 2006 (http://purl.org/net/Weiss); Nicholas Carr, "Sharecropping the Long Tail," *Rough Type,* December 19, 2006 (http://purl.org/net/Carr); Cathy Davidson, "Do-It Yourself, Do-It-for-Everybody," HASTAC April 16, 2008 (http://www.hastac.org/node/1307).

15. This is the slogan that Stuart Brand popularized in *The Media Lab: Inventing the Future at MIT* (New York: Viking, 1987), 202.

16. "A Public Domain Audio Book Library, with Hugh McGuire," interviewed by Paula Bernstein, "The Writing Show," August 23, 2005 (http://purl.org/net/PBernstein).

17. M. M. Bakhtin, *The Dialogic Imagination: Four Essays,* trans. Michael Holquist (Austin: University of Texas Press, 1981), xix, 263.

Learning from LibriVox   213

18. "Browse by Category: Audio Book, Human-Read" (http://purl.org/net/ABhr).
19. McGuire gives reasons for releasing LibriVox files into the public domain without control by license: "Why Public Domain and Not Creative Commons?" (http://purl.org/net/McGuire).
20. See http://www.archive.org/advancedsearch.php.
21. And there are other uncertainties to consider, such as the risk of count-inflation caused by robots; Project Gutenberg addresses that hazard ("Top 100," http://purl.org/net/top100), but the Internet Archive does not. Contributors' forums at both LibriVox and the Internet Archive also report recurrent counter outages lasting a week or more, which muddy the results.
22. McGuire reported 3,227 "completed projects" as of March 9, 2010 (http://purl.org/net/goal). I have posted the raw Internet Archive data for March 22, 2010, on which I base most of my analysis, at http://purl.org/net/LfL, along with an edited version that calculates downloads per day.
23. Richard D. Altick, *Victorian People and Ideas: A Companion for the Modern Reader of Victorian Literature* (New York: Norton, 1973), 192.
24. It was uploaded in July 2006, near the end of LibriVox's first year. A writer for the Wikipedia article on LibriVox noted that "in January 2009" it was "the most downloaded recording."
25. Craig Silverman, "Public Domain Books, Ready for Your iPod," *New York Times,* August 25, 2006, http://purl.org/net/Silverman.
26. Every book or author mentioned in the four paragraphs above figures also in the several lists of top-one-hundred downloads reported for Project Gutenberg as of April 6, 2010 (lists for the previous day, for the previous week, and for the previous month), *except* for most of the books addressed to children and young adults. Only the exceptionally canonical two books by Mark Twain are in high demand in both print and audio formats.
27. Chris Anderson, *The Long Tail: Why the Future of Business Is Selling Less of More* (New York: Hyperion, 2006).
28. See http://purl.org/Net/Slocum.
29. LibriVox completed its first fund-raising drive in March 2010, raising $23,000—enough to meet its small financial needs (http://purl.org/net/goal). Google has annual revenues in excess of $20 billion. In an early assessment for the neoliberal online journal *Reason.com,* Michael Erard engaged Yochai Benkler in speculation about how to monetize LibriVox. "The Wealth of LibriVox: Classic Texts, Amateur Audiobooks, and the Grand Future of Online Peer Production," *Reason.com,* May 2007 (http://purl.org/net/Erard). That has not happened yet.
30. "Google Checks out Library Books" (http://purl.org/net/GoogleBooks). See also "Company Overview" (http://www.google.com/corporate).
31. Dan Capistan, "LibriVox Video Tutorial 01: Introduction" (http://purl.org/net/Capistan). In 2005, at the very start of the LibriVox project, McGuire remarked, "We have no standards at the moment" (http://purl.org/net/PBernstein).
32. McGuire proposes that the test of quality should be made not by LibriVox administrators but by critics after the fact: "eventually someone will put up a site that sifts thru LibriVox audio and finds the really good stuff." "LibriVox: Apologia," February 16, 2008 (http://purl.org/net/McGuire2). However, so far not much has been done along those lines.
33. Aristotle, *Poetics,* trans. Leon Golden (Englewood Cliffs, N.J.: Prentice Hall, 1968), 14 (chap. 6, 1450^b), 51 (chap. 26, 1462^a). In his edition of the *Poetics* (Oxford: Clarendon Press, 1968), D. W. Lucas offered the then-orthodox opinion that the reading in question "presumably means reading aloud either to oneself or to a small circle" (281–282). However, the century-old belief

214 *Michael Hancher*

that in classical times reading was normally done aloud no longer prevails. For a summary of scholarship that documents the early history of silent reading, see William A. Johnson, "Toward a Sociology of Reading in Classical Antiquity," *American Journal of Philology* 121 (2000): 583–627, especially 593–599.

34. For example, Wayland Maxfield Parrish is generous with cautionary advice in *Reading Aloud: A Technique in the Interpretation of Literature* (New York: Nelson, 1933).

35. Stephen Colclough and David Vincent, "Reading," in *The Cambridge History of the Book in Britain*, 6 vols. (Cambridge: Cambridge University Press, 1998–2009), 6:312.

36. These were not identifiable as such in either the LibriVox catalogue or the Internet Archive database; to identify them I resorted to a plain Google search. Results are posted at http://purl.org/net/LfL (third tab).

37. Harmon mined his data from the eighth, ninth, and tenth editions of *The Columbia Granger's Index to Poetry*, also titled *The Columbia Granger's Index to Poetry in Anthologies,* ed. Edith Hazen et al. (New York: Columbia University Press, 1990–1994), a comprehensive listing of poems printed in British and American anthologies.

38. London: Macmillan, 1861.

39. At least one other reader has shared this high opinion of the poem: A. D. Nuttall, Introduction to John Milton, *The Minor Poems in English* (London: Macmillan, 1972), 53. In Harmon's ranking it barely made the top hundred: number ninety-two.

40. So advertised by LibriVox (http://purl.org/net/Kipling). See *The Nation's Favourite Poems*, ed. Griff Rhys Jones (London: BBC Books, 1996), 5, 9. "At the final count it got twice as many votes as the runner-up," Tennyson's "The Lady of Shalott."

41. T. S. Eliot, *The Waste Land: A Facsimile and Transcript of the Original Drafts, Including the Annotations of Ezra Pound* (New York: Harcourt, 1971), 4, 125.

42. Convincingly asserted in the voice of Jemma Blythe, who reads this chapter of *Our Mutual Friend* for LibriVox (bk. 1, chap. 16; http://purl.org/net/OMF).

43. Exemplary but also exceptional inasmuch as Nicholson is a professional actor. Amateur readers may prefer not to attempt such display, and the topic occasions some anxiety in the LibriVox forum; see "Voice Characterizations" (http://purl.org/net/VoiceC). LibriVox policy toward voice characterization is predictably laissez-faire: "In short, you don't have to" (http://purl.org/net/CVA). Practical advice on this and other matters is included in a manual by Robert Blumenfeld published only a year before LibriVox was launched: *Acting with the Voice: The Art of Recording Books* (New York: Limelight Editions, 2004).

44. Available at the Poetry Archive (http://purl.org/net/TSE). See Richard Swigg, "Sounding *The Waste Land*: T. S. Eliot's 1935 Recording," *PN Review* 28 (2001): 54–61. For a detailed appreciation of the 1946 recording see Stefan Hawlin, "'The Waste Land': Text and Recording," *Modern Language Review* 87 (1992): 545–554.

45. Bathon has posted not just one but two readings of the poem, the other one as part of Short Poetry Collection 67 (http://purl.org/net/SPC67). They are different readings, although both date from July 2008.

46. "Having the Guts to Tackle So-Called 'High Literature'" (http://purl.org/net/high). Coleman did not complete or did not post this reading, but she has made many other recordings for LibriVox, which listeners have praised at http://www.anniecoleman.com.

47. These excerpts are all from the LibriVox forum thread "Question of Native Speakers" (http://purl.org/net/question).
48. Jorge Luis Borges, "The Library of Babel," trans. James E. Irby, *Labyrinths: Selected Stories and Other Writings*, ed. Donald A. Yates (New York: New Directions, 1962), 56.
49. Gayatri Spivak, "Translator's Preface" to Derrida, *Of Grammatology*, xi–xii. I once ventured a less sophisticated apology for multiple interpretations: Michael Hancher, "The Science of Interpretation and the Art of Interpretation," *MLN* 85 (1970): 791–802. Recently Peter Kivy has proposed that, especially in the case of fiction, even silent reading is a performance, and that readings of a text will differ just as musical performances of a score differ. *The Performance of Reading: An Essay in the Philosophy of Literature* (Maldon, Mass.: Blackwell, 2006).
50. "LibriVox Community Podcasts," July 23, 2009 (http://purl.org/net/podcasts).
51. "Gutenberg: The Audio Books Project" (http://purl.org/net/GABP); "Radio Gutenberg," *Project Gutenberg Weekly Newsletter,* May 7, 2003, pt. 2 (http://purl.org/net/RG); "About Radio Gutenberg," *Project Gutenberg Weekly Newsletter,* September 17, 2003, pt. 2 (http://purl.org/net/RG2); "ETC—Enigma Technologies Group," *Emacspeak—the Complete Audio Desktop* (http://emacspeak.sourceforge.net).
52. "[I]n August 2005 . . . I was looking for free, full-length audiobooks online for a long car trip. I went to gutenberg.org, but found mostly machine-read stuff there, which I don't like" (http://purl.org/net/Slocum).
53. See http://purl.org/net/ABcg and http://purl.org/net/ABhr.
54. See http://purl.org/net/GABP.
55. Paul Taylor, *Text-to-Speech Synthesis* (Cambridge: Cambridge University Press, 2009), 531. See also Mark Tatham and Katherine Morton, *Expression in Speech: Analysis and Synthesis* (Oxford: Oxford University Press, 2004).

12 A Preliminary Phenomenology of the Audiobook

D. E. Wittkower

Philosophy has been called "a radical asking of the common questions of everyday."[1] Here, our object of inquiry is not one as fundamental to experience as those typical of philosophical inquiry, and our question not quite so common or everyday. Rather than radicalizing general questions such as "What is that?" "Who are you?" or "What time is it?" we will instead ask two interconnected questions:

- What is it like to listen to an audiobook?
- What are we listening to when we listen to an audiobook?

Before turning to the experience of listening to an audiobook, it is worth making a few preparatory notes on the material conditions necessary for the possibility of this experience. Wired or wireless, the audiobook can reach us only through our involvement in a larger technical system, both in the preparation of the experience in question and in the circumstances of the experience itself. The preparation necessary for the possibility of the experience, completed within a larger technical system, may differ in each instance, but a typical preparation might include obtaining an audiobook on CD or through download, adding the audio files to a digital library on a desktop computer, adding the files within a playlist synced to an MP3 player, and updating the MP3 audio library. The circumstances necessary for the possibility of the experience itself will differ as well but invariably include integration in one of a number of larger technical systems, such as listening to the audiobook on a car stereo while driving, on a home stereo while performing domestic tasks, or on an MP3 player while walking or at the gym.

We must also note that the activity is neither isolated nor all-consuming: in fact, if we are to understand the experience of listening to an audiobook, we should not assume that the convergence of intermixed and simultaneous activities has no bearing on the phenomenology of listening, or that coincident activities would not have different effects on the experience. Thus, in a full phenomenology of the audiobook, we would have to consider listening as an experience sufficiently situated and specific to be attuned to the

A *Preliminary Phenomenology of the Audiobook*   217

influence of convergent activities but general enough to be able to provide a resonant shared notion of a 'what it's like' for audiobook listening.[2] This most general understanding of the experience of audiobook listening exhibits many distinct although interrelated movements:

1. The audiobook is a temporal object of experience;
2. The audiobook is spoken;
3. The audiobook has a speaker;
4. The audiobook is started, stopped, and restarted;
5. The audiobook forms a context of physical and social experience.

Owing to space limitations, I will concentrate in this chapter on the audiobook as a temporal object of experience, as this is directly relevant to phenomenological discussions of aural experiences originating with Edmund Husserl. The remaining movements will then be addressed more briefly, and the reader welcomed to consider these commentaries as spurs, notes, or proposals for future research.

1. THE AUDIOBOOK IS A TEMPORAL OBJECT OF EXPERIENCE

The audiobook is audible and auditory. This will obviously distinguish it from the written work of which it is a performance, and the specific time-boundedness of the auditory object must be addressed in order to make sense of what we are listening to when we listen to an audiobook. At the same time, while we will compare the audiobook to previously theorized auditory objects of experience, such as music or the speech of a present other, we must distinguish it from these other objects as well.

"All sensation takes place in time," Walter Ong has noted, "but sound has a special relationship to time. . . . There is no way to stop sound and have sound. I can stop a moving picture camera and hold one frame fixed on the screen. If I stop the movement of sound, I have nothing."[3] Even the film, though, does not really exist as an object of experience within its still frames but is essentially in the movement and flow from one moment to the next. As Maurice Merleau-Ponty put it, "[A] film as a perceptual object . . . is not a sum total of images but a temporal gestalt,"[4] and the perception of its "movement," as with the perception of a melody rather than individual notes, is really the primary and fundamental content of our experience of these objects:

> melody does not perceptibly change when transposed, that is, when all
> its notes are changed while their interrelationships and the structure of
> the whole remain the same. On the other hand, just one single change
> in these interrelationships will be enough to modify the entire make-up

218   *D. E. Wittkower*

of the melody. Such a perception of the whole is more natural and more primary than the perception of isolated elements.[5]

So too, as Don Ihde has put it, "[W]hen I listen to someone speak, I do not ordinarily hear a syllable at a time, or even a word, but I hear the larger melody and flow of speech as an ongoing rhythmic unity."[6] The auditory speech-object is the process of movement between sounds and phonemes. Hence a fuller discussion of how we hear a melody rather than individual notes will allow us to give a "close listening" to the experience of hearing a sentence rather than tones, consonants, and phonemes.

How We Hear a Melody

Each particular sound—say, the note of middle C—is physically present only while it is being actively created by the vibration of the instrument or speaker system. As we experience the C followed by an F, and then a G, a C major tonality is established in the melody. Should the G be followed by a B, we would experience the B as leaning upward toward a return to the tonic, while, had we simply heard a B in isolation, we would experience no such tension. Furthermore, in order to have an experience of the B as a leading tone, we must not merely remember the preceding tones but must continue to feel them as well—but we must feel them as present under erasure for, as John Brough points out, "a melody, whose successive notes were heard all at once as now, would not appear as a melody at all, but as a crash of simultaneous sound."[7] No longer foreground but not yet absent to perception, the notes that are no longer physically present to the eardrum must be phenomenally present to the listener in order to form the background against which the primary impression of the sounding note appears. It is only this presence-under-erasure of the absent which makes it possible to hear a melody rather than a series of mere tones or a clashing cacaphonic muddle.

Husserl describes this as retention—sharply distinguished from memory. Retention is a kind of primary remembrance in which we maintain what just was as a continuing presence to experience, which relativizes the ongoing primary perception of the senses. Memory as we usually use the term is not the presence of a still-perceived 'just-having-been,' but rather a prior 'now' which appears to us only through our recall of it—in Husserl's words, "*not perceived, i.e. self-given, but presentified.*"[8] Perception of objects—such as the melody—which appear in several parts, only one of which is primally present at any moment, requires retention, not memory. Merleau-Ponty makes the same point in a different way:

> If the past were available to us only in the form of express recollections, we should be continually tempted to recall it in order to verify its existence . . . whereas in fact we feel it behind us as an incontestable acquisition.[9]

A *Preliminary Phenomenology of the Audiobook*   219

The presence of a perceived object of experience includes, in addition to a 'now' and a 'just-having-been,' a primordial unity with a future as a 'just-about-to-be.' In the prior example, the experience of the B as a leading tone requires not only a felt carrying-along of the 'just-having-been' but also a projective hearing in which the C that is not heard is experienced in its absence within our hearing of the B. The presence to experience of the B as a tone pushing us toward a return to the home tone of C is *constructed by* the presence of the having-just-been but *consists of* the presence to experience of the just-about-to-be: the C which is not heard, or which is 'heard' as not-yet-present. In harmonies this is felt even more clearly: the movement I–IV–V–vi is experienced as a false resolution precisely because the vi chord is heard as superimposed against the tonic chord established by the dominant chord as an expectation. The vi chord sounds false to the ear not upon reflection or as an intellectual judgment, but rather it is felt as false from the moment the tones sound because it is heard as failing to match up with the tonic chord present to experience at that moment as the anticipated resolution that we are precisely *not* listening to. This presence in the 'now' of an expected future is discussed by Husserl as *protention* and is the futural equivalent of retention, as Thomas Clifton has explained:

> Protention is the term for a future which we anticipate, and not merely await. Awaiting, like recollection, implies a disengagement from the present, whereas, experientially, the now which we perceive is colored by the way we intend the future. Intending a future with respect to a given event means to attach significance to that event in proportion to the way the present and future are attached to, yet distinguishable from, each other.[10]

In listening to speech, too, we certainly do not merely await to hear what words will "arrive" next but instead actively intend the future in modified ways from one phoneme to the next. This is clearly the case when listening to the speech of a present other, as the future is projected forth by context, relationship, body language, and so forth, but this structure of active anticipation and construction of meaning is also present in a full and vibrant way while listening to recorded speech. As we will see, when we listen to the audiobook, we hear every word as along with the words that have been and as against the words that could have been instead, just as surely as, in the melody, we hear each note with the notes which preceded it and against the notes which might have followed instead.

How We Hear a Sentence

Processes of retention and protention are necessary for the listener's comprehension of the spoken word: each new phoneme is heard as relativized by the phonemes preceding it and construct for us a protended anticipation of

220 D. E. Wittkower

the words likely to follow. The adjective alerts the listener to a substantive to follow; the pronoun projects forward a verb. The listener actively constructs the meaning of sentences as the phonemes are sounded and replace one another through time: in order for the subject to be heard as the subject, the listener must hear it along with the not-yet-presence of the predicate which it, as subject, implies will follow. The predicate only appears to the listener as a predicate insofar as the listener retains the subject of the sentence as the just-having-been, which is the background upon which the predicate appears; the predication of the predicate inheres in the absent presence of the retained subject.

All of this is true of the written word as well but in differing ways. The written word is put into motion, so to speak, by the action of the reader. The reader moves forward across the page, replacing the phonemes present within the 'now' of the inner voice at her own pace, circling back to reread as necessary. The spoken word, when containing clauses and conditionals, must be heard by the listener as a series of related points, each of which must be retained by her and actively reconstructed as the succession of phonemes continue to bring further meaning to earlier components. Consider this sentence as it would have to be understood if spoken:

> Consider (imperative action, protends an object) this (protention prolonged: what is it?) sentence (protended object supplied; imperative must be retained in order to contextualize the intended encounter of this object) as (modifies retained imperative action "consider") it (pronoun calling for retention of substantive "this sentence") would (clarifies retained modification "as" of retained imperative "consider"—the listener now knows we are going to consider the sentence "as" something in some counterfactual form yet to be determined) have (the listener hears /æ/ rather than /ə/, signaling that this "have" does not primarily modify the "would"—as in the spoken "would've," which uses a schwa—but will instead modify something which is to follow. If the speaker is American, this word will be pronounced /hæf/, indicating that this "have" is not the "have" of possession, which is /hæv/ in both UK and US English, but will instead form the idiomatic "have to" of necessitation) to (with retained "have" forms idiom of necessitation, protending a subject to be necessitated yet to be determined) be (infinitive verb fragment, the listener must still wait for more context) understood (that which is necessitated by the "have to" is supplied, and the retained phrases "have to" and "to be" can now be used to connect supplied content "understood" with object "sentence" under imperative "consider") if (indicates that the specific nature of counterfactualism, implied previously by "would," will now be supplied) spoken (retained sentence now placed under counterfactual conditional supplied).

Protention and retention are both different from conscious or intentional recall and expectation, and this breakdown of the process of listening is not

A Preliminary Phenomenology of the Audiobook   221

meant to represent the self-aware movements of the mind but instead meant to clarify and make present to awareness the unnoticed and unreflective process of structured listening and active contextualization which makes understanding possible. This structured listening constructs a number of simultaneous timelines. The subject is given, protending a predicate. But then, a modifying clause is given to the subject, and we must maintain our protention of predication while modifying the retained subject. Having circled back, we may again move forward in the construction of meaning. As each word replaces the last in the succession of 'nows,' we construct the meaning of the sentence through a nonlinear cycle of emerging protentions which are variously resolved into the retained content, and the overall meaning of the sentence emerges out of the circling back of elements upon one another, as we might see water as flowing downstream even though it does so through a complex and meandering process of moving up, down, and backward through ripples and eddies on the surface.

2. THE AUDIOBOOK IS SPOKEN

In the written word, the particular modes of relevance of one word upon another are not communicated through grammatical roles alone but also take place through the occult actions of punctuation marks. In the spoken word, similar signals are given through precisely timed pauses and changes in tone. The commas used to offset modifying or explanatory clauses, such as those surrounding this aside, are intended to be heard differently, and to construct meaning differently, than those within a list. The colon indicates content: that which follows it loops back upon and superimposes on that which precedes it. The modifying or explanatory clause—set off by commas or em dashes, like this—is lowered in pitch relative to the primary "timeline" of the sentence. Some words are emphasized in volume or enunciation in order to signal to the listener that these words are essential to the retrospective reconstruction of the meaning of the sentence in question. Words in subordinate clauses and noun phrases are run together subtly in order to indicate their unification as objects distinct from other "moving parts" within the overall claim. Parentheticals are uttered sotto voce (at half voice, like this).

Punctuation marks may seem far clearer than the pauses and vocal modulations of the spoken word, but it is not obvious that they have specifiable meaning. It seems just as likely that they notify us simply that something is supposed to happen at a given point in the sentence, and—like "reading" vowels in Hebrew—the reader is depended on to be able to tell based on context what is supposed to be happening. Today's punctuation usages are formalized and do not always track the rhythms which lend speech its intelligibility. Turning back to earlier forms of written English, we can see punctuation which is less a formal feature of writing and more an encoding of speech. For example, consider a passage from John Stuart Mill's *Utilitarianism*:

222   D. E. Wittkower

> Against this doctrine [the Greatest Happiness Principle], however, arises another class of objectors, who say that happiness, in any form, cannot be the rational purpose of human life and action; because, in the first place, it is unattainable: and they contemptuously ask, what right hast thou to be happy? a question which Mr. Carlyle clenches by the addition, What right, a short time ago, hadst thou even to be?[11]

Whereas this passage closely tracks the affordances of speech in aiding the listener's active construction of meaning, it is still clearly *composed* and far different from speech as extemporaneously spoken.

To speak with someone, that is, to speak with a particular, well to speak in the way that we really do talk most of the time, requires that there's a lot of back and forth and often (well, I do this—you probably do too), if you really pay attention to what someone says, we'll start a sentence three or four times before finishing it. And then start back up in the middle again! And when the speaker moves on from one point to another without finishing the first thought, maybe we know where she was going, or, if we don't, we forget about it because we're concerned with communicating with the person in front of us! The words are just a means to that end, and if there are a few loose ends at the end, who cares! (—and plus, there's no evidence, right?) Spoken words move their cargo like ants pulling along a bit of bread: the ants fall down, some drop it, others keep going, some peel off to go do something else, and some of them push it the wrong way, and little by little, the bread moves on down the line.

The written word is fully available to the reader,[12] to be engaged with at her own pace and in the order and level of care that she prefers. The spatial presentation of writing allows for a nonlinear visual encounter because space, unlike the successive presentation of time, contains and co-presents its elements. The reader may circle back, repeat, review. And so, in contrast to the way spoken word functions between present conversationalists, a written thought must be completed and consistent before it is expressed.

In between the starting and stopping of playback, the audiobook follows its own rhythm and pace in a context-insensitive and user-independent way. Listening to an audiobook is not like listening to a person speak—persons speaking to persons make eye contact, pause to invite signs that the listener is paying attention, use body language to emphasize or change meanings, and um and hem and haw. The audiobook proceeds at the same inexorable rate while the audience drifts in and out of attention.

(Please read this paragraph backward from the end.) .paragraph this in simulate to tried have I which experience this is It .something missed we've find we if sentence the of beginning the to back look simply cannot we because ,end the at together all it piece to passed just has what of enough remember to working actively ,procession their on carry words the while on going is what out work to attempt must We .sound of nature momentary the of difficulty inherent the exacerbates understanding and meaning create to take-and-give interpersonal the use to inability This .needed when back circle and listener the to respond to ability the without ,relentlessly forward continues narrator The .language written or spoken either of affordances the of many lacks audiobook The

The audiobook, as an audio performance of the written word, contains the determinate and preconsidered meaningfulness of the written word but without the affordance of nonlinear options for reader engagement. However, the richness of human speech seems to be sufficient compensation to support comprehension, even without the give-and-take of listening to a present other. Not only are the guiding rhythms of speech reintroduced, substituting for punctuation marks—their pale written equivalent—but additionally every word is made replete with meaning through its intonation. As Ihde has observed,

> For the reader who comes upon the word on a page, the field and its unsaid significance is a dark obscurity. . . . But if this word is *spoken*, there is already a certain potential field and presence of unsaid significance in the voice. If "Adam" is said in an angry voice, imploringly, or in a quiet whisper, each sounded presence allows the "bare word" to emerge from some of its obscurity in the sounding of its presence.[13]

Similar to Heidegger's observation that Dasein always finds itself having a mood (*Stimmung*), we may observe that the voice always has some kind of attunement. Just as "the pallid, evenly balanced lack of mood . . . is far from nothing at all," so too is the word spoken with no inflection and a flat affect just as full of meaning in its performance as if spoken animatedly.[14] The voice cannot but carry with it an emotional component, even when that component is emotionlessness. Marshall McLuhan noted that "[t]here are not many ways of writing 'tonight,' but Stanislavsky used to ask his young actors to pronounce and stress it fifty different ways. . . . The written word spells out in sequence what is quick and implicit in the spoken word."[15] The audiobook, although it contains this narrative description of what is emotively present in the spoken word, contains the replete modulations of the spoken word as well.

The pause, too, plays a great role in aiding the construction of meaning. The pause can function as a grammatical marker, signaling when to bind together meanings with preceding substantives, or when to expect further conditionals, modifiers, actions, and so forth. Pauses serve not only as signals to engage in these forms of synthesis and expectation but also as opportunities to do so. When the narrator moves along too quickly, or without suitably lengthy pauses at constitutive interstices, we very easily become confused and fall behind. The longer pauses which come at the end of sentences, paragraphs, or sections serve a similar role, except that they signal the completion of a larger process of construction and provide the

224   *D. E. Wittkower*

opportunity for the listener to bind together a larger set of meanings. As Husserl points out, these finial pauses are not experienced as silence:

> One speaks of the dying or fading away etc., of the content of sensation when veritable perception passes over into retention. Now, according to the statements made hitherto, it is already clear that the retentional "content" is, in the primordial sense, no content at all. . . . The retentional sound is not actually present but "primarily remembered" precisely in the now.[16]

Consider the natural pause which occurs at the end of a classical performance. It is surely possible for an audience member to applaud too soon, but this rarely occurs. Instead, the audience members seem on the whole to have an agreement about when the pause necessary to the piece has elapsed, or they simply await the downward return of the conductor's baton. The duration of this pause is rightly regarded as a part of the composition, for applause too early is heard as an interruption despite the fact that sound is no longer being produced. Without this pause, the music stops but does not end; the binding together of sound into unitary temporal experience requires this pause, and thus there can only be an ending in the sense of coming to fruition when there is an appropriately timed pause which, as the ending of the piece, is as integral to the experience as any note sounded within it.[17] The appropriate duration is dictated by the mental reverberation required by binding the experience, not by a physical echo which may be present. It is likely that a haunting piece which trails off into a lonely and hopeless pianissimo would require a longer pause before applause than a louder piece with less emotional depth, even if the latter is performed in a very live room and the former in a more muted space. Unlike the physical reverberations of the echo, the mental reverberation of retentional meaning-binding in the pause grows louder as the pause extends. Or, at least, up to a certain point—certainly the pause can be too long, at which point the listener has finished attending to what has just been heard and has become distracted by other events, or the silence ceases to retain what came before and begins to protend what is about to occur. In the concert hall, we await the drop of the conductor's baton, and at some point we are no longer still 'listening' to the now-absent music but begin instead to think, "What's going on? Should I clap? Maybe it isn't over yet . . ."

In order to properly bring sentences, paragraphs, and chapters to fruition, the narrator of an audiobook must similarly pause for the right amount of time and do so for the same reasons. Should the pause be too short, comprehension is inhibited and the listener becomes confused or disengaged. Like the conductor holding her hand aloft, the narrator can signal to the audience not to move on, not to be distracted, and not to stop paying attention. For this reason, it may be that audiobooks have special value to offer to poetry, for readers may have difficulty lingering properly over phrases, and the audiobook forces an appropriate reflective duration (even if the reflection itself does not always take place). As Nick Piombino put it, "[T]he aural ellipses of the contemporary poem ensure that there will be spaces for invention on the part of the listener. . . . this is all the more important in contemporary life where there is so much talking and so little listening."[18] When we read the written poem, we are 'talking' and 'listening' to our 'inner voice,' and unless we make a serious effort to internally perform the poem, it is very easy to fail to hear the poem at all. Having the poetic work performed provides a structure to support the listener's active listening: she must wait, and she may then be more likely to wonder and protend and reflect. This effect extends to poetic and dramatic passages in prose works as well.

Surely, here too the pause can be too long. We are trained by radio to be bewildered by "dead air" in a way that we are not in the concert hall, and when there is any somewhat long pause, we begin to be distracted by our surroundings or to ask whether the track has ended, whether something has gone wrong with the playback, or whether it's time to insert the next CD.

Here, the amount which can be carefully and precisely covered within a single book chapter is at an end. In order to make some attempt at appropriately broad coverage of the chapter's topic, as previously mentioned, I will make some briefer and more informal commentaries on other aspects of a phenomenology of audiobooks.

Thus far, we have seen how listening to an audiobook requires a listening which binds together past, present, and future in an active construction of meaning. This process, while immensely complicated, is one to which we are well accustomed from its similarity to communication with a present other. We have also seen how pauses and intonations strongly aid comprehension of complex written prose, not necessarily intended to be read aloud, even when the affordances of the written page are removed.

Taken together, we might expect these aspects of audiobook listening to result in a displacing or entrancing experience. There is much work to do and attention demanded, and there is a flow of future with past into present which follows no rhythm but its own—and all of this is superimposed onto a visual field and embodied interactions related to the auditory world of the audiobook in only the most accidental and arbitrary way. This overall depiction of audiobook listening is already implied by what we have discussed to this point in the chapter, but the following will lend it further support.

3. THE AUDIOBOOK HAS A SPEAKER

The audiobook is a performance, and both the performance and the performer contribute much to the listening experience. But what exactly is part of the experience is not as clear as it might seem and depends on the listener as well as the performer. As Ihde has noted,

226   D. E. Wittkower

in a highly concentrated "narrow" focus I get certain sounds in the other's speech but may find it almost impossible to note what was said; and contrarily in a "broader" focus, as in attending to what is being said, I may miss or barely be aware of the aspirated *s* which is characteristic of the other's speaking style.[19]

Professional audiobook narrators are selected for their ability to perform with either a neutral or content-appropriate accent, in which the goal, presumably, is to minimize the likelihood that the listener's focus will be drawn by these formal aspects of the performance rather than by the content which it is meant to represent. Authors who narrate their own works seem to be coached in the expected style.

The free recordings available online at LibriVox give us an opportunity to see whether and to what extent such formal variances influence our listening; LibriVox audiobooks are recorded by volunteers, and anybody with any kind of voice or accent may choose to record any public-domain work.[20] Although other listeners disagree, I have personally never found it distracting to hear P. G. Wodehouse performed with an American accent and see no reason why the Southern American accent should be limited to Southern genre pieces rather than, for example, a history of England or the Christian Bible.[21] Listening to Kirsten Ferreri's recording of sections from *The Antichrist* on LibriVox was strange to me at first, but, in less than a minute, I noticed that I was no longer listening to a woman reading Nietzsche but was instead listening simply to Nietzsche. Alternately, listening to Gesine's recording of Schopenhauer's *Über die Weiber* did not produce the same transparency—that a woman had chosen to voice Schopenhauer's most misogynist essay reminds the listener of the performer's presence as a mute agent behind the voice, and the performer's active personal silence in the verbatim production of words which she must clearly disavow makes the materiality of her voice productively obstructive rather than transparent.

Some narrators purposefully add distinctive vocal characteristics as an attempt to highlight and enhance content—"doing voices," as for example with Jim Dale's award-winning narration of J. K. Rowling's Harry Potter books. In some cases the "voices" are simply a binding together and representation of the content already within the written word; in other cases the "voices" are more a creative superaddition supplying new content.

Altogether, the voice itself may be present in three primary ways: counterpunctual, consonant, and dissonant. It may be present as a representation and enhancement of content, much as a counterpoint supports a melody while creating new content in accordance with its form. It may be present although transparent, fading into the background of the listener's experience, allowing the listener to focus simply on the content, much as consonant notes accompany and harmonize with a melody, simply drawing out what is already in it. Or, it may be present in an obstructive form, whether in a purposeful and productive form, as in the example above of Gesine's Schopenhauer, or in an accidental and purely disruptive form, as might be the case with a title that has poor recording quality or a vocal characteristic which the listener is for some reason unable to allow to fade into the background. In either case, the voice is similar to dissonant notes which clash against and sour a melody—interesting and deepening the experience when this is the intended effect but less so when unintended or poorly done.

These three modes of interaction between form and content—counterpunctual, consonant, and dissonant—apply to physical and social contexts of listening as well. Listening to poetry on one's iPod may be given a strong counterpoint by walking through woods; may be simply consonant with driving, allowing the experience of the road to fade away into the background; and may be dissonant with the commuter crowd, either in a surreal and interesting manner or in a manner simply annoying and distracting.

4. THE AUDIOBOOK IS STARTED, STOPPED, AND RESTARTED

The listener must initiate the process of playback when listening to an audiobook, at which time the vocal performance follows its own predetermined schedule. The driver or the walker must plan ahead for the intended overlapping of experiences not only through the presence of audio files, with an appropriately integrated technological system of converting these files to sound waves, but also through the initiation of playback prior to the intended experiential convergence. The listener may experience frustration in starting playback in medias res, fumbling through CDs at a red light or trying to navigate MP3 directories while keeping pace.

If the driver does not specifically start and stop audiobooks but simply uses the powering on and off of the stereo as a stop and start button, the activity of driving is fully enclosed within playback: playback resumes upon starting the engine, and the driver must first attune to the audiobook, then turn to the road, and, once the driving process is complete, the playback continues until it too is halted. The walker, too, has experiences akin to these "driveway moments," in which the walker may continue on the exercise machine past the end of a planned amount of time or distance, waiting for an opportune and hard-to-anticipate moment of narrative resolution.

In the great majority of cases, the duration of playback is far longer than the duration of activities engaged in along with playback. The audiobook might reside in the driver's car or the walker's MP3 player for several weeks and be played back over many commutes or exercise sessions. For this reason, along with those in the preceding paragraphs, it is appropriate to say that listening forms the context in which the driving and walking occur rather than the other way around. In Merleau-Ponty's visual terminology, the listening is

228   D. E. Wittkower

the figure, and the driving or walking is the background. This conclusion may sound strange: we more often speak of listening to an audiobook while driving than of driving while listening to an audiobook. Still, this inversion is well supported by other common experiences: for example, that audiobooks may be most often listened to while on daily commutes or long road trips, situations in which little attention to the road is needed. It seems, further, that the very purpose of many who listen to audiobooks while at the gym—I suspect nearly everyone who does so—is precisely to move the process of exercise into the background in order to undergo it without so distinctly experiencing it. And thus the audiobook *forms* a context for physical and social experience rather than being experienced *within* a physical and social context.

Michael Bull has made observations in support of this point:

> Listening frees up the eyes to observe and imagine, thus differing from the traditional reading of a book, in which the reader is visually engaged in the text. . . . The text becomes a continuous flow of sound on to which he adds a level of physicality in the act of imagination. The sound print of the book is imposed on the silence of the world around him.[22]

In the case considered here, the audiobook listener looks around a café, imagining that the people present are characters in the text. Clearly, there are many other ways that listening to an audiobook will condition physical and social experiences, depending upon the kind of listening involved and the kind of environment in which that listening takes place.

Ihde has discussed the orienting role of the background rhythms of nature and of the technosphere—the bird calls which signal the time of day, the hum of fluorescent bulbs which provide a context for paperwork.[23] When I plug my ears, I remove this context and its cues, and I replace them with auditory events occurring in a different environment and a different space. It may be that I am to some subconscious extent aware of the contours of that absent space to which I am listening in some dim shadow of the resonances made clear by composer Alvin Lucier's classic *I Am Sitting in a Room*—at least, I am aware that it is a space different from the one in which I am embodied and navigate, for it does not change its direction when I turn my head, nor does it fade as a I walk, or change its resonance as I move from one room to another or go outside. In both time and space, the audiobook offers us an alternate and independent world that is literally experienced, without even considering the more metaphorical 'other-worldly' effects of narrative and imagination.

5. THE AUDIOBOOK FORMS A CONTEXT OF PHYSICAL AND SOCIAL EXPERIENCE

Some time ago, I walked through the grounds of the Bergianska trädgården in Stockholm while listening to a recording of Ralph Waldo Emerson's essay "Self-Reliance." Was one part of this experience supposed to enhance the other? Why is this "romantic" to say so? My memory of listening to Peter Kropotkin's *Conquest of Bread* associated with the woods around a particular stretch of Interstate 77 is no less distinct, nor is my memory of listening to William Sangster's *Umbrellas and Their History* while in a grocery store parking lot. Surely these moments cannot stand out in my mind due to any substantive connection between the physical experience and content of the audio context in which that experience occurred.

Less memorable is my experience of listening to David Hume's *Enquiry Concerning Human Understanding* while on the elliptical and the exercise cycle, not because there was less of a connection, or less of interest to remember from the book, but instead due to an excess of familiarity. I have met both Hume's text and the elliptical in different circumstances, and I can easily think of Hume without the gym coming to mind—but when I return to Emerson, the Bergianska trädgården comes along with it, as I have (as Hume would have put it) made them contiguous in my experience without diluting that contiguity through a multiplicity of other unrelated associations. "Custom," as Hume said, "is the great guide of human life."[24]

Certainly, as Bull has noted, audiobook listening changes the way we perceive our social environment.[25] To his example of the listener sitting in the café, we might add the listener who watches the bustle of crowds and the listener among the bustle of a crowd; the listener seated on public transit; the listener in the corner store or supermarket. As noted above, these experiences may be counterpunctual, consonant, or dissonant with the audiobook which provides their context. The difference, it seems to me, may depend on the interpretation of the text in which the listener engages as much as anything else. It is not just one thing to listen to Jane Austen on the subway.

Regardless of how the social environment is experienced by the listener, it is clear that the listener is in some kind of disconnection with the social environment, experiencing it within a context not available to others in that environment. If the context for being-with-others is supplied via earbuds, whatever experience of community the listener has must be a kind of false or imaginary community—a public space interpreted as a private and interior event. And yet the listener is also part of a real but nonlocal community, at minimum a community formed by the work itself: the author, the performer, the listener, and all the other unknown listeners. This community may be indefinite, where the listener might imagine how others reacted to, for example, a controversial event within a plot or claim within a nonfiction work. This community may be well defined, as when a listener has picked up an audiobook on the basis of its bestseller status, was lent it by friends or family, or was recommended it by Oprah Winfrey.

And so here we see three kinds of community within the seemingly solitary and solitude-seeking act of listening to an audiobook in public: a real but nonlocal community which is formed around the aesthetic work;

230 D. E. Wittkower

a local but imaginary community within the listener's privately contextualized experience of others; and a real and local but unexperienced community of audially unavailable mere presence-alongside-others.

There are many further questions which a full phenomenology would address—in the preceding discussion I hope to have provided a solid start to such a phenomenology, along with a sketch of its contours. We have seen that the experience of an audiobook requires active binding of past, present, and future; requires us to construct a timeline separate from that of our physical interactive world; is constructed and bears authoritative expressions akin to written text; is personal and bears emotional attunement akin to spoken word; contains demanding and challenging silences; is borne by a voice which is counterpunctual, consonant, or dissonant; forms a context for physical and social experience; can be used to fade embodied experience into background; binds memory in ways very different from written text, due to the simultaneous experience of an arbitrarily related visual field; and produces unusual forms of isolation-in-community.

NOTES

1. Remy C. Kwant, *From Phenomenology to Metaphysics* (Pittsburgh: Duquesne University Press, 1966), 158. Summary and representation of Maurice Merleau-Ponty's comments from "Interrogation and Intuition," in *The Visible and the Invisible*, trans. Claude Lefort (Evanston, Ill.: Northwestern University Press), 105–107.
2. Similar to many studies of phenomenology, this chapter uses single quotation marks in order to refer to something from within the phenomenological bracketing, or *epoché*. Single quotation marks allow the designation of a thing in its presence-to-experience without implying its absolute reality (as might be the case without any quotation marks) and without implying its illusory nature (as might be the case with double quotation marks). The single quotation marks allow us to signify a thing named while remaining uncommitted about whether this naming is a calling of a thing something which it is or a mere calling of a thing something which it is merely called.
3. Walter Ong, *Orality and Literacy: The Technologizing of the Word* (New York: Routledge, 1982), 31–32.
4. Maurice Merleau-Ponty, "The Film and the New Psychology," in *Sense and Non-Sense*, trans. Hubert L. Dreyfus and Patricia Allen Dreyfus (Evanston, Ill.: Northwestern University Press, 1964), 54.
5. Merleau-Ponty, "The Film and the New Psychology," 49.
6. Don Ihde, *Listening and Voice* (Athens: Ohio University Press), 89.
7. John B. Brough, "The Phenomenology of Internal Time-Consciousness," in *Husserl: Shorter Works*, ed. Peter McCormick and Frederick A. Elliston (Notre Dame, Ind.: Notre Dame University Press, 1981), 272.
8. Edmund Husserl, "The Lectures on Internal Time-Consciousness from the Year 1905," in *Husserl: Shorter Works*, ed. Peter McCormick and Frederick A. Elliston (Notre Dame, Ind.: Notre Dame University Press, 1981), 283.
9. Maurice Merleau-Ponty, *Phenomenology of Perception*, trans. Colin Smith (New York: Routledge, 1998), 418–419. The translation of "*Abschattungen*" is my own.

A Preliminary Phenomenology of the Audiobook   231

10. Thomas Clifton, *Music as Heard: A Study in Applied Phenomenology* (New Haven: Yale University Press, 1983), 62.
11. John Stuart Mill, *Utilitarianism*, 3d ed. (London: Longmans, Green, Reader, and Dyer, 1867), 17.
12. Do you read a footnote immediately, in the middle of a sentence, or afterwards? Where do you go back to when you return to the sentence? Do you have to start back at its beginning? Are you supposed to reread the sentence with the footnote retained as a kind of semi-literal "subtext"? How different this is from the spoken tangential remark!
13. Ihde, *Listening and Voice*, 154.
14. Martin Heidegger, *Being and Time*, trans. John Macquarrie and Edward Robinson (New York: Harper & Row, 1962), H. 134.
15. Marshall McLuhan, *Understanding Media* (New York: McGraw-Hill, 1964), 82.
16. Edmund Husserl, "The Lectures on Internal Time-Consciousness," 281.
17. See Heidegger, *Being and Time*, H. 243–4.
18. Nick Piombino, "The Aural Ellipsis and the Nature of Listening," in *Close Listening: Poetry and the Performed Word*, ed. Charles Bernstein (New York: Oxford University Press, 1998), 70.
19. Ihde, *Listening and Voice*, 89.
20. LibriVox, https://librivox.org. For more on LibriVox, see Michael Hancher's chapter in this volume.
21. It is worth noting that some listeners attempting to use audiobooks for the purpose of language acquisition have found special value in the way that LibriVox recordings represent a variety of different forms of spoken English, and make use of LibriVox recordings specifically to gain access to accents prevalent in spoken English but not favored in commercially produced speech.
22. Michael Bull, *Sound Moves: iPod Culture and Urban Experience* (New York: Routledge, 2007), 40–41.
23. Ihde, *Listening and Voice*, 86.
24. David Hume, "An Enquiry Concerning Human Understanding," from *Enquiries Concerning the Human Understanding and Concerning the Principles of Morals*, ed. L. A. Selby-Bigge, 2d ed. (Oxford: Clarendon Press, 1902), §36, 44.
25. Bull, *Sound Moves*, 40–1.
26. Here, I have in mind Ruud Kaulingfreks and Samantha Warren's discussion of community and solitude in iPod listening, where the first kind of community corresponds to their discussion of Hans-Georg Gadamer's *The Relevance of the Beautiful and Other Essays* (Cambridge: Cambridge University Press, 1986), and the third kind corresponds to their discussion of Jean-Luc Nancy's *The Inoperative Community* (Minneapolis: University of Minnesota Press, 1991). See "Mobile Clubbing: iPod, Solitude, and Community," in *iPod and Philosophy*, ed. D. E. Wittkower (Chicago: Open Court, 2008), 167–179.

Contributors

Charles Bernstein is the editor of *Close Listening: Poetry and the Performed Word* (Oxford University Press, 1998) and the author of *All the Whiskey in Heaven: Selected Poems* (Farrar, Straus, & Giroux, 2010) and *My Way: Speeches and Poems* (The University of Chicago Press, 1999). He teaches at the University of Pennsylvania, where he is codirector of PennSound (writing.upenn.edu/pennsound), a vast archive of downloadable poetry recordings.

Jason Camlot is Associate Professor and Chair of English at Concordia University in Montréal. His critical works include *Style and the Nineteenth-Century British Critic* (Ashgate, 2008) and *Language Acts: Anglo-Québec Poetry, 1976 to the 21st Century* (coedited with Todd Swift; Véhicule Press, 2007). He is also the author of three poetry collections, most recently, *The Debaucher*. His critical articles have appeared in such journals as *Postmodern Culture*, *Book History*, and *ELH*.

Michael Hancher is Professor of English at the University of Minnesota and current President of the Dictionary Society of North America. He has published numerous essays on British Victorian writers and artists, as well as articles on intention and interpretation, speech-act theory, pragmatics, and the law. His work on pictorial illustration includes *The Tenniel Illustrations to the "Alice" Books* (Ohio State University Press, 1985) and several studies of illustrated dictionaries. Recent articles include "Grafting *A Christmas Carol*" in *SEL* (2008) and "Definition and Depiction" in *Word and Image* (2010).

K. C. Harrison teaches literature in the Department of Postsecondary Teaching and Learning at the University of Minnesota, Twin Cities. She recently completed a dissertation at Yale University entitled "Tales Twice Told: Sound Technology and American Fiction after 1940," and has articles forthcoming on the shared acoustics of William S. Burroughs and Amiri Baraka, and Thomas Pynchon's interest in Ishmael Reed.

234   *Contributors*

Michael S. Hennessey is the Editor of PennSound and Jacket2 (http://jacket2.com), as well as a Visiting Assistant Professor of English and Comparative Literature at the University of Cincinnati. Recent critical publications include essays on Charles Bernstein's "1–100" in *English Studies in Canada* and on Ted Berrigan and Harris Schiff's *Yo-Yo's with Money* in *Interval(le)s*, with work forthcoming in *The Salt Companion to Charles Bernstein* and *The Journal of Electronic Publishing*. His poetry has appeared in *EOAGH, Cross Cultural Poetics, Elective Affinities*, and *Jacket* as well as the chapbooks *Last Days in the Bomb Shelter (17 Narrower Poems)* and *[static]*.

James Jesson is Assistant Professor of English at La Salle University, where he specializes in modern and contemporary drama. He has held fellowships at the Lilly Library at Indiana University and at the University of Texas's Harry Ransom Humanities Research Center. His publications include work on Beckett's *Embers* and on writing pedagogy and writing center praxis. He is currently completing a book manuscript on literary, cultural, and institutional influences on British and American radio drama.

Sara Knox teaches in the School of Humanities and Languages at the University of Western Sydney, and is a member of the Writing and Society Research Group. She is the author of *Murder: A Tale of Modern American Life* (Duke University Press, 1998). Her most recent publications include a study of the figure of the ghost in the work of Hilary Mantel in *Australian Feminist Studies* (2010) and an analysis of media "first responders" to Hurricane Katrina in *Cultural Studies Review* (2008). Her novel, *The Orphan Gunner* (Giramondo, 2007), won the 2009 Asher Literary Prize and was shortlisted for the Commonwealth Writer's Prize and the Age Book of the Year.

Jesper Olsson is a Swedish Academy researcher at the Department of Literature, Stockholm University, and is currently writing a book on audiotape and the tape recorder in postwar aesthetic practices. In 2005 he published the book *Alfabetets användning*, on Swedish concrete poetry in the 1960s. He has written extensively on contemporary poetry, avant-garde aesthetics, and media history. He also coedits volume 3 of the forthcoming *A Cultural History of the Nordic Avant-Gardes*, and is an editor of the journal *OEI*.

Brigitte Ouvry-Vial is Professeur des Universités at Université du Maine in France, where she teaches twentieth-century literature and children's literature. She is a former student of Ecole Normale Supérieure in Paris and received her Ph.D. from Columbia University. After a book and numerous articles on the French poet and painter Henri Michaux, she

Contributors   235

is doing research on contemporary print culture in France, specifically on editing and publishing as an act of textual interpretation. As Literary Director for Editions L'Inventaire, cofounded in 1993, she also publishes major foreign contemporary writers and poets in French translations. She is currently directing the "Women in Books" section (publishers, librarians, printers) for the *Dictionnaire encyclopédique universel des femmes créatrices*, to be published in 2011.

Matthew Rubery is Lecturer in Nineteenth-Century Literature at Queen Mary, University of London. He is the author of *The Novelty of Newspapers: Victorian Fiction after the Invention of the News* (Oxford University Press, 2009), which won the European Society for the Study of English (ESSE) First Book Award 2010. His previous work on sound includes "Play It Again, Sam Weller: New Digital Audiobooks and Old Ways of Reading" in the *Journal of Victorian Culture* (2008), and he is currently working on a project entitled *The Untold Story of the Talking Book*.

Jeffrey Severs is Assistant Professor of English at the University of British Columbia. His essays and interviews on Philip Roth, Thomas Pynchon, and Norman Mailer are published or forthcoming in *Studies in American Fiction*, *Pynchon Notes*, and *The Mailer Review*. He is also coeditor, with Christopher Leise, of *Pynchon's* Against the Day: *A Corrupted Pilgrim's Guide* (University of Delaware Press, 2011).

Justin St. Clair is an Assistant Professor of English at the University of South Alabama, where he specializes in postmodern fiction and sound culture studies. His recent publications include articles on Thomas Pynchon's *Against the Day*, Naguib Mahfouz's *Arabian Nights and Days*, and the obscure American folk musician Wee Willie Shantz. He is currently working on a book-length study of sound in the postmodern novel.

Garrett Stewart is the James O. Freedman Professor of Letters at the University of Iowa and an elected member of the American Academy of Arts and Sciences. His work on the audiobook and its reverberations for prose style reconvenes the topics of several of his previous books on literary poetics, prose fiction, and both media and narrative theory, including a particularly direct convergence of *Reading Voices: Literature and the Phonotext* (University of California Press, 1990) and *Novel Violence: A Narratography of Fiction* (The University of Chicago Press, 2009), which received the 2010 Perkins Prize from the International Society for the Study of Narrative. His next study takes up, by contrast, the abject silence of altered or fabricated book sculpture under the title *Bookwork: Medium to Object to Concept to Art* (forthcoming from the University of Chicago Press, 2011).

236   Contributors

D. E. Wittkower teaches philosophy and interdisciplinary studies at Coastal Carolina University, and writes on the relevance of German philosophy to applied ethics and new media. He is editor of volumes such as *iPod and Philosophy* (Open Court, 2008) and *Facebook and Philosophy* (Open Court, 2010), as well as author of articles and book chapters including "Revolutionary Industry and Digital Colonialism" in *Fast Capitalism* (2008), "Method Against Method: Swarm and Interdisciplinary Research Methodology" in *Social Identities* (2009), and "On the Origins of the Cute as a Dominant Aesthetic Category in Digital Culture" in *Putting Knowledge to Work and Letting Information Play* (Center for Digital Discourse and Culture, 2010). He has also recorded a dozen audiobooks with LibriVox.org, and has contributed to the recording of two dozen more.

Index

"n" indicates reference to a note
"f" indicates reference exclusively to a figure

24 Hour Psycho, 66

A

abridgment, 6, 12, 155n3, 168–169, 200
Acker, Kathy, 104n3
Adam, Alison, 154
affect, sound and, 127–128, 137
African origins: *Dreams from My Father*, 165, 166, 167–168, 170
African Americans: oral expression, print and sound, 14, 143, 144, 147–148, 150–151, 152, 157n45, 161, 172
albums: works for children, 186–187
Albums du Père Castor, Les, 178, 179
Alexander, Joy, 193
Alice's Adventures in Wonderland, 203
alienation: own voice from another source, 73n25
All Poets Welcome, 76
All the Year Round, 32–33
Allen, Donald, 86
Allen, Jane (pseud.), 51
Allen, Woody, xiii, xiv
alphabet: transcriptive use, xvi
American Foundation for the Blind, 5, 6
American Printing House for the Blind, 5
Anderson, Benedict, 158n50
Andrews, Malcolm, 32
animal talk, 183–184, 196n10
Anne of Green Gables, 203, 206
Antichrist, The (Nietzsche), 226
Antin, David, 69
antiphony, 145, 152–153, 154, 157n45
AppSessions LLC, 201–202
Architectural League, 80
archival recordings, 8

Aristotle, 205, 213n33
art as process, 57, 145–146
Ateliers du Père Castor, Les 178
Audacity of Hope, The, 159
Audible audiobooks, 132, 133, 135, 137, 138, 141n39
audience. *See* listeners
Audio Arts, 70, 71, 74n48
Audio Publishers Association, 8, 9
audiobook: definition, 1; etymology, xv; standardization of term, 8
audiobooks, hybrid: novel and score, 92–106
audiocassettes, 8, 70–71
audiograph, 183
audiotext, 13, 20n42
aural manipulation, 104
authenticity, 144, 147, 148
author and reader: hierarchical relationship 150, 189–190
author's voice, 26
authorial attribution, 48, 57
authorship: doubling of, 128, 130, 132–137, 138–140; radio adaptations of novels, 48, 49–57
automation of writing, sound recording as, 39
Awakening, The (Chopin), 154

B

Baddeley, V. C. Clinton, 6–7
Baker, Houston, 146, 147, 151, 156n13
Bakhtin, Mikhail, 47, 201
Bakulè, Frantisek, 178, 186
Baldwin, James, 173
Barrymore, Lionel, 54, 55–56
Barthes, Roland, 95, 160–161
Bassett, Caroline, 139

238 *Index*

Battis, William Sterling, 27, 28, 29, 30–32, 34, 35, 36–37, 38–40
Baucom, Ian, 153
Beats, the, 67, 73n27, 85, 86, 88
Bellamy, Edward, 113–114
Beloved, 147, 150
Benjamin, Walter, 146, 152
Benson, Sheila, 88
Bentinck, Anna, 138, 139–140
Bentley, Thomas, 35–36
Bernstein, Charles, 13, 89
Bible, the: LibriVox, 202–203
Birkerts, Sven, 3, 11, 15
Black Mountain poets, 86
black sound: sonic Afro-modernity, 162
black voices: commercial profit, 144, 147–148
Blackburn, Paul, 64
Blackton, J. Stuart, 30
Bolter, Jay David, 25–26, 27, 46, 47, 104n2
book scores, 92–108
books: material construction, 47–48; physical objects, 149–150
Books for the Adult Blind Project, 19n18
Books in Motion, 8
Books on Tape, 8, 133
Boon, Marcus, 77
Borges, Jorge Luis, 209, 211
Bougnoux, Daniel, 191
Bowles, Paul, 67
Brainard, Paul, 92–93, 100
Brautigan, Richard, 85–86
Brent, Linda, 151
British Broadcasting Corporation, 6–7
Brodsky, Joseph, 133, 134
Brough, John, 218
Brown, Claudia, 152
Browning, Frank, 160–161
Bruner, Jerome, 187
Bryan, William Jennings, 30
Bull, Michael, 2, 11, 127, 139, 228, 229
Burroughs, William S., 67–69, 86, 87, 88
Bush, George W.: reading ability, 159

C

Caedmon Records, xiv, 8, 84–85
Cage, John, 63–64
call-and-response, 145, 152, 157n45
Calvino, Italo, 190
Camlot, Jason, 128, 133

Campbell, Timothy C., 45
Campbell (soup manufacturer), 45–46, 51, 52, 53–54, 54–56, 57
Campbell Playhouse, 45–46, 48–49, 50, 51–56, 57
captive listener, 11
Cash, Johnny, 96, 97
Cassady, Neal, 67
cassettes, audio, 8, 70–71
Cave, Nick, 104n4
CBS network, 49
CDs: le Carré's novels, 112, 123; Père Castor, 180
celebrity: Orson Welles's self-creation, 49
celebrity narrators, 5, 13–14
Chappell, Ernest, 54, 55
characters, literary, 44, 129, 148–149; performed, 28, 30–35, 36–40, 48, 49, 56; Victorian, 28, 30–40, 44; works for children, 183–184, 185, 187, 189, 190; *Northline*, 94–98, 99–100, 102, 103; *Tess of the d'Urbervilles*, 135–137, 138; *Trådnytt*, 61–62; *War and Peace*, 129
"Charge of the Light Brigade, The", 27
Chautauqua, 30–31
children: audiobooks for, 178–198; books for (LibriVox), 203–204; sound in stories for, 183–186
Chivers audiobooks, 131
Chopin, Henry, 64–66, 68, 70
Chopin, Kate, 154, 158n52
Christmas Carol, A, 52–56
Chromosome (Giorno and Moog), 78
cinematic soundtracks, 93–95, 98–99
Cinquième saison, 70
Classic Hundred Poems, The, 206
classics, 6–7, 45–46, 50, 54, 200; children's, 179, 180, 186–187, 190
Classiques Albums, 194
Clay, Steve, 76
Clifton, Thomas, 219
Clinton Baddeley, V. C., 6–7
close listening, 13
Colclough, Stephen, 206
Collins, Philip, 32
commercial constraints: audiobooks, 200
commodification: radio drama, 54–55, 56, 57
community, imagined, 153–154, 158n50, 229–230

Index 239

commuting and audiobooks, 8, 142n42, 154, 227, 228
compact discs. *See* CDs
comprehension: school students and audiobooks, 156n18
concentration levels: audiobooks, 3, 11, 14, 153, 193
Connor, Steven, 2, 127, 128
Conquest of Bread, 229
Conrad, Joseph, 134
consumer interest: audiobook publishing, 155n5
copyright, 5, 111, 200, 203, 212n9
Corwin, Norman, 57
Cugoano, Ottobah, 150
cummings, e e, 81
Curry, Samuel Silas, 27, 36, 37
cut-ups: tape recording, 67–68, 69

D

Danielewski, Mark Z., 92
David Copperfield, 6, 35–36, 38, 135, 203
Davidson, Frederick, 109, 130, 132–133, 134, 135, 141n39
Davis, Frank Marshall, 163, 166–167, 171, 176n23
Day Lewis, Cecil, 44
"Death Be Not Proud", 206
Decameron, 203
decontextualisation, 131, 141n28
DeLillo, Don, 95–96, 105n13
Derrida, Jacques, 13, 20n41, 151–152, 209–210
Dewey, John, 35
Dial-A-Poem, 77, 80–84
Dickens, Charles, 6–7, 27, 28–40, 52–56, 109, 208
Dickensian Magazine, 35
Didion, Joan, 68
diegetic sound, 94, 95–98
disability: attitudes toward, 2; print (LibriVox), 200
disembodiment: broadcast voice, 57
dissonance: *Dreams from My Father*, 172
Dombey and Son, 207
Douglass, Frederick, 151
"Dover Beach", 206
Dracula, 47, 112, 113, 203
drama, radio, 44–60; relationship to novel, 48–49
Dreams from My Father, 159–177
driving, audiobooks and, 15, 139, 146, 216, 227–228

Du Maurier, George, 28
Dubey, Madhu, 148

E

ear: vulnerability, 127, 140n3
eavesdropping: le Carré's novels, 111, 116, 118, 121, 124, 125
eBay: LibriVox titles, 201
Edison, Thomas, 1, 3–5, 25, 40n2, 62
Edison cylinder, 25
editing: tape, 64 71
Education nouvelle, 178
educational records, 28–29
educational role: children's literature, 186–189, 196
educational technology: origins, 29
Eigner, Edwin, 32
ekphrasis, 46
Electronic Sensory Poetry Environments, 78, 79–80, 83
Elegiac Sonnets and Other Poems (Smith), 204
Eliot, T. S., 208–209
Ellison, Ralph, 162, 166, 171, 173, 176n34
elocution, 27, 32, 36, 199, 211n3
Emacspeak, 210
Emma, 203
emotion: speech, 83, 129–130, 131, 137, 223, 224, 230; synthesis, 210–211
emotional labor: solo narration, 129–130
Enigma Technologies, 210
Enquiry Concerning Human Understanding, 229
EPI (Exploding Plastic Inevitable), 79
Equiano, Olaudah, 150
Eschman, Mike, 210
ESPEs, 78, 79–80, 83
Euripides, xiv
exercise, audiobooks and, 227, 228
Exploding Plastic Inevitable, 79

F

Fables (Aesop), 203, 204
Fables for the Frivolous, 204
Faucher, François, 178–179, 186, 187
Faucher, Paul, 178–179, 186, 187, 189, 196
Faust, 207
Favreau, Jon, 175n9
Ferlinghetti, Lawrence, 85

240 *Index*

fictional characters performed, 28, 30–35, 36–40, 48, 49, 56
film: perceptual object, 217–218
film sound, 93–95, 98–99
First Person Singular, 45–46
Flammarion, 179, 188f
fluency: school students and audiobooks, 156n18
Foley, Barbara, 168, 171–172, 172–173, 176n23, 176n28
format: audiobooks, 179–180; translation of, 132
France: audiobooks for children, 178–198
Fraser, Ian, 6
Frykholm, Amy Johnson, 155n4
Furlong, William, 70, 71, 74n48

G

game, reading as, 193–196
Garleck, Pamela, 137
Garnett, Constance, 133–135, 141n39
Gates, Henry Louis, Jr., 150, 151, 161
Genette, Gérard, 47–48, 94
Gibson, Flo, 13, 135–136, 139–140
Ginsberg, Alan, 67, 81, 85, 86, 88
Giorno, John, 70, 76–91
Giorno Poetry Systems, 70, 76–77, 82, 84–89
Gissing, George, 33
Gitelman, Lisa, 14, 45
Gold, Ron, 83
Golden Treasury of the Best Songs and Lyrical Poems in English, The, 207
Goldsmith, Kenneth, 84, 86, 87, 89
Gooding, Mel, 71
Goodman, Nelson, 110–111
Google, 210
Gorbman, Claudia, 93, 94–95, 98, 99
Gordon, Douglas, 66
Gramophone, Film, Typewriter, 114
gramophones, 8, 35–36, 170. *See also* records, flat disc
Green, Eileen, 154
Griffin, Farrah Jasmine, 147–148
Griot Audio, 152
griots, 147, 152
Gronniosaw, Ukawsaw, 150
Grusin, Richard, 25–26, 27, 46, 47, 104n2
Guillory, John, 27, 30
Gysin, Brion, 67, 68, 69

H

Hachette, Louis, 187
Haggard, Merle, 96–97
Hannity, Sean, 164, 175n19
Happenings, 78
Hard Times, 109
Harding, John Wesley, 92
Hardy, Robert, 130
Harold D. Smith Collection, 29
Harry Potter books, 226
Haunted (Poe), 92
Havelock, Eric, xiv
headphones as "cocoon", 11
hearing, xiv, 40, 73n25, 123–124, 132, 192, 193, 218–221. *See also* listening
Heidegger, Martin, 223
Hell on Ice, 47
Helms, Hans G., 69
Henderson Journal, 30–31
Hepworth Company, 35–36
heteroglossia, 201, 208
Hetzel, Jules, 187
Heure Joyeuse, L', 190, 192
Heyer, Paul, 49
Hightower, John, 81
Hilmes, Michele, 49, 54
Histoire de mes malheurs, 204
Hoffman, Abbie, 83
Holdridge, Barbara, 84, 85
Holiday, Billie, 168
"Home Thoughts from Abroad", 206
Homer, xiv
hooks, bell, 152
Hörlesen, 70
House of Leaves, 92
Household Words, 32–33
Houseman, John, 46
Huckleberry Finn, 48, 203
Hugo, Victor, 25
Huizinga, Johan, 194
Hume, David, 229
Husserl, Edmund, 217, 218, 219, 224
hybrid audiobooks: novel and score, 92–106
hypermediacy, 25–26, 27, 46, 47, 57

I

I Am Sitting in a Room, 228
I Lost My Girlish Laughter, 50, 51, 52
iClassix, 201–202
iconotexts, 185

identity: children's development, 187, 190; performance of, 161, 167; personal, voice and, 67
ideology: implications of narrator's voice, 14
"If", 207
Ihde, Don, 218, 223, 225–226, 228
illustrated books for children, 189
Illustrated London News, 32
imagination: auditory, 192, 193, 228; play and, 194
immediacy, 25–26, 46, 47, 192
impersonation: oratory, 30–32, 34–35
In the Native State, 57–58
intellectual engagement: audiobooks, 154
interception: le Carré's novels, 115, 116, 118–119, 121, 122, 123
internationalism: Giorno Poetry Systems, 77
Internet: digital audio formats, 8–9; poetry, 88, 89
Internet Archive, 201, 202, 204, 211n2
interpretation, oral. *See* narrators' voice
intimacy: poetry, 82; reading, 149; sound, 26, 149; vocal delivery, 12, 34, 53, 66, 125
intonation, 117, 125, 130, 131, 209, 223, 225
Invisible Man (Ellison), 166, 171, 173, 176n34
iPhones, 201–202
iPod, 8–9, 227
iTunes, 212n13

J
"Jabberwocky", 207
Jack, Steven, 140
James, Robin, 71
Jane Eyre, 203
Jarvis, Martin, 129
Jason, Neville, 132–133, 141n39
Jazz (Morrison), 149, 150, 151, 152
Jekyll and Hyde, 27, 28
Jensen, Rich, 71
Jesson, James, 128
jingles: children's stories, 184
Jobert, Marlène, 185, 196n15
John Giorno Band, 87, 88
Johnny Guitar, 78–79
Johnson, Bengt Emil, 69–70
Johnson, Richard, 129
Joie par les livres, La, 192
Joyce, James, 15
Junior Classics, The, 203

Jurgensen, John, 105n8

K
Kahn, Douglas, 2, 144, 185
Kane, Daniel, 76, 80
Kaphan, Morgan, 34
Kaufman, George, 51–52
Keller, Helen, 5
Kerouac, Jack, 67, 73n27, 85
Kindle, 10
Kingsolver, Barbara, 148
Kittler, Friedrich, 62, 72n3, 111, 112–113, 114, 115, 116, 119, 120, 123
Kivy, Peter, 110–111
Kozloff, Sarah, 145, 149
Kreilkamp, Ivan, 26–27, 32, 33, 39
"Kubla Khan", 206
Kurzweil Reading Machine, 9

L
Lacan, Jacques, 62, 72n3
language, written: status and function, 150–151
Largehearted Boy, 105n8
Lastra, James, 2
LaVine, Heidi, 104n1
Le Carré, John, 109–126
Lecat, Lisette, 13
Lecture comme jeu, La, 193–194
Lee, Brenda, 97, 98, 101, 103
LeGuin, Ursula K., 104n3
Leonard, Elmore, 92
Library of Congress Books for the Adult Blind Project, 5, 25
LibriVox, 154, 199–215, 226–227, 231n21
linguistics: literature and sound technology, 119–123
listener as interlocutor, 37–38, 39
listeners, radio, 45
listening: deep (audiobooks challenged), 3; *Dreams from My Father* (leitmotif), 164–165, 166, 168, 169, 170, 173; experience of (audiobooks), 216–218, 223–230; private nature of (modern audio products), 199, 200; *See also* hearing
literacy: freedom and power, link to, 150–151, 157n42
literary recordings, emergence of, 29
literature, recorded, 62
Livraphone, 179

242 *Index*

Looking Glass War, The, 114–116
Los Angeles Times, 88
Love Hall Tryst, 92
Lucier, Alvin, 228
Lurie, John, 92
Luxor, 61–62
Lyceumite, 30–31
"Lycidas", 207
Lydenberg, Robin, 68

M

Macherey, Pierre, 171
Mackey, Nathaniel, 146, 147, 156n13, 172
Macmillan, Roy, 137–138
Magnephone, 61
mail-order, 8
Malanga, Gerard, 79
Mallarmé, Stéphane, 15
manipulability: tape recording, 64–71
Mann, Michael, 118
Mann, Ron, 88
marketing, soundtracks as, 93–94, 104, 105n8
Marlaguette, 183–184, 196n10
Marsh, Joss, 35–36
Marxist analysis: *Dreams from My Father*, 171, 172–173
Mason, Michael, 104n1
Masters, Jill, 134
Mathews, Charles, 32, 39
Matz, W. B., 35
Maude, Aylmer, 133, 134–135, 141n39
Maude, Louise, 133, 134–135, 141n39
Maximum Ride, 105n8
Mayor of Casterbridge, The, 137
McCaffery, Steve, 66
McGuire, Hugh, 205, 206, 210, 212n12
McLuhan, Marshall, 65, 81–82, 192, 223
media culture prophesied, 112–114
Mekons, 104n3
melody, perception of, 217–218, 218–219, 226, 227
Mercury Theatre, 45–58
Merleau-Ponty, Maurice, 217–218, 227–228
metadiagetic sound, 94, 99–100
Meyer-Kalkus, Reinhart, 70
Michka, 179, 180f, 196
Miller, Edward D., 57
Miller, J. Hillis, 38
Misérables, Les, 25

Mission Song, The, 111, 119–123, 124
Moby Dick, 203
Modern Oliver Twist, A, 30
Montaigne, Renee, 85
Moog, Robert, 78
Morrison, Toni, 144, 146–147, 148–150, 151, 154, 159, 161, 174n4
Morse code, 114, 115, 116
Most Wanted Man, A, 118
moving pictures: Giorno Poetry Systems, 88
MP3, 8, 40, 132, 135, 201, 216
Müller, Gerda, 187
Mullen, Haryette, 147–148
Muller, Frank, 13, 110, 112, 115, 116, 117
Museum of Modern Art (New York), 81
music: book scores: insight into emotions, 96, 97–100; children's stories, 184, 186; pauses, 224; shared, 147, 152
music hall, 33
musicking, 146, 156n13
musique concrète, 63, 64
Muzak, 94

N

Nabokov, Vladimir, 133
Nagy, Gregory, xiv
narration, pace of: audiobooks, 3, 11, 12, 134, 153, 193, 222, 223
narrative: elaboration on, 68–69; pictures and, 186–187, 194–195
narrative theory, film sound and, 94
narrator's voice: Barack Obama, 159–177; John le Carré's novels, 110, 112, 114, 115–116, 117–118, 119–123, 124–125; Leo Tolstoy's novels, 128, 129, 130, 132–135, 137, 141n39; LibriVox, 199, 201, 205–206, 207–211, 226–227; textual reception, 13–14, 143, 221, 223–224, 224–227. *See also* reception of literature: oral delivery; Thomas Hardy's novels, 128–129, 130–131, 135–137, 137–138, 138–140
narrators, celebrity, 5, 13–14
National Library of Canada, 29
Naxos audiobooks, 137, 138
Negroponte, Nicholas, 191
Nesmith, Michael, 104n3

New American Poetry, The: 1945–1960, 86
New York Public Library, 9
New York School poets, 82, 86
New York Times, 80, 81
Nielsen, Aldon Lynn, 147
Noise, Water, Meat, 144
noise: LibriVox recordings, 201
noises: stories for children, 184–186, 196n10
nondiegetic sound, 94, 98–99
Northline, 92–106
nostalgia, 145
novels: early recordings, 5, 6–7
Nussbaum, Martha, 146

O

objectification of sound, time and events, 63–4, 66, 67, 72n12
"Ode to Autumn", 206, 207
Ogg Vorbis, 201
O'Hara, Frank, 82
Oliver Twist, 203
Olson, Charles, 81
Ong, Walter, 12–13, 65, 145, 147, 149, 151–152, 153, 157n42, 217
Onyango, Hussein, 169–170, 171, 176n28
Oprah's Book Club, 146, 147, 153, 158n52
oral and written cultures: dichotomy, 13, 151
oral interpretation. *See* narrators' voice
oral performance, Victorian, 27, 30–35
orality: African American, 143, 144, 147–148, 150, 152; historical xiii–xiv, 12–13, 20n41, 65, 147–148; poetry, 76; primary, 65, 145, 147, 151, 153; secondary, 12, 65, 145
OU, 65, 70
Our Mutual Friend, 207
Oyelowo, David, 120, 125
"Ozymandius", 206, 207

P

P. S. editions (Harper Perennial), 100, 102
pace of narration: audiobooks, 3, 11, 12, 134, 153, 193, 222, 223
Page, Patti, 97, 98, 101, 103
Paradise Lost, 204
paratext, 14, 15, 47–48, 50–53, 57
Parrain, Nathalie, 187

participative capacity: audio transmission, 145, 153, 154
passivity: audiobook listening, 10–11, 128
Patchen, Kenneth, 85
Pathé Records, 34
Patterson, James, 105n8
pauses in narration, 221, 223–224, 225
Peake, Richard Brinsley, 32
Peirce, C. S., 64
Penguin Island, 204
Peoria Daily Star, 30–31
Père Castor, Le, 178–198
Perfect Spy, A, 112, 116, 118, 123
performance: audiobook as, 146, 199, 223, 225–227; music, 224; poetry, 65–66, 69, 77, 81, 87; reading as, 110–111; reading aloud as, 13, 26, 27, 32, 33–34, 53, 128–129, 131, 205
performance of identity, 161, 167, 170, 173
Perloff, Marjorie, 82
Pernice, Joe, 104n4
Perrault, Charles, 183
Personism, 82
Persuasion, 206
phenomenology: audiobooks, 216–231
Phillips, Rodney, 76
phonograph, 1, 3–5, 25, 26; Ellison's image, 162, 165, 166, 168, 170, 173
phonographic books, 3, 4f, 25, 26, 27, 62
Phonographies, 162
phonography, 33, 63
physical experience, audiobook and, 228–230
physical labor: solo narration, 129–130
Picard, Michel, 193
picture books, 185, 186, 189
pictures: children's stories, 185, 186–187, 189, 190, 191, 192
Pilgrim's Progress, 204
Piombino, Nick, 225
pitch: voice: children's stories, 184
Platform Magazine, 31, 36–37
play, books as, 193–196
playback, 66, 111, 145, 222, 227
pluralism, political: *Dreams from My Father*, 160, 171, 172–173
Poe (Annie Decatur Danielewski), 92
Poems Every Child Should Know, 203
poésie sonore, 64–66, 68–69

244 *Index*

poetry, spoken, xv-xvi, 3–4, 8, 27, 36, 64–66, 69–71, 224–225; Giorno Poetry Systems, 70, 76–77, 82, 84–89; LibriVox, 206–209; radio, 83; rock and roll and, 87; tape recording, 64–71; telephone, 80–84
Poetry Experiment, The, 83–84
Poetry in Motion (Mann), 88
Poetry Project at St. Mark's Church (New York), 76, 78–79, 82–83
political activism: Dial-A-Poem, 80, 81
politics: *Dreams from My Father*, 160, 162, 163, 164, 167, 168, 170, 171–173
Pollyanna, 203
Poole, John, 32
Portelli, Alessandro, 151
Potter, Paul, 28
Poulsen, Valdemar, 61
preservation: sound recording of voices, 56
Pride and Prejudice, 203
primary orality, 65, 145, 147, 151, 153
Principia Ethica, 204
process over finished art object, 57, 145–146
Project Gutenberg, 200, 201, 204, 205, 210, 211
projective verse, 81
protention: anticipated future, 219–221, 224, 225
protosemantic: poetics, 66
Public Domain, 45
publishing: collective process, 187–189
punctuation marks, 221
Pynchon, Thomas, 104n4

Q

quality: LibriVox recordings, 205, 213n32
Quist, Harlin, 195

R

racism, 163–164
radicalism, Obama's attitude to, 162, 171, 176n23
radio: Algerian, 153; literature on, 11; talking books, 6–7
radio drama. *See* drama, radio
radio poetry. *See* poetry, radio
Radio Free Poetry, 83
Radio Gutenberg, 210
Radio Hanoi, 83

Radway, Janice, 155n4
Random House Audio, 159–160
Random House Incorporated, 51, 52
Raspberry, 78
"Raven, The", 210
Reader, The (Schlink), 110
reader and author: hierarchical relationship, 150, 189–190
readers, audiobook audiences as, 110
reading, communal, 199–200, 202–203; solitary and shared, 153, 191, 199–200
reading as performance, 110–111, 215n49
reading for children: audiobooks, 189–196; LibriVox, 203–204
readings, multiple: LibriVox, 206
readings, public, 145; poetry (New York), 82; Victorian, 26–27, 32, 52, 53, 109
real, trace of the: tape recording, 64, 66, 71
Rebecca, 48–49
reception of literature: oral delivery, 1, 10–12, 13–15, 17, 70, 71, 143, 145. *See also* narrator's voice: textual reception
record albums: poetry, 84–86
Recorded Books, 8, 110, 123, 152
recording, magnetic: theme in fiction, 61–62
records, flat disc, 25, 38, 42n54; long-playing, 8
Reed, Roxanne, 147, 154, 158n52
Reiner, Rob, 14
remediation, 47, 104n2; books to radio drama, 47–48, 57; definition, 46; film sound, 93, 94–100; literature into sound, 25–43, 46
replay speed, 135–136
representative status: Barack Obama, 171, 172
retention: primary remembrance, 218–221, 224
Return of Sherlock Holmes, The, 203
Return of the Native, The, 203
Revolution in Writing, 45
Rexroth, Kenneth, 85
Ricard, René, 79
Richmond Fontaine, 93, 94, 100
Rippy, Marguerite H., 52
rock and roll, poetry and, 87
Rodger, Ian, 45
Roney, Marianne, 84

Index 245

Rorty, Richard, 146
Rosenblat, Barbara, 192
Rothenberg, Annie Coleman, 209
Royal National Institute for the Blind, 6
Rubery, Matthew, 128, 192
Russia House, The, 123–124
Ruy-Vidal, François, 195

S

sacred stories, 172–173
sales, audiobook, 9
Samuels, David, 166, 171, 176n23,
    176n34
Satellite Radio Poets, 83–84
Saussure, Ferdinand de, 209
Schaeffer, Pierre, 63
Schafer, Murray, 128, 192
Schjeldahl, Peter, 83
Schlink, Bernhard, 110
schools: market for records, 29
Schor, Jane, 51
Schulman, Silvia, 51
Schwartz, Hillel, 127
Schweighauser, Philipp, 183, 184
Scientific American, 3–4
Screen Test Poems, 79
secondary orality, 12, 65, 145
Secret Agent, The, 201
*Secret Location on the Lower East Side,
    A*, 76
Sedaris, David, 131, 145
"Self-Reliance" (Emerson), 228–229
Sense and Sensibility, 203
sensuousness: books, 11
sentences: comprehension, 219–221,
    231n12
September on Jessore Road, 88
Shaw, Lytle, 82
Shepard, Richard E., 80
Sheridan, Thomas, 27
Shore, Emily, 206
shorthand, 33, 39
silence, 117, 170, 171, 224
silent reading, conceptualization of, 3
silent reading user interface (SRUI), xiv
Silksoundbooks, 19n20
simultaneity, children and, 192
slave narratives, 144, 150, 161
Small, Christopher, 146, 156n13
Smith, Harold D., 29–30, 34–35, 37,
    38, 39
social experience, audiobook and,
    229–230
Soft Skull Press, 88–89

solitude, accompanied, 139, 229–230
Sommerville, Ian, 68
Sonnet 43 (Browning), 206
Sonnet 106 (Shakespeare), 206
Sonnet 116 (Shakespeare), 207
Sontag, Susan, 78, 80
sound: children's stories, 180, 183–186;
    compression, 132; culture and,
    1–2; *Dreams from My Father*,
    164–167, 169, 170; power, 127;
    spacialization, 63–64; Toni Mor-
    rison's novels, 144, 145, 147,
    149, 150, 151, 154
sound poetry, 64–66, 68–69
sound recording: automation of writ-
    ing, 39; surveillance, 109–126
Sound Recording Committee, 6
sounding, 146, 156n13
soundtracks, film, 93–95, 98–99
soup and radio drama, 45–46, 54–55,
    56, 57
spatialization of sound, 63–64
spatial arrangement: literary texts,
    14–15
Speaight, Frank, 34
speech, perception of, 218, 219–221,
    222–227, 230
speed, replay, 135–136
speed reading, 12
Spencer, Len, 27, 28
Spivak, Gayatri, 209–210
spoken recordings: generic categories,
    29, 41n14
spoken word, perception of, 218,
    219–221, 222–227, 230
"Spring and Fall" (Hopkins), 206
St. Dunstan's, 6
St. Mark's Poetry Project (New York),
    76, 78–79, 82–83
Stebbins, Genevieve, 27
Sterne, Jonathan, 2, 40, 56, 132
Stevens, Wallace, 207–208
Stevenson, Robert Louis, 27, 28, 47,
    50–51, 55, 56–57
Stewart, Garrett, 33
Stewart, Jon, 1
Stoppard, Tom, 57–58
storage capacity of sound recording, 26;
    flat discs, 25, 38; phonographs,
    5, 40n2
stories, sacred, 172–173
storytelling: children's, 178–198; cul-
    ture of, 12, 53, 152
Stow, Simon, 146

246 Index

structured listening, 221
structured silences, 171
Subduing Demons in America, 88–89
surveillance, sound recording as, 109–126
Svengali, 27, 28
Swiss Family Robinson, The, 203
synchronicity: book score, 95, 100–101, 105n9; film soundtrack and image content, 94–95
synthetic voice, 9–10, 210–211

T

talk poems, 69
talking books: trope, 144, 148–149, 150–151, 152, 157n40, 161
Talking Books Program, 5, 8
talking records, 29
tape recorders, 61, 62–75, 114; John le Carré's novels, 117, 118, 119
tape recording, 62–75, 114; identity production, 67
telegraphone, 61
telephone: poetry, 80–84
television, 114, 143, 145, 148, 153
temporality: experience of audiobooks, 217–221
Tennyson, Alfred, 27, 36
Tess of the d'Urbervilles, 135–137, 137–138, 139–140
Text Synchronized Audio, 201–202
text-to-speech technology, 9–10, 210–211
theatre, pantomime: influence on Dickens, 32
Thigpen, Lynne, 152
"Thirteen Ways of Looking at a Blackbird", 207–208
This is Spinal Tap, 14
Thomas, Dylan, 8, 57, 84–85
Thompson, Emily, 2
Thorne, Stephen, 138
"Tiger, The", 206
time, flow of, 166, 217–221
Tinker, Tailor, Soldier, Spy, 111–112, 119
Tishomingo Blues, 92
Tolstoy, Leo, 128, 133
Tom Sawyer, 203
tradition, creation of image of, 54–55, 56
Trådnytt, 61
translatability, xiv–xv
translation, literary, xiv–xv, 129, 131, 132–135, 141n39

translation of format, 132
Treasure Island, 46–47, 49, 50–51, 55, 56
Tree, Herbert Beerbohm, 27, 28
Trilby, 28
Tristram Shandy, 15
Twain, Mark, 5, 48
typewriter: nonalphabetic telegraphy and the, 114; poetry, 81–82

U

UbuWeb, 89
Über die Weiber, 226–227
Ulysses (Joyce), 15
Umbrellas and Their History, 229
Under Milk Wood, 57
Under the Greenwood Tree, 128–129, 130–131, 138
Understanding Media, 81–82
Unheard Melodies, 93, 94–95, 98, 99
Up Above the Sky, 67

V

Vache orange, La, 181f, 183, 184–185
Valéry, Paul, 65
Velvet Underground and Nico, 79
Venus in Furs, 204
verse, spoken, xv–xvi, 3–4, 8
Victor Talking Machine Company, 27, 29–30, 34–35, 36, 37, 38, 40n13, 42n54
VideoPaks, 88
Village Voice, 83
Vincent, David, 206
Virtual Gender, 154
Vishner, Mayer, 83
visual environments, audiobooks and, 15
Vitagraph Company, 30
Vlautin, Willy, 92–106
vocal versatility, 28, 33
"vocalization" of printed page, 11
voice: narrator's. *See* narrator's voice; natural and recorded (distinction), 144; personal identity and, 67
voicing: interpretive act, 14, 120, 128–129, 131, 134, 139, 140
volunteers: LibriVox, 154, 200–201, 204–205, 206, 211n2, 212n12, 226

W

Wadoswki, Hélène, 179
Waldman, Anne, 83

Walker, John, 27
walking, audiobooks and, 136, 139, 216, 227–228
Wallace, David Foster, 15
War and Peace, 129, 130, 132–135, 137, 141n39
War of the Worlds, The, 47
Warhol, Andy, 79
Warsh, Lewis, 83
Waste Land, The, 208–209
Wayne June Voice Talent agency, 131
WBAI-FM, 83–84
We Hold These Truths, 57
Web 2.0: LibriVox, 200, 201
Weekly Poetry Project, The, 206–209
Weheliye, Alexander, 147, 161–162
Welles, Orson, 7, 45–60, 128
White Noise, 95–96, 105n13
whites, Obama's attitude to, 163–164, 171, 176n23
Whitman, Walt, 171–172
Why Read the Classics?, 190
Wilhelm Meister's Wanderjahre, 204
Williams, Bransby, 27, 28, 33–35, 36–37
Williams Mix, 63–64
Winfrey, Oprah, 146, 229
wireless: writing machines, 45
wiretapping: le Carré's novels, 110, 116, 118

Woloch, Alex, 39
Woman in White, The, 205
women: *Dreams from My Father*, 168–169
Works Progress Administration, 5
Worthen, William B., 57
WPAX, 83
Wright, Jeremiah, 162, 163, 164, 173, 176n34
writing machines: wireless, 45
written and oral cultures: dichotomy, 13, 151
written language: audiobooks and, 217, 223, 230; experience of, 220, 221–222, 223, 225; status and function, 150–151
Wyatt, Eustace, 45

Y

Yeats, W. B., xv–xvi
You Got to Burn to Shine, 84
Young, John, 145, 146–147, 150, 161
YouTube, 161, 162–163, 164

Z

Zimmerman, Walter, 132–133, 133–134, 135
Zurbrugg, Nicholas, 62, 70